Property of Zeresa

Easy CorelDRAW!™

Stephen R. Poland

QUE

Easy CorelDRAW!

Library of Congress Catalog No: 94-66172

ISBN: 1-56529-780-6

96 95 94 6 5 4 3 2 1

Interpretation of the printing code: the rightmost double-digit number is the year of the book's printing; the rightmost single-digit number, the number of the book's printing. For example, a printing code of 94-1 shows that the first printing of the book occurred in 1994.

Screen reproductions in this book were created with Collage Plus from Inner Media, Inc., Hollis, NH.

Publisher: David P. Ewing

Associate Publisher: Corinne Walls

Publishing Director: Lisa A. Bucki

Managing Editor: Anne Owen

Product Marketing Manager: Greg Wiegand

Credits

Acquisitions Editors
Thomas F. Godfrey III
Nancy Stevenson

Product Director
Jim Minatel

Production Editors
Chris Nelson
Pamela Wampler

Editors
Lorna Gentry
Patrick Kanouse

Technical Editor
Robert Beatty

Book Designer
Amy Peppler-Adams

Cover Designer
Jay Corpus

Production Team
Stephen Adams
Angela Bannan
Claudia Bell
Kim Cofer
Anne Dickerson
Karen Dodson
Bob LaRoche
Beth Lewis
Andrea Marcum
Nanci Sears Perry
Linda Quigley
Ryan Rader
Caroline Roop
Michael Thomas
Robert Wolf
Lillian Yates

Indexer
Michael Hughes

Composed in *Stone* and *MCPdigital* by Que Corporation

About the Author

Stephen R. Poland is an entrepreneur in the toy and novelty industry and a computer consultant specializing in writing about application software topics for IBM PCs, PC compatibles, and the Apple Macintosh. He uses CorelDRAW! extensively to promote his business, producing engineering drawings and marketing materials such as mechanical drawings, electronic schematics, package designs, and sales brochures.

Steve is the author of the *10 Minute Guide to the Mac* and a contributing author to several other computer books including *Microsoft Office 6 in 1, The Idiot's Guide to Buying and Upgrading Computers,* and *The First Book of Personal Computing.*

Acknowledgments

I wish to express my appreciation to the others who helped me complete this book. Jim Minatel, Product Development Specialist at Que, developed the manuscript and gave careful guidance and insightful suggestions for improving the structure and presentation of the material; and Chris Nelson, Production Editor at Que, managed the book through the production process and also helped clarify confusing procedures and explanations. Thanks to Pamela Wampler, who managed the copy edit process and caught my occasional inconsistencies. Special thanks to Nancy Stevenson and Tom Godfrey, Acquisitions Editors and keepers of the schedule, for arranging this project and for keeping me honest in regard to manuscript delivery dates and percentages.

Many thanks go to the technical editor, Robert Beatty, who ensured the technical accuracy of this book and who helped us keep track of the differences between CorelDRAW! 3 and CorelDRAW! 4. Special thanks to the production staff who turned dozens of word processing files and hundreds of screen captures into this printed book.

Trademark Acknowledgments

Contents at a Glance

Contents

Part III: Viewing and Selecting Objects 74

Part IV: Modifying Objects 94

Part V: Adding and Editing Text 134

Part VI: CorelPHOTO-PAINT and CorelCHART Basics 154

Part VII: Sample Documents 196

Index 208

Action Index 214

Introduction

What You Can Do with CorelDRAW!

CorelDRAW! is one of the most robust and full-featured graphics programs for the PC. With its easy-to-use drawing tools, hundreds of fonts, and thousands of clipart images and symbols, you can quickly and easily create documents ranging from simple one-page drawings and diagrams to elaborate newsletters and charts.

Specifically, you can use CorelDRAW to perform these operations:

- *Draw lines, circles, boxes, and polygons.* CorelDRAW's set of drawing tools enables you to create an infinite variety of shapes and objects. For example, using CorelDRAW's Bézier tool, you can make connect-the-dots-like objects, or you can use the Pencil tool to draw freehand lines like you would with pencil and paper. Creating precisely sized circles and rectangles is simple using the Ellipse and Rectangle tools. All the while, as you draw, CorelDRAW tells you how long, wide, and tall your lines and other objects are.

- *Add color fills to shapes.* Once you've created the parts of your drawing using the drawing tools, you can fill them with color, selecting from hundreds of color choices in Corel's Color Palette. For more interesting effects, you can try a patterned fill, such as a brick wall pattern or a polka dot pattern. With CorelDRAW, you can experiment with color fills and patterns until you find just the look you want.

- *Add text.* If your drawing calls for text elements, CorelDRAW has the tools you need. Adding a text label to a drawing is simple using the Text tool. You can change the look of the text by selecting from over 750 fonts, or rotate the text so it runs up the side of the page. Creating documents such as newsletters and brochures is a snap using CorelDRAW version 4.

- *Zoom in on a drawing.* CorelDRAW's Zoom tool enables you to zoom in on a portion of your drawing to show more detail. If you're creating objects with small dimensions and exacting detail, the Zoom tool is indispensable. You also can zoom out from your drawing to show the entire page. Although zooming out does not show you the details of your drawing, it does allow you to see where objects are placed on the page. No matter what size drawing view you have zoomed to, you can use all of CorelDRAW's drawing and editing tools.

- *Print your drawing.* Once you've created your drawing, you can print it to see how it looks on paper. If you need to make changes to your drawing, you can revise it and print again.

- *Edit objects.* If the line you drew is not positioned correctly, you can drag its endpoint to a new location. Other objects are just as easy to edit. You can reshape an ellipse to a circle, stretch a square into an elongated rectangle, and change a circle to an arc.

- *Change line thickness.* Using CorelDRAW's Outline tool, you can vary the thickness of the lines you draw. For example, you can create a decorative border by drawing several large rectangles inside one another and then increasing the thickness of each rectangle's border.

- *Check spelling.* Whether you have numerous paragraphs of text in a newsletter, or just a few words on a letterhead, you can run a spell check to search for misspellings. The spell check feature can give you extra confidence because you know that your documents do not contain misspelled words.

- *Create a chart.* Using CorelCHART!, you can graph numeric data to track sales trends, monitor market share, or even display your child's growth over the years. CorelCHART provides a worksheet where you enter and change the numbers you want to chart. Once you've entered the numeric data, you can choose from among dozens of chart types to display your data.

- *Paint a picture.* If you like painting more than drawing, CorelPHOTO-PAINT! provides the tools to create and edit bitmap painting. Using tools such as the Pointillist brush, you can imitate the great painting masters. Other painting tools enable you to create different artistic effects, such as using the Smudge tool to smudge and smear an area of your painting, mixing the colors as if they were oils on a canvas.

The tasks in this book cover CorelDRAW! 3 and CorelDRAW! 4. Screen shots are from version 3 unless otherwise noted. Steps and features that are different in CorelDRAW! 4 are indicated in steps and notes.

Task Sections

The Task sections include numbered steps that tell you how to accomplish certain tasks, such as creating a new drawing or modifying an object. The numbered steps walk you through a specific example so that you can learn the task by actually doing it.

Big Screen

At the beginning of each task is a large screen shot that shows how the computer screen will look after you complete the task, or that shows a feature discussed in that task, such as a menu or dialog box.

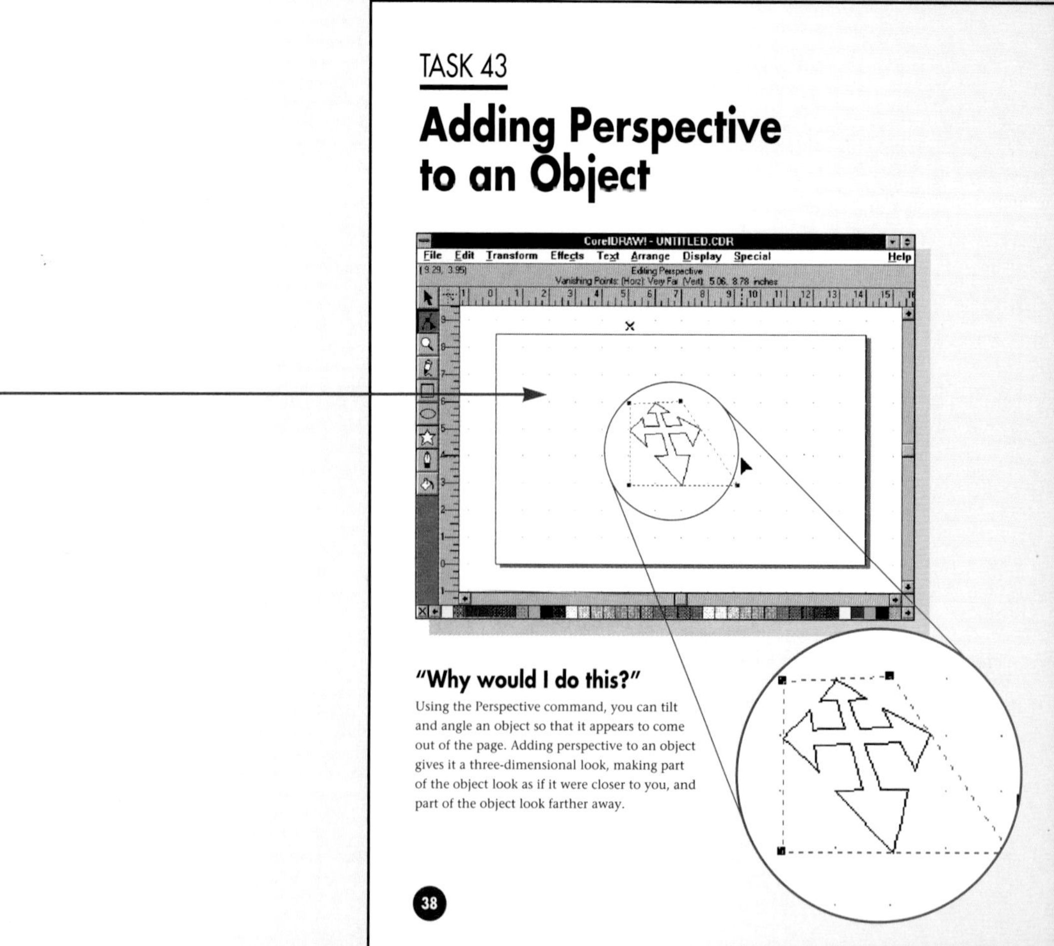

TASK 43
Adding Perspective to an Object
CorelDRAW! - UNTITLED.CDR
File Edit Transform Effects Text Arrange Display Special Help
"Why would I do this?"
Using the Perspective command, you can tilt and angle an object so that it appears to come out of the page. Adding perspective to an object gives it a three-dimensional look, making part of the object look as if it were closer to you, and part of the object look farther away.
38

Step-by-Step Screens

Every task includes a screen shot for each step of a procedure. The screen shot shows how the computer screen looks at each step of the process.

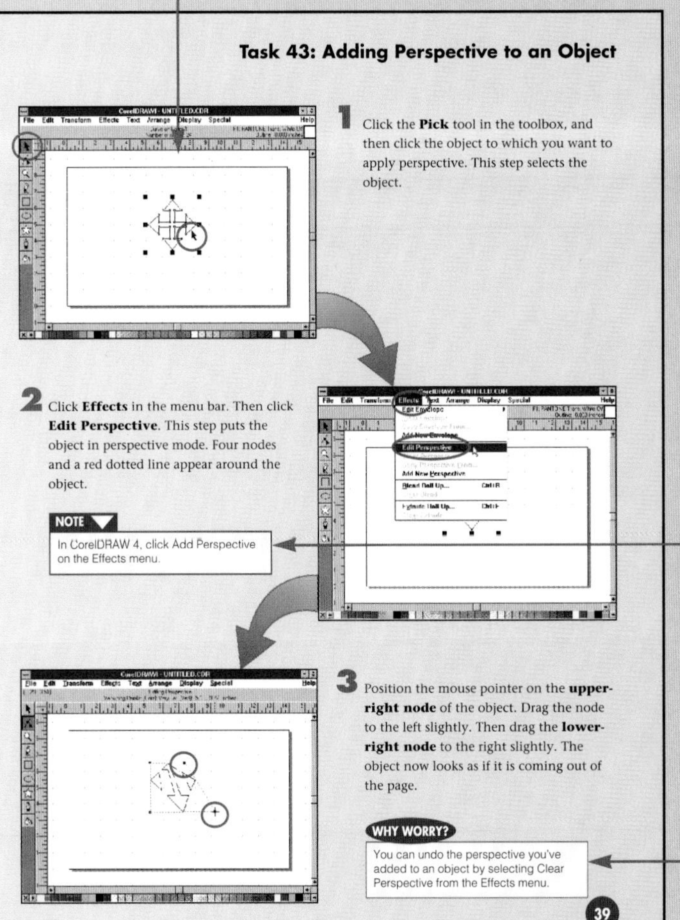
Task 43: Adding Perspective to an Object
1 Click the **Pick** tool in the toolbox, and then click the object to which you want to apply perspective. This step selects the object.
2 Click **Effects** in the menu bar. Then click **Edit Perspective**. This step puts the object in perspective mode. Four nodes and a red dotted line appear around the object.
NOTE
In CorelDRAW 4, click Add Perspective on the Effects menu.
3 Position the mouse pointer on the **upper-right node** of the object. Drag the node to the left slightly. Then drag the **lower-right node** to the right slightly. The object now looks as if it is coming out of the page.
WHY WORRY?
You can undo the perspective you've added to an object by selecting Clear Perspective from the Effects menu.
39

General Notes

Many tasks include short notes that tell you a little more about certain procedures. These notes define terms, explain other options, and so on.

Why Worry? Notes

You may find that you've performed a task, such as moving drawing object, that you don't want to do after all. The Why Worry? notes tell you how to undo certain procedures or get out of a situation.

CorelDRAW! - UNTITLED.CDR
File Edit Transform Effects Text Arrange Display Special
Help
Drawing in Freehand Mode on Layer 1
(1.39, -3.34)
CorelDRAW! - UNTITLED.CDR
File Edit Transform Effects Text Arrange Display Special
New
Open... Ctrl+O
Save Ctrl+S
Save As...
Import...
Export...
Insert Object...
Print... Ctrl+P
Print Merge...
Print Setup...
Page Setup...
Exit Ctrl+X
C:\CORELDRW\AUTOBACK\AMZMAIL1.CDR
C:\CORELDRW\DRAW\CARD1.CDR
C:\CORELDRW\DRAW\SALES1.CDR
C:\CORELDRW\DRAW\BC1.CDR
Help
CorelDRAW! - UNTITLED.CDR
File Edit Layout Effects Text Arrange Display Special
Help
New From Template
File Name:
*.cdt
3_fold2.cdt
b_day.cdt
bank_bc.cdt
catalog1.cdt
coreldrw.cdt
cover.cdt
job.cdt
lunch.cdt
meeting1.cdt
Directories:
c:\corel40\draw\template
c:\
corel40
draw
template
Drives:
c:
List Files of Type:
CorelDRAW! Template (*.cdt)
OK
File Edit Layout Effects
(3.88, 6.01)

PART I

CorelDRAW Basics

Part I of this book introduces you to CorelDRAW basics. Before you can create your own drawings, you need to know how to find your way around the CorelDRAW screen, work with the menus and dialog boxes, and use the drawing tools.

Before you can use CorelDRAW, the program must be installed on your system. CorelDRAW, along with CorelCHART and CorelPHOTO-PAINT, are Windows-based applications, so you'll need to make sure you have Microsoft Windows installed on your system, as well. This book's tasks cover CorelDRAW versions 3 and 4.

To start CorelDRAW from the Windows Program Manager, you simply double-click the program icon. Exiting is just as easy—you use CorelDRAW's Exit command.

When you start CorelDRAW, a *drawing window* appears in the center of the screen, with a menu bar at the top and a toolbox positioned at the left. The drawing window resembles a sheet of paper. This is where you'll create the objects and other images that make up your drawing. As you'll learn in this part, you can choose the size of the drawing window, as well as its orientation.

The *menu bar* at the top of the screen lists the CorelDRAW menu names. Like other Windows applications, CorelDRAW menus contain the commands that you use to manipulate, modify, and manage your drawing. Some menu commands open submenus, listing additional options for that command.

The *toolbox* located to the left of the drawing window holds the tools you use to create objects such as circles, rectangles, lines, and other shapes. Each tool is represented by a small picture (an *icon*) of the tool's real-world counterpart. For example, the Pencil tool contains a pencil, the Ellipse tool contains an ellipse, and the Text tool contains a capital letter A.

The first tool in the toolbox is the Pick tool. You use the Pick tool to select or move objects in your drawing.

Some tools in the toolbox, such as the Zoom tool, help you control how you view your drawing as you work. Tools such as the Pen tool and Fill tool control the color and

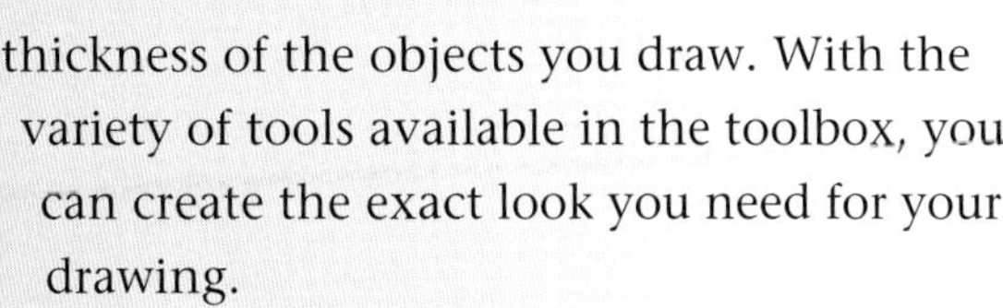

thickness of the objects you draw. With the variety of tools available in the toolbox, you can create the exact look you need for your drawing.

A few of the tools in the toolbox open a *fly-out menu* when selected. A fly-out menu is a set of additional tools relating to a specific function or task. For example, the Pen fly-out menu displays tools for controlling the thickness, color, shading, and style of the line drawn with the Pen tool. Selecting the thick line option on the Pen fly-out menu causes the Pen tool to draw a thick line. Or, if an object is selected, the thick line option widens the object's outline.

CorelDRAW offers innovative *roll-up windows*. Roll-up windows are similar to dialog boxes; however, roll-up windows can remain on-screen while you work. The Text roll-up window, for example, enables you to choose the font, size, and alignment of the text you type using the Text tool. As you type text in your drawing, the Text roll-up window remains open, allowing you to apply the option in the roll-up window to the text you type. To set aside the window temporarily, you can "roll it up," leaving only the thin title bar of the window. Next time you need to modify text, simply "unroll" the window. You do not have to return to the Text menu on the menu bar and reopen the roll-up window.

As you work in CorelDRAW, you will undoubtedly make a drawing mistake, or choose the wrong menu command. Fortunately, CorelDRAW's Undo command lets you undo the results of the last operation or command you performed.

Part I also tells you how to use CorelDRAW's Help system. The Help menu offers extensive help on all aspects of using and understanding CorelDRAW. You can look up a command by name, or learn a procedure step by step using the Help system.

TASK 1

Starting and Exiting CorelDRAW

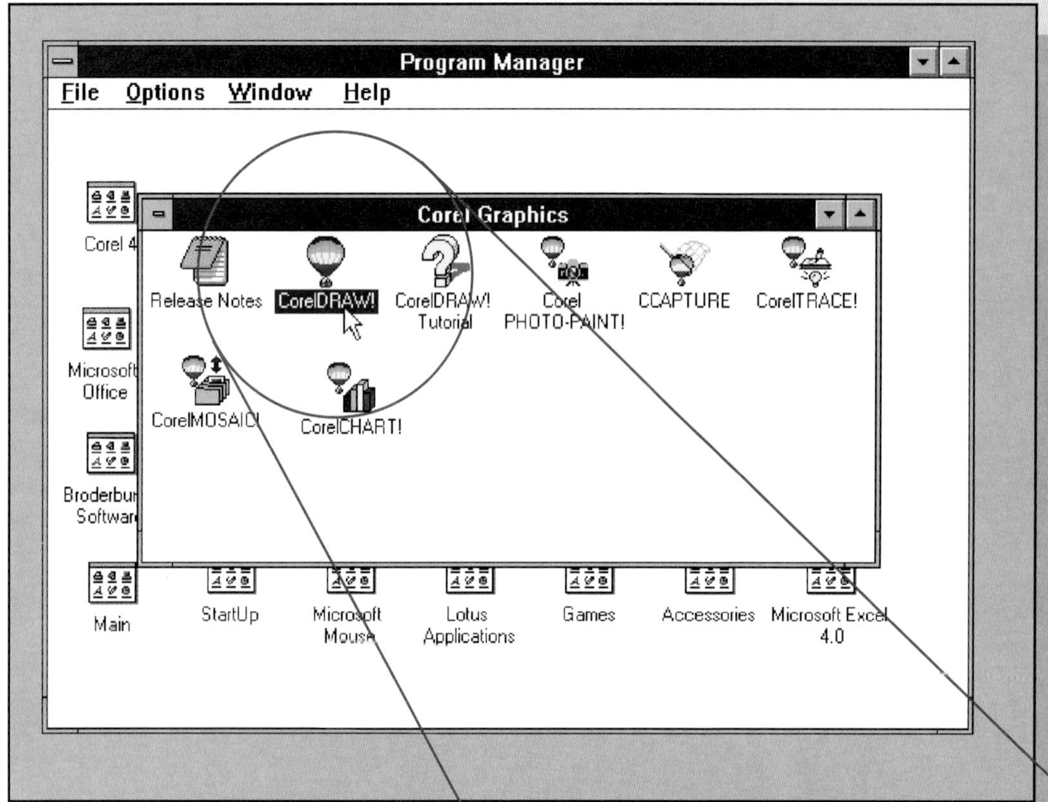

"Why would I do this?"

The CorelDRAW application is represented by a hot-air balloon icon. As with other Windows applications, you can start CorelDRAW by double-clicking the icon. The CorelDRAW icon and the icons for Corel's other programs, such as CorelCHART, are placed in a window called Corel Graphics. (In version 4, the group is called Corel 4.)

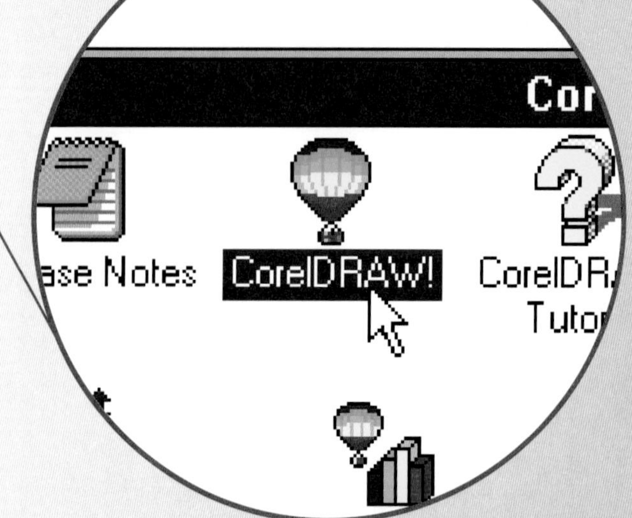

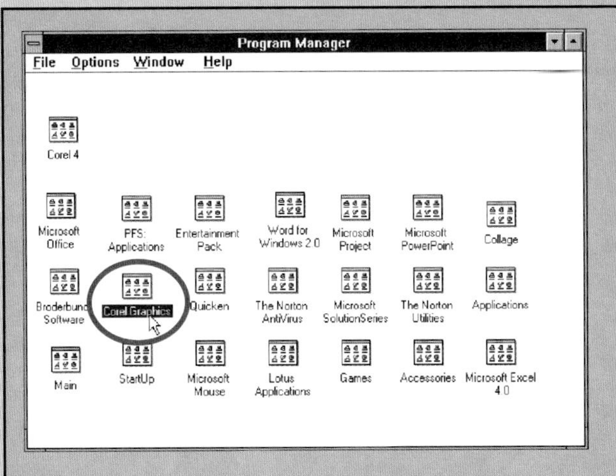

1 Double-click the icon labeled **Corel Graphics** (or **Corel 4**) in the Program Manager window. This step opens the Corel Graphics (or Corel 4) program group window.

NOTE

Each Corel program is represented by an icon. If a full installation is performed, you see icons for CorelDRAW!, CorelCHART!, CorelSHOW!, CorelMOVE! (version 4), CorelMOSAIC!, CorelPHOTO-PAINT!, CorelTRACE!, and CCAPTURE in the program group window.

2 Double-click the **CorelDRAW!** icon in the Corel window. This step starts CorelDRAW. The main CorelDRAW window appears on-screen.

NOTE

You can use the keyboard to start Corel by pressing Ctrl+Tab until the Corel 4 icon is highlighted, and then press Enter. Press the right-arrow key until the CorelDRAW icon is highlighted, and press Enter again.

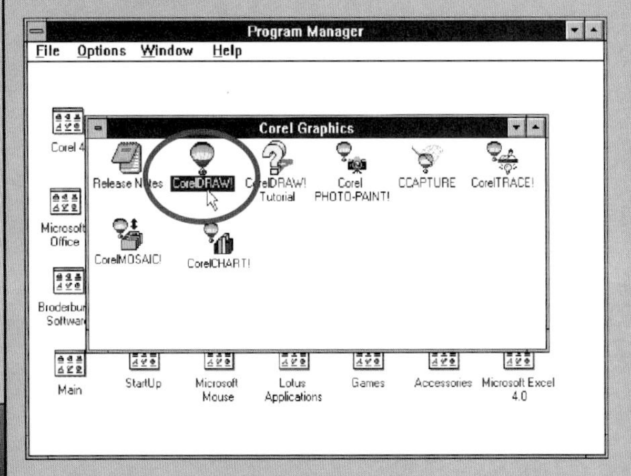

3 To exit CorelDRAW, click **File** in the menu bar. Then click **Exit**.

NOTE

To exit quickly, double-click the Control box in the upper-left corner of the window.

TASK 2

Using a Roll-Up Window

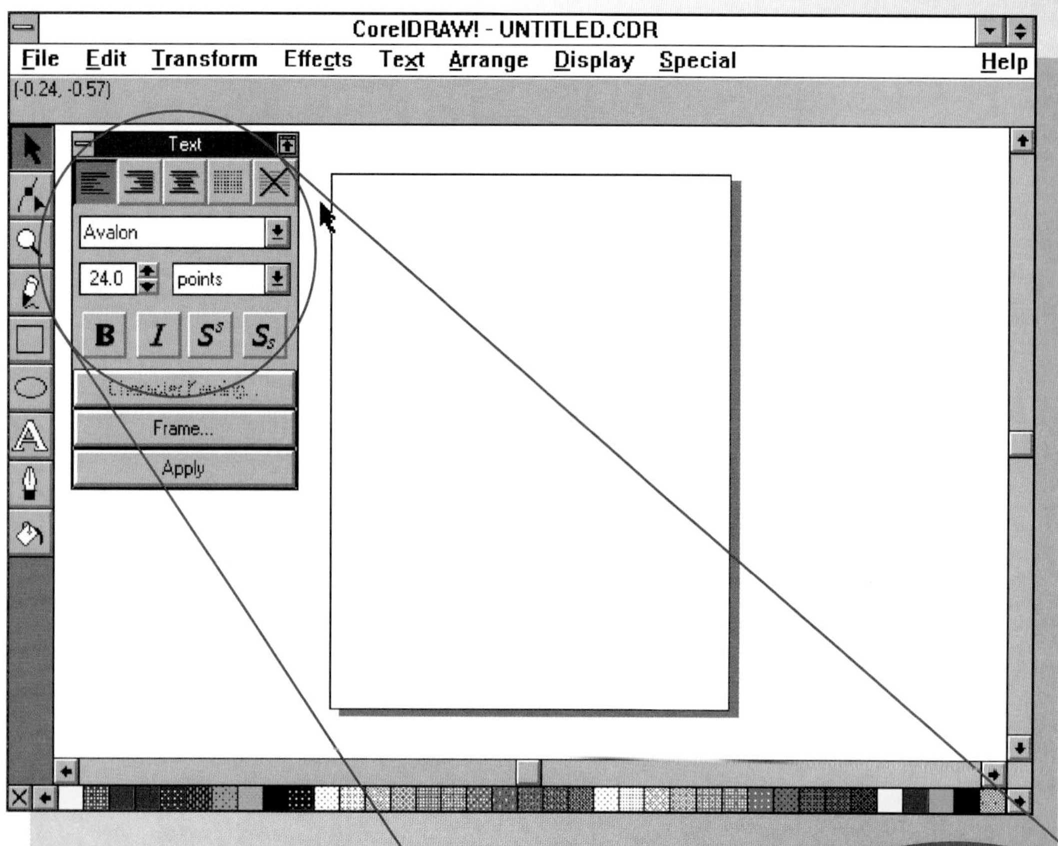

"Why would I do this?"

Roll-up windows are special dialog boxes. Like other dialog boxes in Corel, roll-ups contain many options for a particular procedure. Unlike normal dialog boxes, roll-ups can remain open while you work. Each time you need to access the commands in a roll-up window, you simply change the settings. As the name implies, a roll-up window can be "rolled up," leaving only the title bar of the window on-screen. Your work area remains uncluttered, yet the roll-up commands are within reach. The next time you need to access the option in the dialog box, you simply unroll the roll-up window.

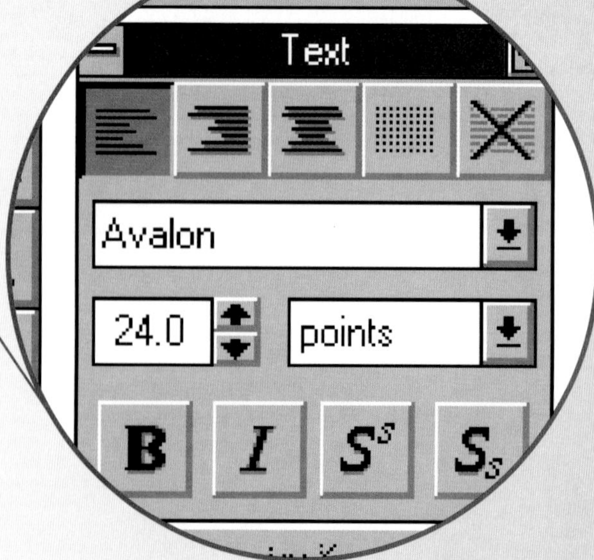

Task 2: Using a Roll-Up Window

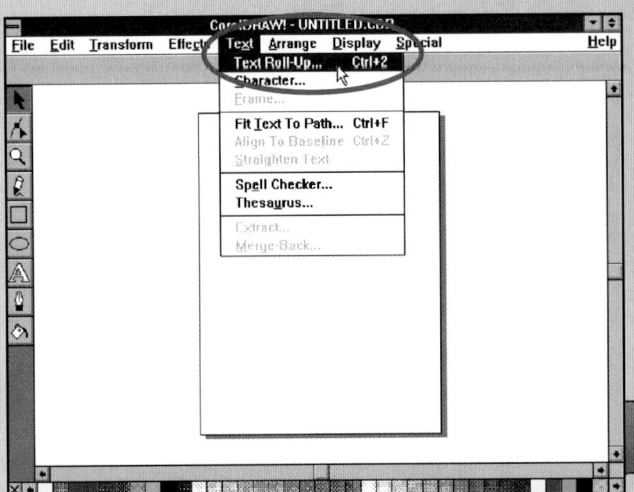

1 Click **Text** in the menu bar. Then click **Text Roll-Up** in the Text menu. The Text roll-up window appears.

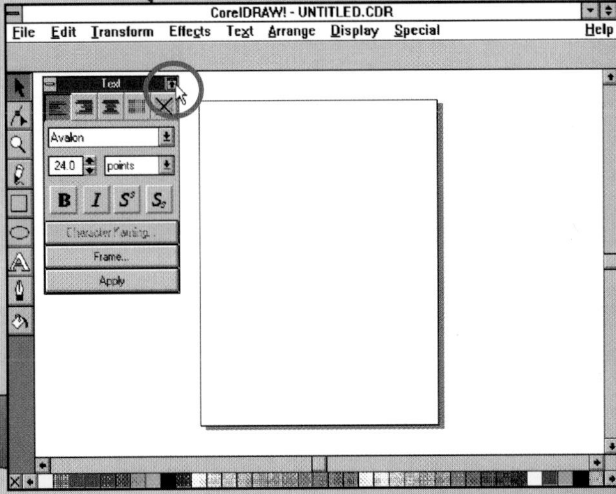

2 Click the **up arrow** in the upper-right corner of the roll-up window. The window rolls up, leaving only the title bar of the window.

3 Click the **down arrow** on the right side of the roll-up window's title bar. The window opens.

Task 2: Using a Roll-Up Window

4 Click the **control box** in the upper-left corner of the window. The window control menu appears. Then click **Arrange**. The window rolls up and is placed in the upper-right corner of the CorelDRAW window.

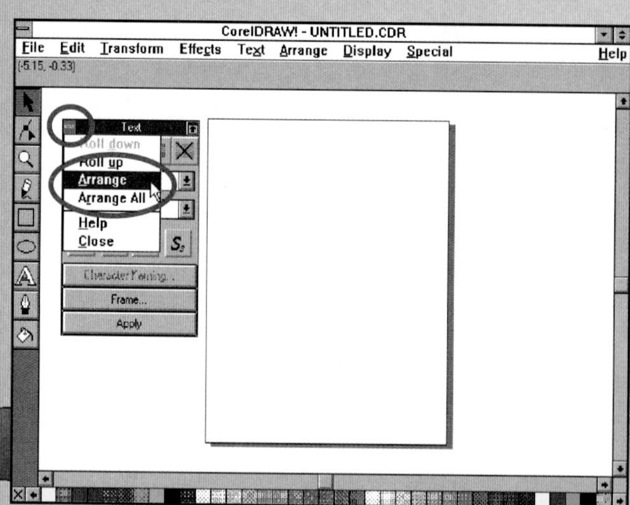

NOTE

You also can move a roll-up by dragging it by its title bar. The roll-up can be open or closed.

5 Click the **control box** in the title bar of the roll-up window. The window control menu appears.

6 Click **Close**. The roll-up window closes and disappears from the screen. To work with the roll-up window again, click **Text Roll-Up** on the **Text** menu.

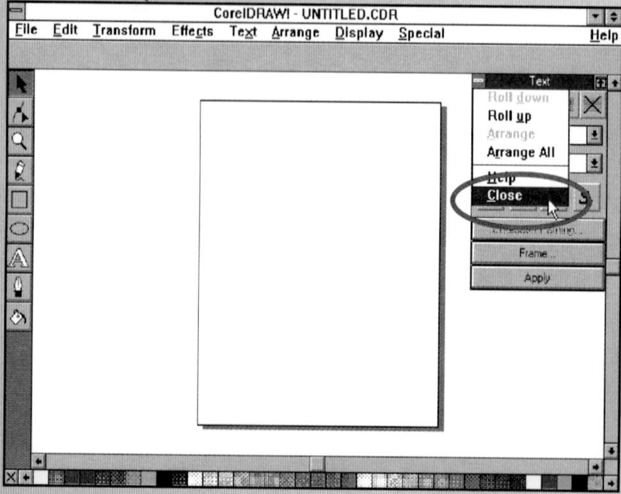

TASK 3

Using the Toolbox

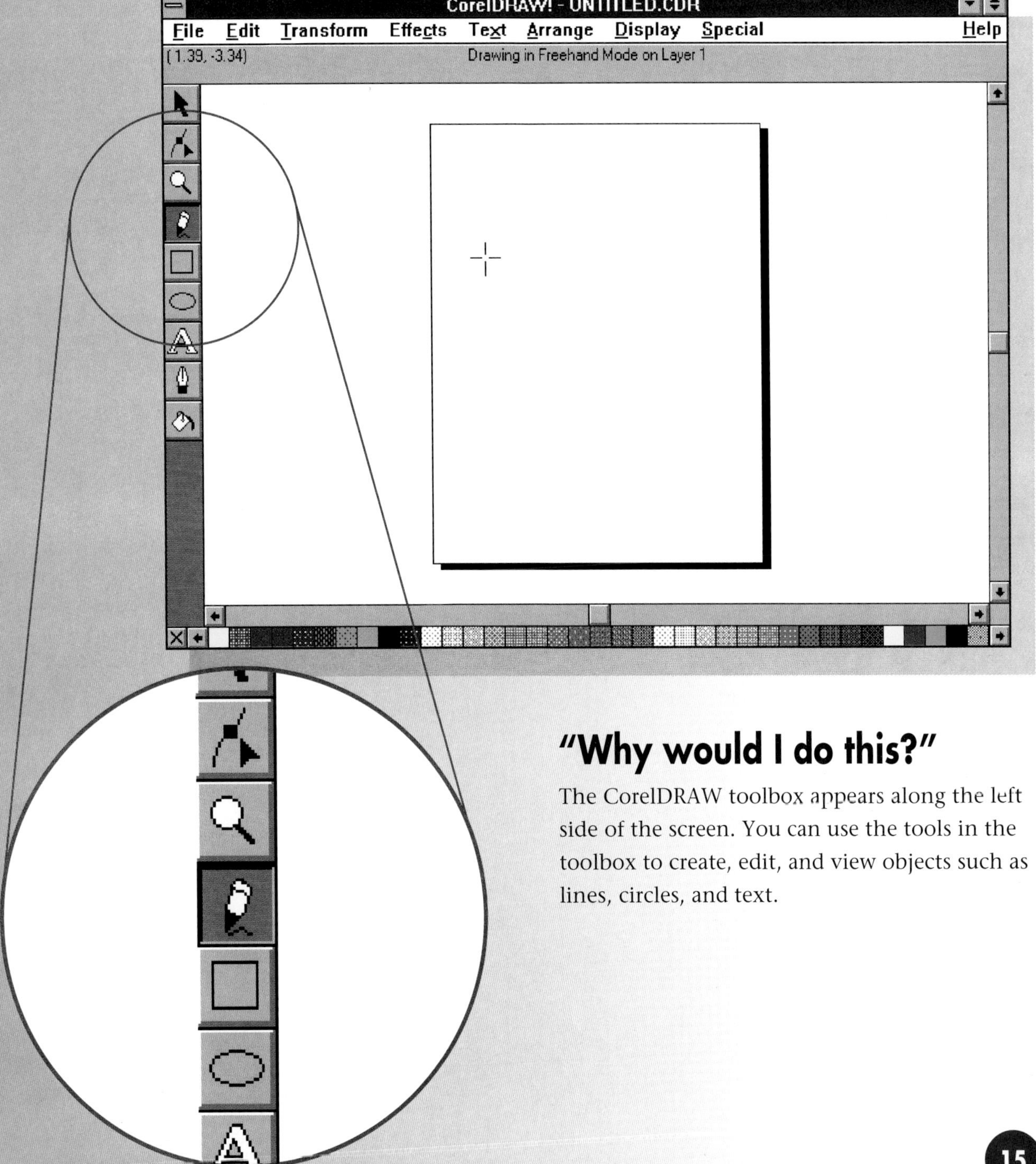

"Why would I do this?"

The CorelDRAW toolbox appears along the left side of the screen. You can use the tools in the toolbox to create, edit, and view objects such as lines, circles, and text.

Task 3: Using the Toolbox

1 Click the **Pencil** tool on the CorelDRAW toolbox. This step selects the Pencil tool.

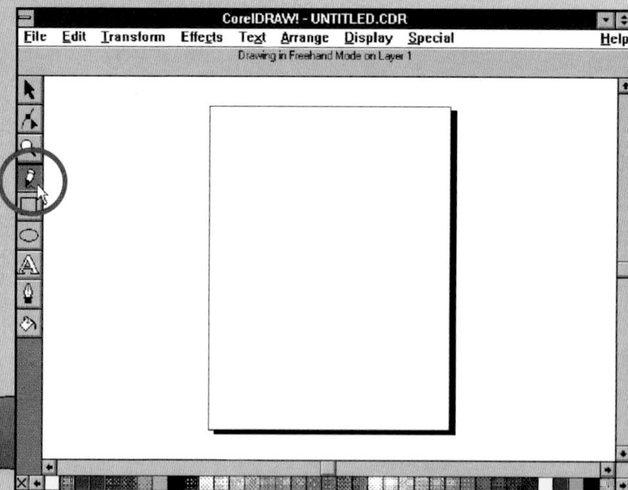

2 Move the mouse pointer to the CorelDRAW drawing area. The mouse pointer changes to a crossbar.

NOTE

The pointer takes many different shapes, depending on the tool that is selected from the toolbox. For example, it appears as a magnifying glass when the Zoom tool is selected, and as an arrowhead when the Node tool is selected.

3 Move the mouse pointer back to the toolbox. The pointer changes back to an arrow.

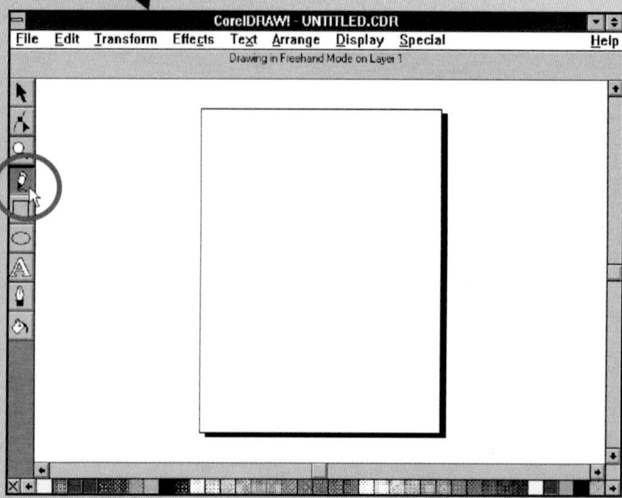

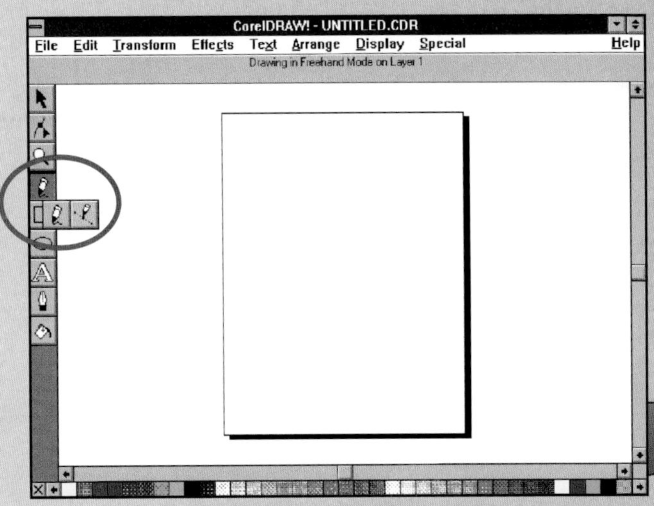

4 Click the **Pencil** tool and hold down the mouse button until a fly-out menu appears displaying additional Pencil tool options.

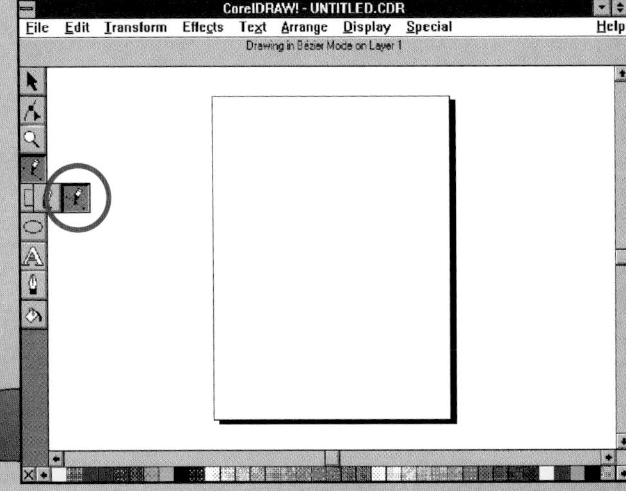

5 Click the **Bézier** tool. The Bézier tool appears in the toolbox in place of the Pencil tool.

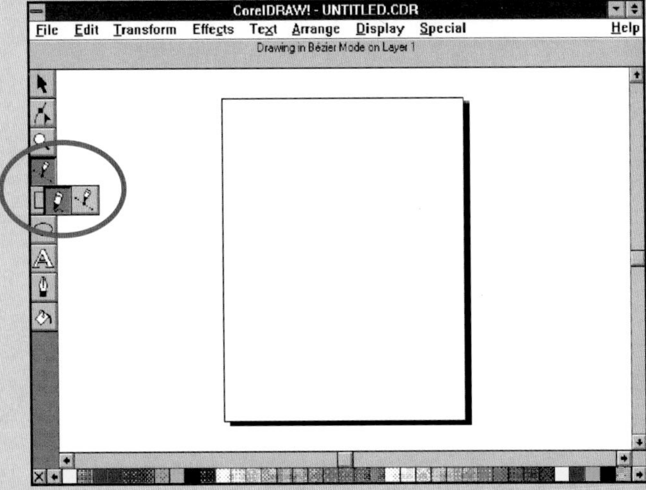

6 Click the **Bézier** tool until the fly-out menu appears. Click the **Pencil** tool. The Pencil tool replaces the Bézier tool in the toolbox.

TASK 4

Creating a New Drawing

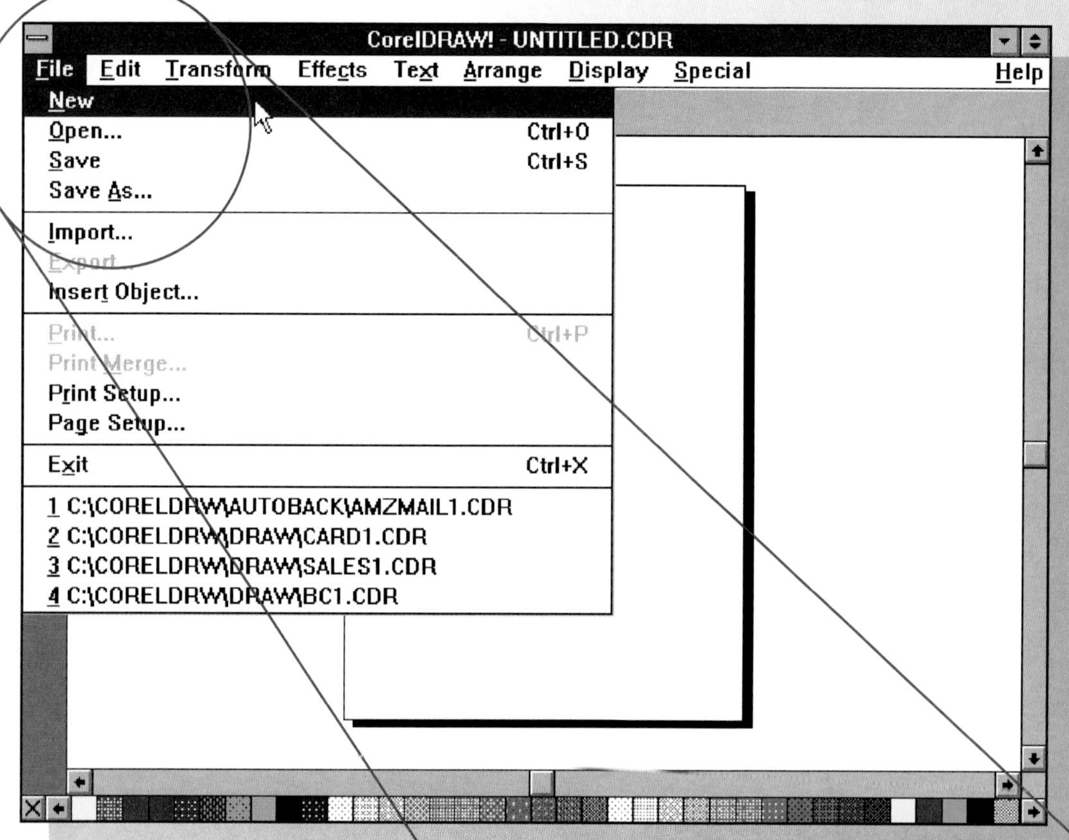

"Why would I do this?"

Each time you start CorelDRAW, a new drawing is created. You can begin drawing when the drawing window appears. If you are working with a drawing and want to start a new one, you can create a new blank drawing and either save or discard the current drawing. This task shows you how to create a new drawing.

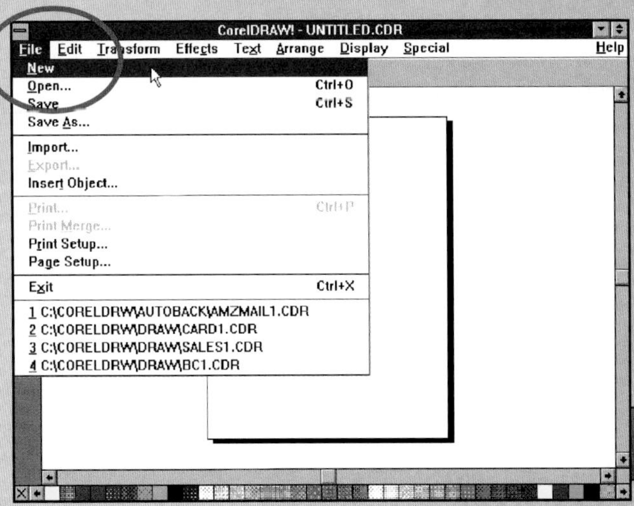

1 Click **File** in the menu bar. Then click **New** in the File menu. This step displays a blank CorelDRAW screen. If you were working on a drawing when you selected the new command, CorelDRAW displays a window asking if you want to save the changes to the current drawing.

2 Click **Yes** to save changes to your current drawing. Click **No** to discard the current drawing.

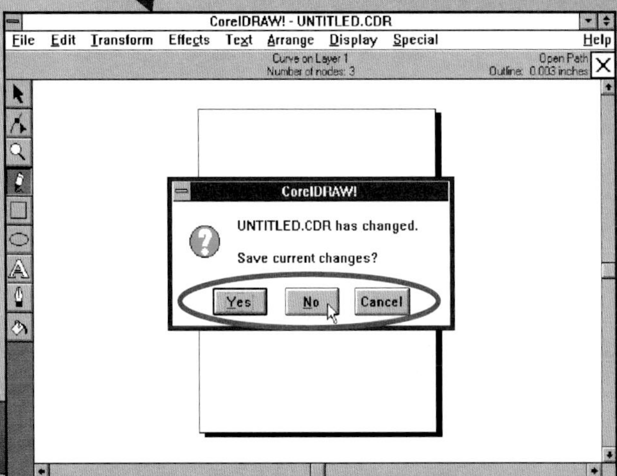

WHY WORRY?

If you have not made any changes to the current drawing, CorelDRAW creates a new drawing without prompting you to save the changes to the current drawing.

3 CorelDRAW clears the drawing window. You can now create a new drawing.

TASK 5

Creating a New Drawing Using a Template (version 4)

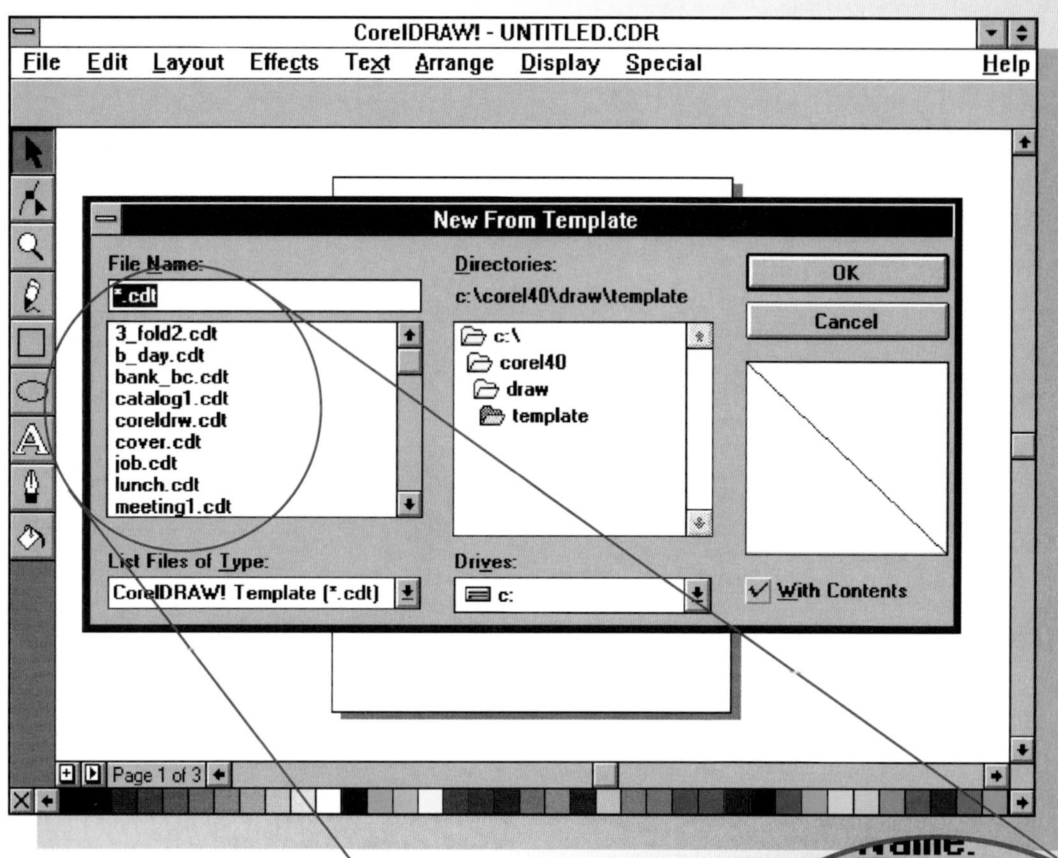

"Why would I do this?"

If you are working with CorelDRAW version 4, you can use templates to quickly create drawings. *Templates* are premade files that contain basic drawing objects and text. CorelDRAW 4 provides several templates, including a newsletter template and the help-wanted flier described in this task. You can easily modify the template drawing and text to meet your own needs.

Task 5: Creating a New Drawing Using a Template (version 4)

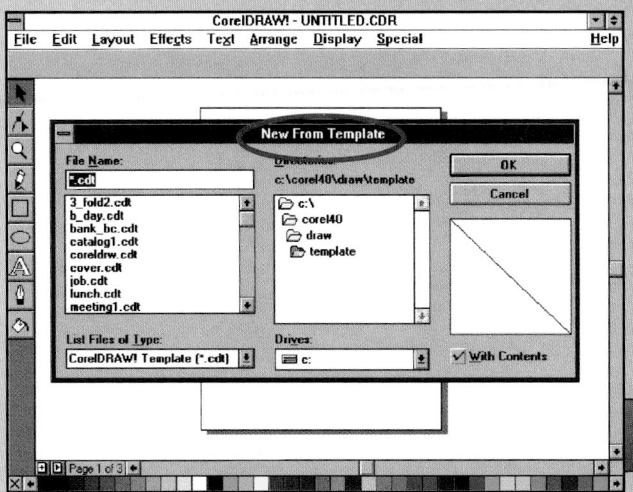

1 Click **File** in the menu bar. Then click **New From Template** in the File menu. The New From Template dialog box appears on-screen. A template is a collection of styles and can contain graphics and/or text. Each new drawing you begin uses the default CORELDRW.CDT styles template.

2 In the File Name box, click **JOB.CDT.** A preview image of the template appears on the right side of the dialog box. When you have selected the template you want to use, click **OK.**

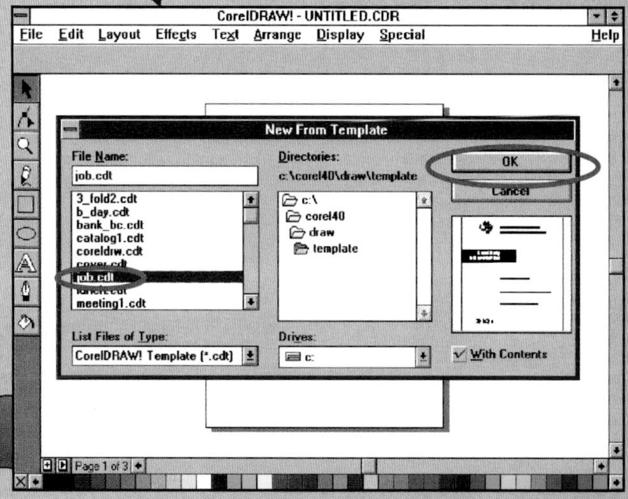

3 CorelDRAW places a new drawing on-screen containing the contents of the template. You can now add your own objects and text to the drawing.

TASK 6

Setting Up a Multipage Document (version 4)

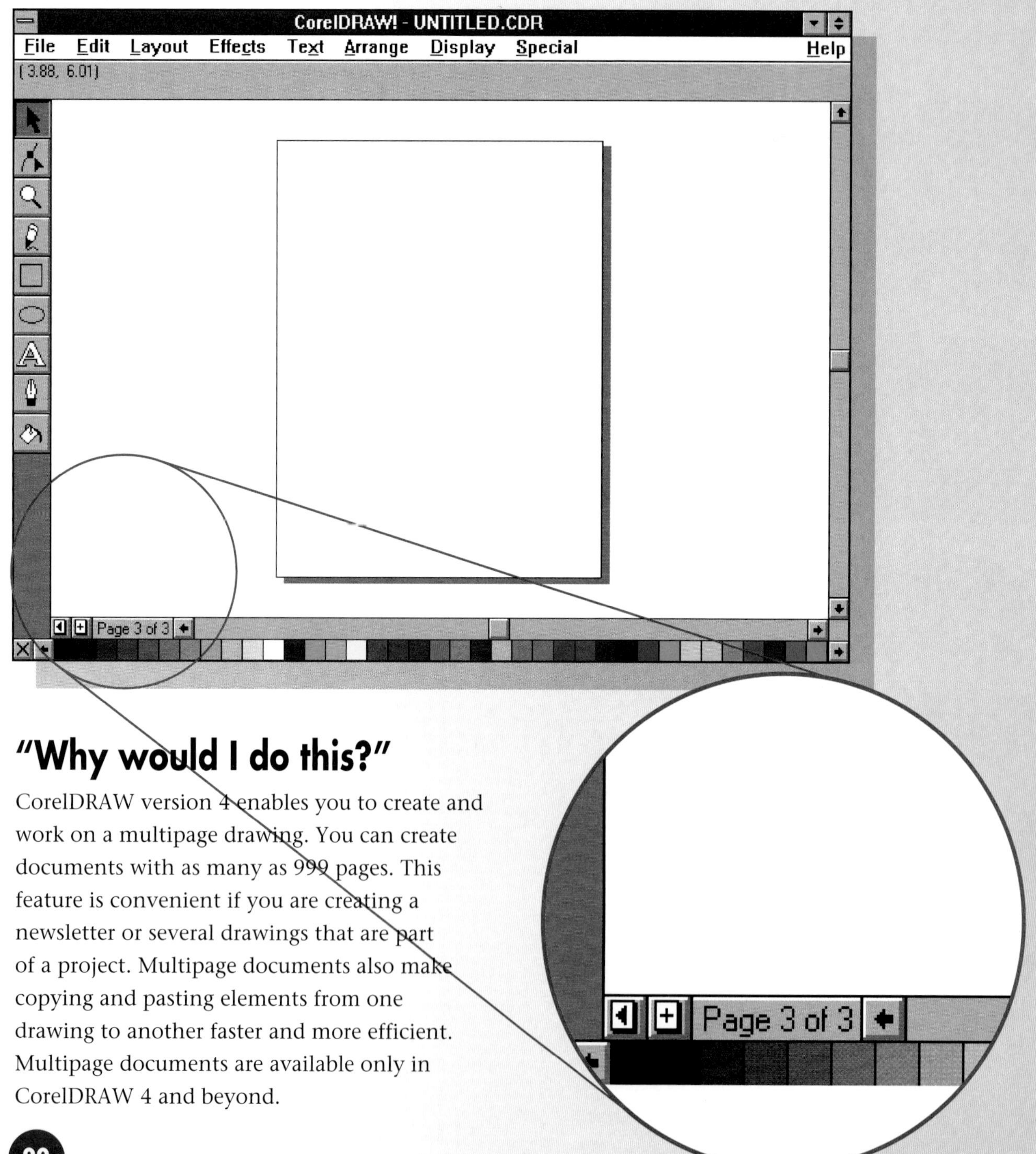

"Why would I do this?"

CorelDRAW version 4 enables you to create and work on a multipage drawing. You can create documents with as many as 999 pages. This feature is convenient if you are creating a newsletter or several drawings that are part of a project. Multipage documents also make copying and pasting elements from one drawing to another faster and more efficient. Multipage documents are available only in CorelDRAW 4 and beyond.

Task 6: Setting Up a Multipage Document (version 4)

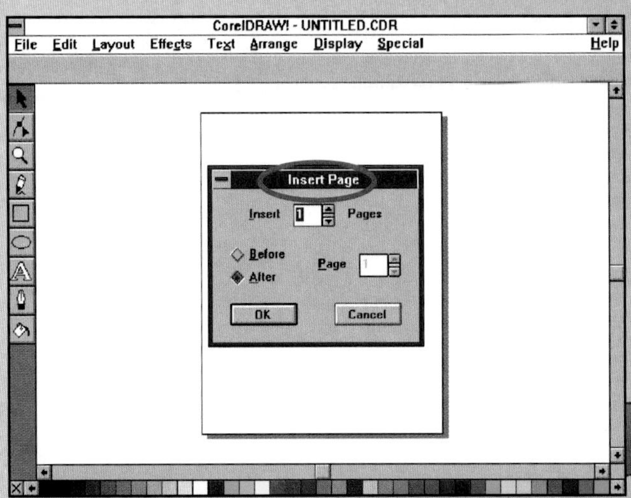

1 Click **Layout** in the menu bar. Then click **Insert Page** in the Layout menu. This step opens the Insert Page dialog box.

2 Type **2** next in the Insert Pages text box. This step tells CorelDRAW to add two new pages to your document.

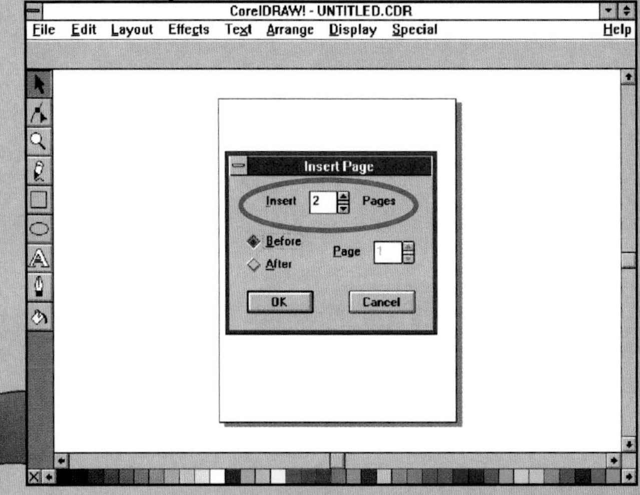

3 Click the **After** option. This step adds the new pages after the current page.

NOTE

If you want to add pages before the current page, click the Before option in the Insert Pages dialog box.

4 Click **OK**. CorelDRAW inserts two new drawing pages after the current page. Icons at the bottom left of the screen indicate that there are three pages in the document and you are currently on the third page.

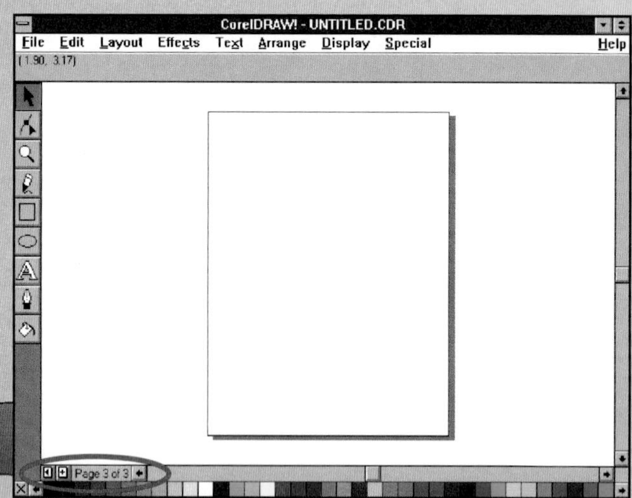

NOTE

In a multipage document, CorelDRAW displays page icons at the bottom left of the screen. These icons identify the number of pages in the document and which page is currently in view.

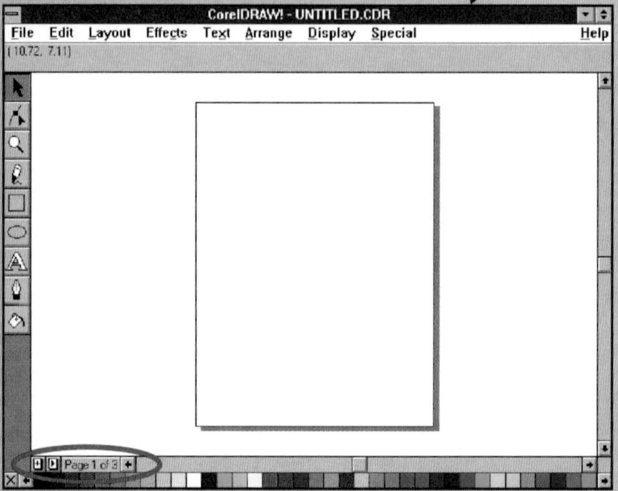

5 Click the **left arrow** icon, at the lower-left corner of the screen, twice. This step changes the display to show the first page of the document.

TASK 7

Specifying the Paper Size and Orientation

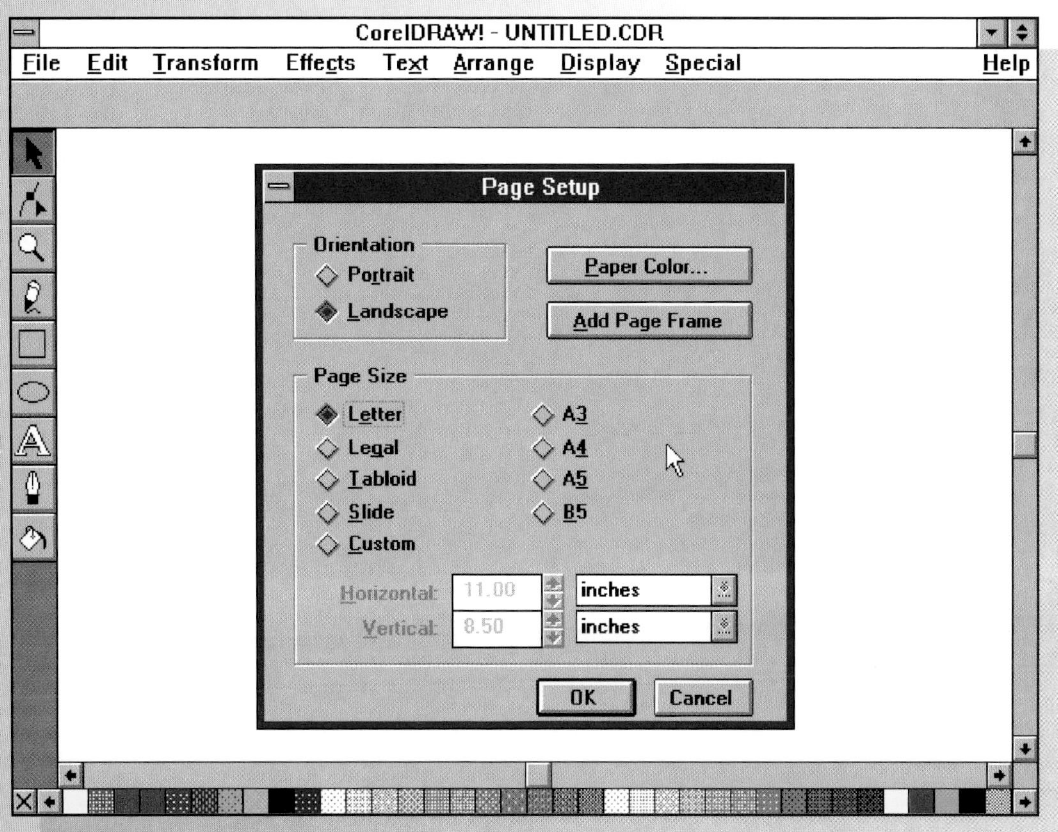

"Why would I do this?"

CorelDRAW's paper size settings allow you to choose among several paper sizes. You can choose among paper sizes such as letter size, 11 by 17 Tabloid size, or a custom size of your own choosing. The page orientation setting sets the drawing area so that it is either taller than it is wide, or wider than it is tall.

Task 7: Specifying the Paper Size and Orientation

1 Click **File** in the menu bar. Then click **Page Setup** in the File menu.

NOTE

If you are working in CorelDRAW 4, choose Page Setup from the Layout menu to access the Paper Size and Orientation options.

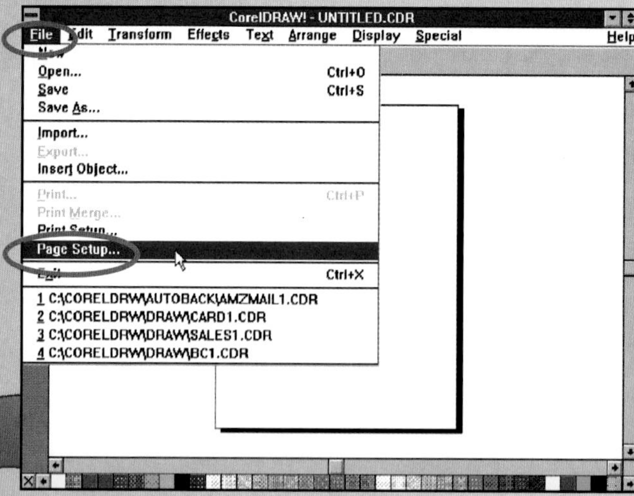

2 The Page Setup dialog box appears. By default, the page is set to a standard size letter (8 1/2 by 11 inches) in portrait orientation.

3 Click **Landscape**. This step changes the page orientation from portrait (taller) to landscape (wider). The horizontal and vertical dimensions displayed at the bottom of the dialog box change to reflect the new orientation.

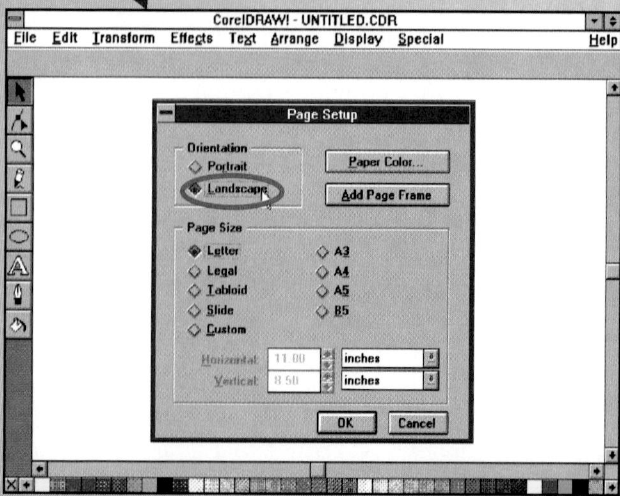

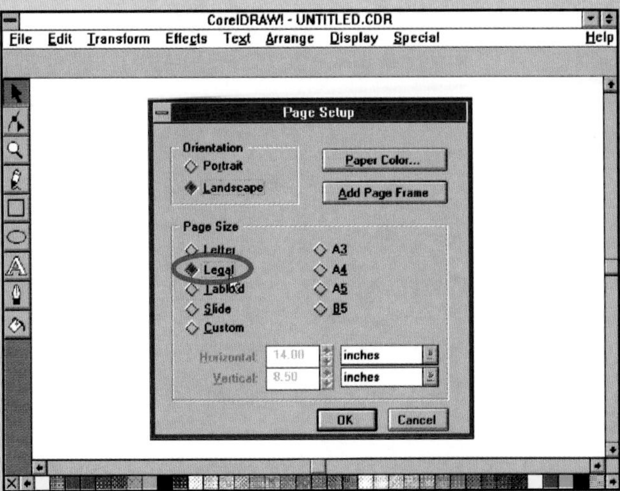

4 Click **Legal.** This step changes the paper size to legal.

5 Click **OK.** The drawing window widens to reflect the new paper size.

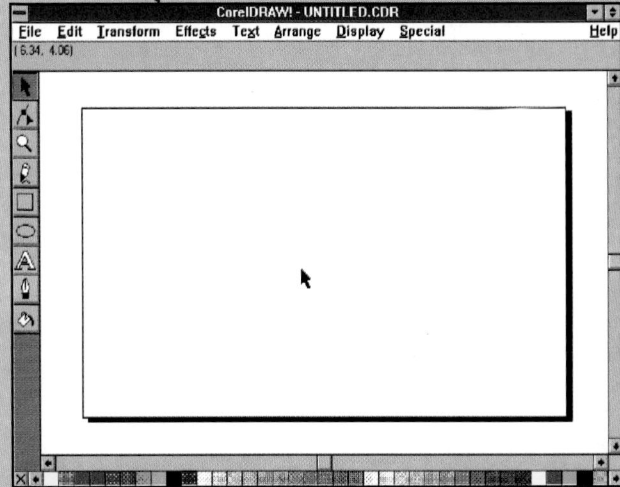

TASK 8

Printing a Drawing

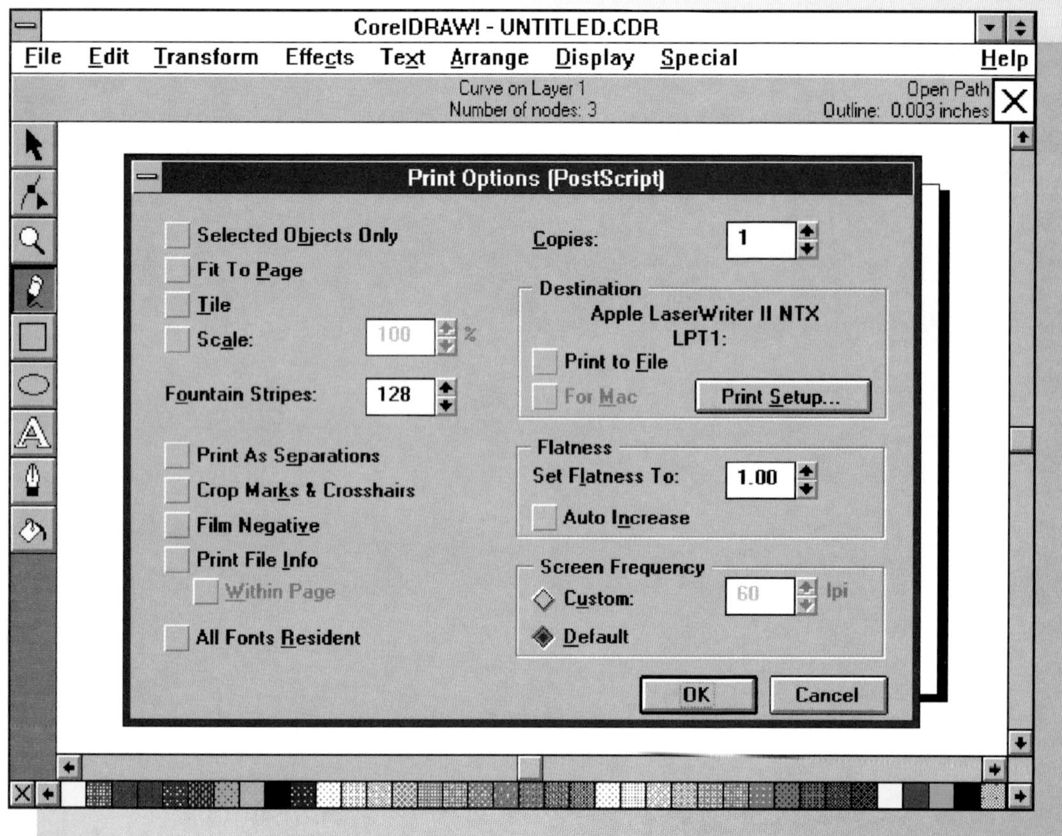

"Why would I do this?"

In CorelDRAW, you can print your drawings using a basic procedure. By using several print options in the Print Options dialog box, you can enhance how your printouts look.

Task 8: Printing a Drawing

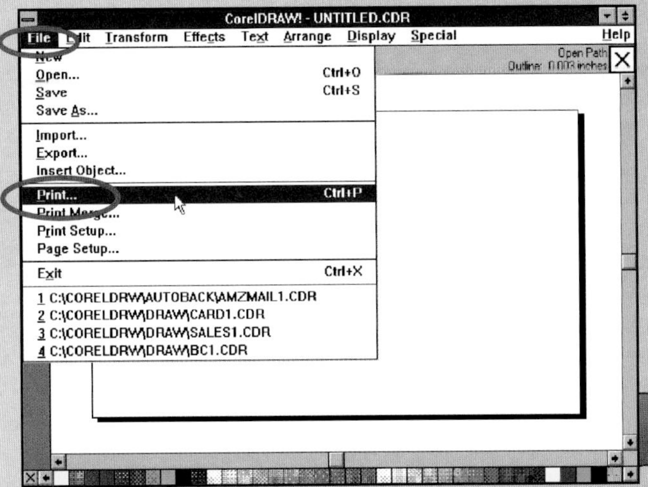

1 Click **File** in the menu bar. Then click **Print** in the File menu.

2 The Print Options dialog box appears. To print the current drawing, click **OK**.

WHY WORRY?

Don't be concerned if your Print Options dialog box looks different from the one in this task. The dialog box changes slightly depending on the kind of printer you have installed. You can still follow the task to print your drawing.

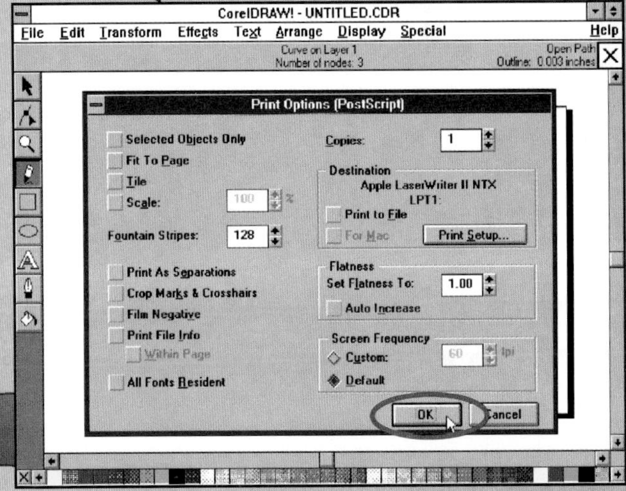

3 While the drawing is printing, Corel displays a message box telling you that it is printing. When the printing is done, the message box will disappear.

WHY WORRY?

To cancel a print job once it has begun, click the Cancel button in the CorelDRAW! Is Printing window.

TASK 9

Changing the Screen Display

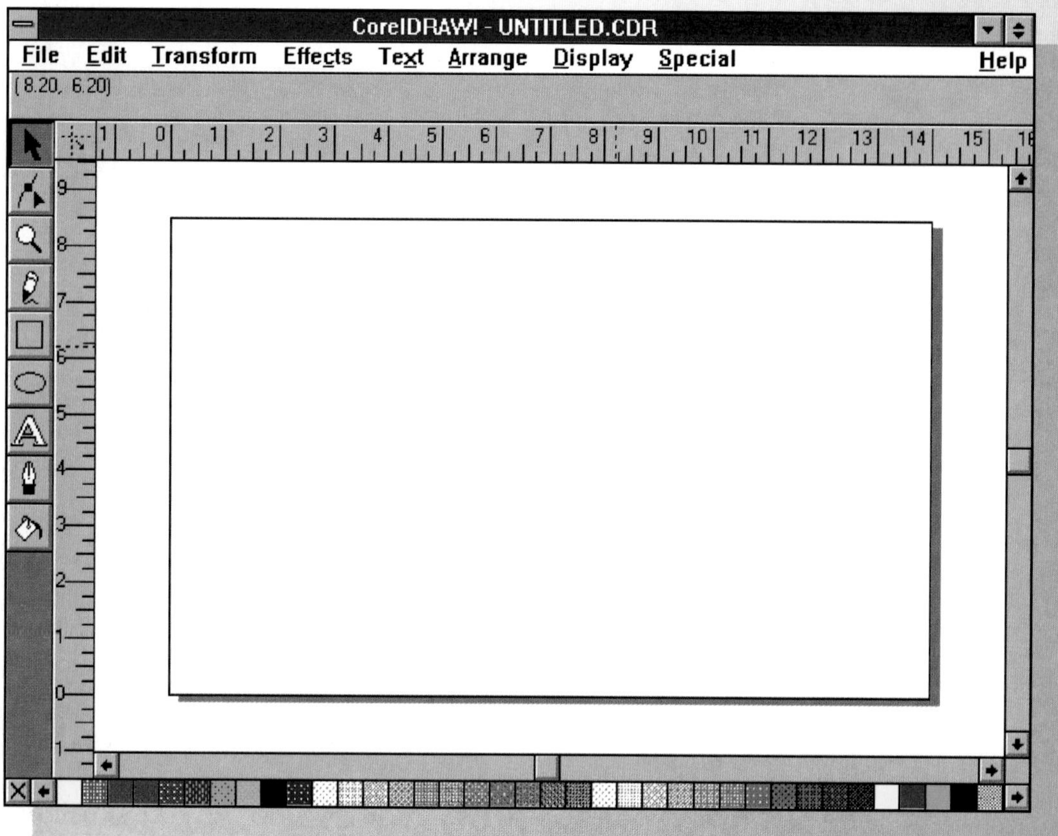

"Why would I do this?"

As you work, you can change the CorelDRAW screen display to suit your needs. For example, you can turn on horizontal and vertical rulers to help you measure and place objects. You can turn on a status line that displays information about the object you're working with. And you can change the display to see what your drawing will look like when you print. This task shows you how to use these display features.

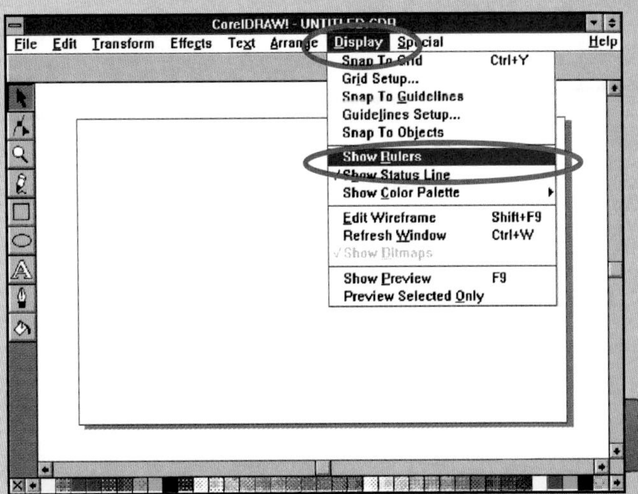

1 Click **Display** in the menu bar. Then click **Show Rulers**. This step toggles CorelDRAW's rulers on and off. If a check mark appears next to the Show Rulers option on the Display menu, the rulers are turned on.

2 Click **Display**. Clicking the **Show Status Line** toggles the status line on and off. The check mark next to the option indicates that the status line is turned on. The status line is displayed between the menu bar and the drawing window, and provides information about the selected object or the action you are currently performing.

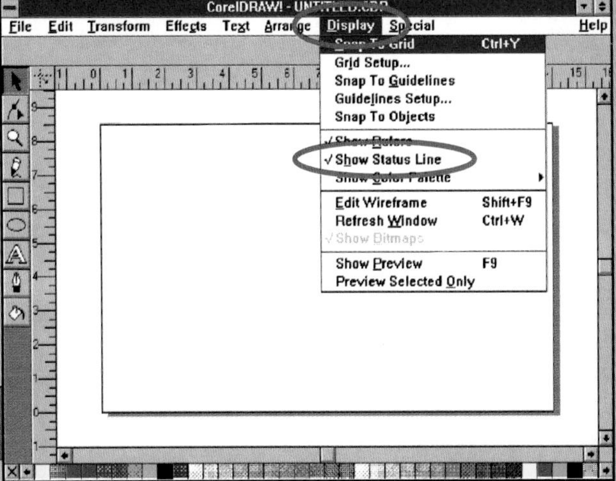

3 Review the CorelDRAW screen. Notice the rulers displayed at the top and left of the drawing window, and the status line displayed at the top of the screen.

NOTE

You can preview your drawing by selecting Show Preview on the Display menu. Show Preview removes all menus and tool boxes from the screen. When finished, click the right mouse button to return to the CorelDRAW drawing window.

TASK 10

Setting Up a Grid

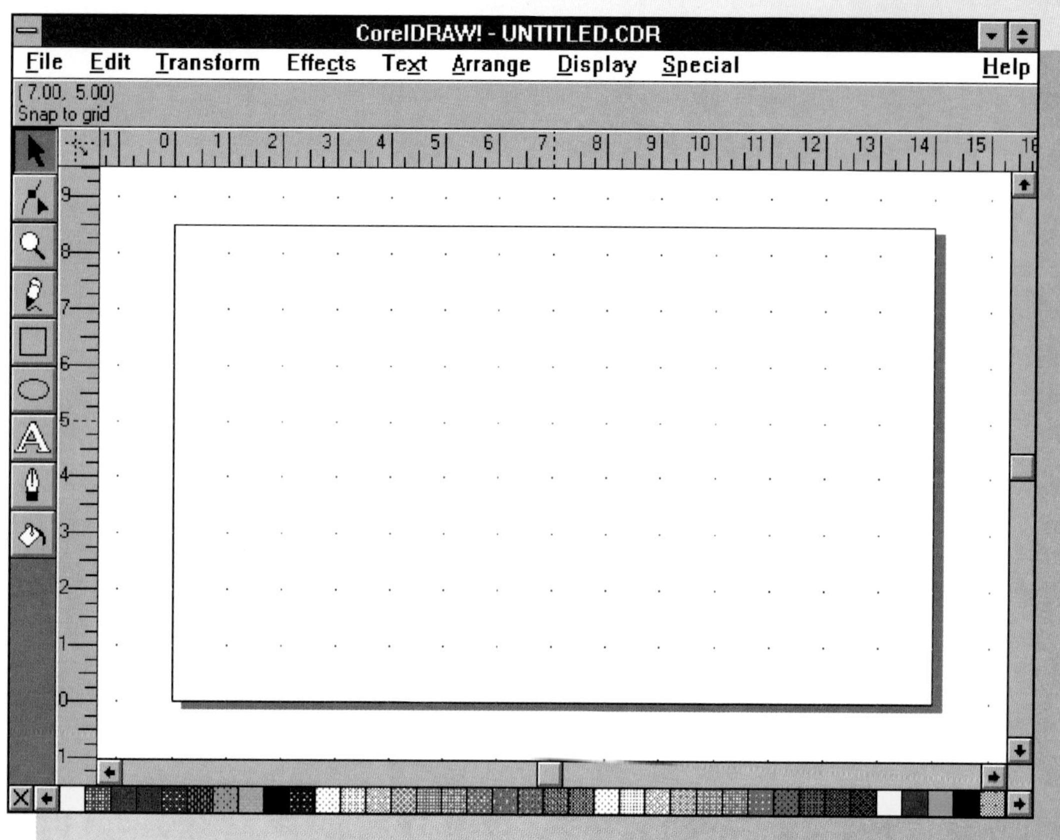

"Why would I do this?"

Like a piece of graph paper marked evenly with rows and columns, CorelDRAW's Grid feature places dots on the drawing window at even intervals. The grid enables you to precisely place and draw objects in the drawing window. Turning on the Snap To Grid feature gives you more control by helping you place objects exactly on grid points. You'll notice this feature when you place an object in the drawing window and the object jumps slightly to the nearest grid point when you release the mouse button.

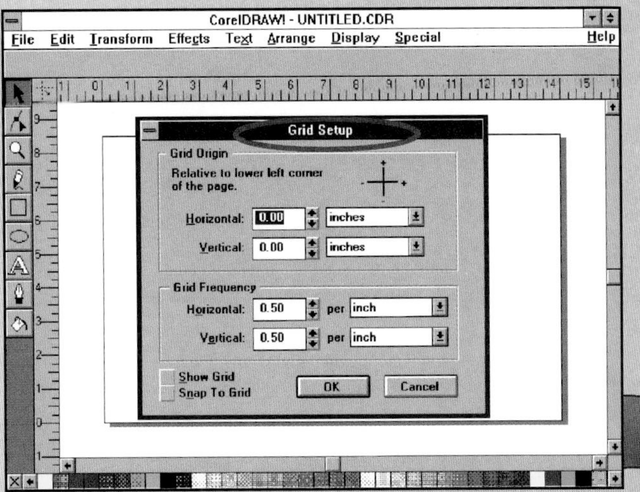

1 Click **Display** in the menu bar. Then click **Grid Setup** to display the Grid Setup dialog box.

NOTE

If you are using CorelDRAW 4, the Grid Setup option is located on the Layout menu.

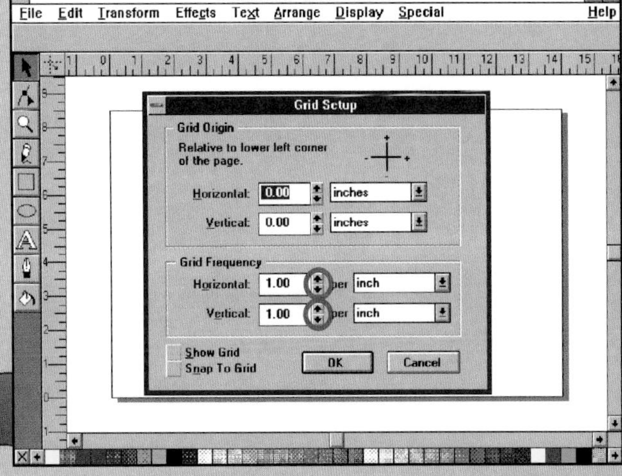

2 In the Grid Frequency section, click the Horizontal setting **up arrow** once. Click the Vertical setting **up arrow** once. These steps set the number of grid lines per inch. The horizontal and vertical settings are set to 1 line per inch.

NOTE

Changing the Grid Frequency also changes the measuring increments on CorelDRAW's rulers. To turn on the rulers, click Show Rulers on the Display menu.

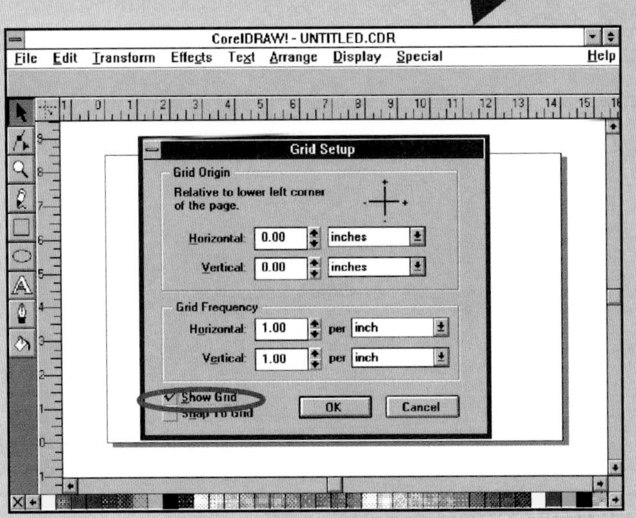

3 Click the **Show Grid** check box in the lower-left corner of the dialog box. This step turns on a series of dots representing the grid in the drawing window. A check mark appears next to the Show Grid check box.

4 Click the **Snap To Grid** check box. With the Snap To Grid feature turned on, objects you place in the drawing window are automatically aligned to the grid.

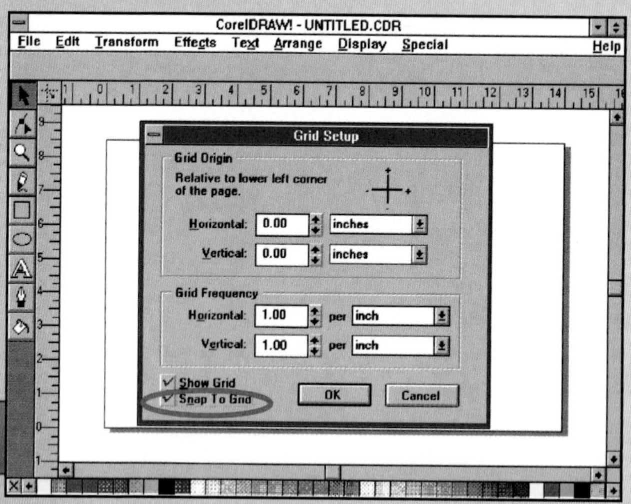

WHY WORRY?

Sometimes the Snap To Grid feature can prevent you from placing an object where you want it. If you find that an object keeps jumping to the nearest grid point instead of dropping where you want it, try turning off the Snap To Grid feature.

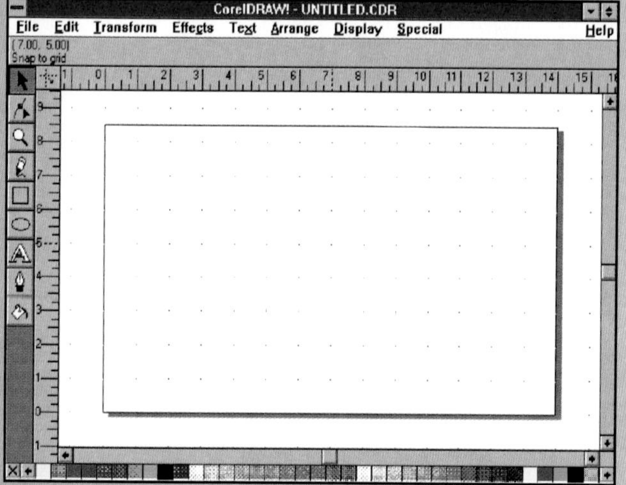

5 Click **OK** to accept the changes in the dialog box. The drawing window is displayed with the grid showing.

TASK 11

Undoing Mistakes

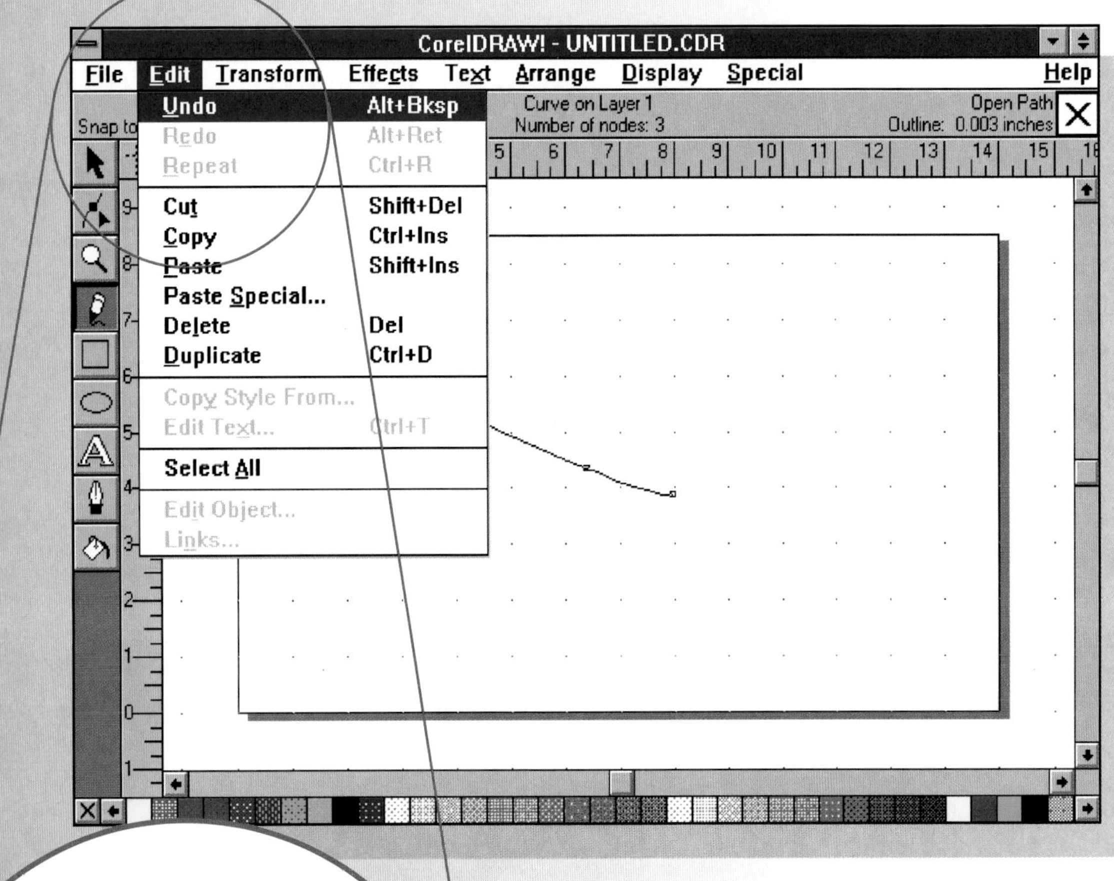

"Why would I do this?"

CorelDRAW version 3 enables you to undo the last action you performed. Whether you deleted a line by mistake or changed the color of an object inadvertently, the Undo command will reverse your last action. If you change your mind again, the Redo command will redo the last action you made. With CorelDRAW version 4, you can undo your last 99 actions.

Task 11: Undoing Mistakes

1 Click the **Pencil** tool in the drawing toolbox. Move the mouse pointer to the drawing window. The mouse pointer changes to a crossbar pointer.

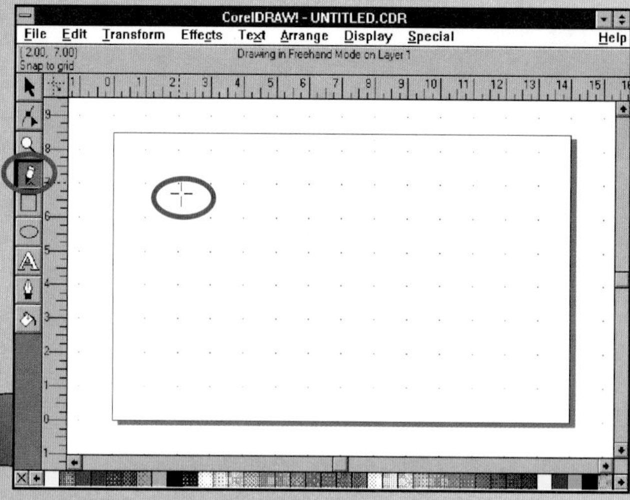

2 Press the left mouse button and drag the crossbar to create a line. This step creates a freehand line in the drawing window.

3 Release the mouse button. This step completes the freehand line.

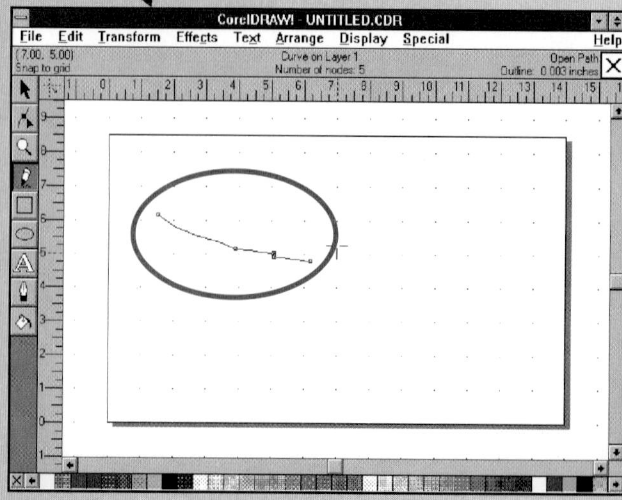

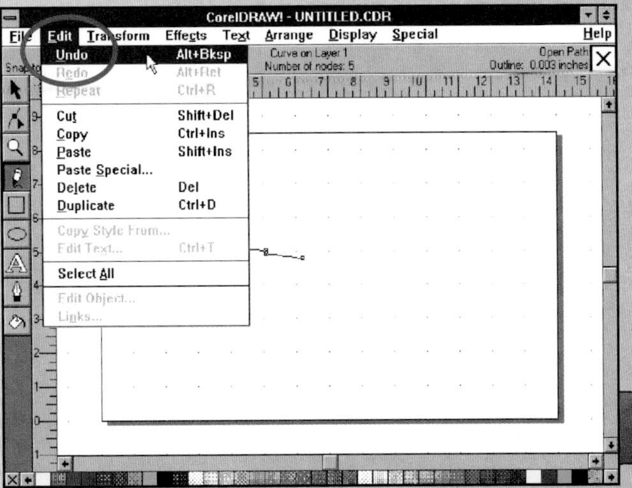

4 Click **Edit** in the menu bar. The Edit menu appears.

5 Click **Undo** in the Edit menu**.** This step removes the freehand line you just created.

> **NOTE**
>
> Not all actions can be undone. For example, you cannot undo zooming or scrolling, or opening, saving, or importing files.

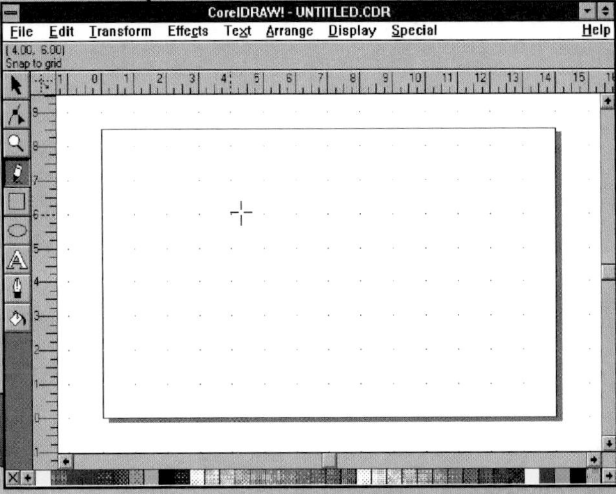

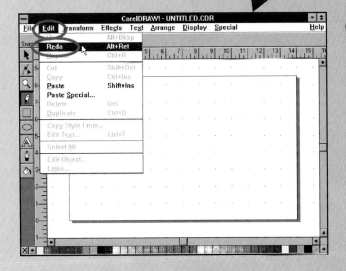

6 Click **Edit** and then click **Redo**. This step redoes the undo you just did. Or, this step cancels the last Undo operation. In this case, Redo replaces the freehand line in the drawing window.

> **NOTE**
>
> In CorelDRAW 4, the name of the Undo command in the Edit menu changes to identify the last action. `Can't Undo` appears when an action can't be undone.

TASK 12

Saving a Drawing

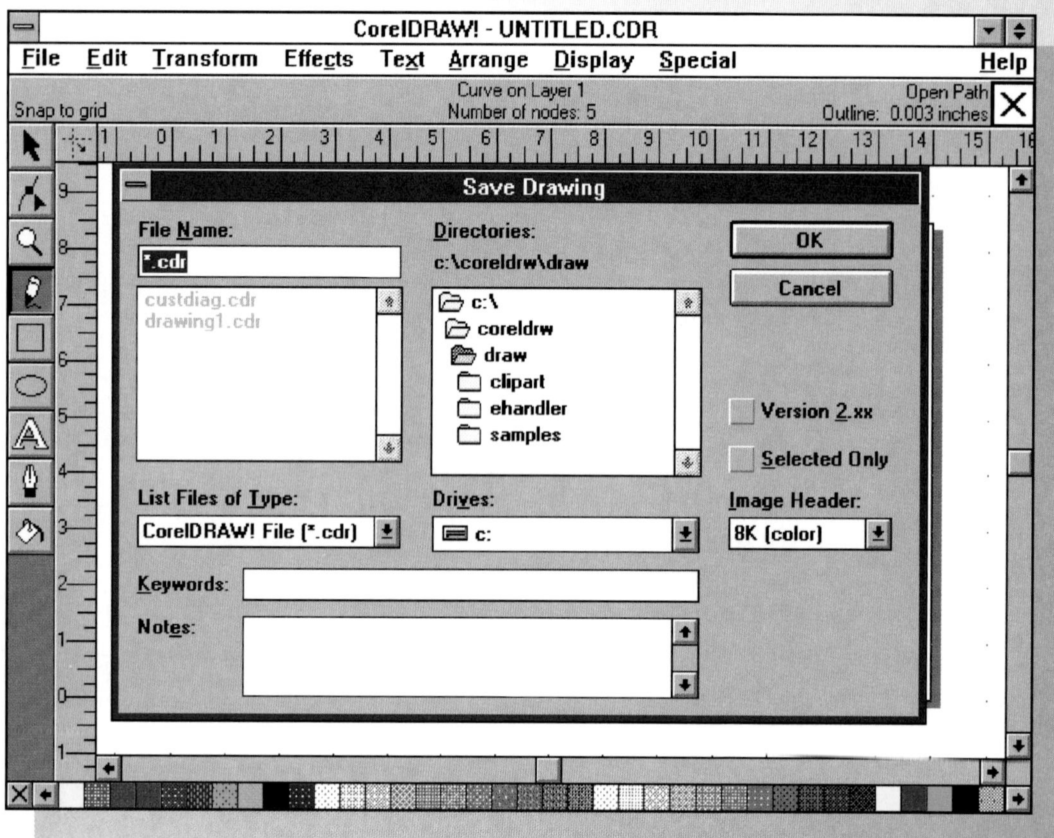

"Why would I do this?"

While you're working on a drawing in CorelDRAW, the drawing is stored in the computer's memory. If you turn off the computer, or if a power loss occurs, the drawing will be lost. Saving your drawing stores it on disk. When you need to work on the drawing again, you can open it from the disk. If you are making extensive changes to a drawing, you should save your work frequently.

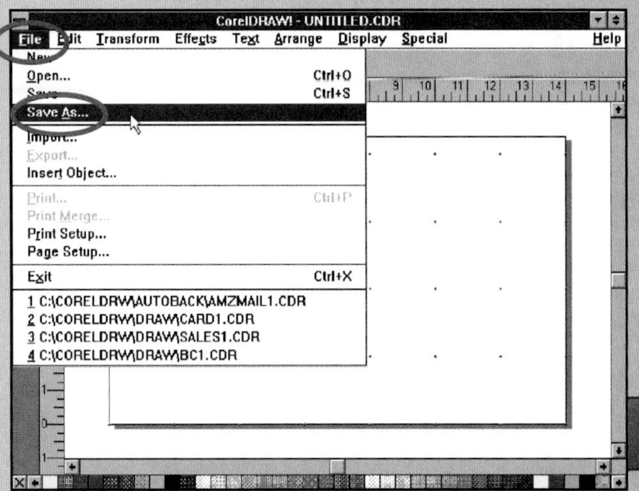

1 Click **File**, and then click **Save As**.

2 The Save Drawing dialog box appears. Type **DRAWING1** in the File Name text box. You can type up to eight characters. CorelDRAW adds the CDR extension automatically.

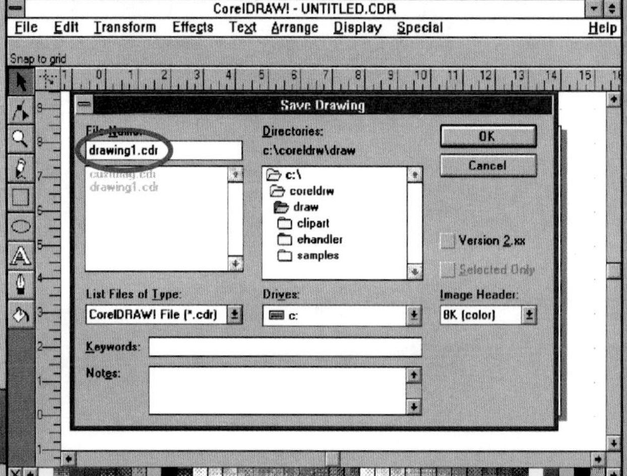

NOTE

After you have named your file in the Save Drawing dialog box and saved the file, you can save the file quickly next time by clicking Save on the File menu.

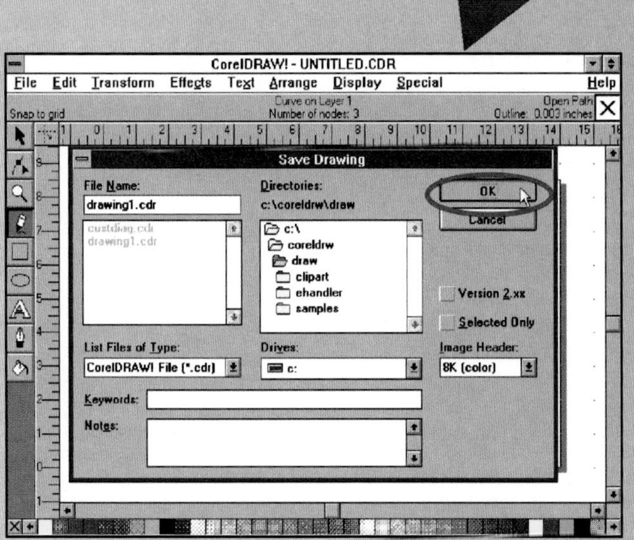

3 Click **OK**. This step accepts the file name and saves your drawing to the disk. The file name, `DRAWING1.CDR`, appears in the title bar.

WHY WORRY?

If you type a file name that already exists, CorelDRAW displays an alert box, asking `Replace Existing File?`. Click Cancel to return to the Save Drawing dialog box, and then type a new file name.

TASK 13

Opening an Existing Drawing

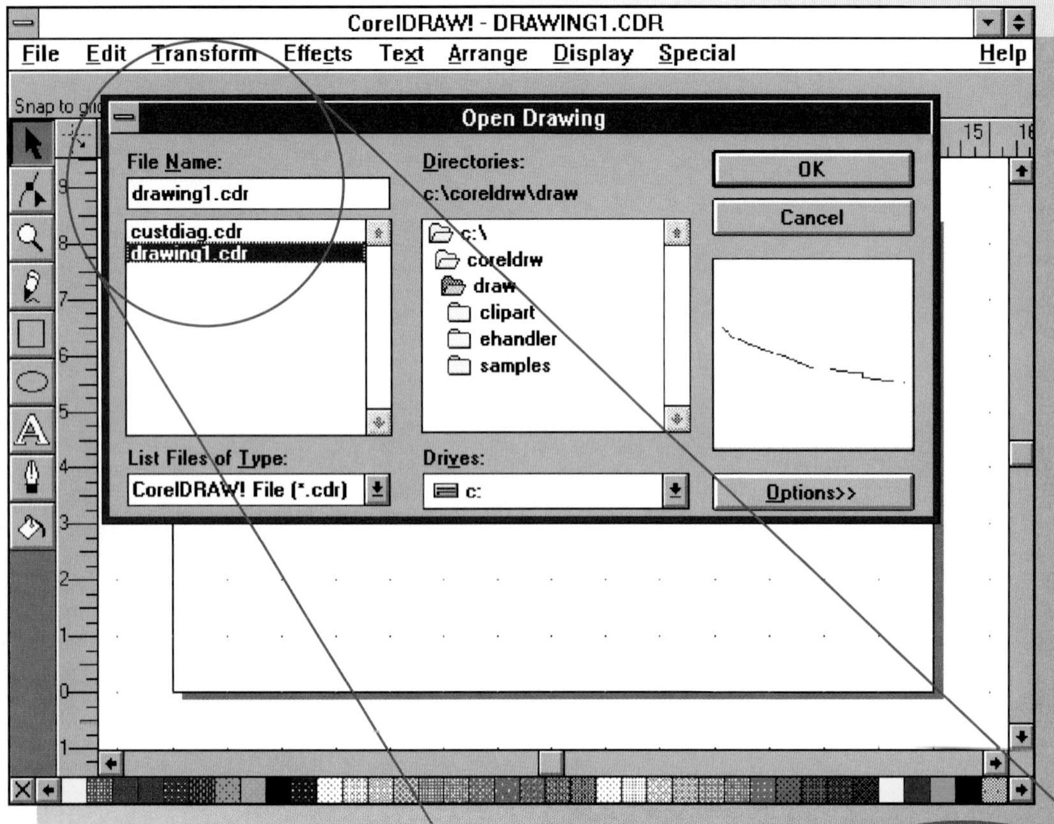

"Why would I do this?"

CorelDRAW displays a new blank drawing when you start the program. To work on a drawing you saved previously, you need to retrieve the drawing from disk. CorelDRAW's Open dialog box enables you to navigate through the directories and file names on your disk and display a small preview image of each file as you select it. This task shows you how to open a drawing saved to disk.

Task 13: Opening an Existing Drawing

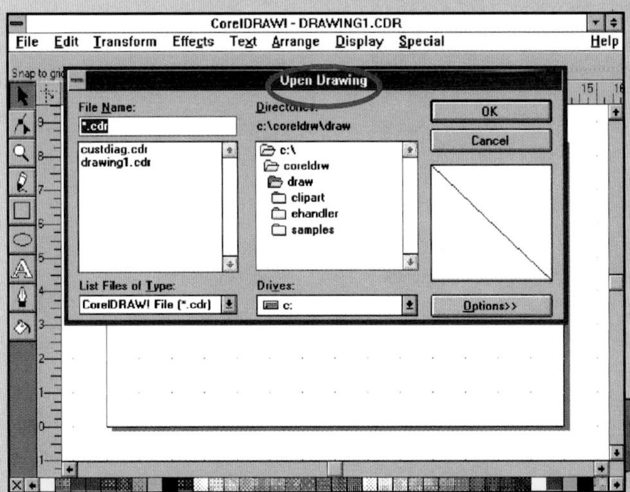

1 Click **File** in the menu bar. Then click **Open** in the File menu. The Open Drawing dialog box appears.

2 In the File Name list box, click a file name. If necessary, click the **down scroll arrow** in the File Name list box to locate the file name. A preview of your drawing appears on the right side of the dialog box.

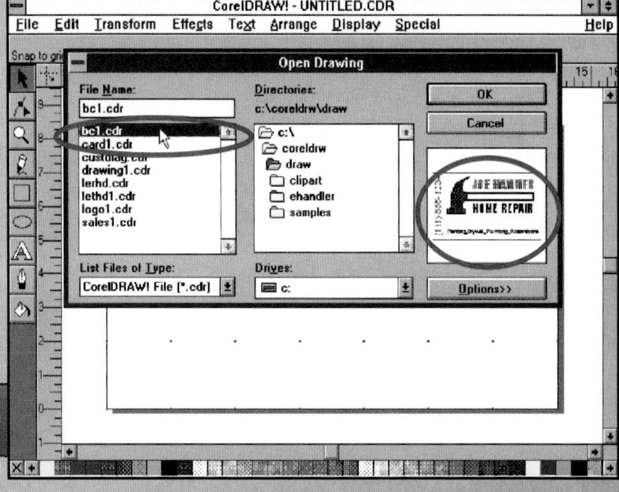

3 Click **OK.** CorelDRAW displays the drawing in the drawing window. The file name appears in the title bar.

TASK 14

Getting Help

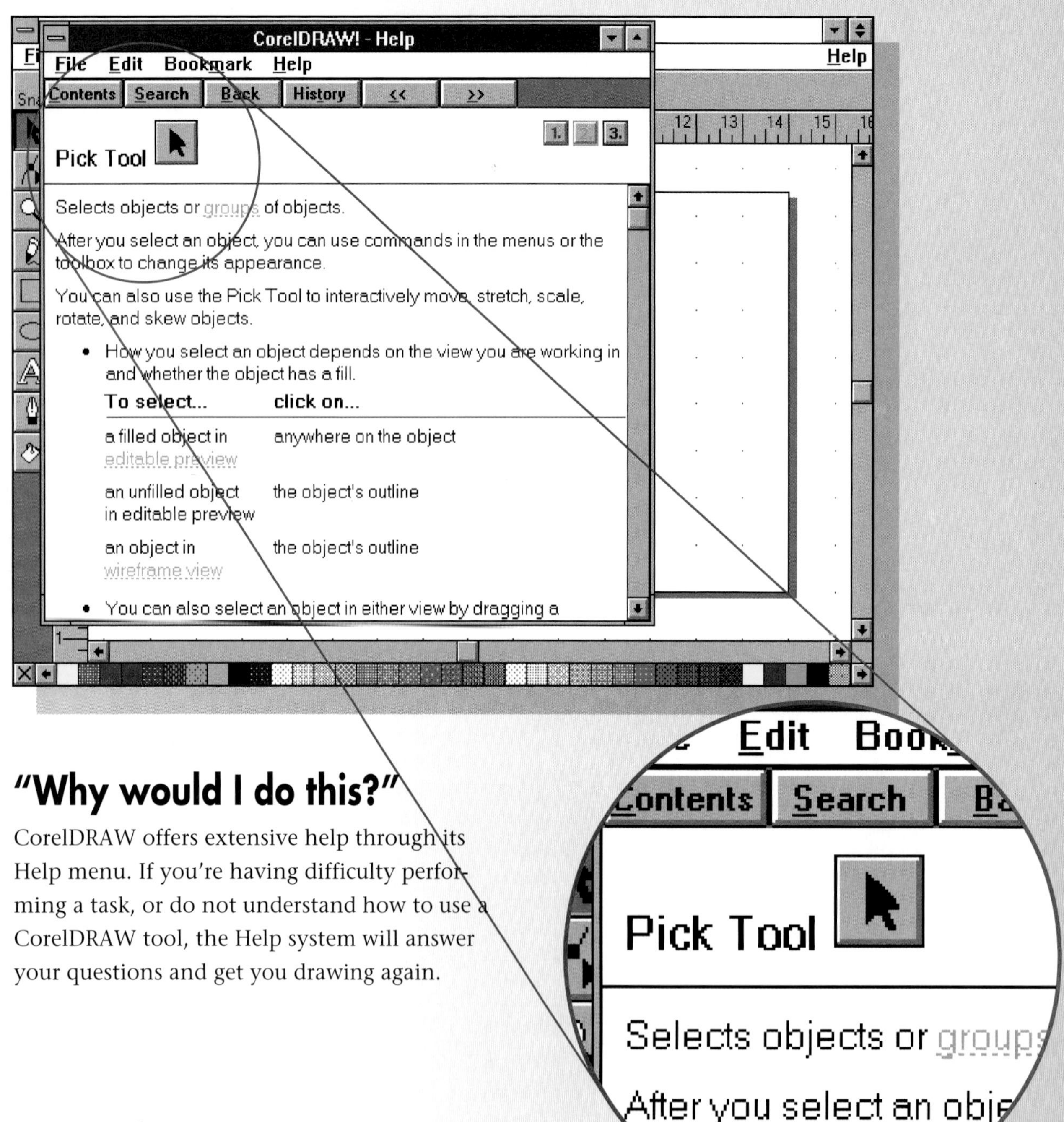

"Why would I do this?"

CorelDRAW offers extensive help through its Help menu. If you're having difficulty performing a task, or do not understand how to use a CorelDRAW tool, the Help system will answer your questions and get you drawing again.

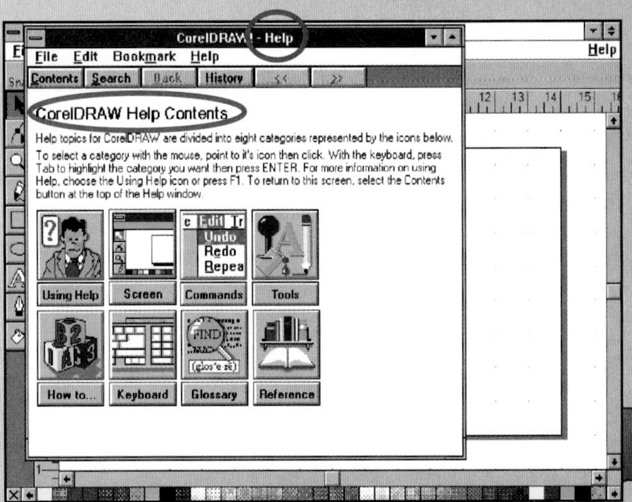

1 Click **Help** in the menu bar. Then click **Contents** in the Help menu. CorelDRAW opens the Help Contents window. The name of the help window appears in the title bar.

2 Point to the **Tools** icon. The pointer changes to a hand. Click the left mouse button. The Tool help menu appears.

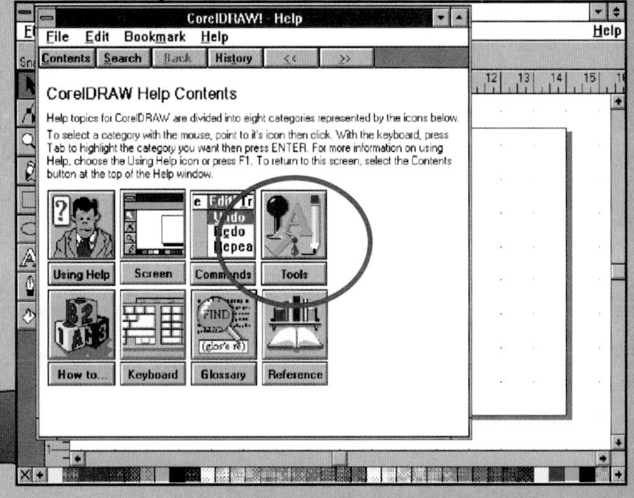

3 Click the **Pick Tool** icon. This step displays the help window for CorelDRAW's Pick tool. Each help window gives you information on a particular task. Click again to close the Pick Tool information window.

4 Click the highlighted word **groups** in the first line of the help window. A definition window appears, displaying the definition of *groups*. Click the left mouse button again to close the definition window. Defined words appear highlighted and with a dotted underline.

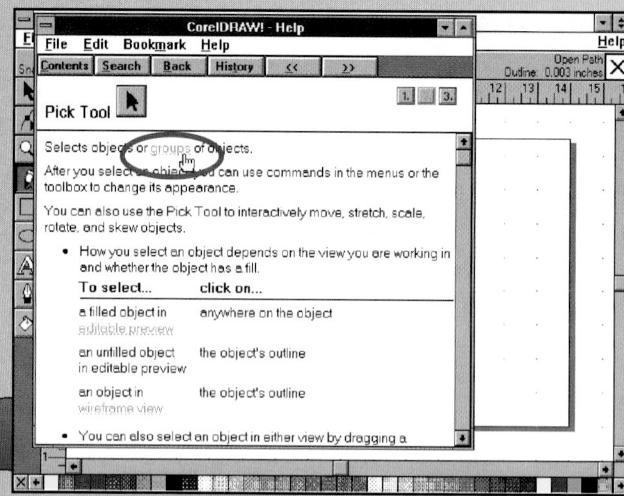

5 Click the **1. 2. 3.** icon in the upper-right corner of the Help window. A list of How To topics appears.

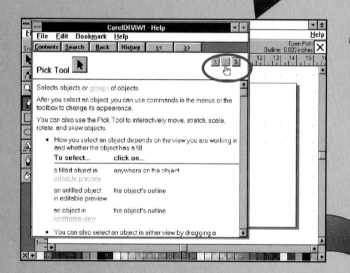

6 Click **Select an Object** in the How To list. The help window is redisplayed showing the help information for Selecting an object. Click the **Back** button at the top of the help window to return to the Pick Tool information window.

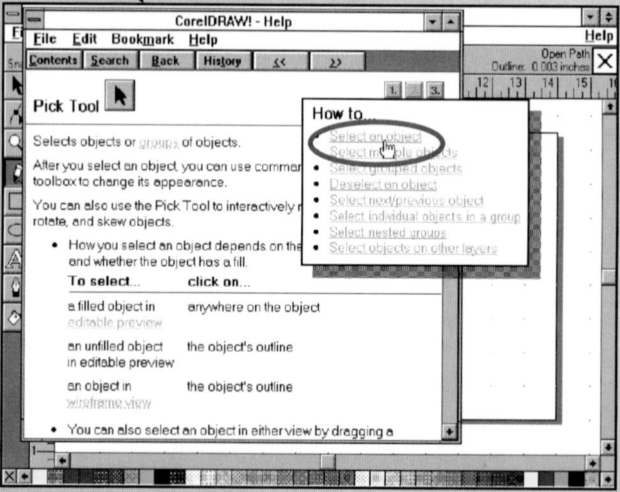

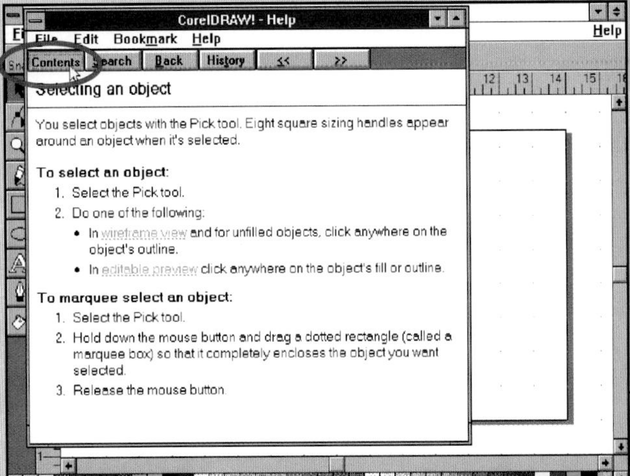

7 Click the **Contents** button at the top of the help window. This step displays the CorelDRAW Help Contents window again.

> **NOTE**
>
> You can quickly find help for commands and operations by clicking the Search button at the top of the help window. Then type the name of the command you need help for and double-click the topic that best fits the one you're looking for.

8 Click **File** in the menu bar. Then click **Exit** in the File menu. This step closes the help window and returns you to the drawing window.

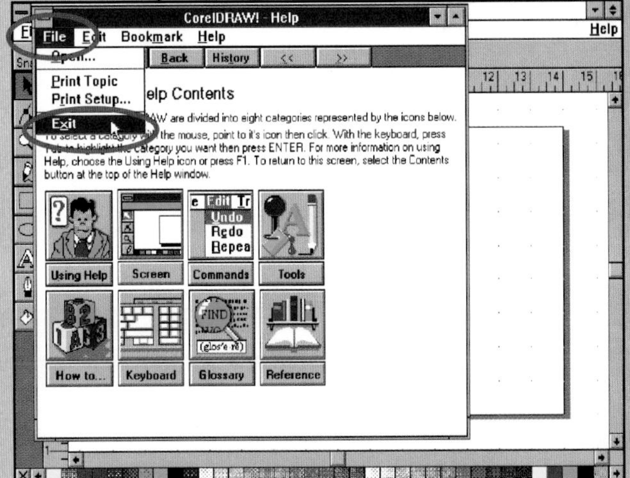

CorelDRAW! - DRAWING1.CDR
File Edit Transform Effects Text Arrange Display Special
Help
Rectangle on Layer 1
(12.00, 2.00)
Snap to grid
CorelDRAW! - DRAWING1.CDR
File Edit Transform Effects Text Arrange Display Special
Help
(13.00, 6.00)
Snap to grid
Ellipse on Layer 1
Width: 3.00 Height: 2.00 Center: (11.50, 7.00) inches
Fill: PANTONE Trans. White CV
Outline: 0.003 inches
CorelDRAW! - DRAWING1.CDR
File Edit Transform Effects Text Arrange Display Special
Help
(7.53, 3.75)
(13.00, 6.00)
Snap to grid

PART II

Learning the Drawing Tools

In Part I of this book, you learned the basics of CorelDRAW—using menus, dialog boxes, roll-up windows, and the toolbox. Part II shows you how to start drawing with the drawing tools in the toolbox.

Drawing basic shapes such as lines, circles, and rectangles is simple when you use the tools in the toolbox. When you examine sample images, you can see that complex images are created by combining simple shapes such as lines, circles, curves, and rectangles. The tasks in this part show you, step by step, how to draw these objects using CorelDRAW's drawing tools.

As you learned in Part I, the toolbox contains the drawing tools used to create shapes in CorelDRAW. The Pencil tool is one of the most frequently used tools in the toolbox. Using the Pencil tool, you can draw a freehand line like you would using a pencil. As you drag the pencil-shaped pointer across the drawing page, a freehand line is created, weaving and jagging as wildly as you move the pointer. To create straight lines using the Pencil tool, you simply plant the beginning point of the line with a mouse click, move the pointer, and click again to plant the end of the line segment. Combining freehand lines and straight line segments gives you the components needed to create intricate objects and images.

More complex shapes such as curves are easily created using the Bézier tool. Bézier was a famous mathematician who liked drawing curves, but he did not have the luxury of using CorelDRAW's Bézier tool. The Bézier tool, located on the Pencil tool's fly-out menu, enables you to draw an infinite variety of curves. By following the curve-drawing task in this part and with a little practice, you can create curves Bézier would be proud of.

If you want to create a perfect circle or an ellipse, the Ellipse tool is just what you need. The Ellipse tool draws both ellipses and circles. If you remember your geometry, an *ellipse* is just an oblong circle. Holding down the Ctrl key on the keyboard forces the Ellipse tool to draw a perfect circle as you drag the tool in the drawing window.

You'll use the Rectangle tool to draw rectangles and squares. As with the Ellipse tool, you can use the Ctrl key to force the Rectangle tool to draw a perfect square.

The Node tool enables you to reshape the objects you've drawn. A *node* is the point at which the outline of an object changes direction. For example, a square has four nodes, one at each corner. By moving a node, you change the location where the object's outline changes direction. For line segments, nodes start and end the segment. A circle or ellipse has two nodes, one at the beginning of the circle and one at the end. In this part, you'll learn to use the Node tool to create an arc from a circle by dragging the circle's node.

To assist you with creating objects of an exact size, CorelDRAW displays a *status line* at the top of the screen. As you draw lines, circles, and other objects, the status line displays the dimensions of the object and the object's position in the drawing window. Also displayed in the status line is the color an object is filled with, and the line thickness of an object's outline. The status line is indispensable if you need to draw objects of a specific size and color.

CorelDRAW's Symbol tool, located on the Text tool's fly-out menu, gives you access to over 5,000 professionally drawn symbols. Categories ranging from health and environmental to military and office are available. Each category contains dozens of symbols you can place in a drawing. Before you attempt to draw an object, scan the symbols library. You're likely to find the symbol you need. Because symbols are created using CorelDRAW, you can edit and modify them with the tools in CorelDRAW's toolbox.

TASK 15

Drawing a Line

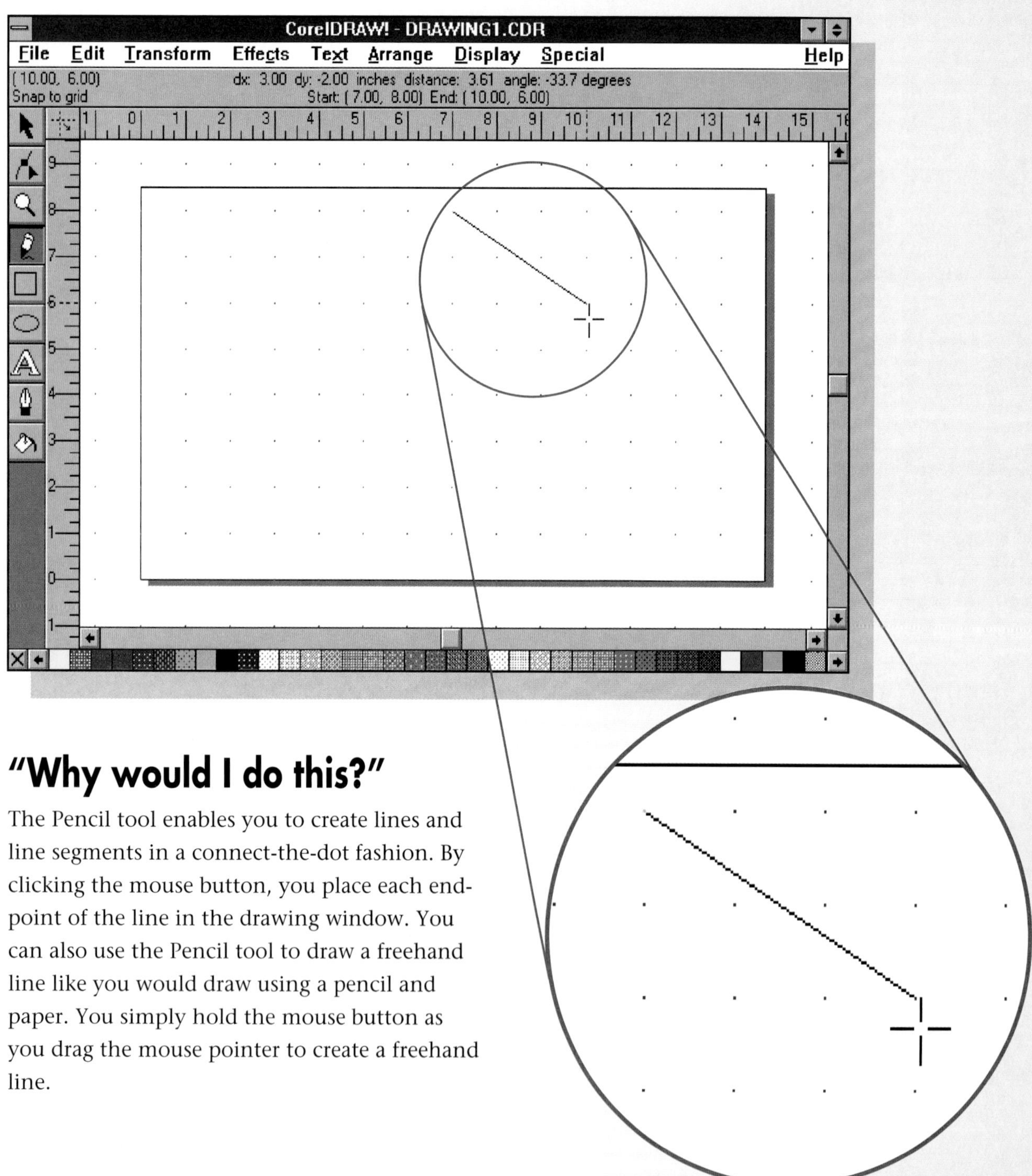

"Why would I do this?"

The Pencil tool enables you to create lines and line segments in a connect-the-dot fashion. By clicking the mouse button, you place each endpoint of the line in the drawing window. You can also use the Pencil tool to draw a freehand line like you would draw using a pencil and paper. You simply hold the mouse button as you drag the mouse pointer to create a freehand line.

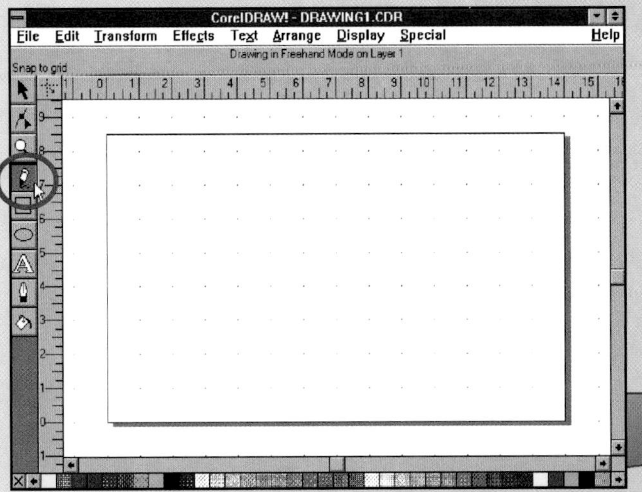

1 Click the **Pencil** tool in the toolbox. This step selects the Pencil tool.

2 Move the mouse pointer to the drawing window. The mouse pointer changes to a crossbar pointer.

> **NOTE**
>
> You can draw anywhere in the drawing window; however, only the portion of your drawing within the page border will be printed. The area outside the page border is called the *pasteboard*.

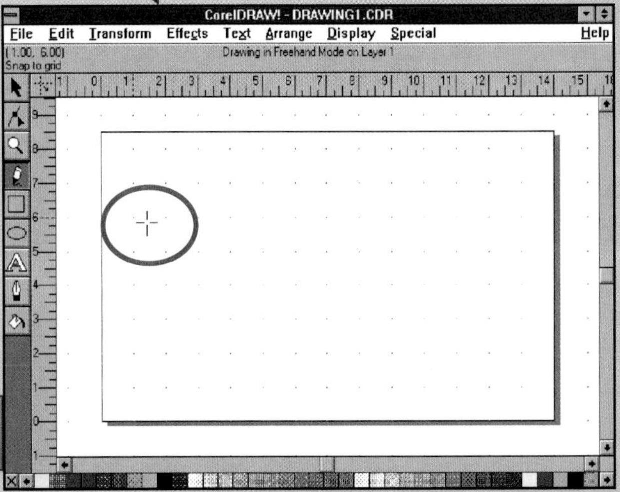

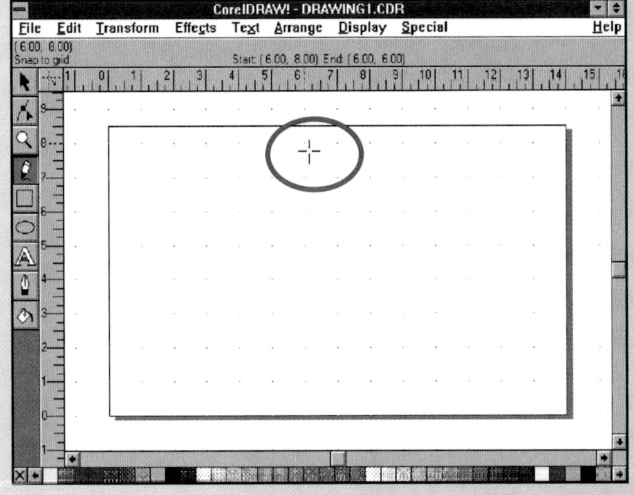

3 Move the crossbar pointer to where you want the line to begin in the drawing window. Click the left mouse button. This step positions the starting point of the line.

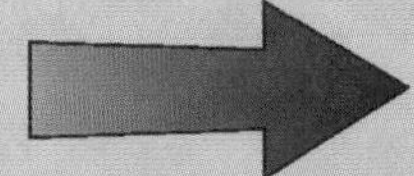

4 Move the crossbar pointer to where you want the line to end. A straight line stretches to meet the crossbar.

NOTE

To draw a freehand line, hold the mouse button and drag the crossbar pointer. A line is drawn by the crossbar pointer. Release the mouse button to complete the freehand line.

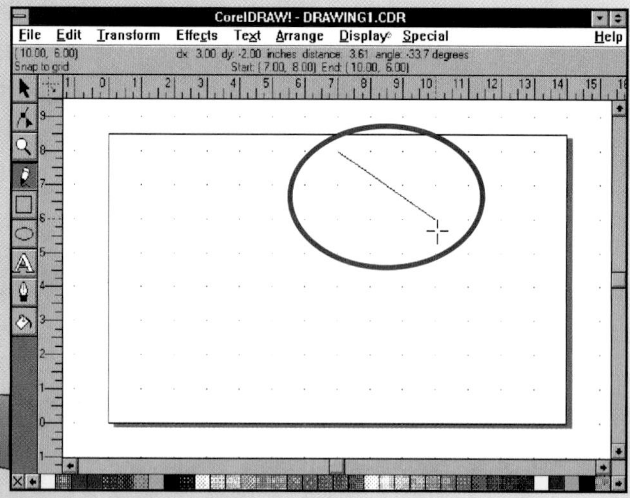

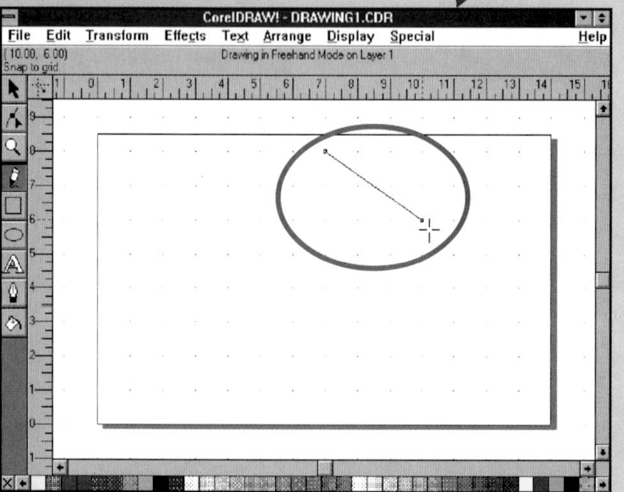

5 Click the left mouse button. This step positions the end of the line. The line is complete.

NOTE

To create another line segment attached to the end of the first line segment, double-click the mouse button in place of step 5 and move the mouse as you did in step 4.

TASK 16

Drawing a Curve

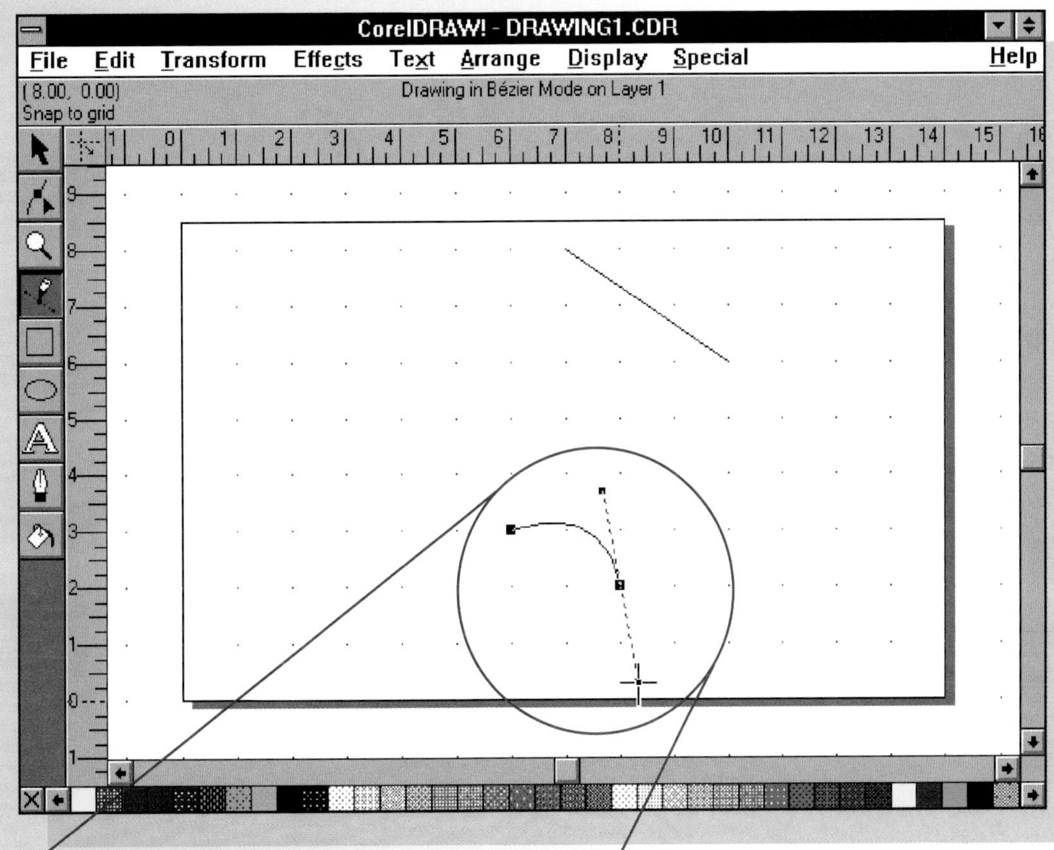

"Why would I do this?"

To create your drawings in CorelDRAW, you'll use a combination of straight lines and curves, as well as closed objects such as circles and rectangles. Drawing a curve is similar to drawing a line. Using the Pencil tool, you place the beginning and ending points of the curve, and then indicate how far to bend the line.

Task 16: Drawing a Curve

1 Click the **Pencil** tool and hold the mouse button until the Pencil tool fly-out menu appears. Two tools appear below and to the right of the Pencil tool.

NOTE

CorelDRAW 4 displays five Pencil tool icons on the Pencil tool fly-out menu.

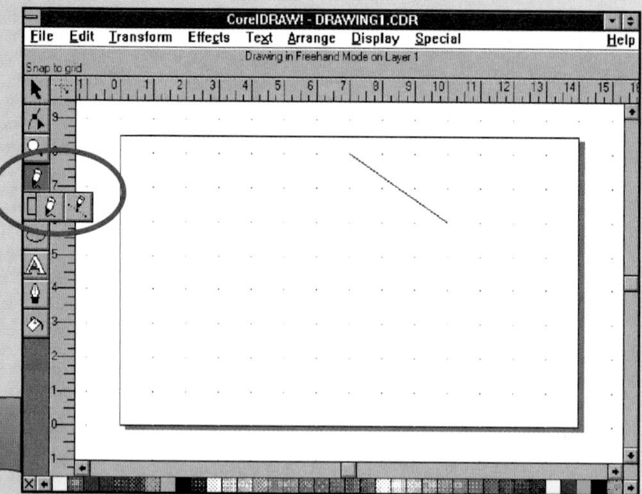

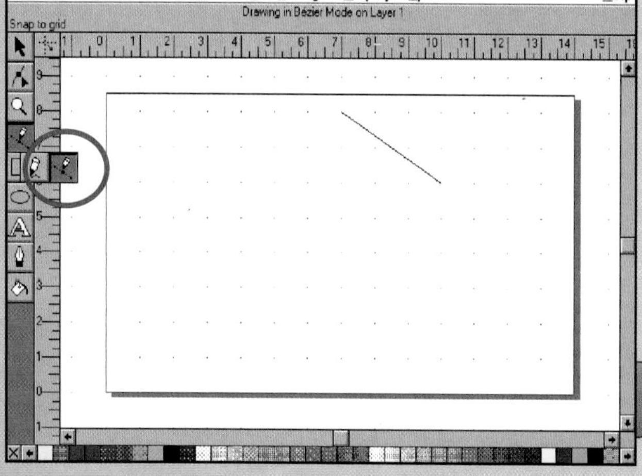

2 Click the **Bézier** tool. This step selects the Bézier tool and puts it in the toolbox, in place of the Pencil tool.

WHY WORRY?

If you click the wrong tool in the fly-out menu, repeat step 1 to reopen the fly-out menu and try again.

3 Move the crossbar pointer to the drawing window. The mouse pointer changes to a crossbar pointer. Click the mouse button. This step positions the beginning point of the curve in the drawing window.

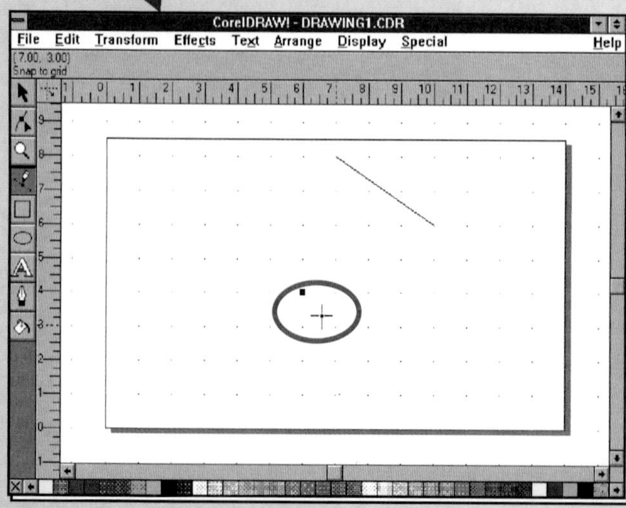

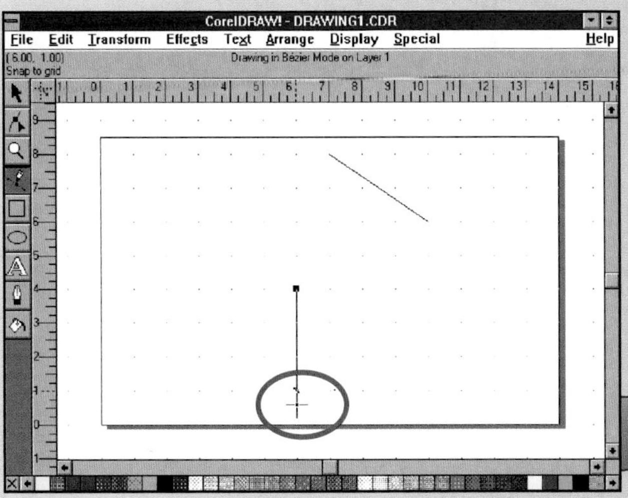

4 Move the crossbar pointer to where you want the end point of the curve. Hold the mouse button.

5 Drag the crossbar pointer. As you drag, two control points appear and move in opposite directions from the curve's end point. The curve of the line becomes greater as you move the control points further from the curve's end point.

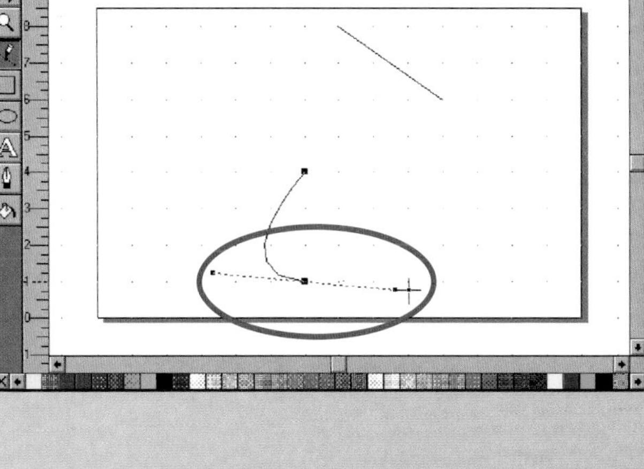

WHY WORRY?

The dotted lines that extend from the control nodes are not part of the drawing. They disappear when you release the mouse button.

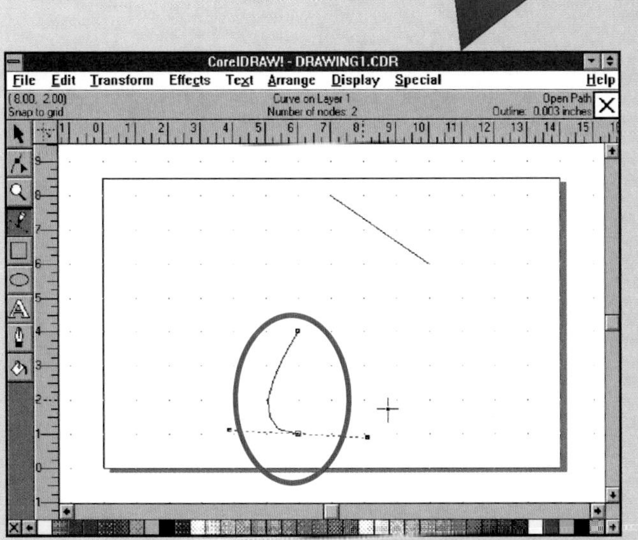

6 When you are satisfied with the curve, release the mouse button. This step completes the first segment of the curve. If you want to add more segments to the curve, repeat steps 3 through 6; otherwise, click the **Pick** tool to complete the operation.

NOTE

As you draw a curve or any other object, the status line at the top of the screen displays a description of the current action.

TASK 17

Drawing a Rectangle or Square

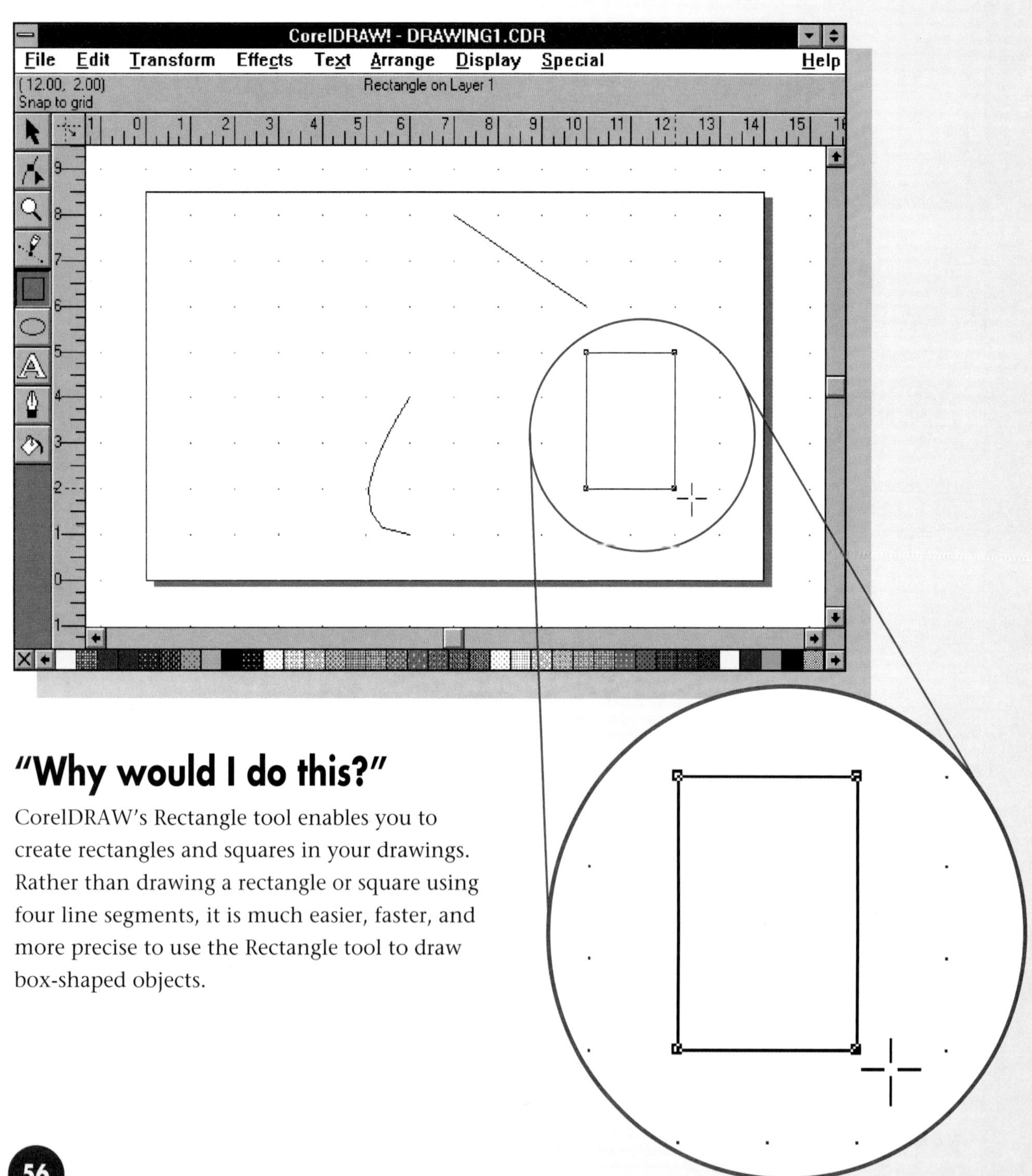

"Why would I do this?"

CorelDRAW's Rectangle tool enables you to create rectangles and squares in your drawings. Rather than drawing a rectangle or square using four line segments, it is much easier, faster, and more precise to use the Rectangle tool to draw box-shaped objects.

Task 17: Drawing a Rectangle or Square

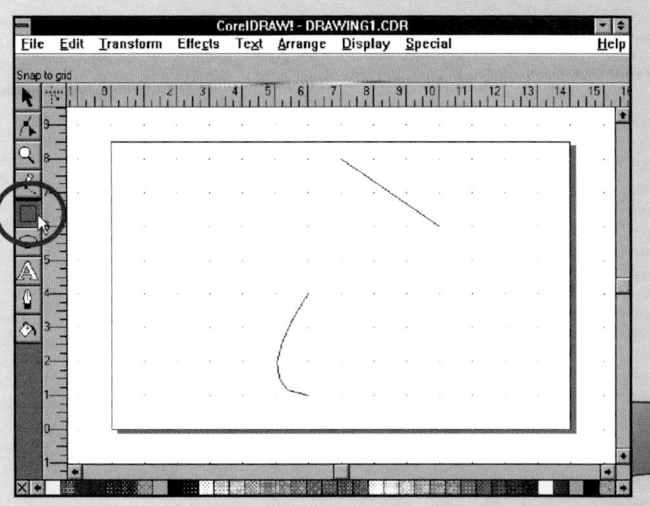

1 Click the **Rectangle** tool in the toolbox**.** This step selects the Rectangle tool. Move the mouse pointer to the drawing window. The mouse pointer changes to a crossbar pointer.

2 Position the crossbar pointer where you want one corner of the rectangle.

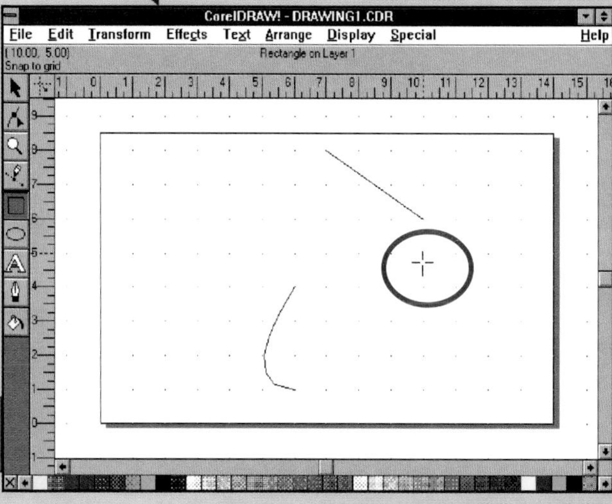

3 Hold the mouse button to start the rectangle drawing mode. To draw a perfect square, hold the Ctrl key before pressing the mouse button. Continue holding the Ctrl key until after step 5.

NOTE

As you hold the mouse button, the status line displays the coordinates and dimensions of the rectangle. The rectangle's size will be 0 inches wide and 0 inches tall until you move the mouse.

4 Drag the crossbar pointer to where you want the opposite corner of the rectangle. If you need a rectangle of a specific size, use the rulers at the top and left of the screen. This step determines the size of the rectangle. As you drag, CorelDRAW draws an outline of the rectangle, letting you see how the rectangle will appear when you release the mouse button.

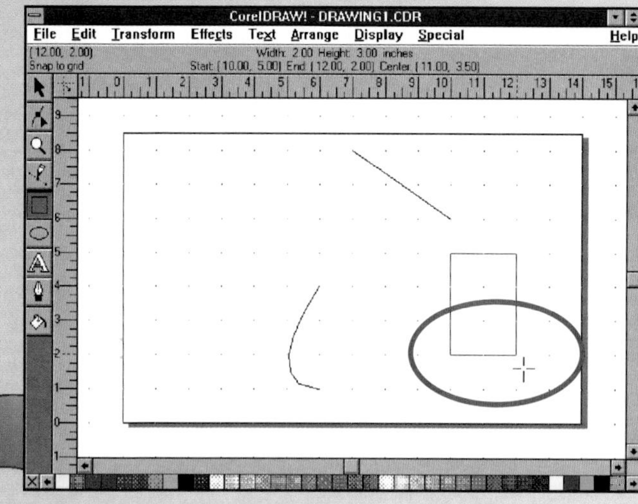

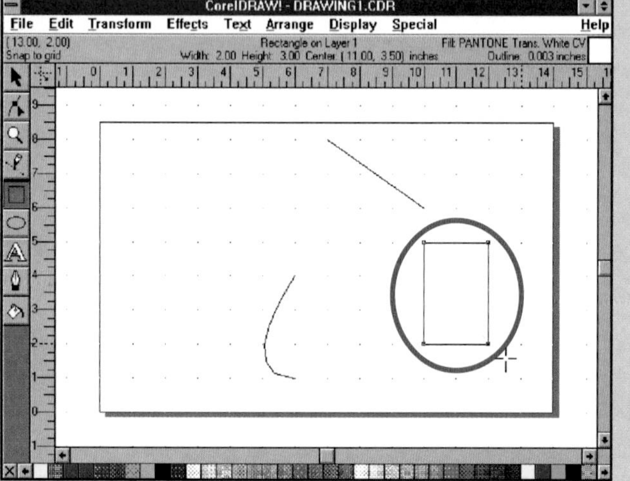

5 Release the mouse button. This step completes the rectangle. If you are drawing a square, you can now release the Ctrl key.

NOTE

If you want to draw a rectangle that starts from the center rather than a corner, hold the Shift key while dragging. This option is helpful if you need to draw a rectangle with its center precisely located in the drawing.

TASK 18

Drawing an Ellipse or Circle

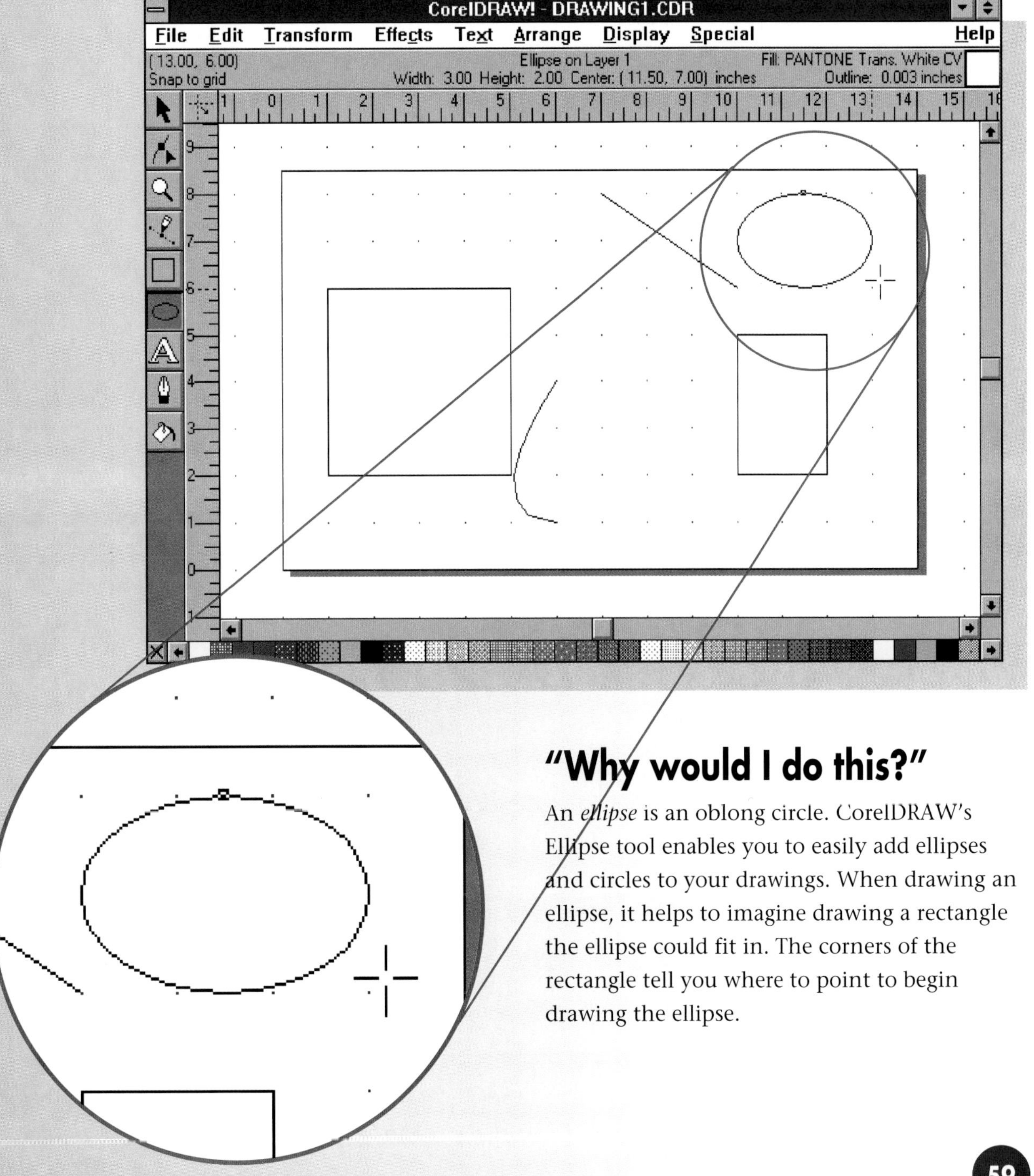

"Why would I do this?"

An *ellipse* is an oblong circle. CorelDRAW's Ellipse tool enables you to easily add ellipses and circles to your drawings. When drawing an ellipse, it helps to imagine drawing a rectangle the ellipse could fit in. The corners of the rectangle tell you where to point to begin drawing the ellipse.

Task 18: Drawing an Ellipse or Circle

1 Click the **Ellipse** tool in the toolbox. This step selects the Ellipse tool. The mouse pointer changes to a crossbar as you move it into the drawing window.

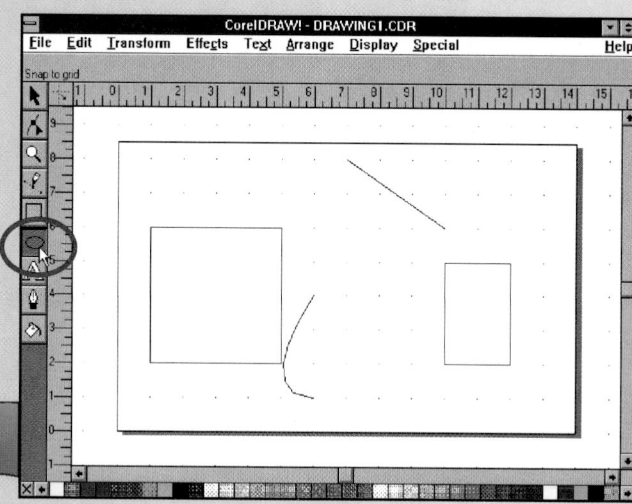

2 Move the crossbar pointer to where you want the ellipse to begin. This step determines where the upper left portion of the ellipse will rest.

3 Hold the mouse button. This step starts the ellipse drawing mode. To draw a perfect circle, hold the Ctrl key before holding the mouse button. Continue holding the Ctrl key until after step 5.

NOTE

As you hold the mouse button, the status line at the top of the screen displays the coordinates and dimensions of the ellipse.

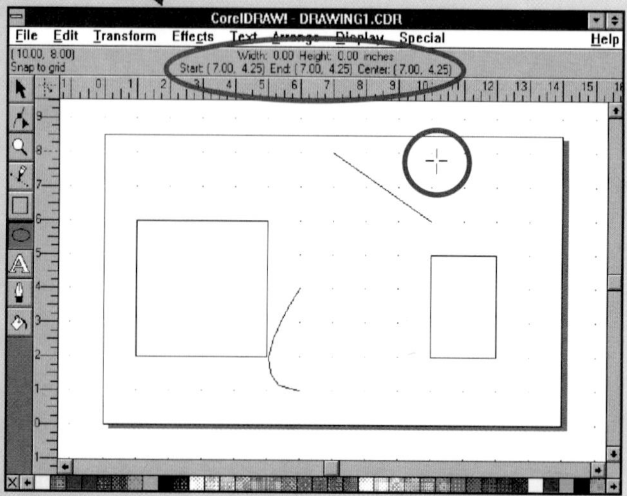

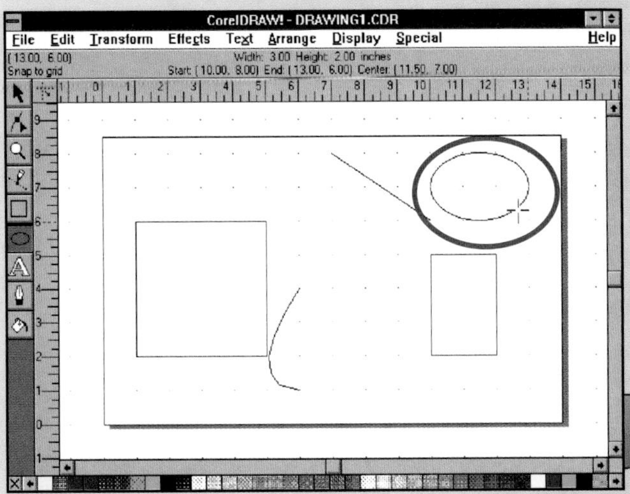

4 Drag the crossbar pointer until the ellipse is the size and shape that you want. As you drag, CorelDRAW draws an outline of the ellipse, showing you how the ellipse will appear when you release the mouse button.

5 Release the mouse button. This step completes the ellipse. If you are drawing a circle, you can now release the Ctrl key.

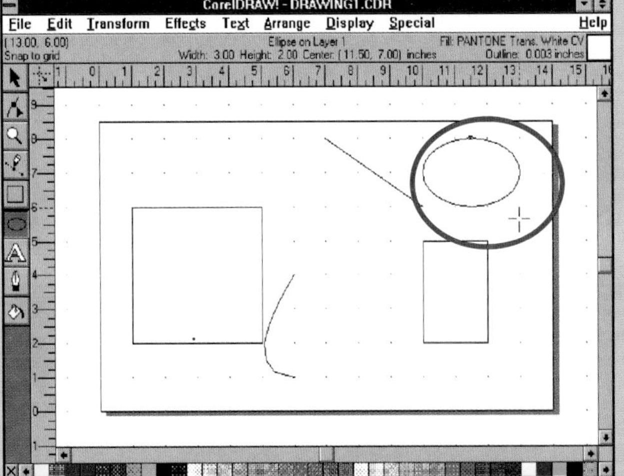

NOTE

If you want to draw an ellipse starting from the center, hold the Shift key while dragging. This option is helpful if you need to draw an ellipse with its center precisely located in the drawing.

TASK 19

Drawing an Arc

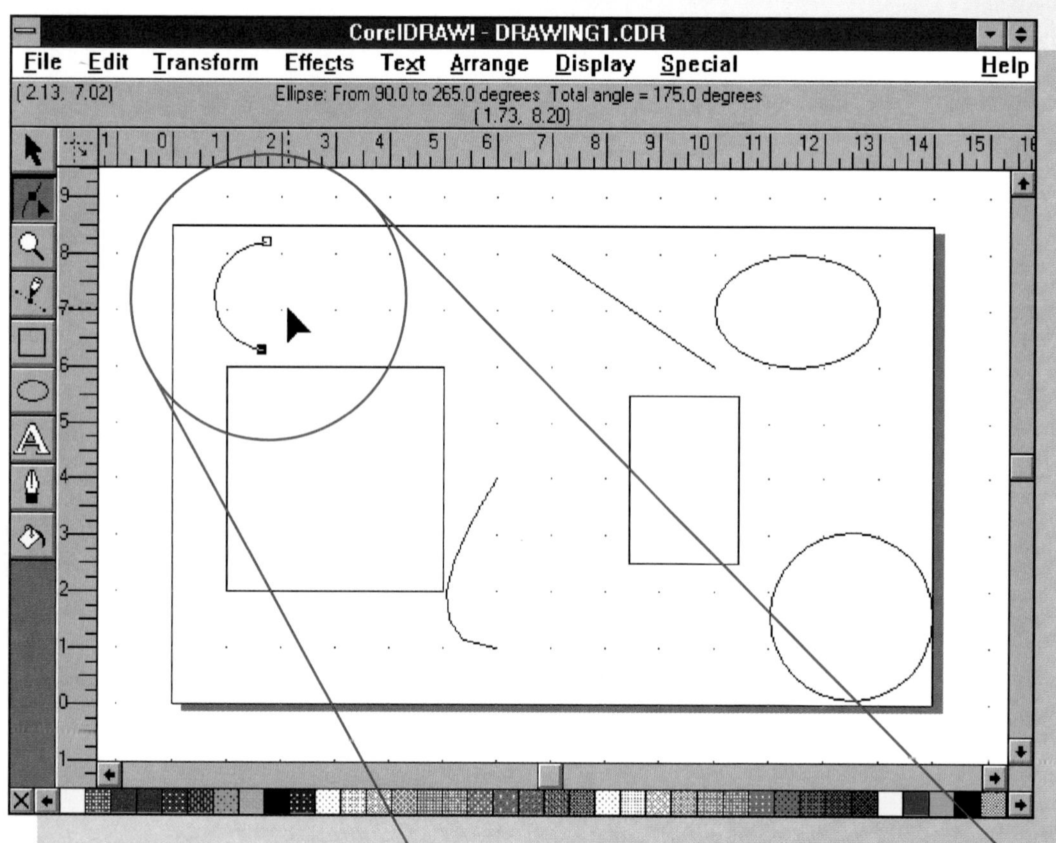

"Why would I do this?"

As you work in CorelDRAW, you might find that you want to draw an exact arc—a portion of a circle or ellipse. By manipulating the nodes of a circle or ellipse, you can easily create an arc. This method is much more precise than trying to create an arc using the Bézier tool from the toolbox.

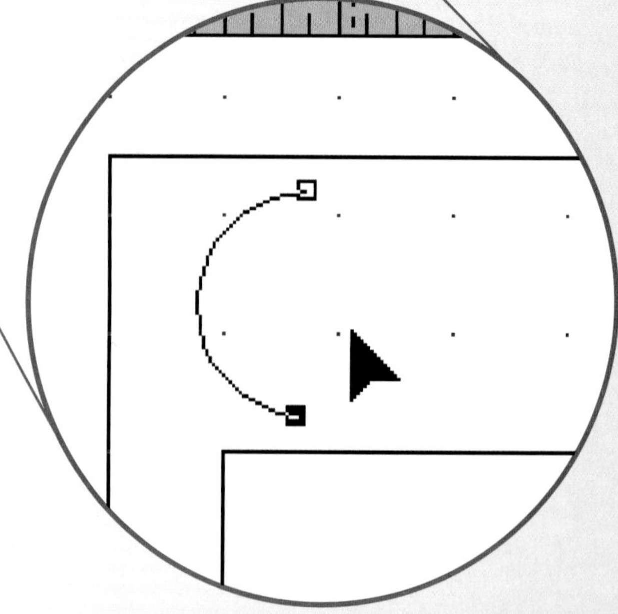

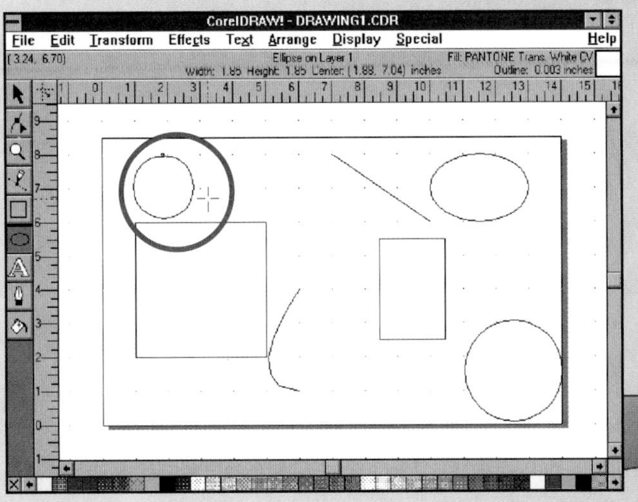

1 Click the **Ellipse** tool in the toolbox. Draw a circle. This step creates a circle from which you'll create an arc.

2 Click the **Node** tool in the toolbox. The pointer changes to a black arrowhead. The Node tool enables you to change the shape of an object by manipulating the object's nodes.

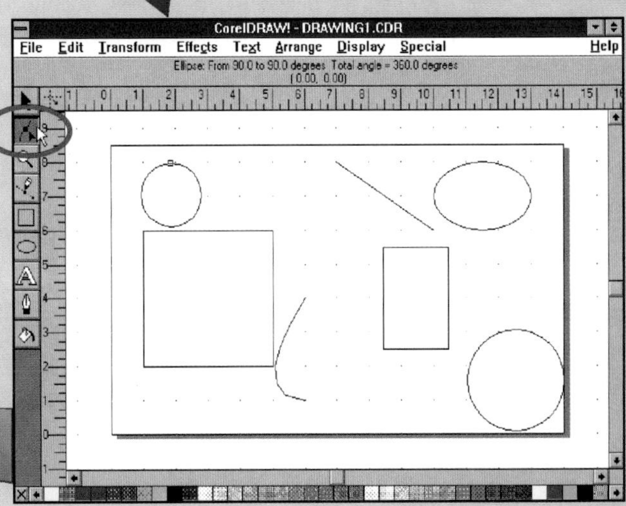

3 Point to the node at the top of the circle. The node appears as a small hollow box.

NOTE

All CorelDRAW objects are made up of nodes. The more complex an object, the more nodes it will contain.

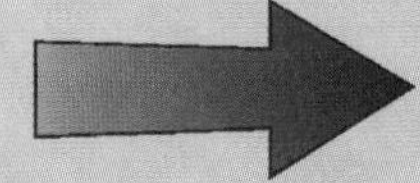

4 Hold the mouse button. This step picks up the node, readying you to move it.

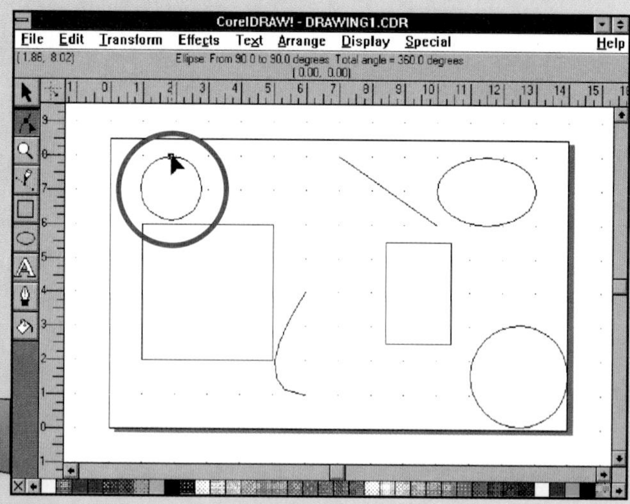

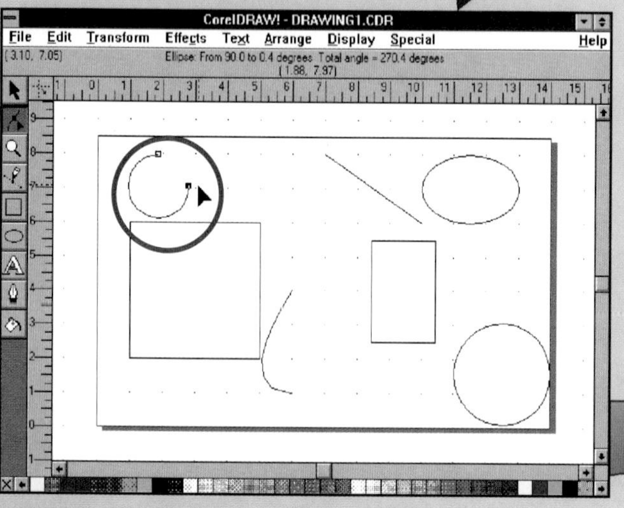

5 Drag the Node tool around the *outside edge of the circle.* As you drag, the edge of the circle disappears. If you drag clockwise, you will see an arc created by deleting part of the circle. If you drag counterclockwise, the circle will disappear and the arc will be created by adding to the circle.

WHY WORRY?

If a pie wedge appears as you drag, the Node tool is on the inside of the circle. Start over, making sure the Node tool is on the outside of the circle.

6 Drag around the circle until you have the arc the size you want, and then release the mouse button. This step completes the process.

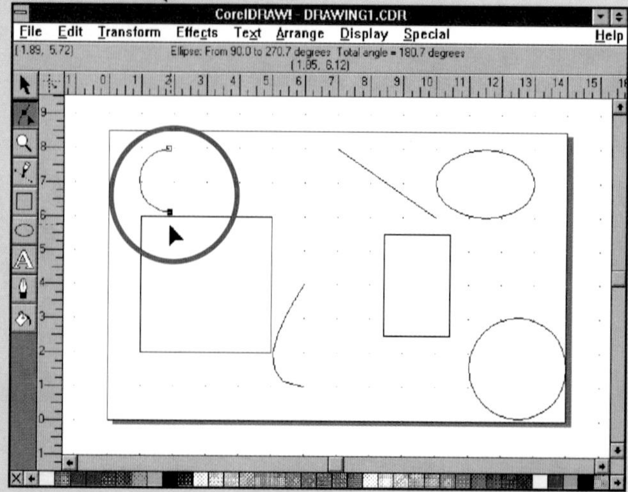

TASK 20

Drawing a Polygon

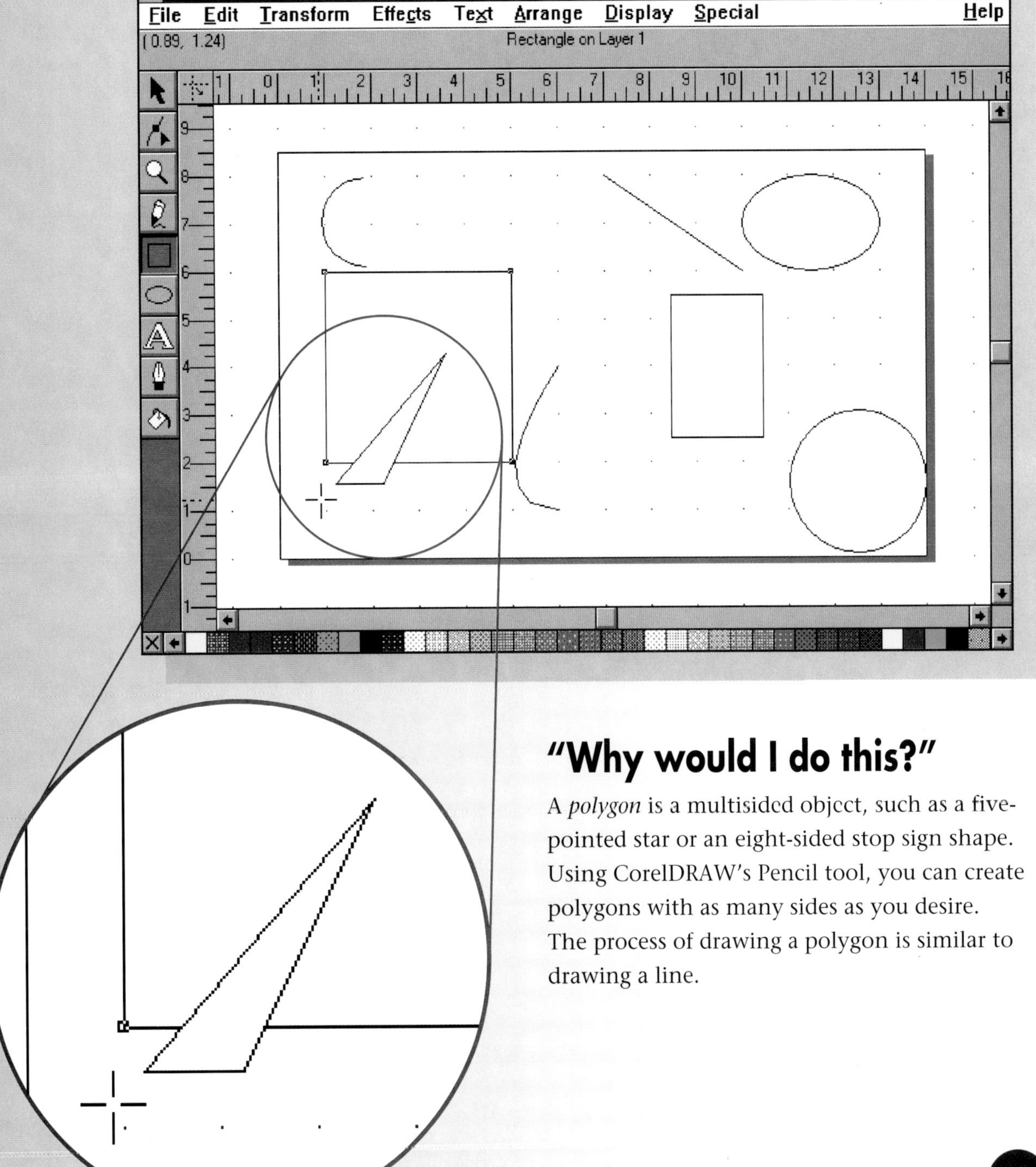

"Why would I do this?"

A *polygon* is a multisided object, such as a five-pointed star or an eight-sided stop sign shape. Using CorelDRAW's Pencil tool, you can create polygons with as many sides as you desire. The process of drawing a polygon is similar to drawing a line.

Task 20: Drawing a Polygon

1 Click the **Pencil** tool. This step selects the Pencil tool, which you'll use to draw a polygon.

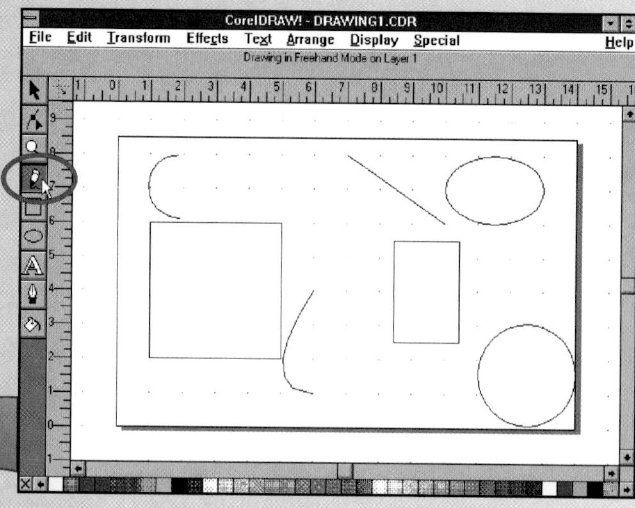

2 Move the pointer to where you want the first segment of the polygon to begin.

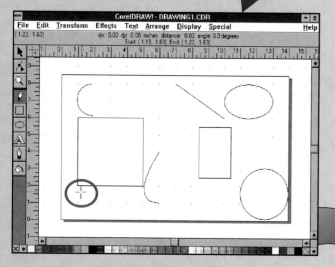

3 Move the crossbar pointer to where you want the first segment to end.

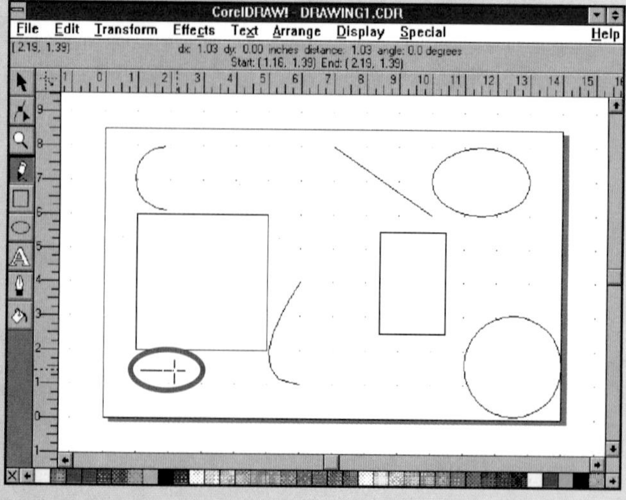

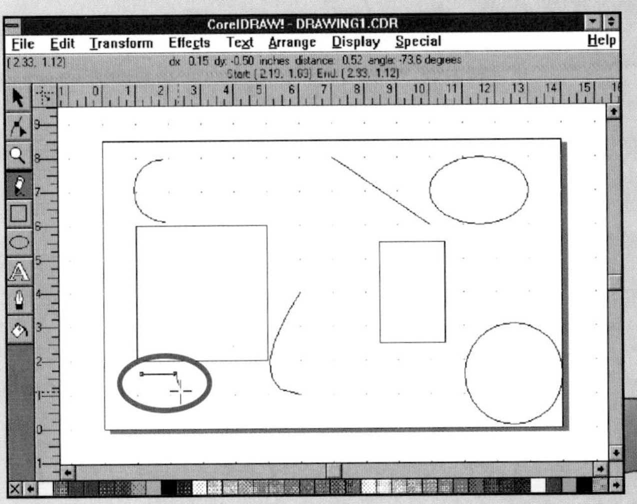

4 Double-click the mouse button. This step sets the end point of the first line segment. A line appears, and the Pencil tool remains selected.

5 Double-click where you want the second segment to end. CorelDRAW draws a second line segment from the end of the first segment to the point where you double-clicked.

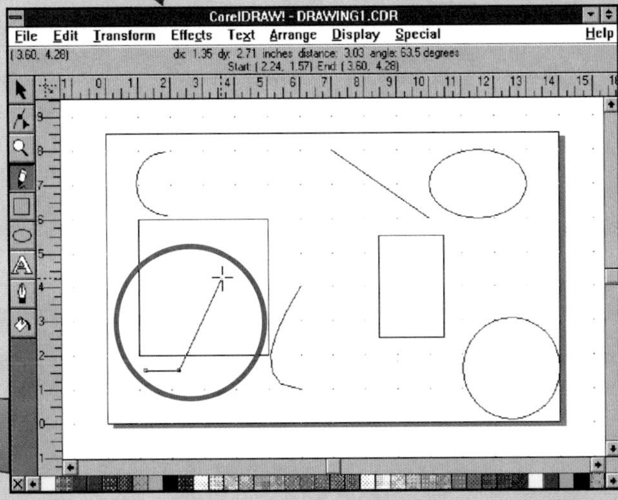

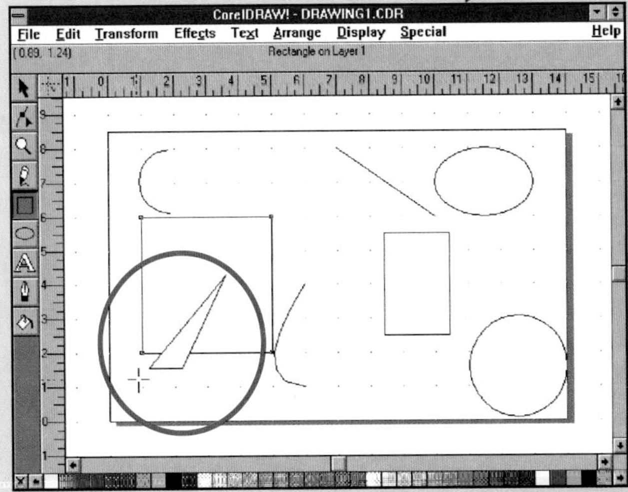

6 Move the crossbar pointer back to the beginning point of the first line segment and double-click. This step completes the polygon.

TASK 21

Adding a Symbol

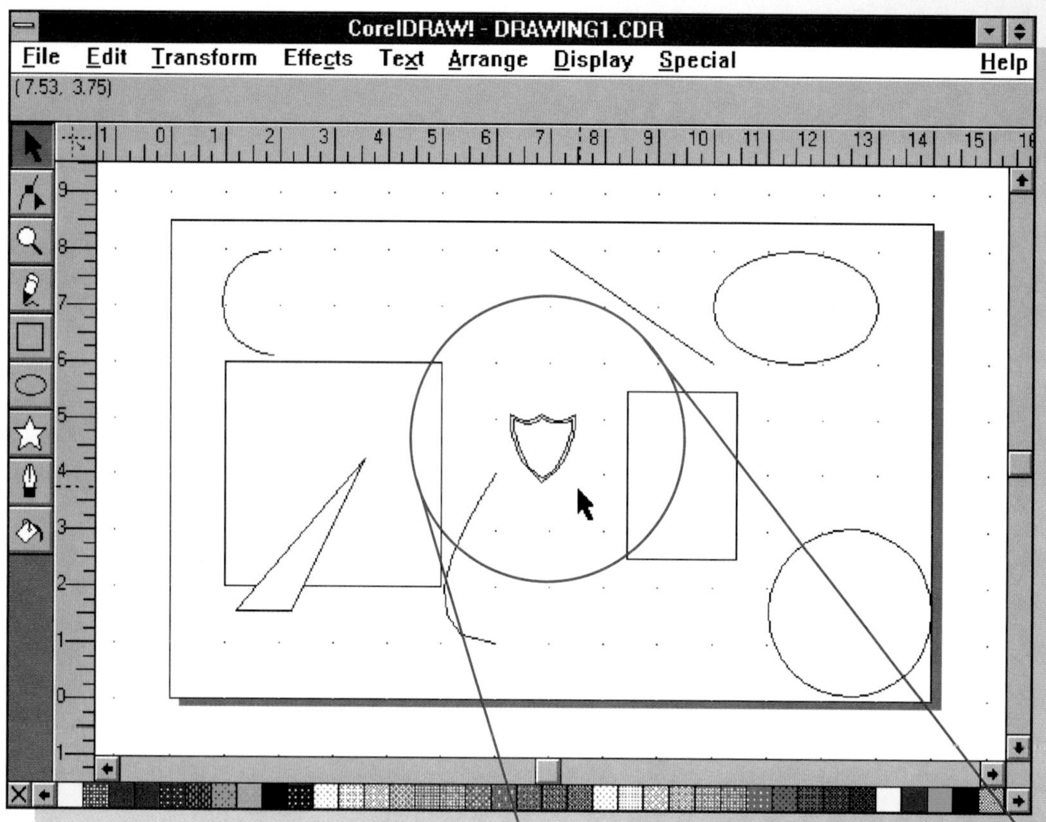

"Why would I do this?"

CorelDRAW provides a symbols window, which contains thousands of professionally drawn symbols relating to electronics and computers, business and science, as well as many more. If you have difficulty drawing an object, look through CorelDRAW's symbol window for the object or an object similar to the one you want. Because CorelDRAW symbols are created using the same techniques you're learning in this book, you can easily modify CorelDRAW symbols to create your own custom images.

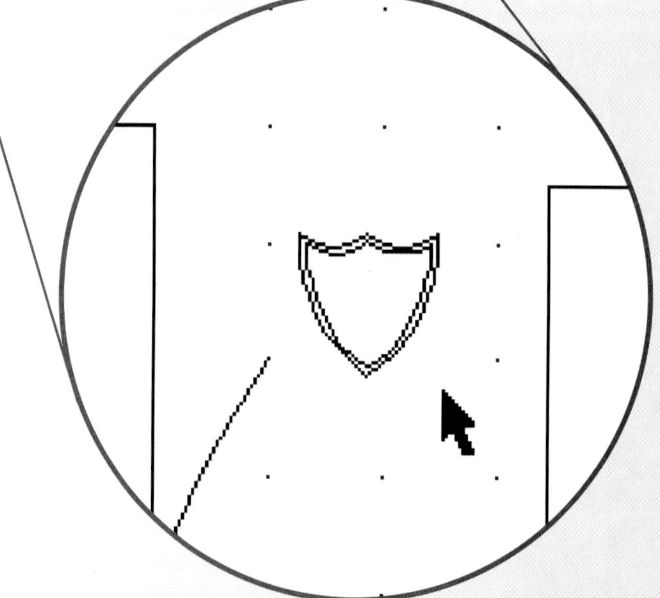

Task 21: Adding a Symbol

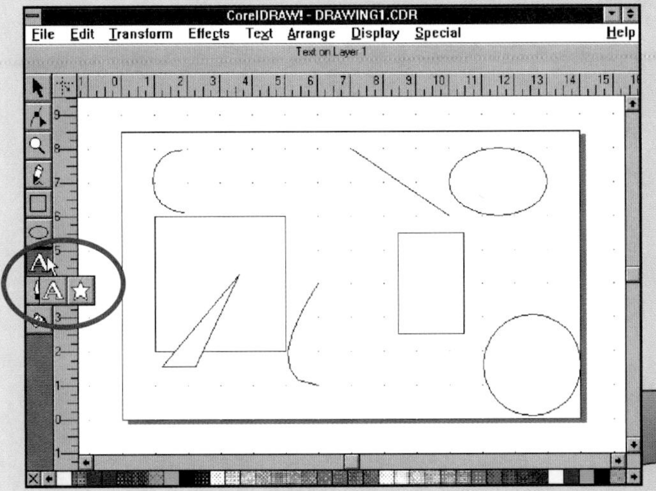

1 Point to the **Text** tool in the toolbox. Hold the mouse button until the fly-out menu appears.

NOTE

The Text tool fly-out menu in CorelDRAW 4 contains a third option for creating paragraph text. This icon is not relevant to this task.

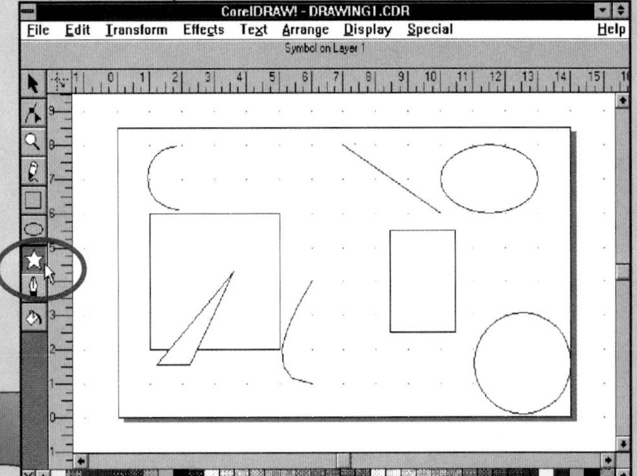

2 Click the **Symbol** tool, which appears on the right side of the fly-out menu. This step replaces the Text tool with the Symbol tool in the toolbox. The Symbol tool is selected.

NOTE

In CorelDRAW 4, clicking the Symbol icon in the fly-out menu opens the Symbol tool roll-up window.

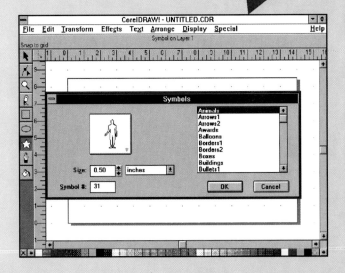

3 Move the mouse pointer to the center of the drawing window and click. This step tells CorelDRAW where to place the symbol and opens the Symbols dialog box.

NOTE

This step is not necessary when adding a symbol in CorelDRAW 4. Continue with step 4.

Task 21: Adding a Symbol

4 Scroll through the list box on the right side of the dialog box to find the category of symbol you want to add. Click the category to select it. The first symbol in the category appears in the preview box on the left side of the dialog box.

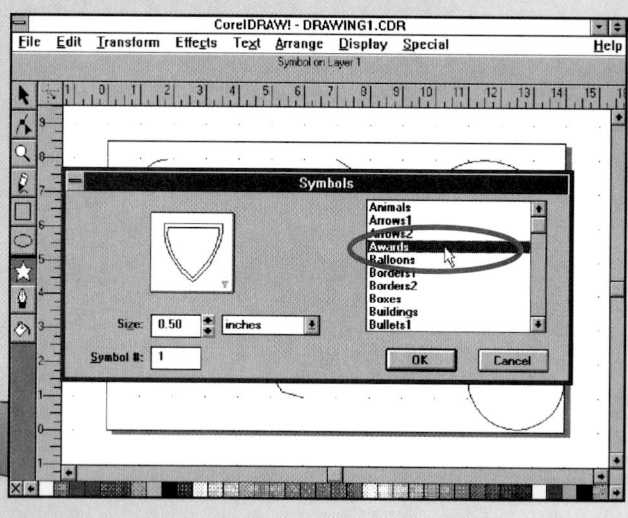

NOTE

For CorelDRAW 4, click on the category drop-down list and select a symbol category. The category's first 18 symbols are shown in the roll-up.

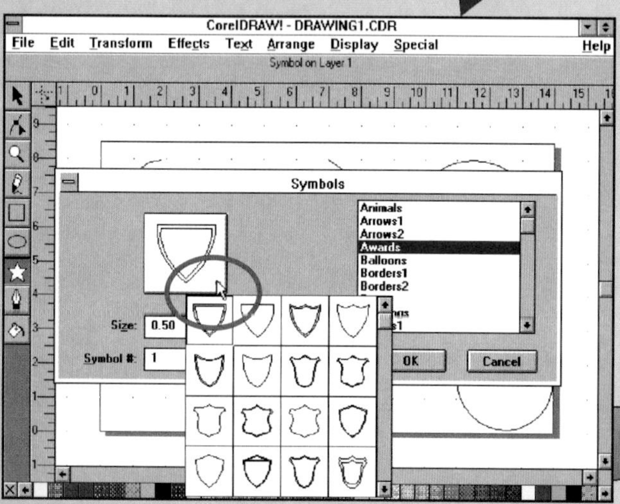

5 Click the symbol in the preview box**.** A list of symbols from the selected category appears.

NOTE

In CorelDRAW 4, drag the symbol you want to the drawing window and release the mouse button. As you drag, the symbol follows the pointer. This step completes adding a symbol in CorelDRAW 4.

6 Click the symbol you want to add. The symbol preview box displays the symbol. Click **OK** to close the Symbols dialog box and place the symbol in your drawing.

NOTE

You can specify the height of the symbol by clicking the up and down arrows in the Size box of the Symbols dialog box. When you choose OK, the symbol is sized accordingly and placed in your drawing.

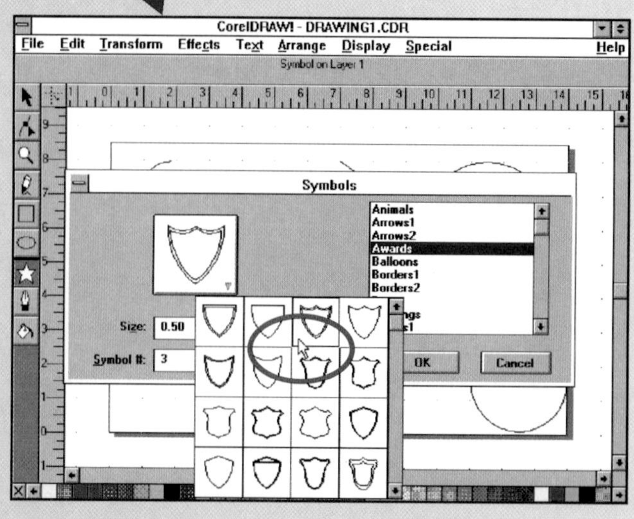

TASK 22

Importing a Clipart Image

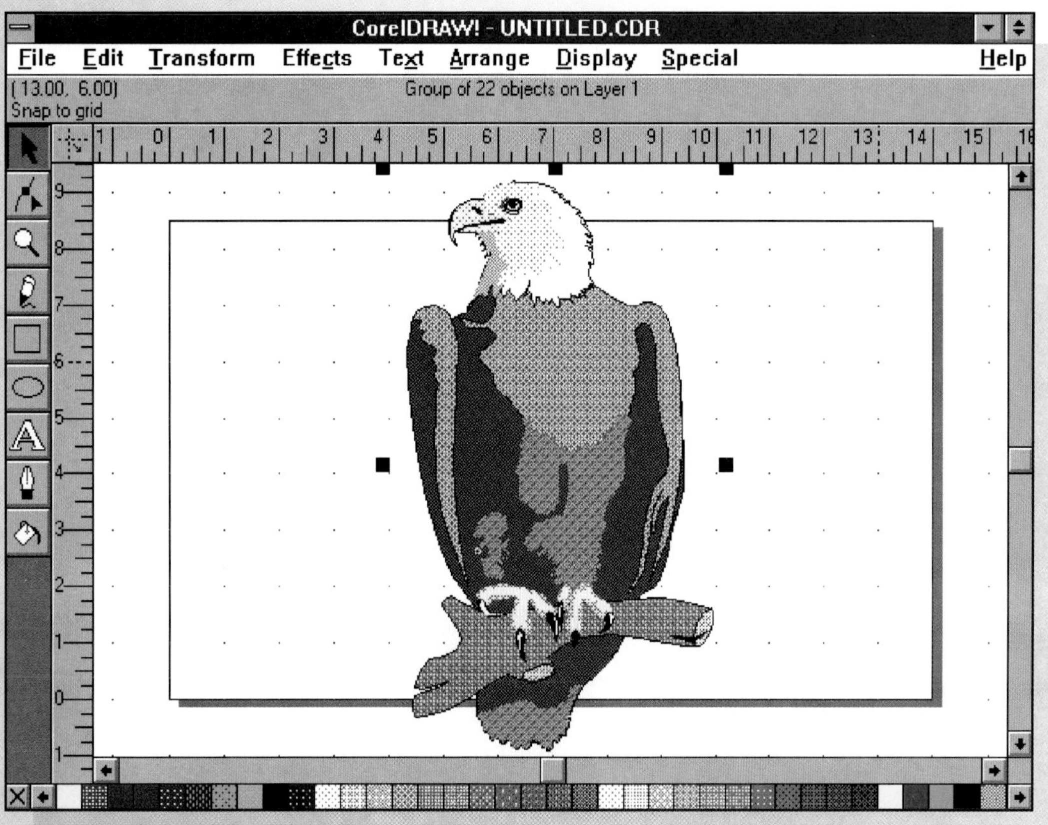

"Why would I do this?"

CorelDRAW 3 comes with over 4,500 clipart images; CorelDRAW 4 comes with thousands more. Clipart categories range from people and celebrities to transportation and sports. When you install CorelDRAW from disk, you install a subset of the clipart available. You'll need a CD-ROM drive to access the remaining clipart images that are supplied on CD in the CorelDRAW package.

Task 22: Importing a Clipart Image

1 Click **File** in the menu bar. Click **Import**. This step opens the Import dialog box.

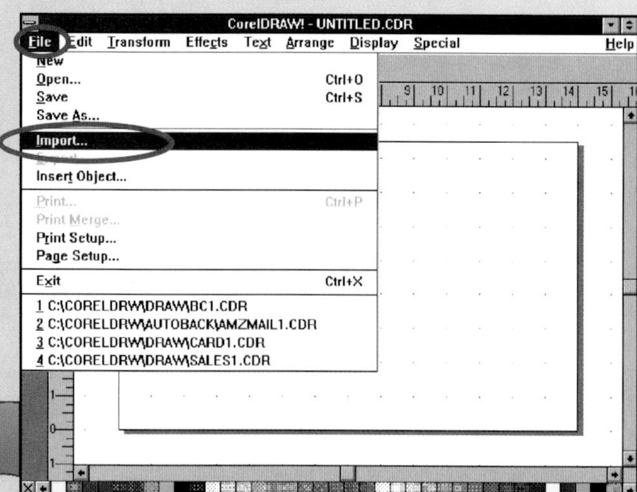

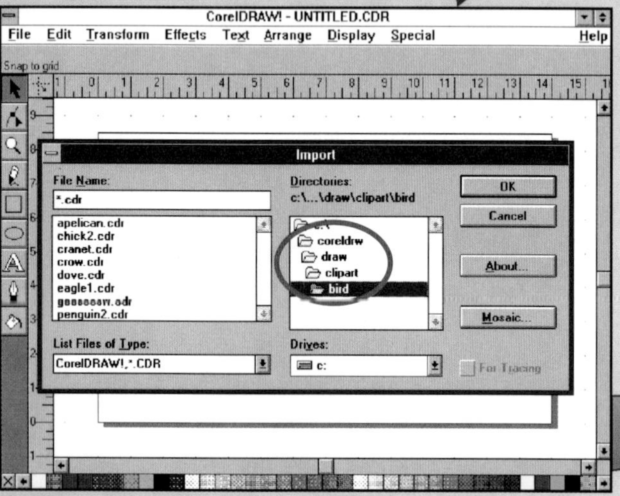

2 Navigate to the **Clipart** subdirectory located under the CorelDRAW subdirectory. Double-click the subdirectory of the category of clipart you want to import. This step displays the clipart files in the File Name section of the dialog box.

WHY WORRY?

If the clipart files do not appear in the File Name section of the dialog box, make sure the List Files of Type box is set to CorelDRAW!,*.CDR.

3 Double-click the clipart file name you want to import. The dialog box closes, and the clipart image is placed in your current drawing.

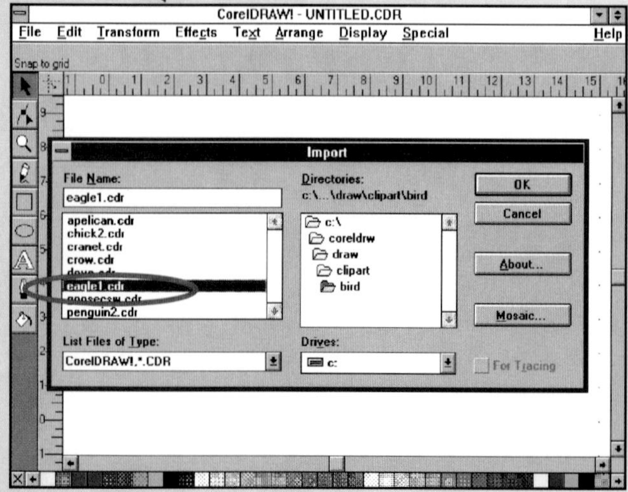

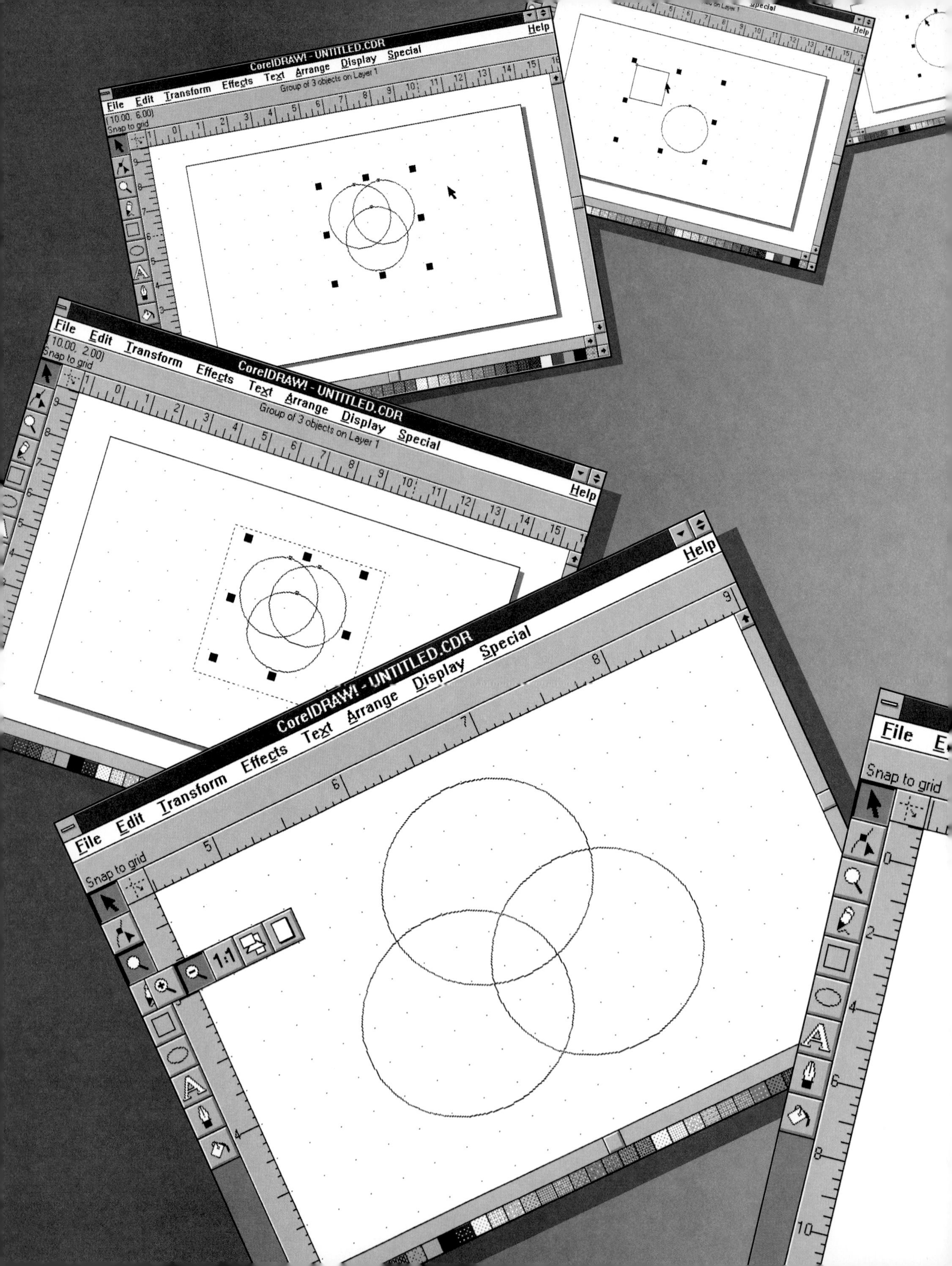
CorelDRAW! - UNTITLED.CDR
File Edit Transform Effects Text Arrange Display Special Help
Group of 3 objects on Layer 1
(10.00, 6.00)
Snap to grid
CorelDRAW! - UNTITLED.CDR
File Edit Transform Effects Text Arrange Display Special Help
Group of 3 objects on Layer 1
(10.00, 2.00)
Snap to grid
CorelDRAW! - UNTITLED.CDR
File Edit Transform Effects Text Arrange Display Special Help
Snap to grid
1:1
File
Snap to grid

PART III

Viewing and Selecting Objects

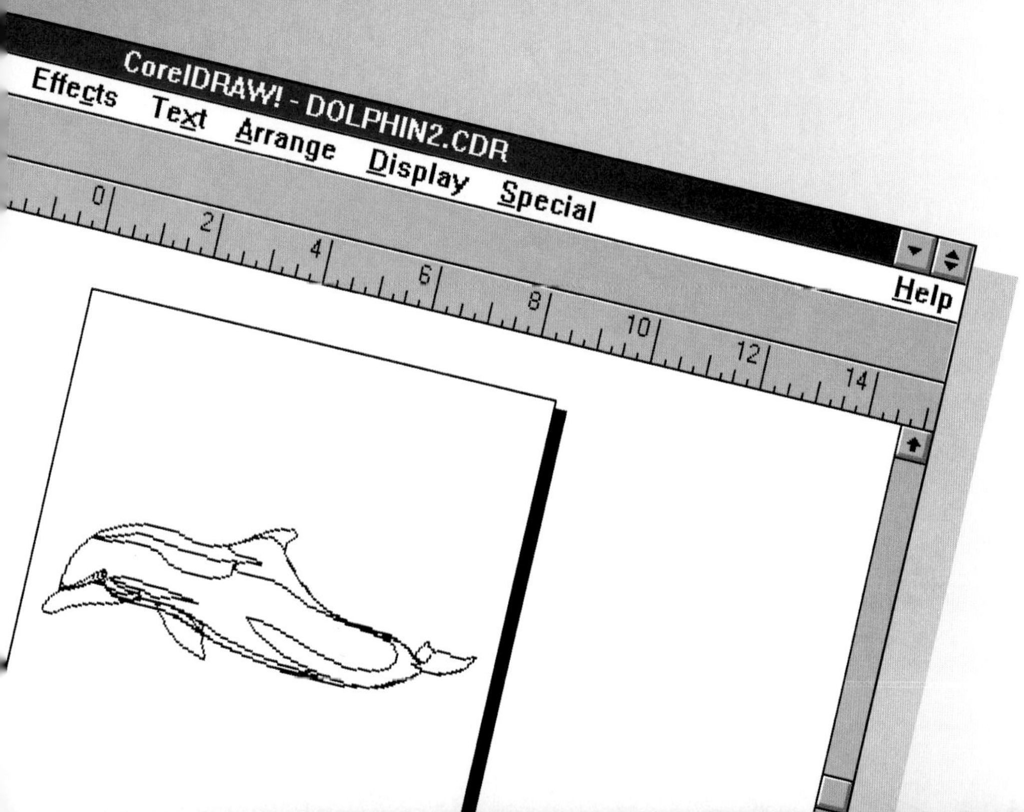

Prior to applying a menu command or an editing tool to an object, you select an object using the Pick tool. This part shows you how to select single and multiple objects, how to use the Zoom tool to enlarge the drawing so you can see more detail, and how to group objects together.

Like choosing a menu command or a tool from the toolbox, you click an object with the Pick tool to select it. To show you that an object is selected, CorelDRAW places eight sizing handles around the object. The sizing handles form an imaginary rectangle around the object. The eight sizing handles represent the eight directions in which the object can be stretched. You'll learn how to stretch (resize) objects in Part IV.

Selecting multiple objects is as simple as selecting a single object. While holding down the Shift key, you click the objects you want to select. As you click each object, sizing handles appear around the group of objects.

To create more complex objects, you'll find that it is helpful to group several objects together so you can work with them as one. Grouping is accomplished by selecting multiple objects using the Pick tool and then choosing the Group command on the Arrange menu. A group can be moved, resized, rotated, and even deleted as one unit. If you need to manipulate one of the objects in the group, you can ungroup it using the Ungroup command.

As your drawings become more detailed, you can use the Zoom tool to enlarge the drawings and see more detail. The Zoom tool, shaped like a magnifying glass, enables you to zoom in on your drawing, making it larger, or zoom out from it, making it smaller.

You can zoom in on the drawing page to show more detail of an object, edit the object, and zoom back out to see the larger picture. To show your drawing at the size it will be printed, you use the Actual Size Zoom tool.

Your computer needs lots of speed and memory to draw and display complex images and objects filled with color and patterns. As your drawing becomes more complex, you might notice that you have to wait while CorelDRAW redraws the screen when you scroll through the drawing window. If your computer is slow, try working in Wireframe view to speed things up a bit. Wireframe view displays all the images in the drawing window without fills, patterns, or varying line thicknesses, which speeds up the display of the images.

Wireframe view is also useful when you are working with numerous filled objects. Many times an object will get covered up by another filled object. Switching to Wireframe view shows all objects as outlines, revealing any objects that might be covered up.

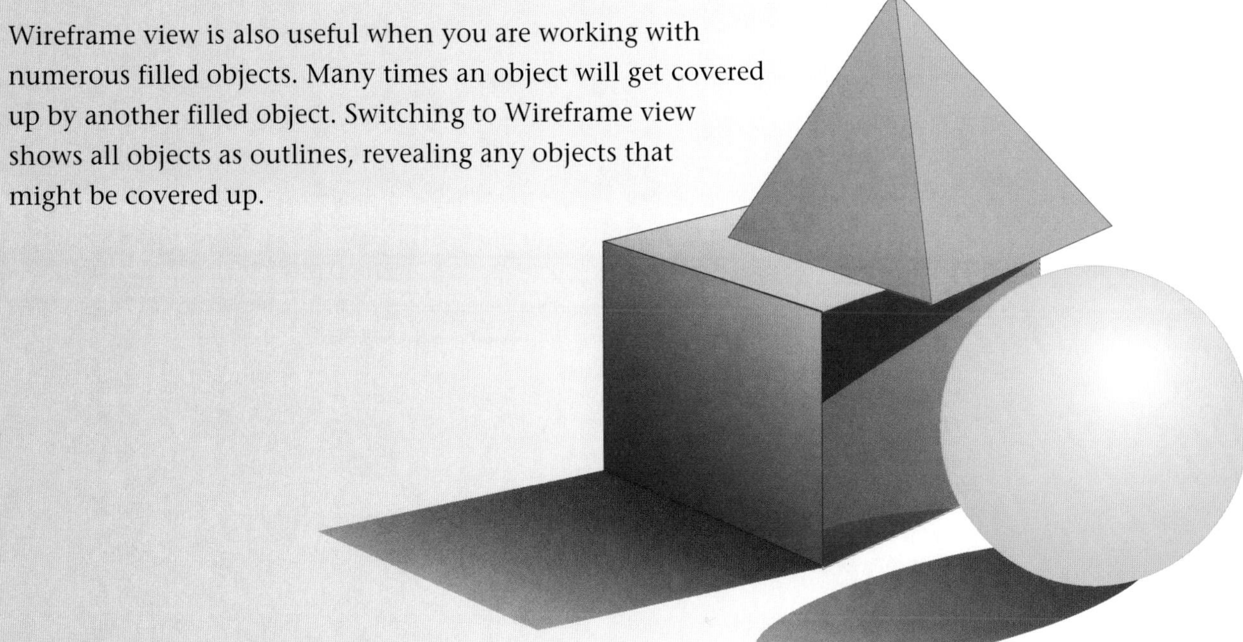

TASK 23

Selecting and Deselecting an Object

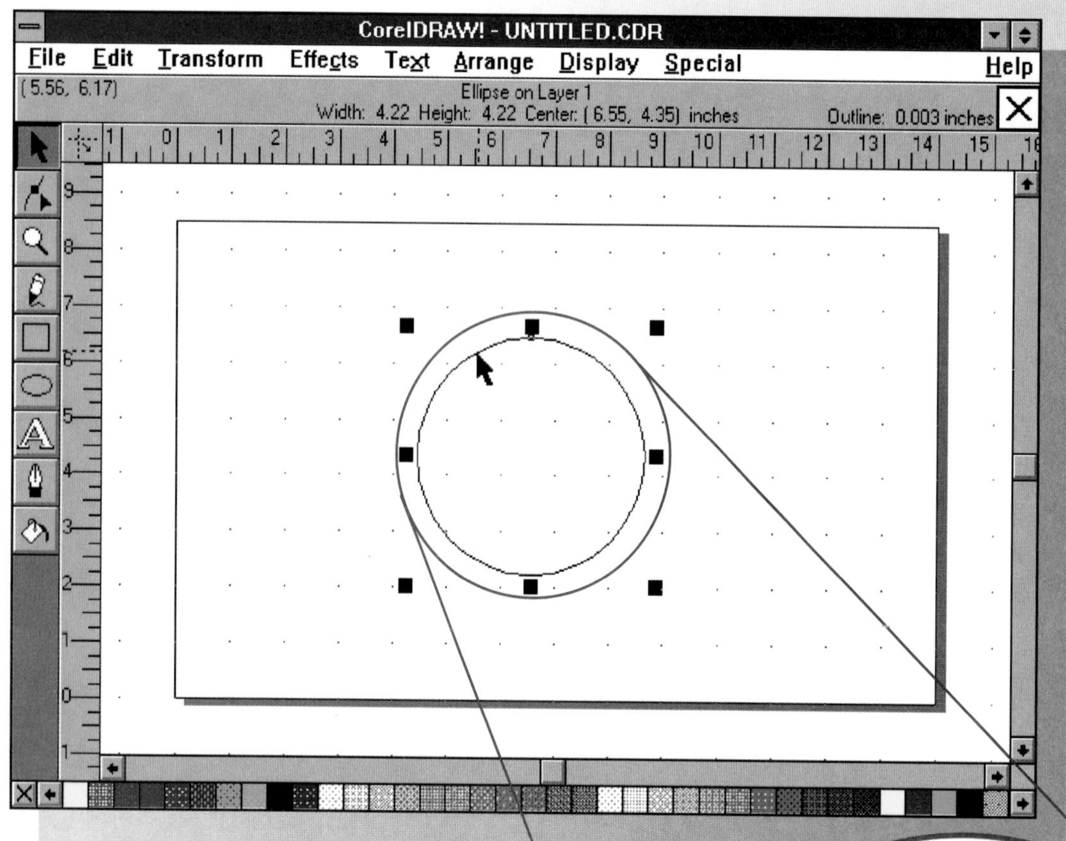

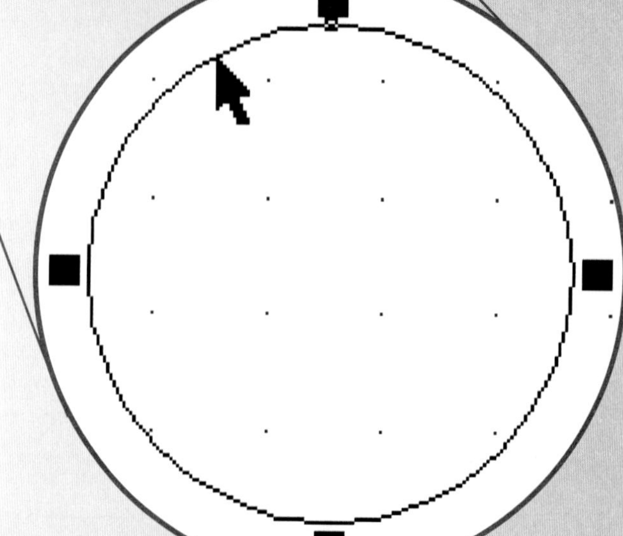

"Why would I do this?"

Selecting an object tells CorelDRAW which object to apply menu commands and mouse actions to. Before you can make any changes to an object, such as stretching it or filling it with a color, you must select it with the Pick tool.

When you create a new object, CorelDRAW selects it automatically so you can work with it immediately. You can tell that an object is selected by the eight sizing handles that appear around it.

Task 23: Selecting and Deselecting an Object

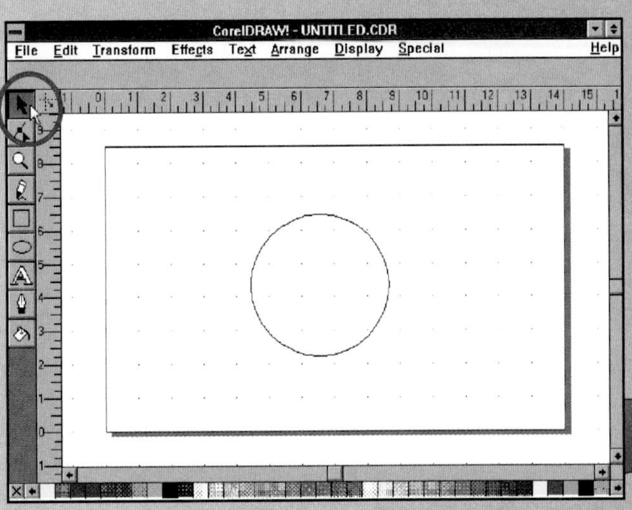

1 Click the **Pick** tool located at the top of the toolbox. This step selects the Pick tool. You'll use the Pick tool to select and deselect all CorelDRAW objects.

2 Click the outline of the object you want to select. This step selects the object. Eight sizing handles appear around the object. The status line indicates that an object is selected by displaying informa-tion about that object.

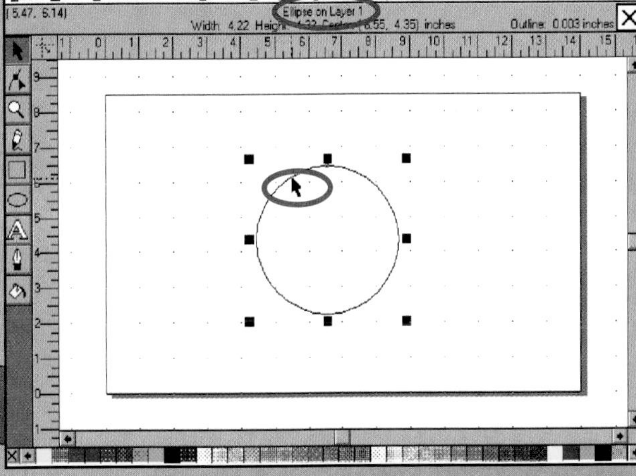

NOTE

To select a filled object, click anywhere on its outline or in its fill color or pattern. Select an unfilled object by clicking the object's outline.

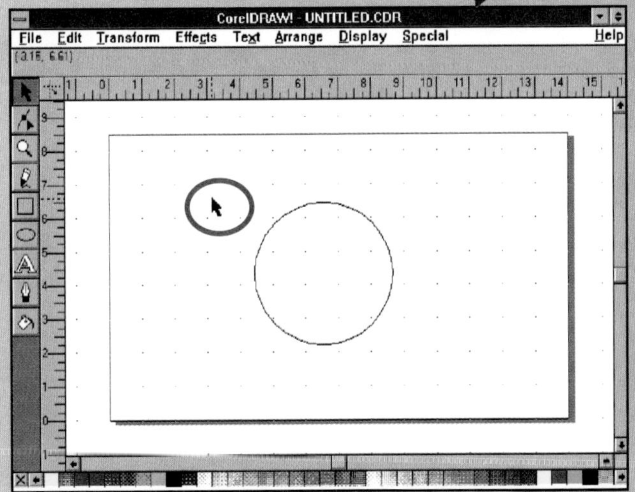

3 To deselect the object, click a blank space on the drawing window. The object's sizing handles disappear.

WHY WORRY?

If you have trouble selecting an unfilled object, make sure you position the very tip of the Pick tool (arrow) on the outline of the object, and then click the left mouse button.

TASK 24

Selecting Multiple Objects

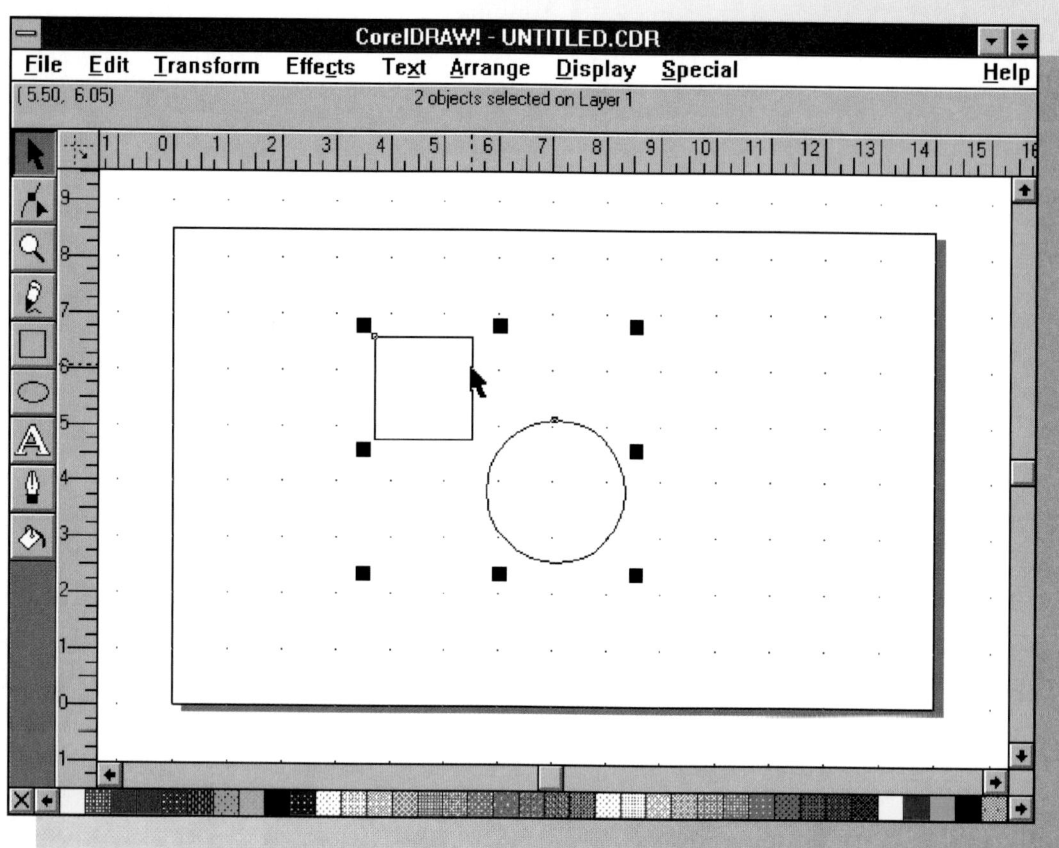

"Why would I do this?"

By selecting multiple objects, you can apply a procedure or command to all of them at one time. For example, if you want to add a color to several objects simultaneously, you first must select each object in the group, without deselecting the others you've already selected.

In this task, you'll select two objects using the Pick tool.

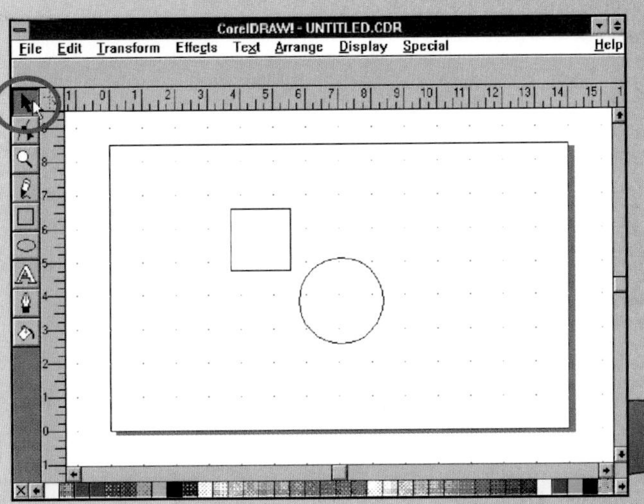

1 Click the **Pick** tool located at the top of the toolbox. This step selects the Pick tool. The mouse pointer changes to a black arrow.

2 Click the first object you want to select. Sizing handles appear around the object.

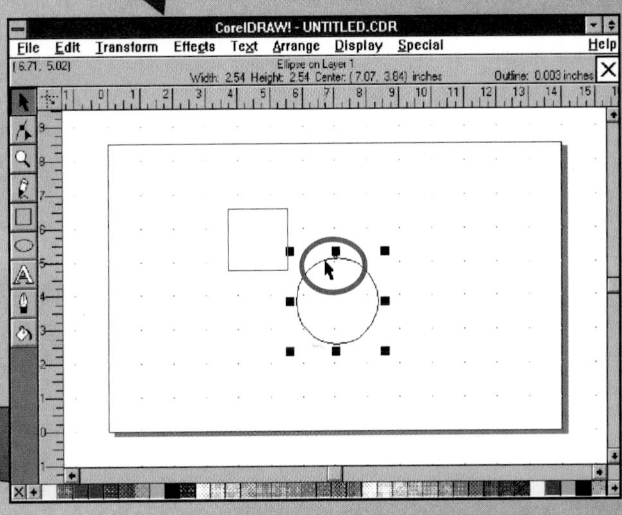

3 Hold down the **Shift** key, and click the next object you want to select. This step selects that object without deselecting the first. The eight sizing handles surround both objects. Both are selected. The status line at the top of the screen indicates that two objects are selected.

NOTE

You can select all the objects in your drawing by clicking Edit on the menu bar and then clicking Select All.

TASK 25

Grouping Objects

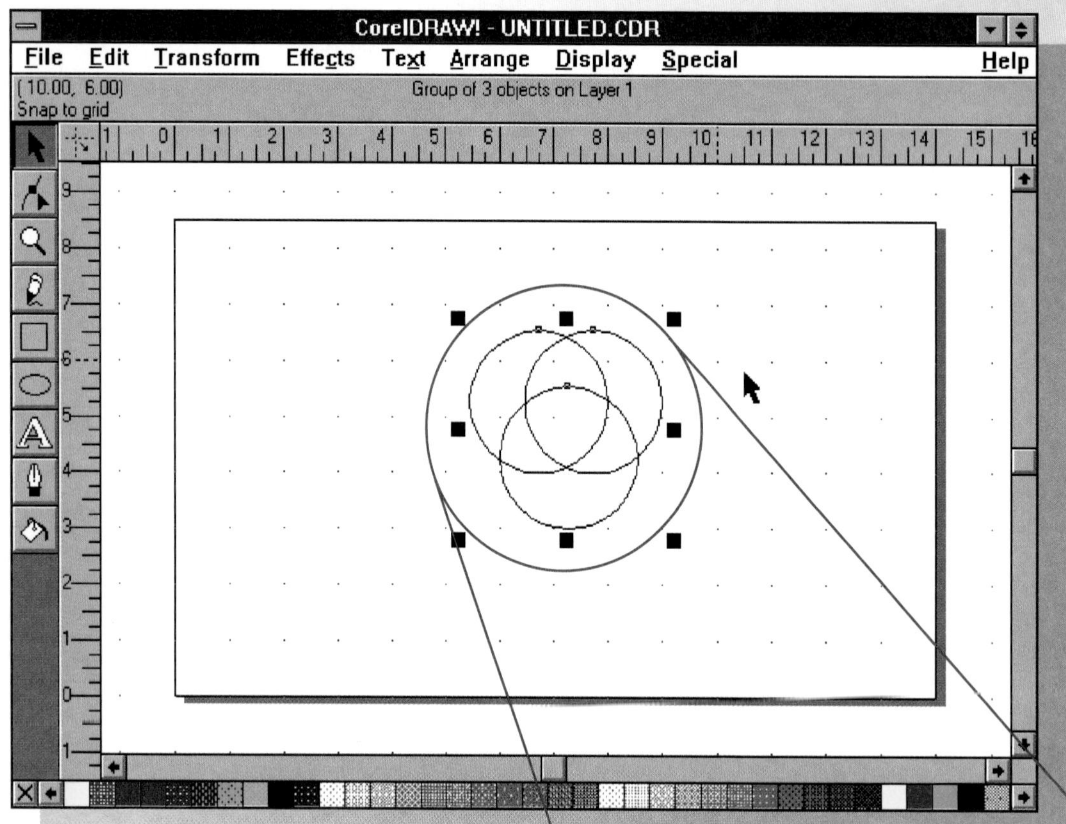

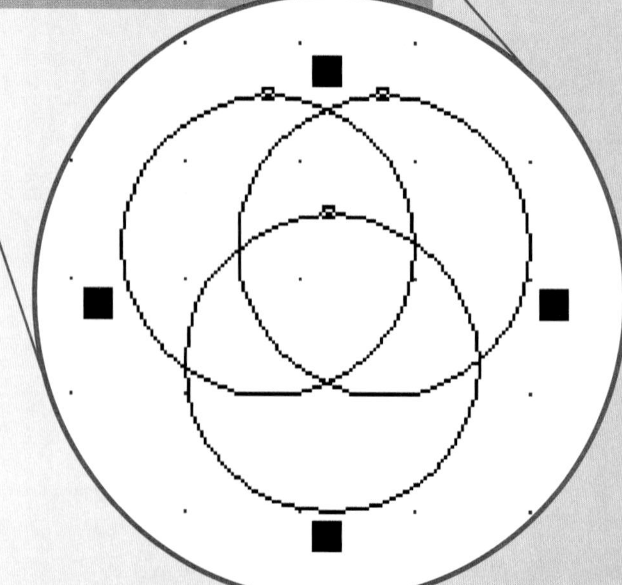

"Why would I do this?"

Most things you'll draw using CorelDRAW are made up of several objects. Once you get them drawn and placed in the drawing window, you want them to remain placed as they are. The Group command binds objects together so they can be moved and manipulated as though they were one object.

Task 25: Grouping Objects

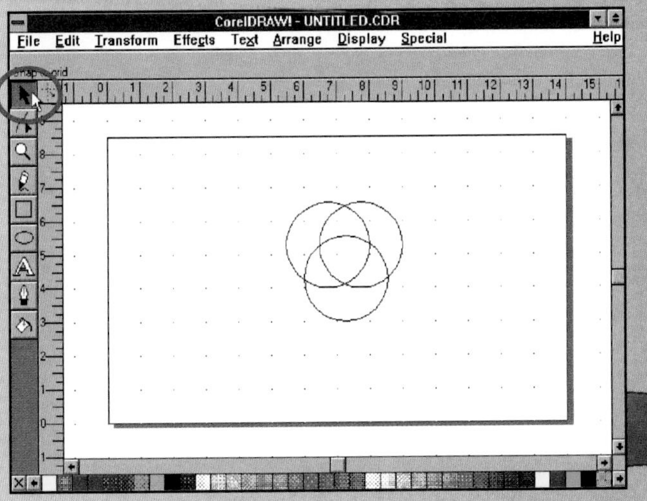

1 Click the **Pick** tool located at the top of the toolbox. Click an empty space in the drawing window. This step deselects all objects.

2 Select the objects you want to include in the group by holding down the **Shift** key and clicking **the objects**. All the selected objects will be surrounded by sizing handles.

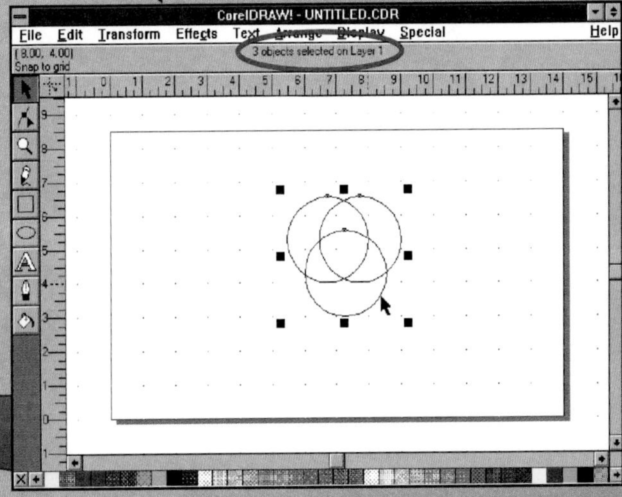

3 Click **Arrange** on the menu bar and then click **Group**. This step groups the selected objects. The status line indicates a group of two objects is selected.

WHY WORRY?

If you need to move or manipulate a single object that is part of a group, you can ungroup the collection of objects and change the object as needed. To ungroup a selected group, select Ungroup from the Arrange menu.

TASK 26

Zooming In on a Drawing

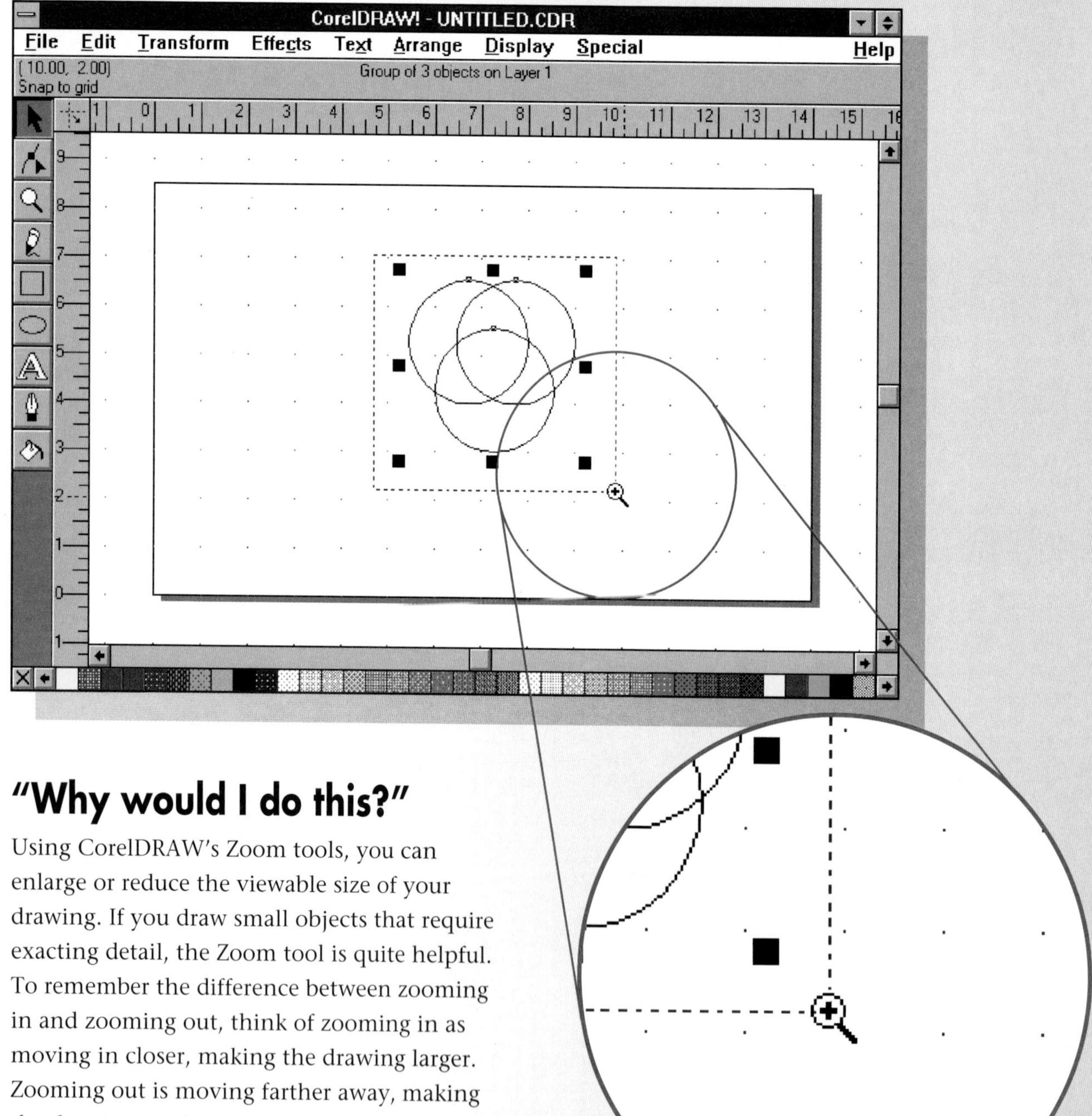

"Why would I do this?"

Using CorelDRAW's Zoom tools, you can enlarge or reduce the viewable size of your drawing. If you draw small objects that require exacting detail, the Zoom tool is quite helpful. To remember the difference between zooming in and zooming out, think of zooming in as moving in closer, making the drawing larger. Zooming out is moving farther away, making the drawing smaller.

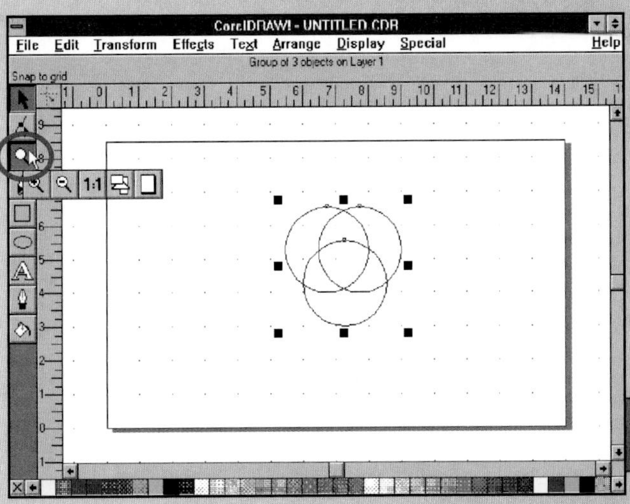

1 Click the **Zoom** tool located on the toolbox. This step opens the Zoom tool fly-out menu. The fly-out menu opens and displays five Zoom tool options.

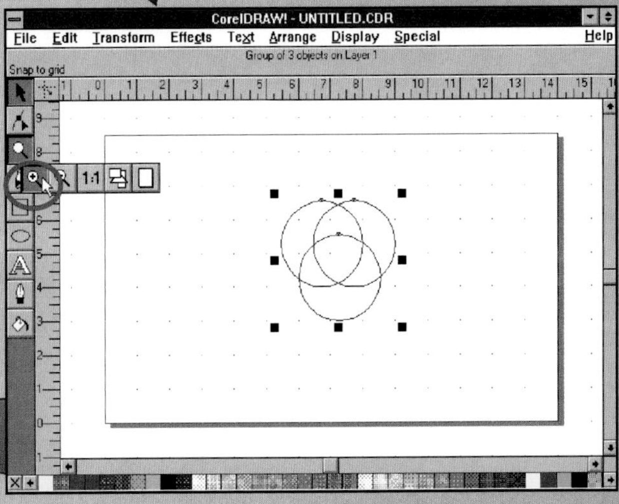

2 Click the **Zoom In** tool on the fly-out menu. This step selects the Zoom In tool. The fly-out menu closes and the Zoom In tool icon is selected.

3 When you move the mouse pointer to the drawing window, it changes to the Zoom In tool (a magnifying glass with a plus sign in it). Move the pointer to one corner of the area you want to zoom in on.

NOTE

When using the zoom tools in CorelDRAW, the drawing window stays the same size, the objects in the drawing window are magnified or reduced.

4 Drag the pointer as if you were drawing a rectangle around the area to zoom. This step selects an area to zoom in on. As you drag, a dashed line rectangle is created.

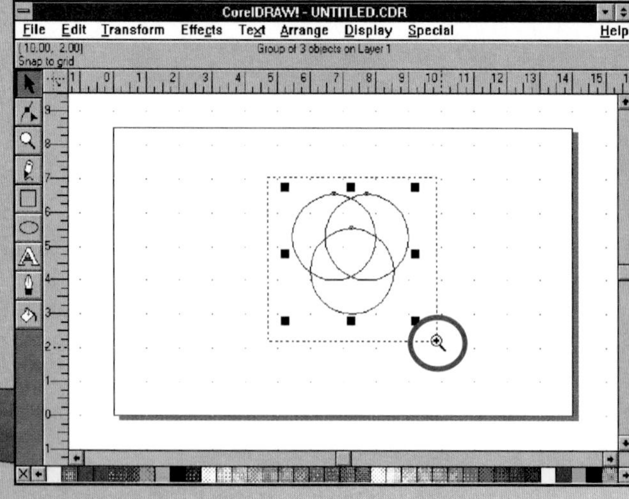

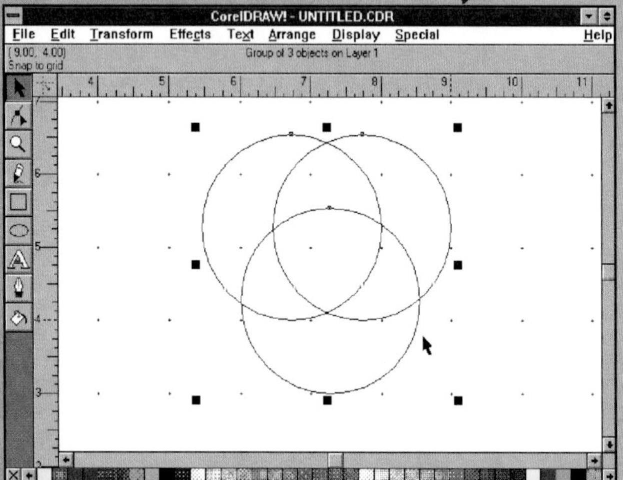

5 Release the mouse button. This step completes the zoom in operation. The drawing window is magnified.

WHY WORRY?

You can easily edit small images by using the Zoom In tool to magnify the image and locate its sizing handles and control nodes.

TASK 27

Zooming Out from a Drawing

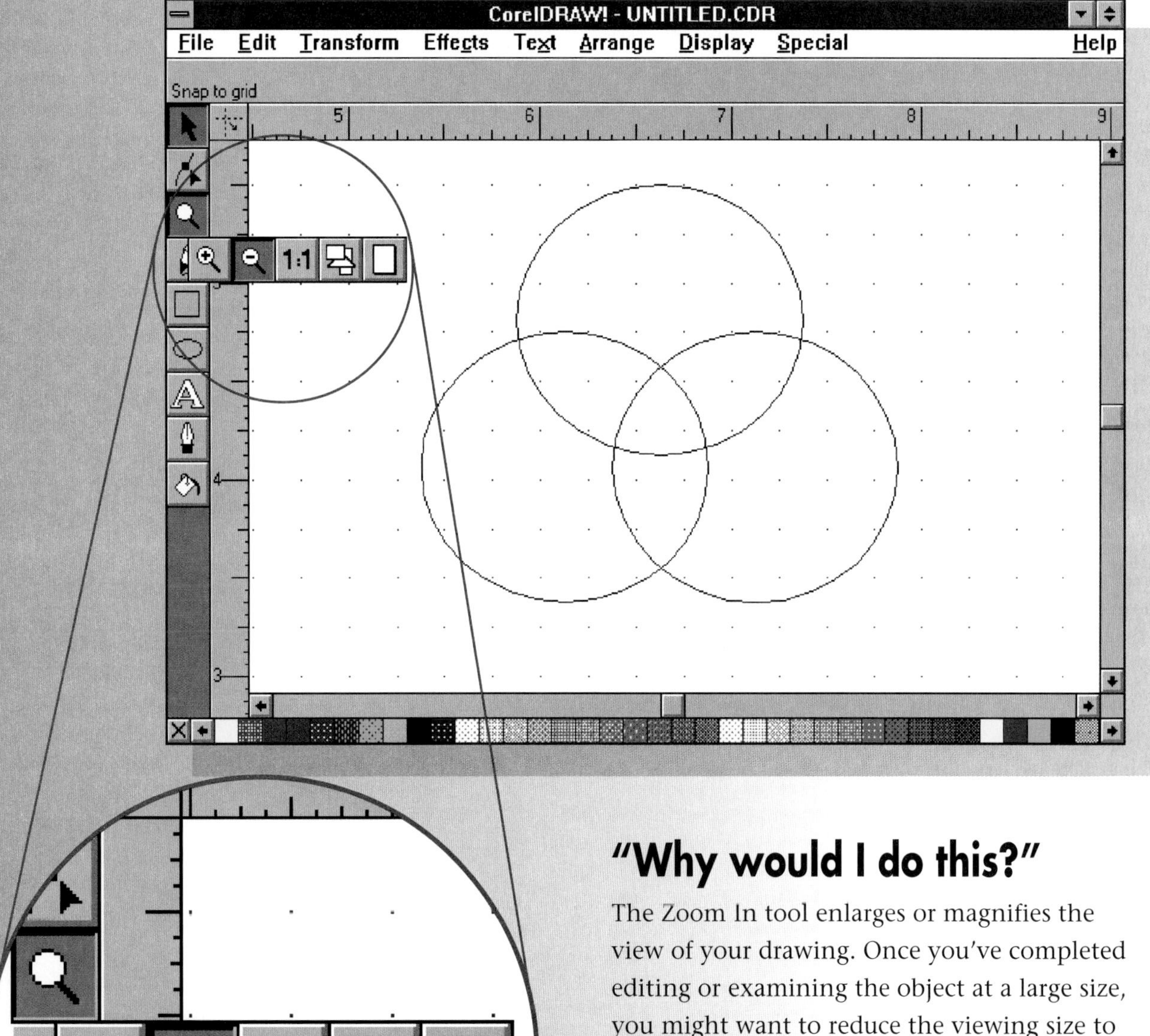

"Why would I do this?"

The Zoom In tool enlarges or magnifies the view of your drawing. Once you've completed editing or examining the object at a large size, you might want to reduce the viewing size to get the big picture of your drawing. The Zoom Out option on the Zoom tool fly-out menu enables you to reduce the viewing size of your drawing, as if you were moving away from the drawing page.

Task 27: Zooming Out from a Drawing

1 Click the **Zoom** tool on the toolbox. This step opens the Zoom tool fly-out menu.

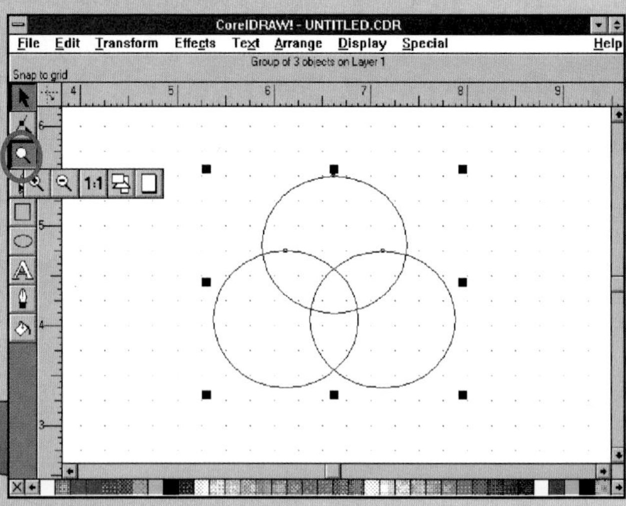

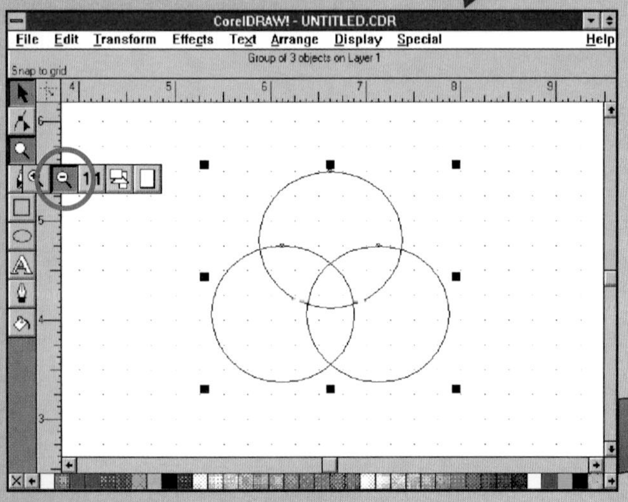

2 Click the **Zoom Out** tool on the fly-out menu. This step selects the Zoom Out tool (the magnifying glass with a minus sign). The view of the drawing window is immediately reduced to the size it was before the last Zoom In operation.

NOTE

If you did not perform a Zoom In on your drawing, selecting Zoom Out reduces the viewing size of your drawing by half.

3 Notice that the rulers at the top and left of the screen are scaled to match the reduced-size drawing view.

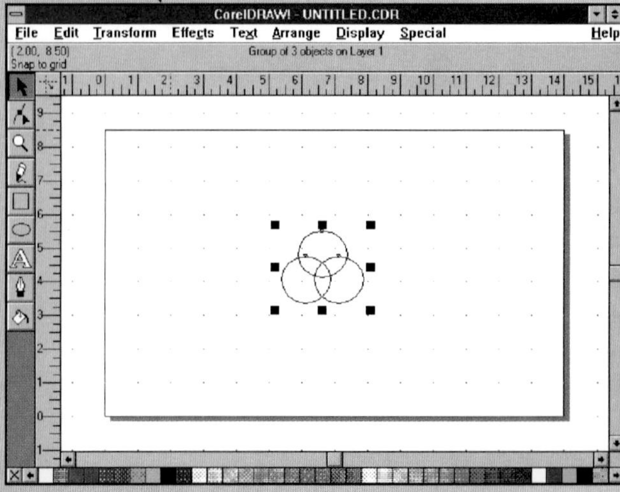

TASK 28

Viewing an Object at Actual Size

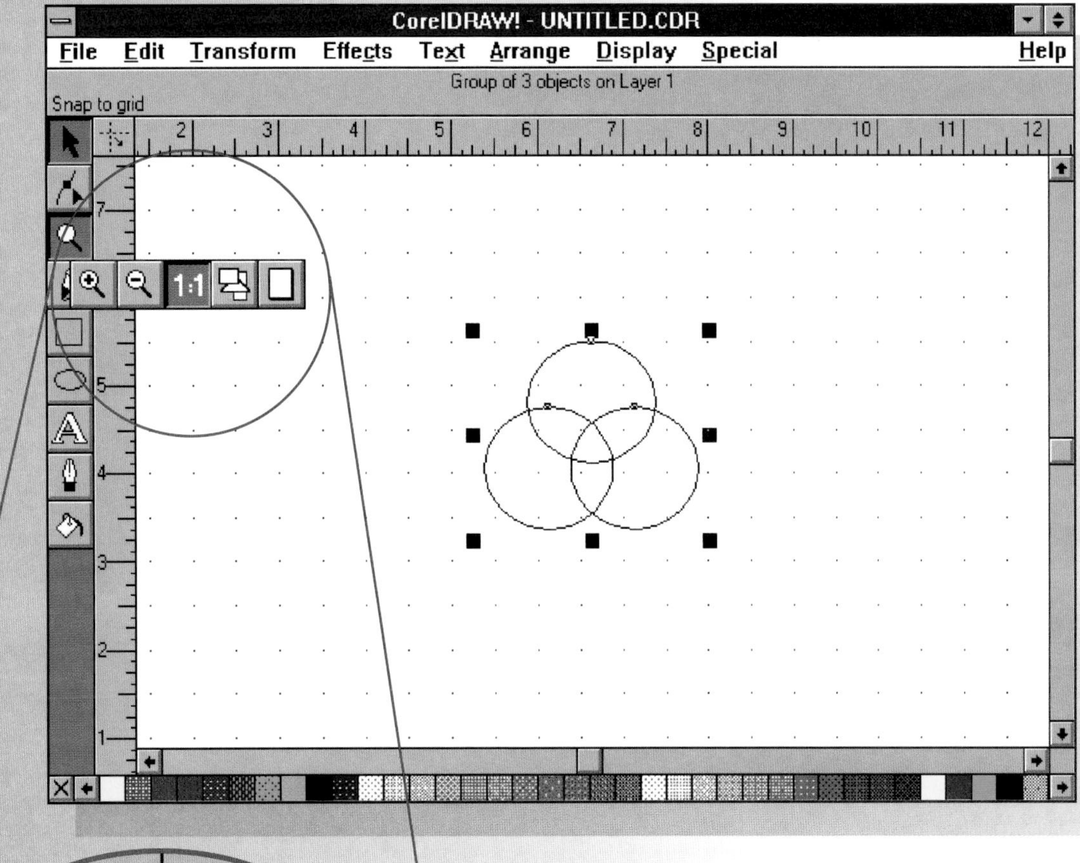

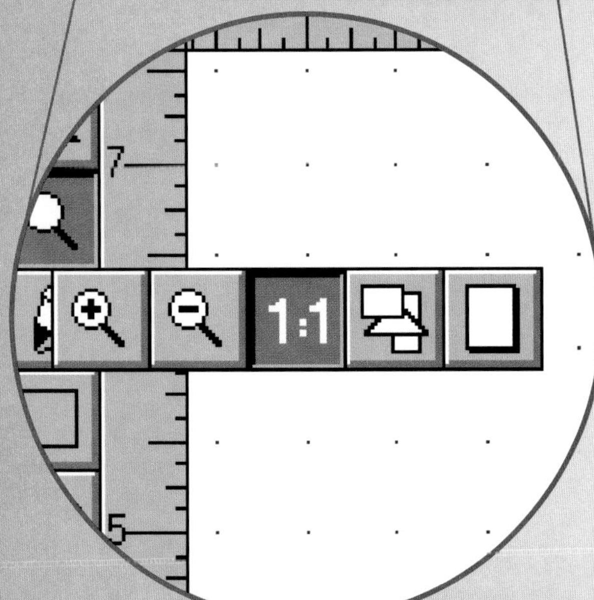

"Why would I do this?"

To see the size your drawing page will be when it's printed, change the view to Actual Size. CorelDRAW's Zoom tool gives you great control over the viewing size of your drawing. Sometimes, you may want to see your drawing displayed at the actual size it will be when you print it. The Actual Size Zoom tool option enables you to instantly change the drawing view to the size your drawing page will be when it's printed.

Task 28: Viewing an Object at Actual Size

1 Click the **Zoom** tool on the toolbox. This step opens the Zoom tool fly-out menu.

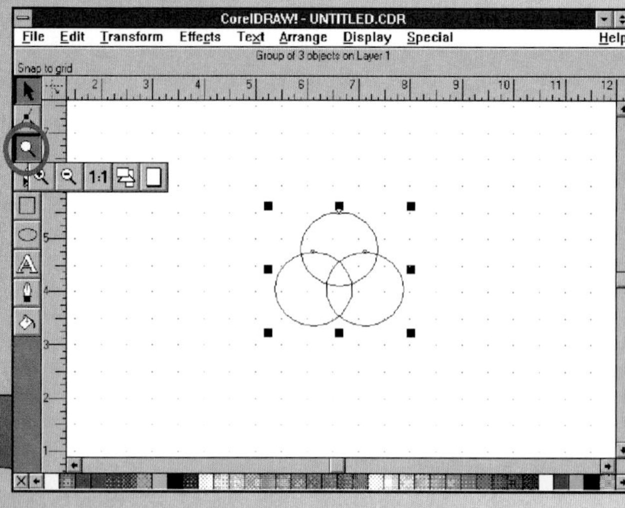

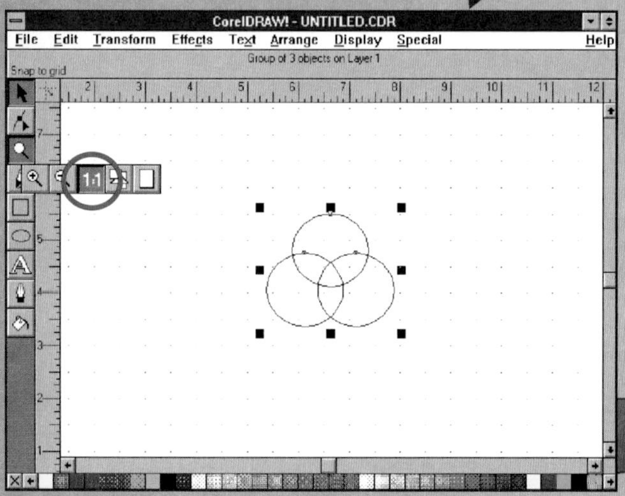

2 Click the **Actual Size** icon (1:1) on the fly-out menu.

3 The CorelDRAW drawing is changed to actual size. This is the size at which your drawing will be printed, unless you make changes in the Print dialog box.

NOTE

When viewing a drawing in Actual Size, the CorelDRAW rulers are true to scale, meaning that one inch on the ruler really is one inch.

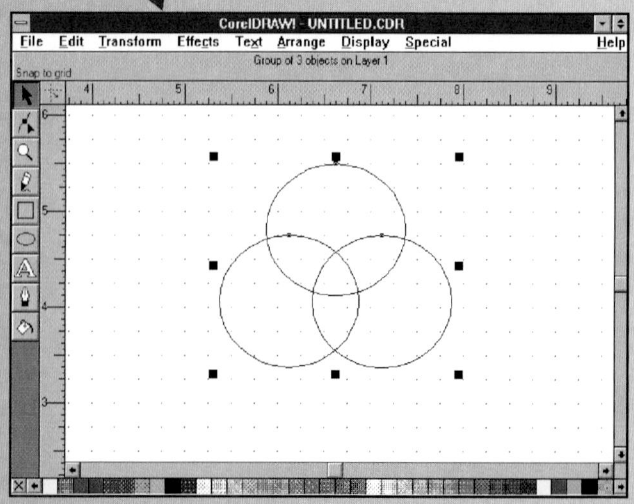

TASK 29

Using Wireframe View

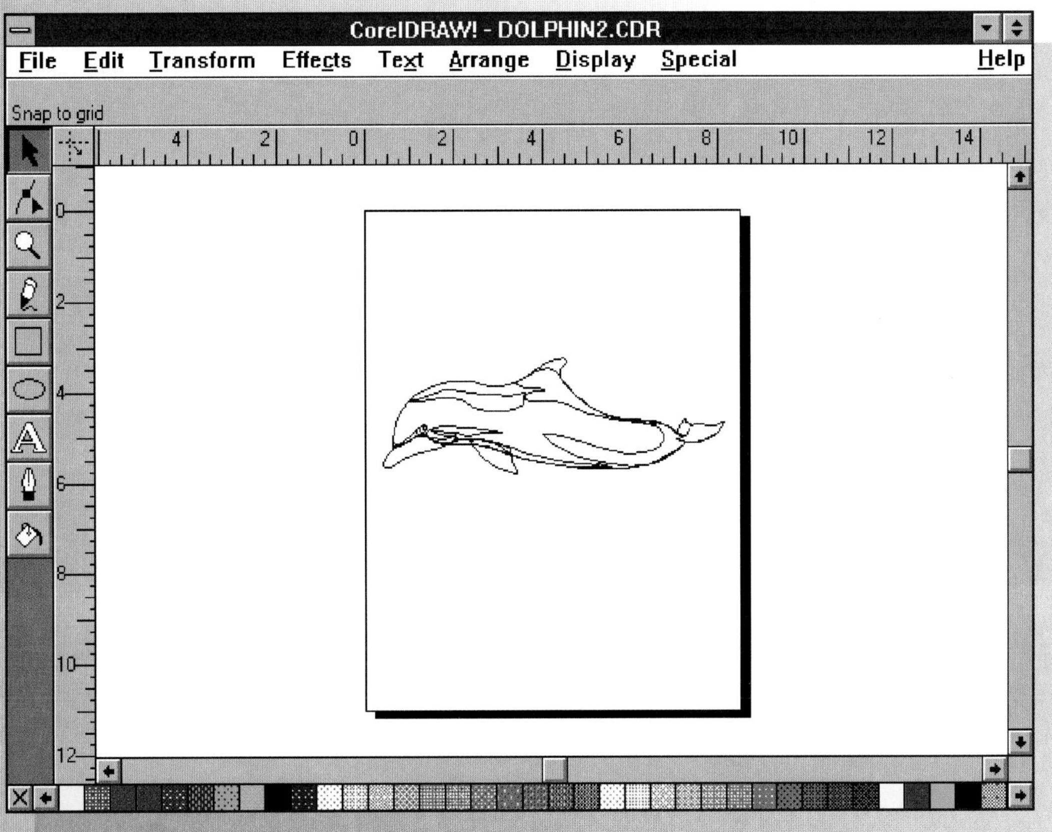

"Why would I do this?"

Normal view shows fills and text attributes as they will appear when printed. However, only the outlines of your objects are displayed in Wireframe view. Since this view takes up less memory than the normal view, Wireframe view speeds up the display of your drawing if you are working on a complex image or a multipage document. Also, you may find that editing wireframes is faster than editing full-color objects.

In this task, you'll load a clipart image and change to Wireframe view.

Task 29: Using Wireframe View

1 Click **File** on the menu bar. Click **Open**. The Open Drawing dialog box appears. Click **Dolphin2.cdr** located in the Mammal subdirectory of the Clipart directory. Click **OK** to load the image. The image of a dolphin displays in the drawing window.

NOTE

Remember that you can view any drawing in Wireframe view. If you have a drawing of your own you want to view in Wireframe view, you can use it instead of Dolphin2.cdr.

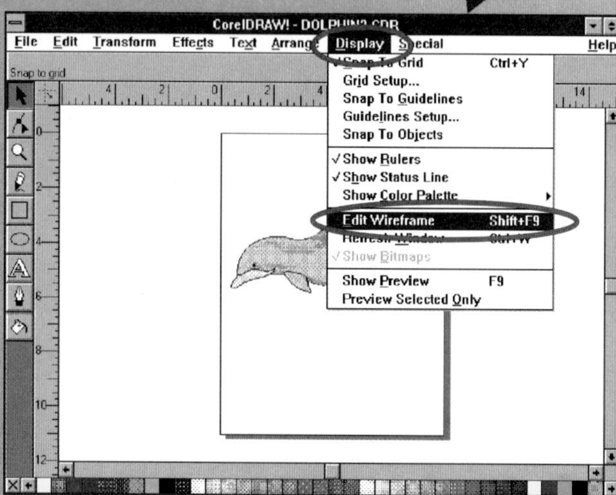

2 Click **Display** on the menu bar, and then click **Edit Wireframe**.

WHY WORRY?

To change back to normal view, click Edit Wireframe again on the Display menu. The view changes back to normal, displaying the image's fill colors.

3 The display changes from Editable Preview to Wireframe view. Notice that none of the fill colors in the dolphin image are displayed.

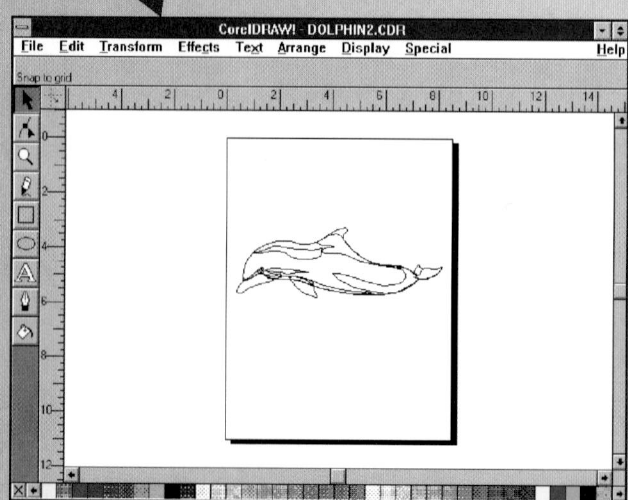

NOTE

The term Editable Preview is Corel's name for the view that shows color fills, patterns, and textures. Remember that you can also use any tool or command in Wireframe view to edit your drawing.

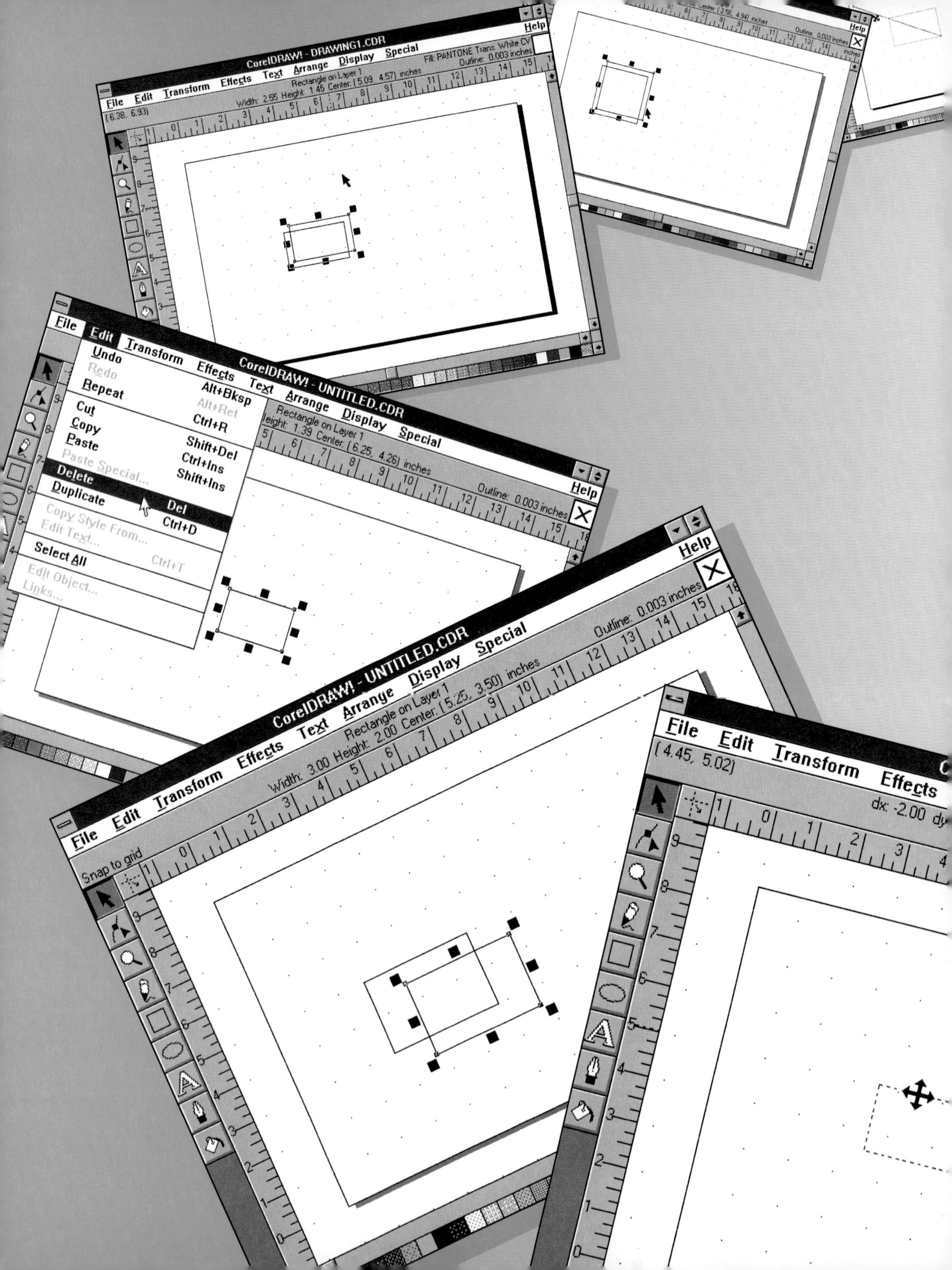

CorelDRAW! - DRAWING1.CDR
File Edit Transform Effects Text Arrange Display Special Help
Rectangle on Layer 1
Width: 2.55 Height: 1.45 Center: (5.09, 4.57) inches
Fill: PANTONE Trans. White CV
Outline: 0.003 inches
(6.38, 6.93)
CorelDRAW! - UNTITLED.CDR
File Edit Transform Effects Text Arrange Display Special Help
Undo
Redo
Repeat
Alt+Bksp
Alt+Ret
Ctrl+R
Cut
Copy
Paste
Shift+Del
Ctrl+Ins
Shift+Ins
Paste Special...
Delete
Del
Duplicate
Ctrl+D
Copy Style From...
Edit Text...
Select All
Ctrl+T
Edit Object...
Links...
Rectangle on Layer 1
Height: 1.39 Center: (6.25, 4.26) inches
Outline: 0.003 inches
CorelDRAW! - UNTITLED.CDR
File Edit Transform Effects Text Arrange Display Special Help
Rectangle on Layer 1
Width: 3.00 Height: 2.00 Center: (5.25, 3.50) inches
Outline: 0.003 inches
Snap to grid
File Edit Transform Effects
(4.45, 5.02)
dx: -2.00

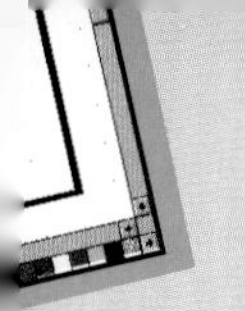

PART IV

Modifying Objects

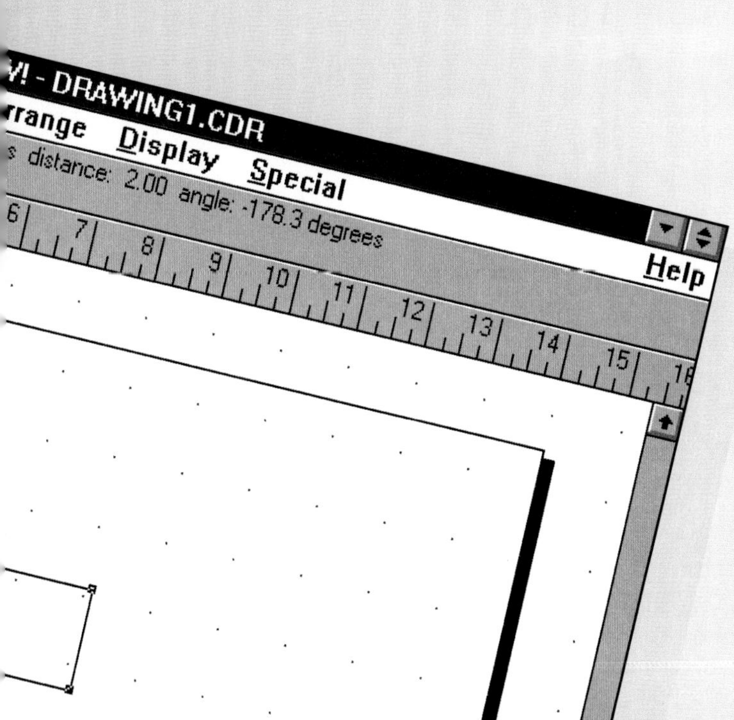

In this part, you'll learn how to use CorelDRAW's editing and viewing tools to modify the objects you draw. For example, you might need to move an object to another part of your drawing, stretch the object lengthwise, or fill it with a color or pattern.

As you add elements to a drawing, you'll find that you need to move them around the drawing window. Using the Pick tool, you can drag objects anywhere in your drawing. As you drag, a dotted outline of the object follows the Pick tool, and the object stays in its original location. Once you move the outline to a new location and release the mouse button, the object jumps to where you moved the outline.

You also may want to copy objects in a drawing. Copying an object to the Windows Clipboard is the easiest way to place an object from another drawing into your current drawing.

To create an exact duplicate of an object in your drawing, use the Duplicate command on the Edit menu. Duplicating creates another copy of the selected object but, unlike copying, it does not copy the object to the Windows Clipboard.

The Clone feature of CorelDRAW 4 offers yet another variation of copying an object. A clone is an exact copy of an object that changes right along with the original. For example, if you create a clone of an ellipse and resize the ellipse, the clone also is resized. Cloning is extremely useful if your drawing calls for repeating objects. Rather than backtracking to change each individual object, you simply change the original and the clones follow suit.

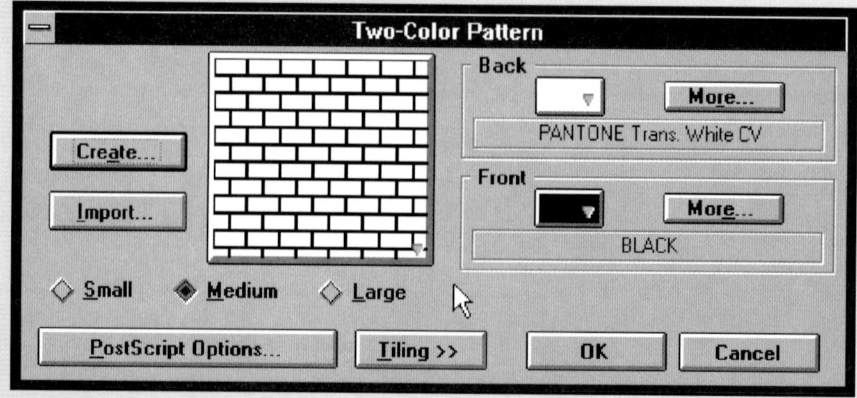

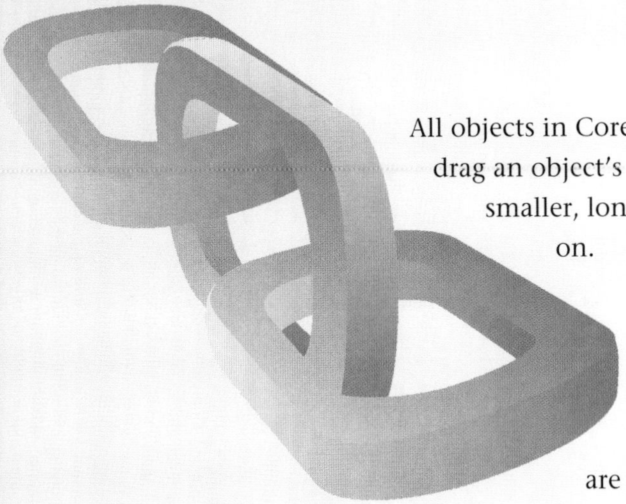

All objects in CorelDRAW can be resized. You can drag an object's sizing handles to make it larger, smaller, longer, taller, shorter, thinner, and so on.

Some objects you create in CorelDRAW, such as rectangles and ellipses, are created parallel to the drawing window—their edges are aligned with the edges of the page. To angle an object such as a square, you use the object's rotation handles. Clicking an object twice displays its rotation handles, which look like double-headed arrows. To rotate the object, drag a rotation handle in the direction you want to rotate. A dotted outline follows the mouse pointer to show you how the object will be rotated.

You can use the Color Palette, located at the bottom of the CorelDRAW screen, to fill closed objects with color. Simply select the object you want to fill, and click a color in the Color Palette. You also can fill objects with patterns, using the two-color patterns available in the Fill roll-up window.

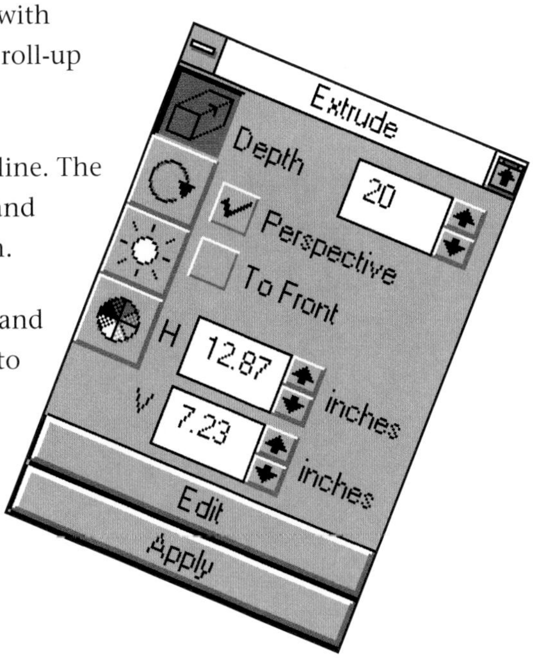

You also can change the color and style of an object's outline. The Pen roll-up window gives you control over the thickness and color of the lines and outlines of the objects you've drawn.

At the end of this part, you'll learn to use two interesting and powerful techniques in CorelDRAW—adding perspective to an object and extruding an object. Adding perspective gives the object depth. Extruding an object makes it appear three-dimensional.

TASK 30

Moving an Object

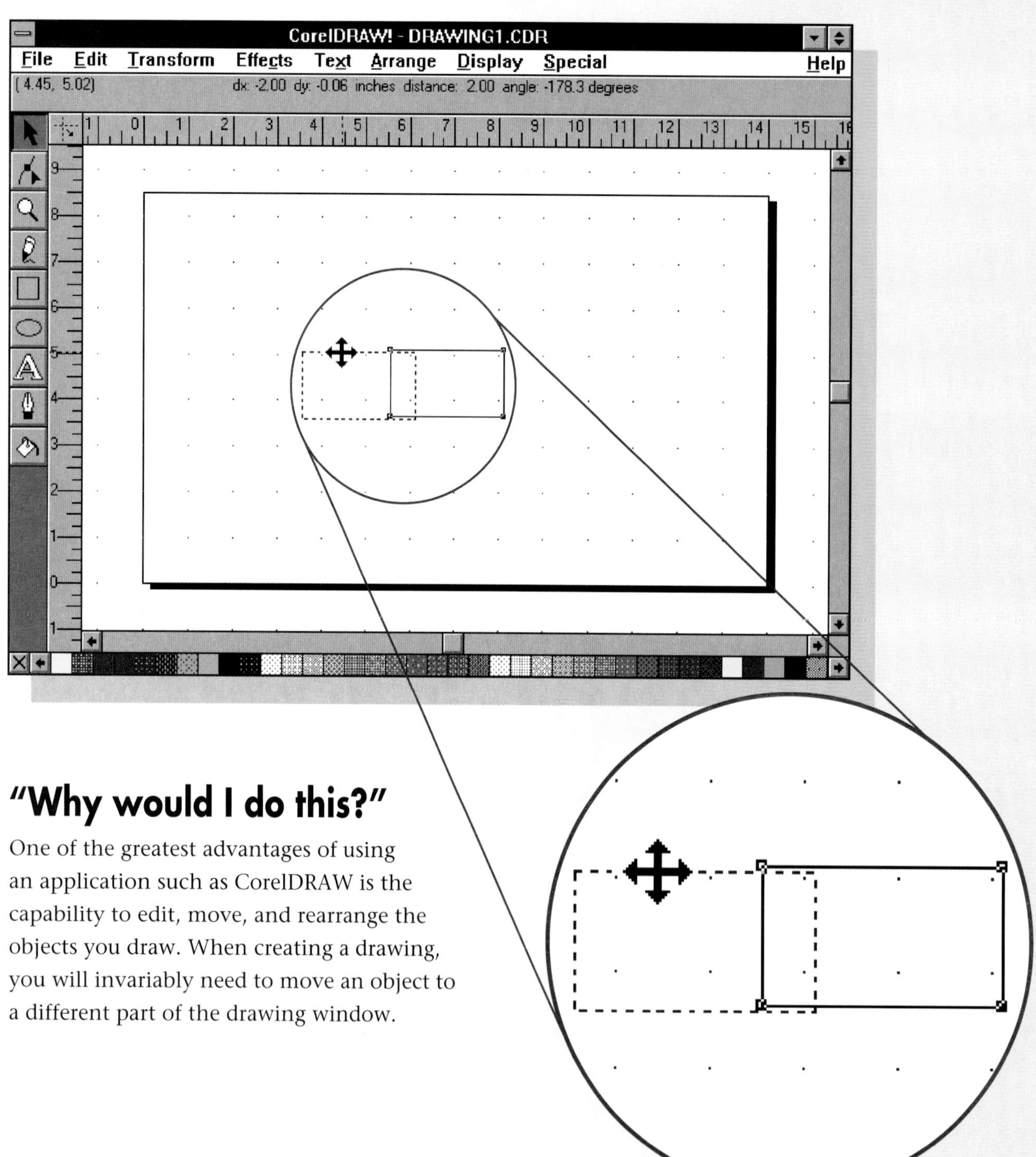

"Why would I do this?"

One of the greatest advantages of using an application such as CorelDRAW is the capability to edit, move, and rearrange the objects you draw. When creating a drawing, you will invariably need to move an object to a different part of the drawing window.

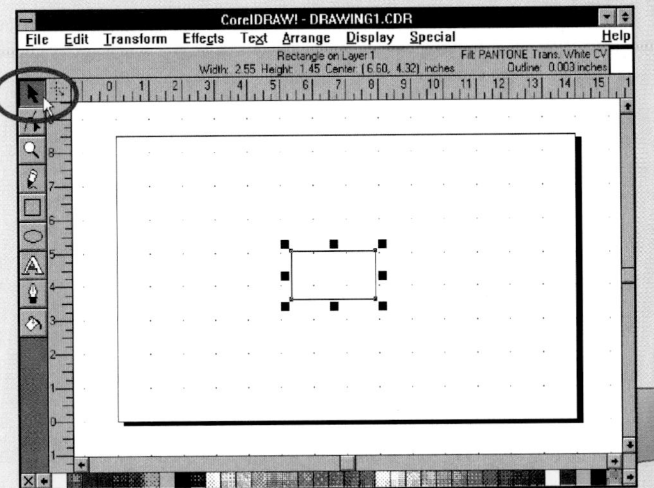

1 Click the **Pick** tool in the toolbox, and then click the object you want to move. This step selects the Pick tool and selects the object.

WHY WORRY?

You can select an unfilled object by clicking anywhere on its outline. To select a filled object, click anywhere on its outline or its fill.

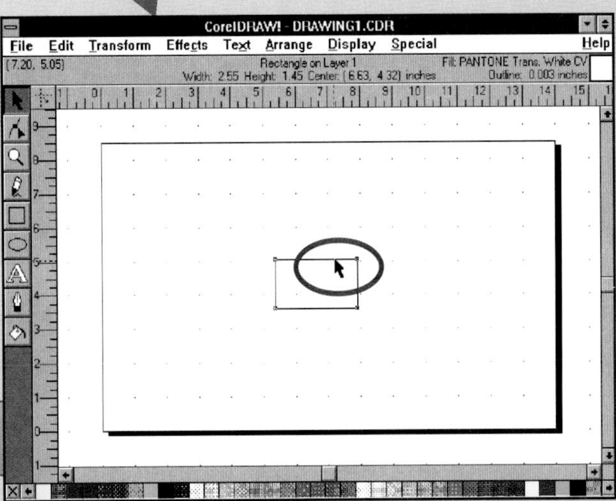

2 Point to the outline of the object and hold the mouse button. This step begins the move operation.

3 Drag the object in the direction you want to move it. As you drag, the mouse pointer changes to a four-headed arrow; a dotted outline of the object follows the pointer. Release the mouse button to drop the object. This step moves the object.

NOTE

The status line indicates how far the object has been moved from its original location.

TASK 31

Copying an Object

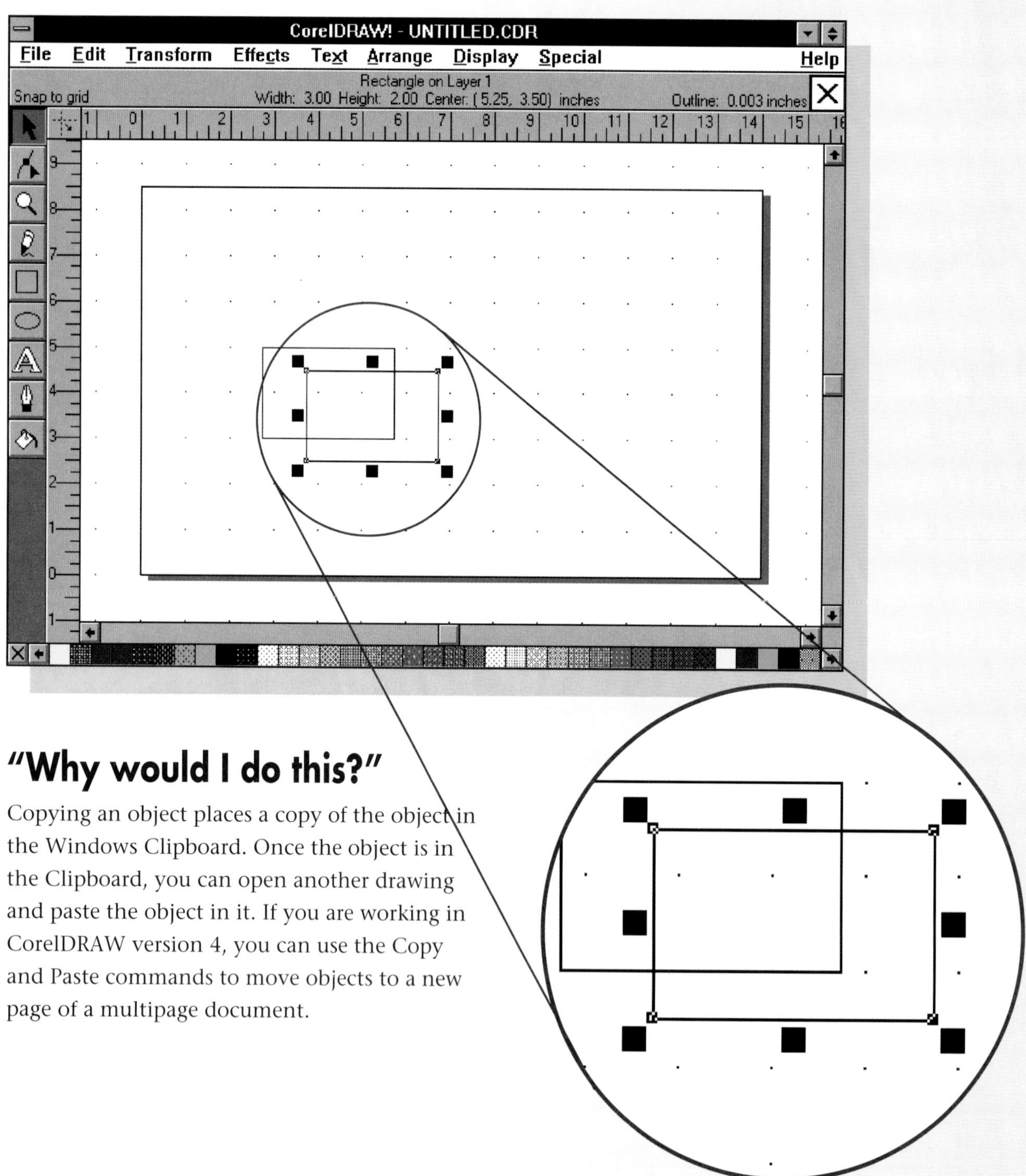

"Why would I do this?"

Copying an object places a copy of the object in the Windows Clipboard. Once the object is in the Clipboard, you can open another drawing and paste the object in it. If you are working in CorelDRAW version 4, you can use the Copy and Paste commands to move objects to a new page of a multipage document.

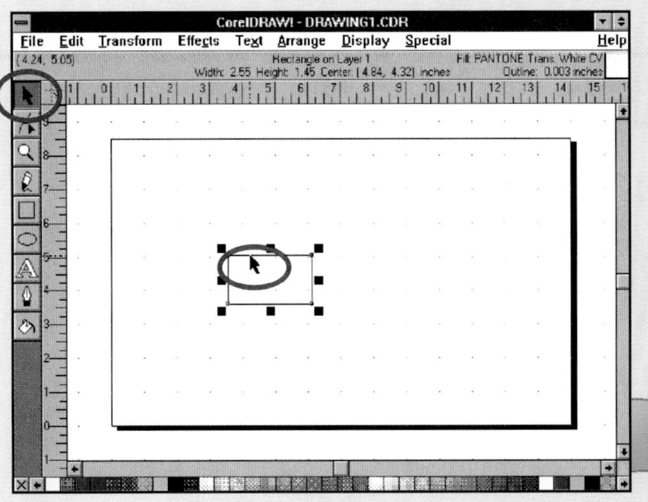

1 Click the **Pick** tool in the toolbox. Click the object you want to copy. The object's sizing handles appear. You must select an object before it can be copied.

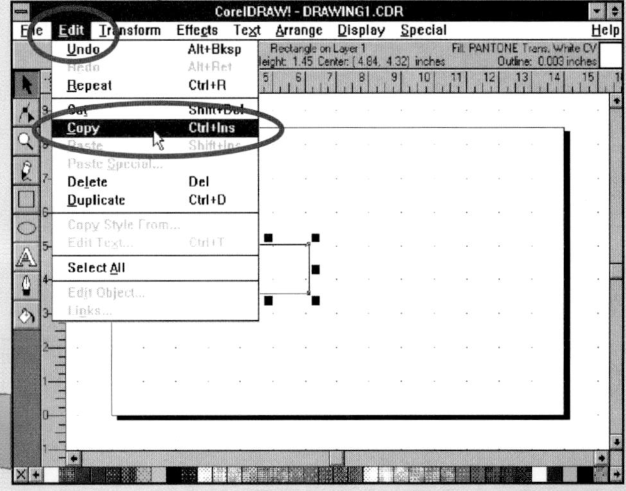

2 Click **Edit** in the menu bar. Then click **Copy**. This step copies the rectangle to the Windows Clipboard. The rectangle remains selected.

NOTE

Once an object is copied to the Windows Clipboard, it remains there until a new object is copied or cut to the Clipboard. You can, therefore, paste an object from the Clipboard as many times as you like.

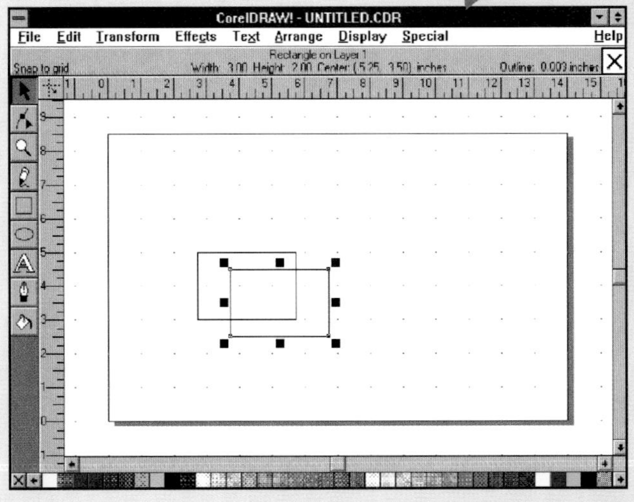

3 Click **Edit** in the menu bar. Then click **Paste**. This step pastes the rectangle on the Clipboard into the drawing window, directly on top of the existing rectangle. To see the two rectangles, drag the pasted rectangle away from the original.

TASK 32

Deleting an Object

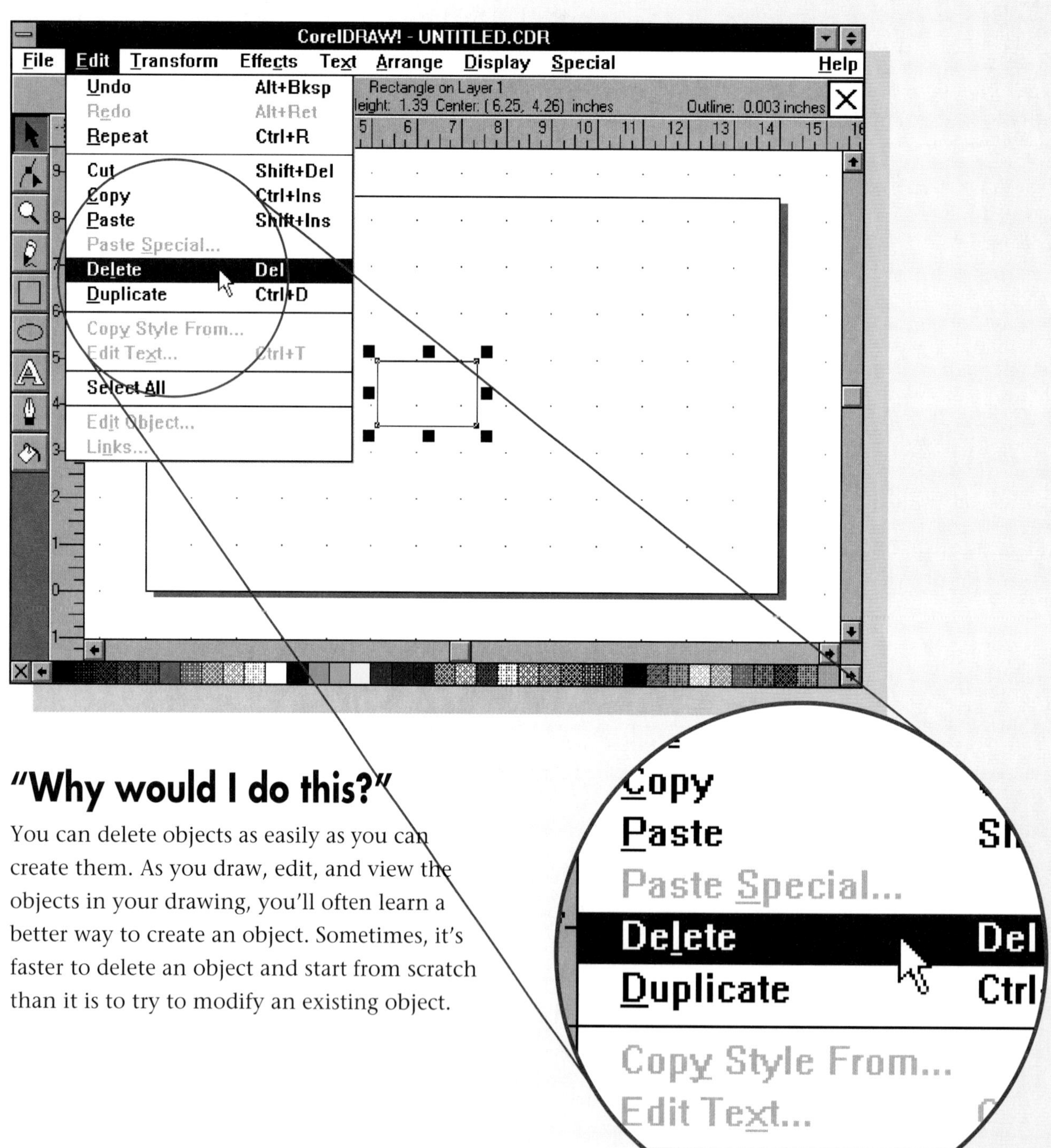

"Why would I do this?"

You can delete objects as easily as you can create them. As you draw, edit, and view the objects in your drawing, you'll often learn a better way to create an object. Sometimes, it's faster to delete an object and start from scratch than it is to try to modify an existing object.

Task 32: Deleting an Object

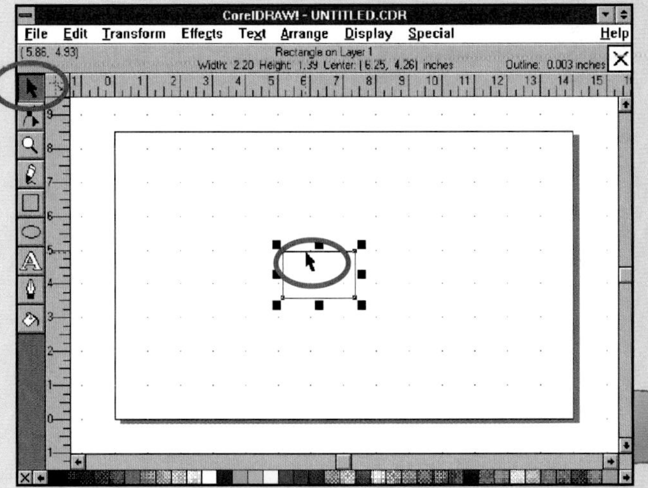

1 Click the **Pick** tool in the toolbox. Select the object that you want to delete in the drawing window. Its sizing handles should appear.

WHY WORRY?

You always can undo a delete operation by clicking Undo on the Edit menu.

2 Click **Edit** in the menu bar. Then click **Delete**. The selected object is deleted.

WHY WORRY?

If you are unsure about deleting an object but want to see what the drawing looks like without it, use the Copy command on the Edit menu to copy the object to the Clipboard. Then delete the object and make any other changes you like. If you need the object back, simply select Paste from the Edit menu to paste the object into the drawing.

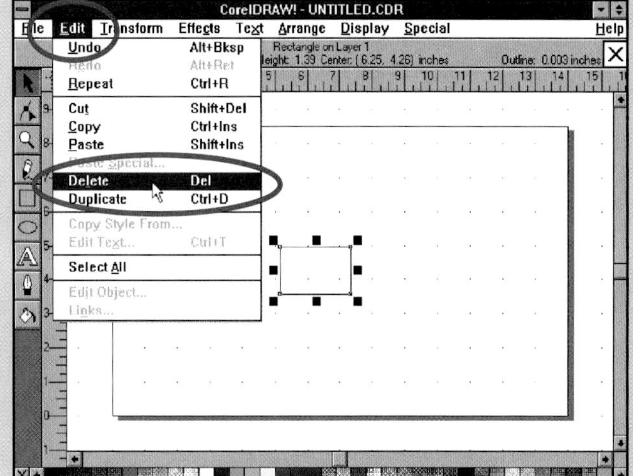

TASK 33

Duplicating an Object

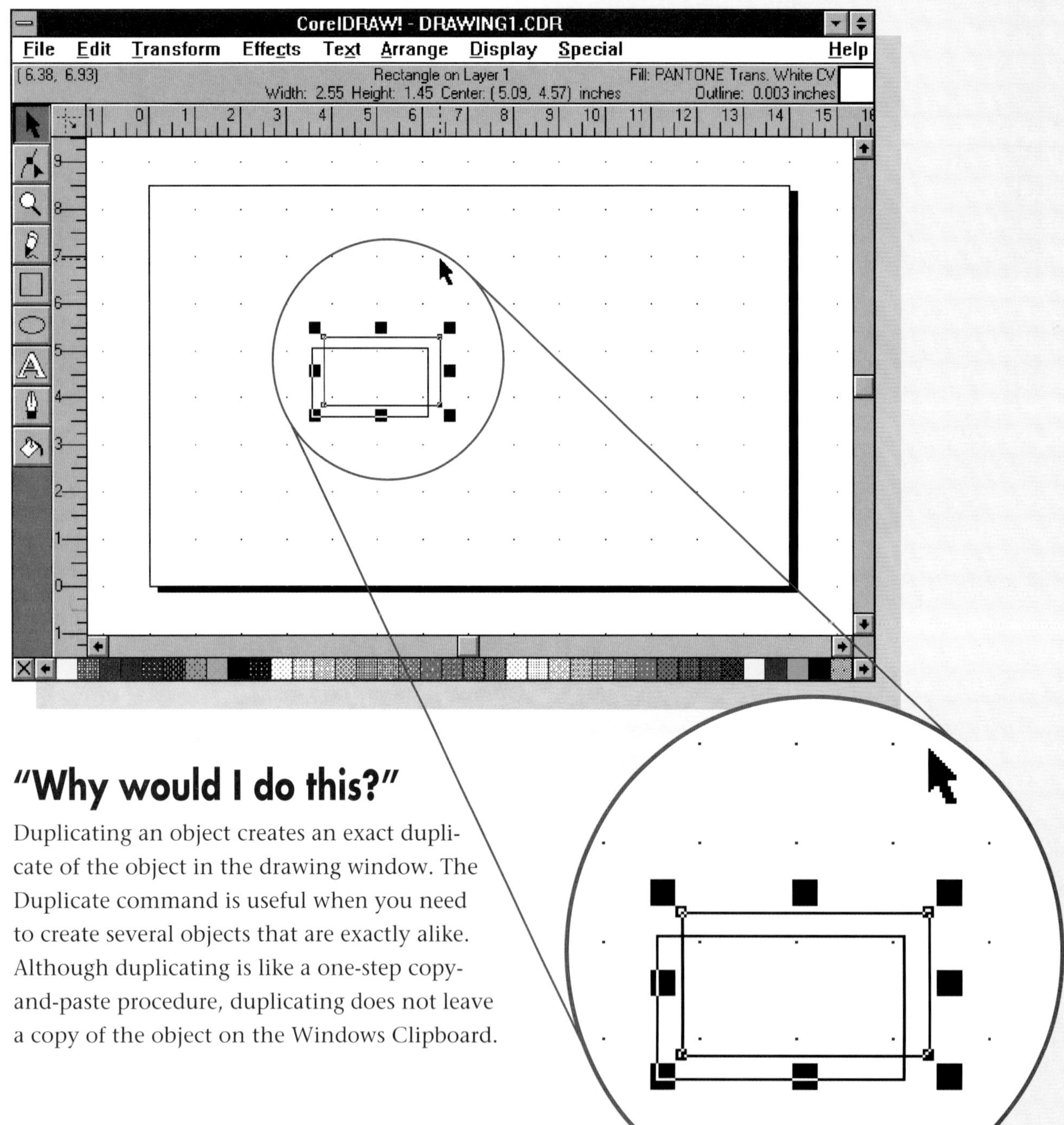

"Why would I do this?"

Duplicating an object creates an exact duplicate of the object in the drawing window. The Duplicate command is useful when you need to create several objects that are exactly alike. Although duplicating is like a one-step copy-and-paste procedure, duplicating does not leave a copy of the object on the Windows Clipboard.

Task 33: Duplicating an Object

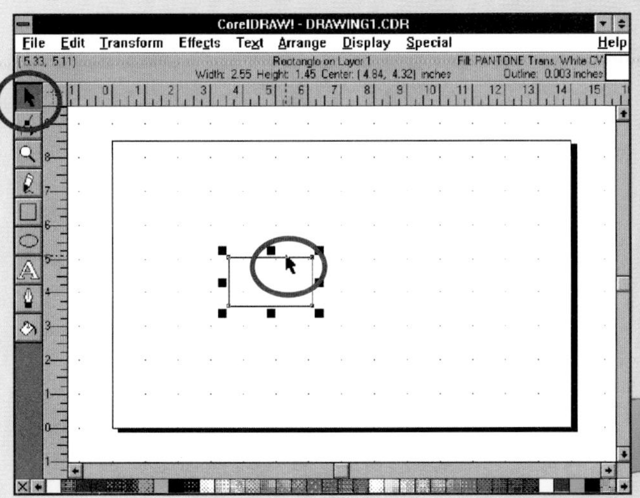

1 Click the **Pick** tool in the toolbox. Click the object you want to duplicate in the drawing window. This step selects the object. Its sizing handles appear.

2 Click **Edit** in the menu bar, and then click **Duplicate**.

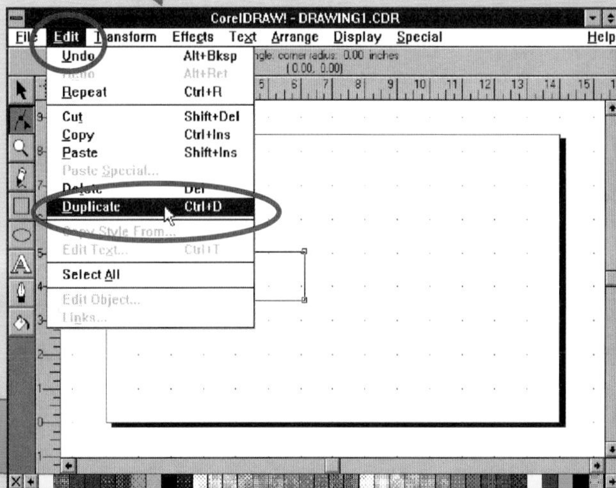

3 CorelDRAW creates an exact copy of the object. The new object is placed slightly up and to the right of the original object. The new object is selected.

NOTE

To adjust the distance duplicated objects are placed from the originals, choose Preferences on the Special menu, and then change the Place Duplicate setting in the Preferences dialog box.

TASK 34

Cloning an Object (version 4)

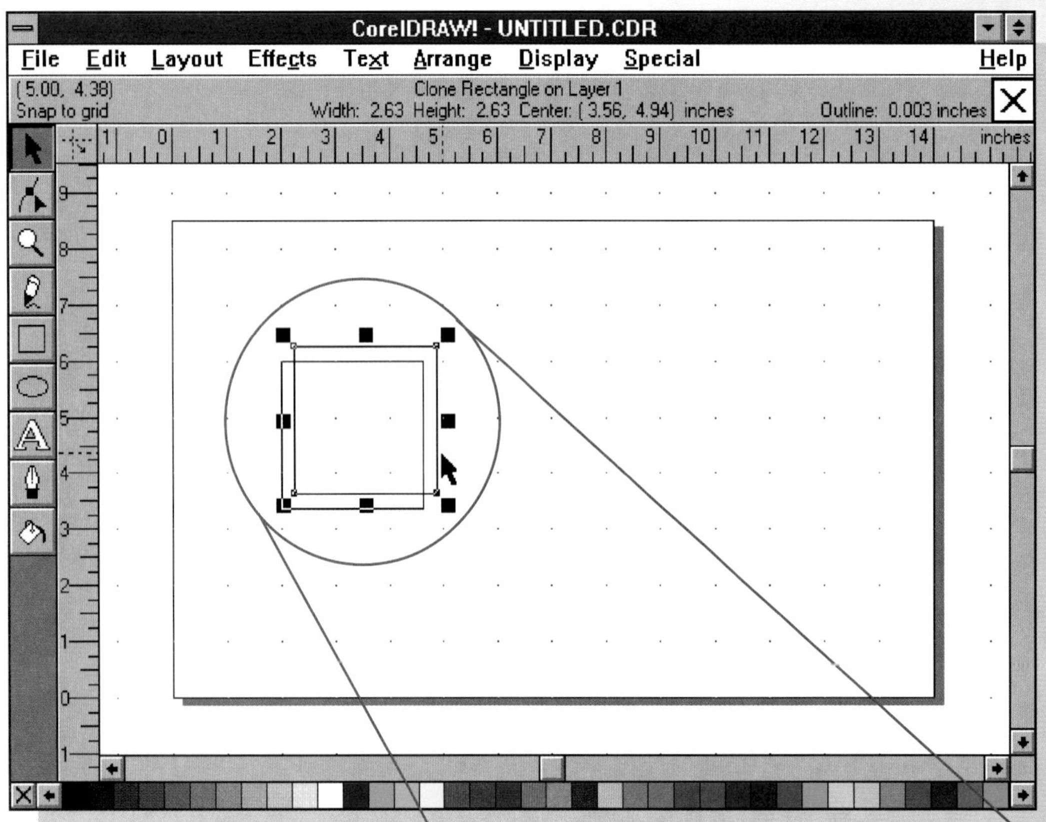

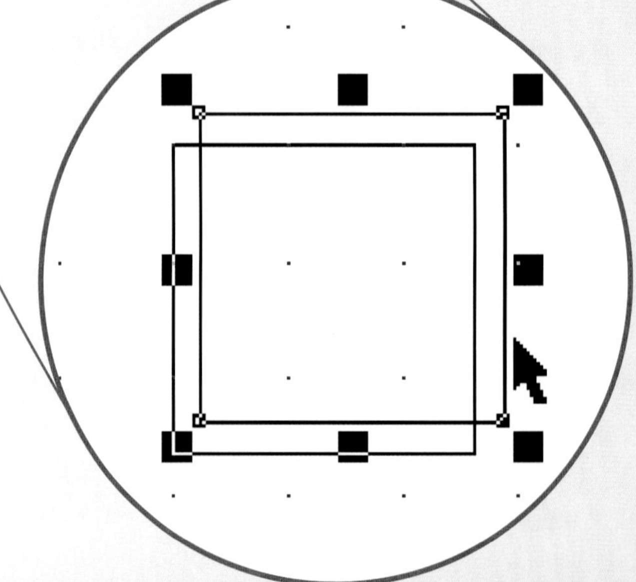

"Why would I do this?"

CorelDRAW version 4 offers an additional method of duplicating an object—the Clone command. Cloning an object is similar to duplicating; however, the Clone command creates an object that mimics the original object. Any changes you make to the original object will automatically be applied to the cloned object.

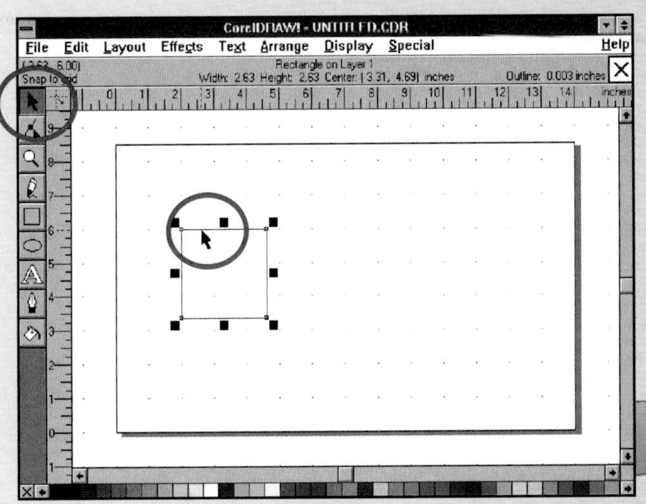

1 Click the **Pick** tool in the toolbox. Click an object in the drawing window to select it. Its sizing handles appear.

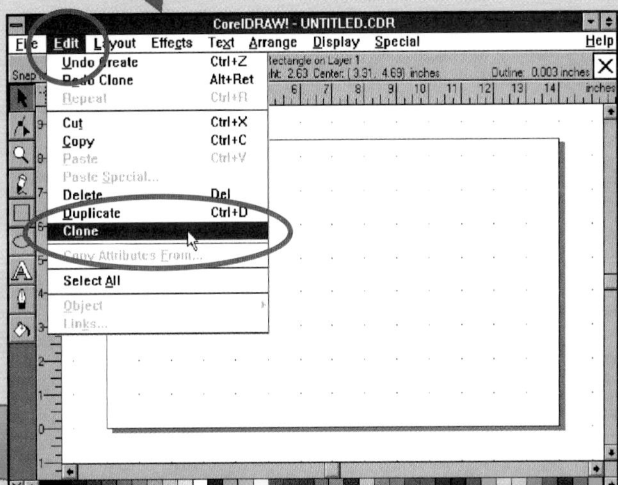

2 Click **Edit** in the menu bar. Click **Clone**. A copy of the object is placed next to the original. The new object is selected.

3 Notice that the status line indicates the selected object is a clone.

NOTE

The remaining steps in this task illustrate how cloned objects mimic the object they were cloned from.

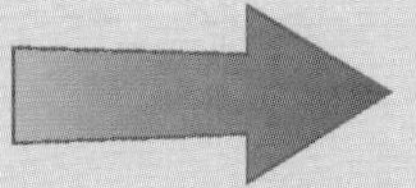

4 Click the first object to select it. Point to the object's upper-left sizing handle, and drag the sizing handle up and to the right to enlarge the object. This step resizes the object.

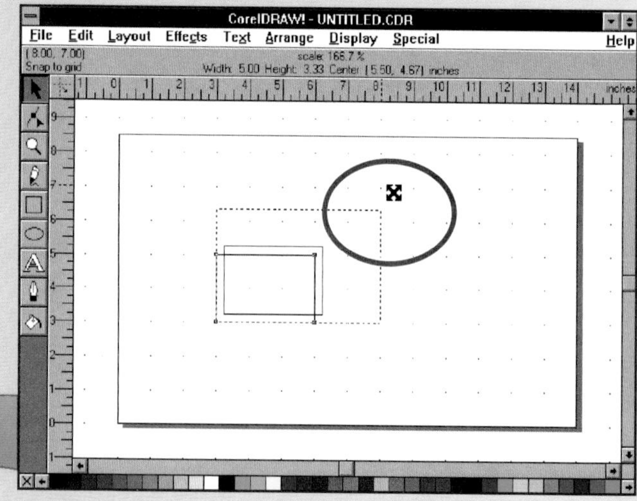

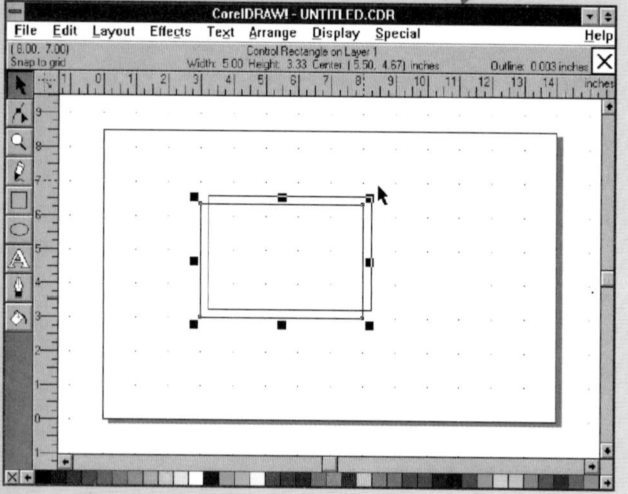

5 Release the mouse button. The cloned object resizes to match the original. Press the **Delete** key. This step deletes the original object and all its clones.

TASK 35

Resizing an Object

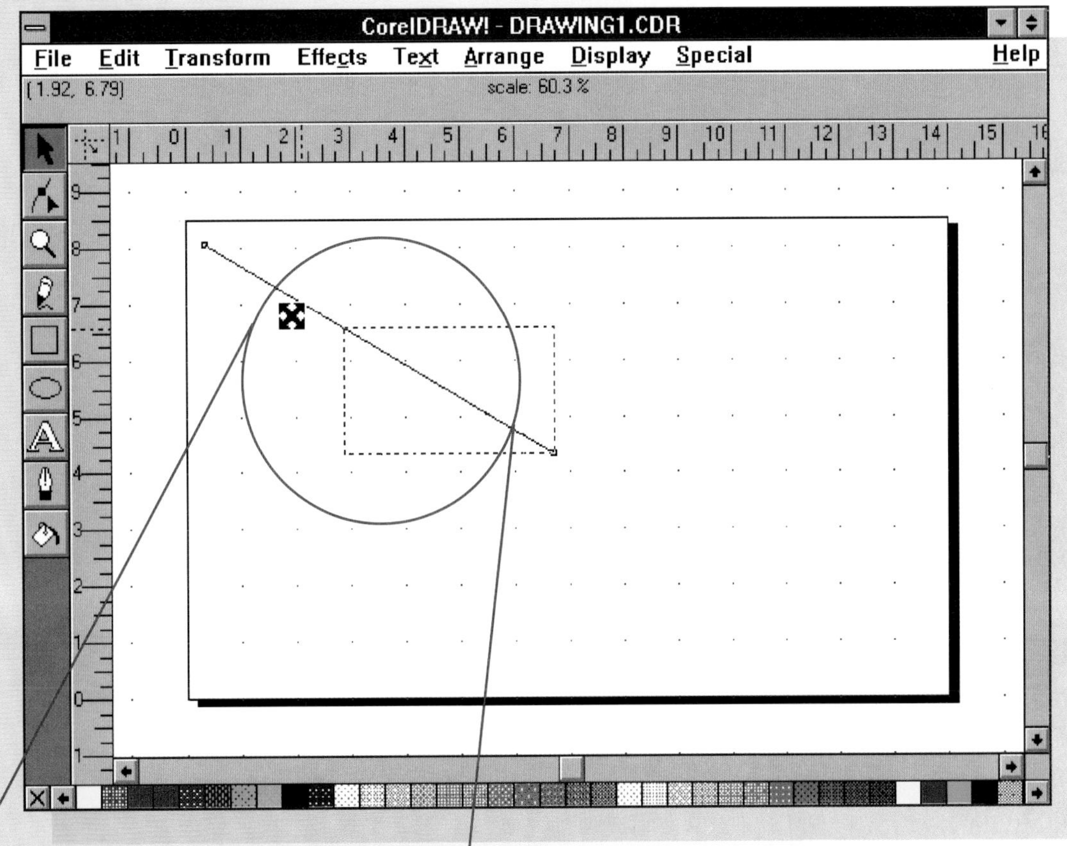

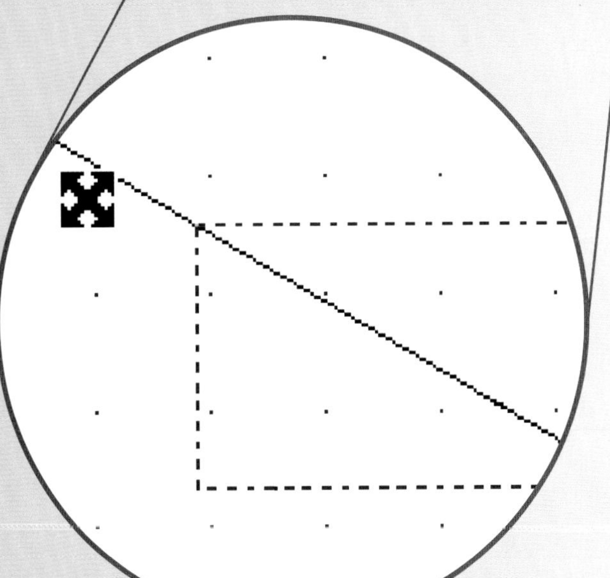

"Why would I do this?"

When you select an object, eight sizing handles appear around the object. By dragging the sizing handles, you can precisely control the size of the object. And by stretching the object in a given direction, you can make it wider, taller, shorter, or thinner. Both individual objects and grouped objects can be resized. If an object is filled with a color or pattern, the object remains filled, no matter how its size changes.

Task 35: Resizing an Object

1 Click the **Pencil** tool in the toolbox. Draw a line from the upper-left corner to the center of the drawing window. This step creates a diagonal line that you will resize in this task.

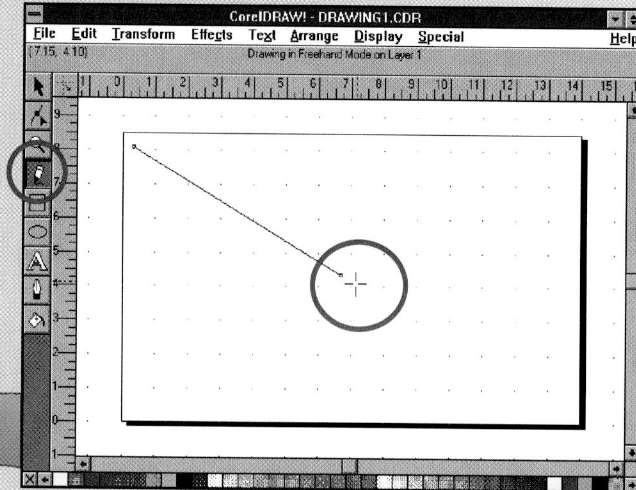

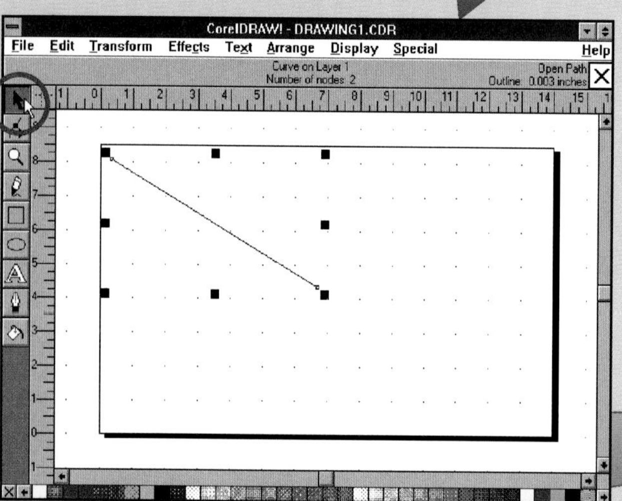

2 Click the **Pick** tool in the toolbox. This step selects the Pick tool. The line's sizing handles appear.

3 Point to the upper-left corner sizing handle of the line. Hold the mouse button. The arrow pointer changes to a crossbar pointer.

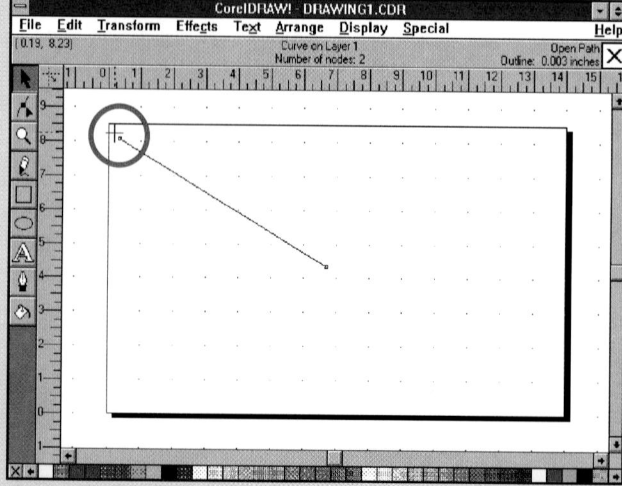

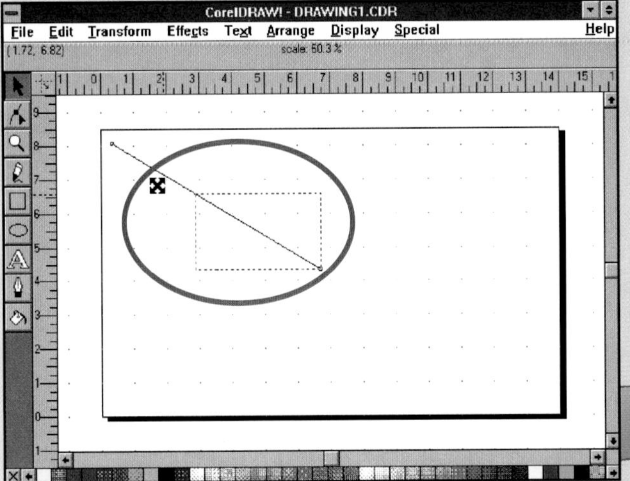

4 Drag the pointer down and to the right. This step resizes the line. As you drag, the line shrinks to meet the crossbar pointer.

NOTE

When resizing an object using a corner sizing handle, the object is always resized proportionally.

5 Release the mouse button. This step completes the resizing of the line.

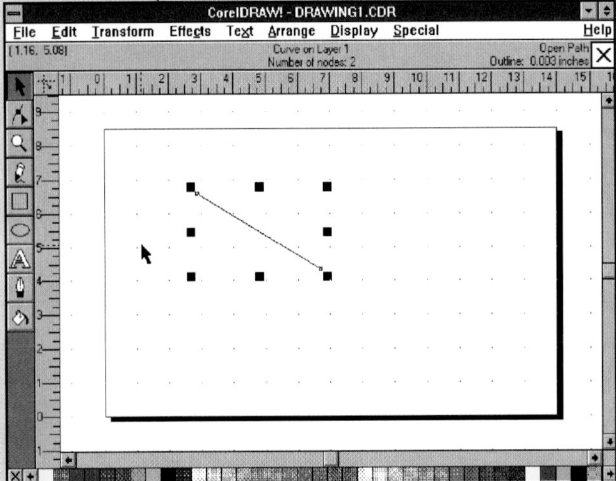

TASK 36

Mirroring an Object

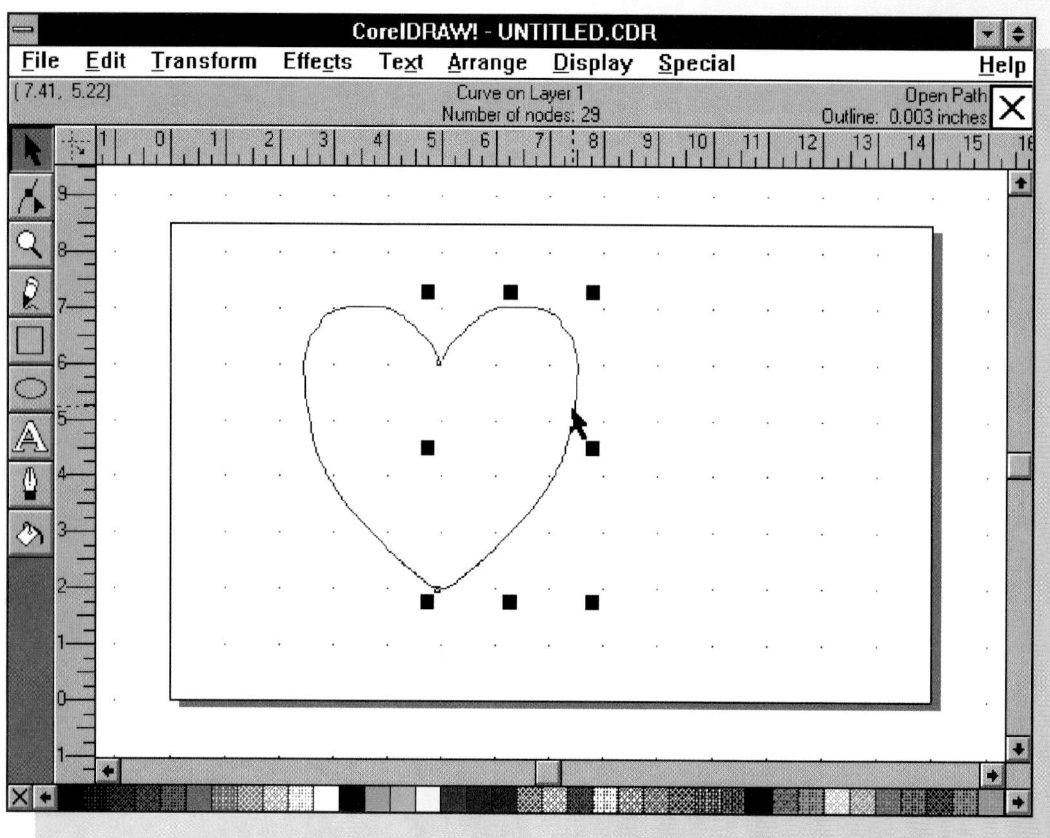

"Why would I do this?"

If you want to create a symmetric drawing, CorelDRAW's Mirror command can assist you. You can flip over objects, from left to right (vertically), or top to bottom (horizontally). Mirroring horizontally turns the object upside down. Mirroring vertically turns over the object, from left to right.

Task 36: Mirroring an Object

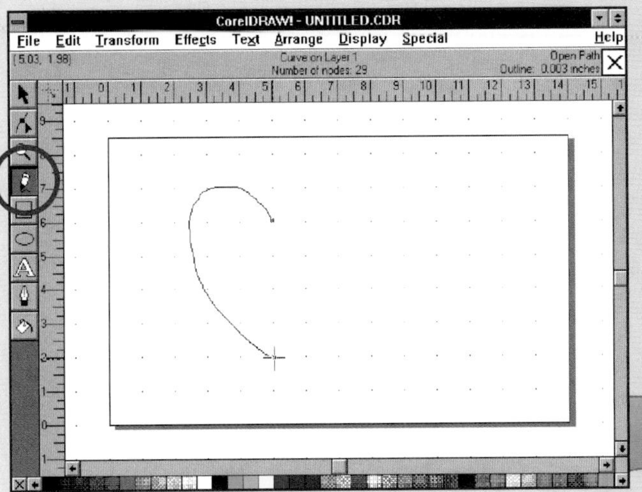

1 Draw or select an object to flip or mirror. In this example, the **Pencil** tool was used to draw half a heart shape in the drawing window.

NOTE

If you are mirroring an object to complete it, remember to draw only half of it. Mirroring will provide the other half. If you are just flipping an object, draw the entire object.

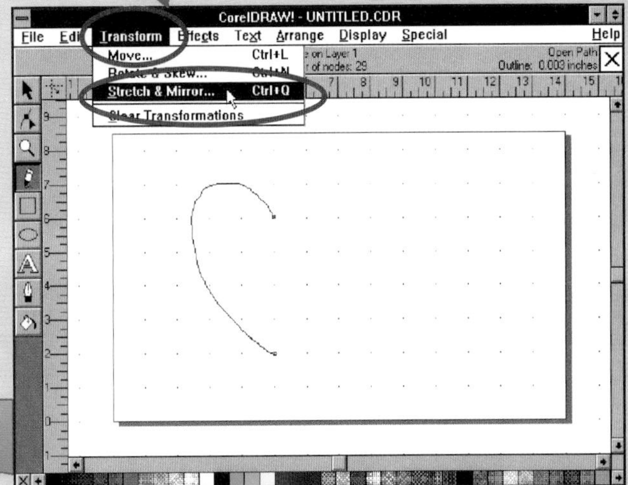

2 Click **Transform** in the menu bar. Then click **Stretch & Mirror**. This step opens the Stretch & Mirror dialog box.

NOTE

If you are using CorelDRAW 4, click Effects in the menu bar, and then click Stretch & Mirror.

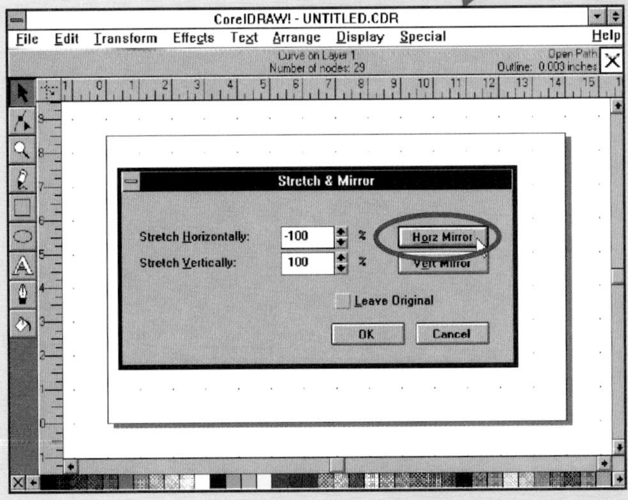

3 Click the **Horizontal Mirror** button. This step tells CorelDRAW to create a mirror image of the selected object. The Stretch Horizontally box displays `-100%`.

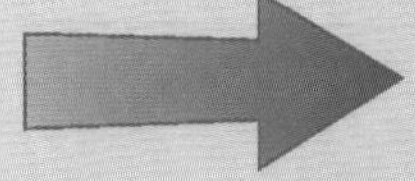

Task 36: Mirroring an Object

4 Click **Leave Original**. This step tells CorelDRAW to leave the original line and create a new line with the mirror effect applied to it. A check mark appears in the Leave Original check box.

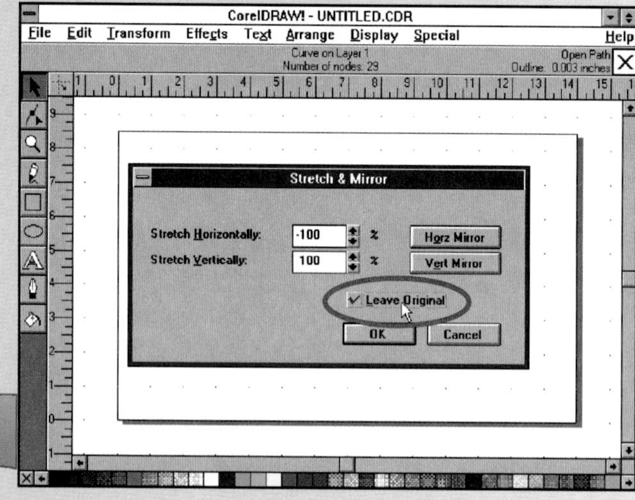

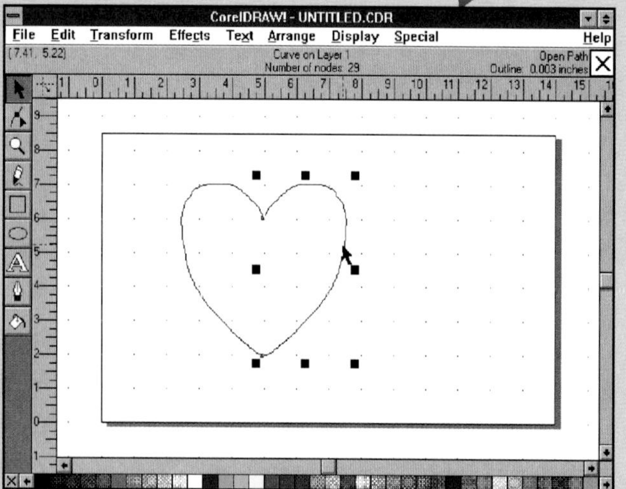

5 Click **OK**. This step accepts the changes in the dialog box. The mirrored line appears directly over the original. The new line is selected. You can drag the new line to the right to complete the heart shape.

TASK 37

Rotating an Object

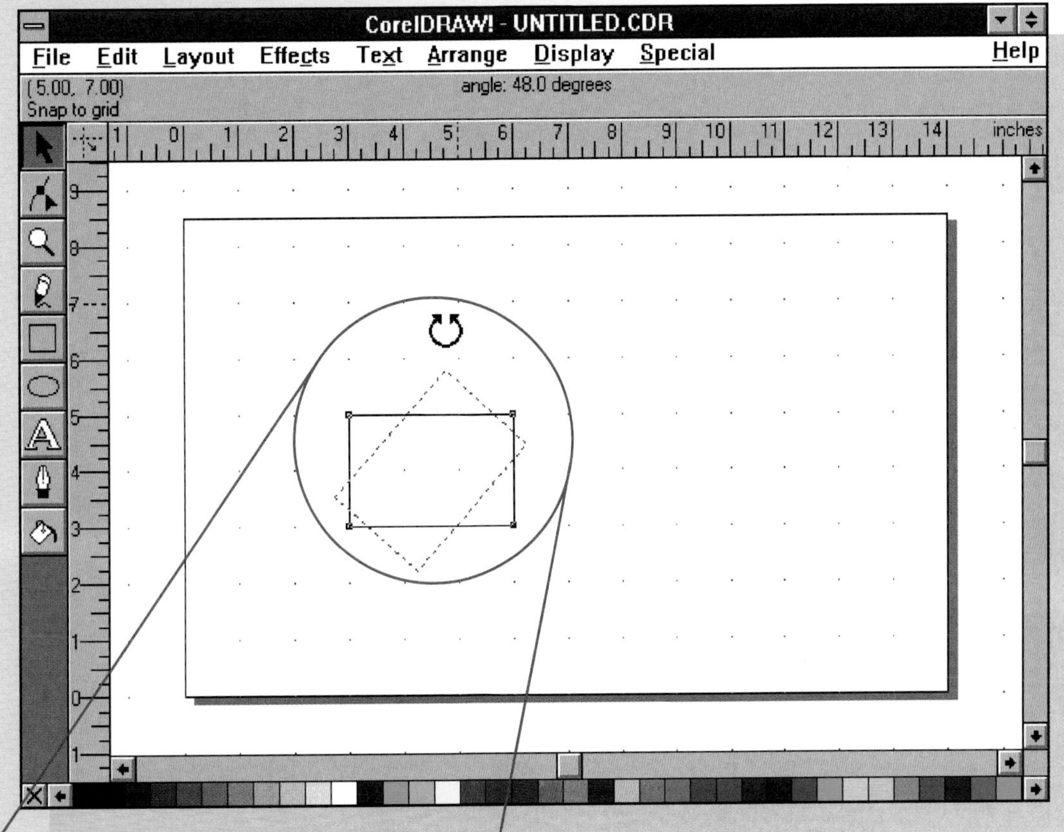

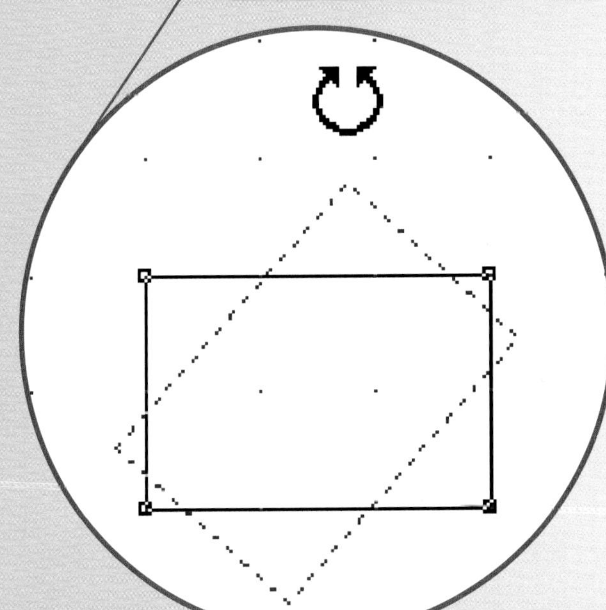

"Why would I do this?"

Objects such as rectangles and ellipses only can be drawn parallel to the edges of the drawing window. If you need an object that is rotated slightly, CorelDRAW enables you to spin the object on its center. You can rotate any object you draw. Even text objects can be rotated.

Task 37: Rotating an Object

1 Click the **Pick** tool in the toolbox, and then click the object you want to rotate. The sizing handles of the object appear.

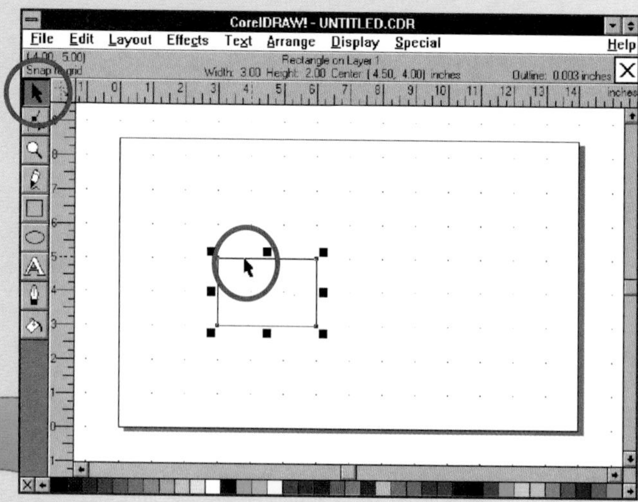

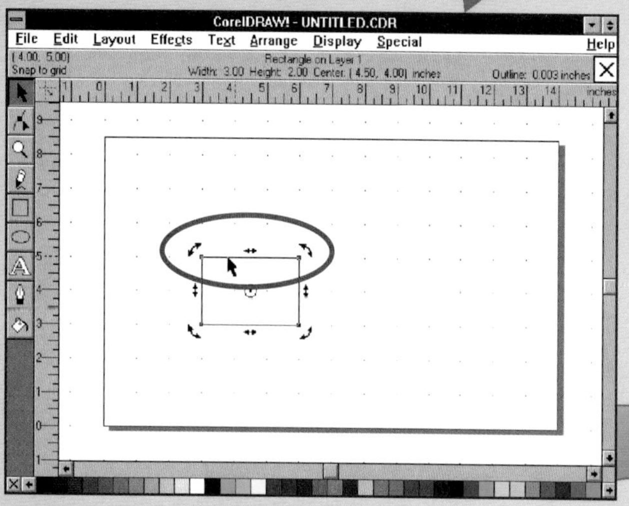

2 Click the object again. This step changes the object's sizing handles to double-headed arrows.

3 Point to one of the double-headed arrows in the corner of the object. Hold the mouse button. This step puts the object in rotation mode. The mouse pointer changes to a crossbar.

NOTE

If you want to skew the shape of an object, drag one of the double-headed arrows in the center of the object's border left or right. The object will slant in that direction.

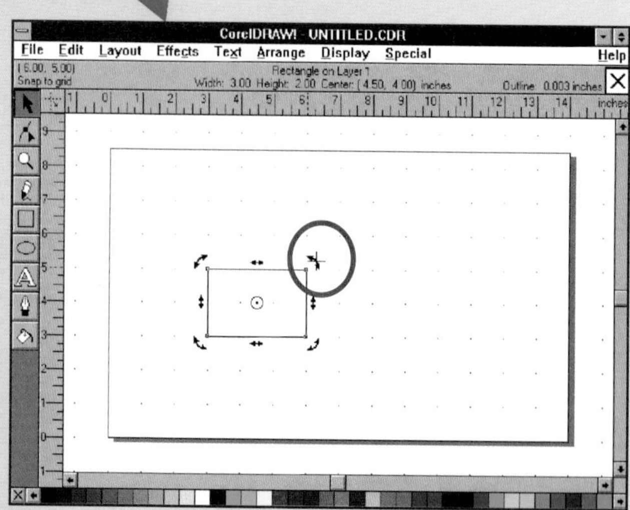

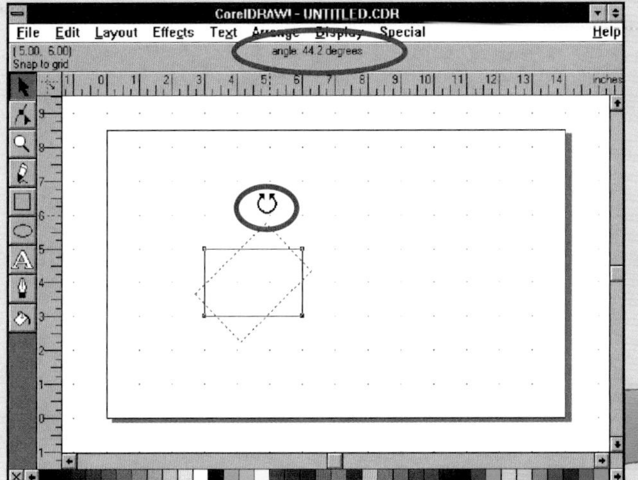

4 Drag in a circular motion around the line. This step rotates the object. As you drag, the bounding rectangle of the object shows the rotation; the angle of rotation is shown in the status line.

NOTE

If you want to rotate an object by an exact degree, click Rotate & Skew on the Transform menu and type the rotation degrees in the Rotate & Skew dialog box.

5 Release the mouse button. The object is rotated and selected.

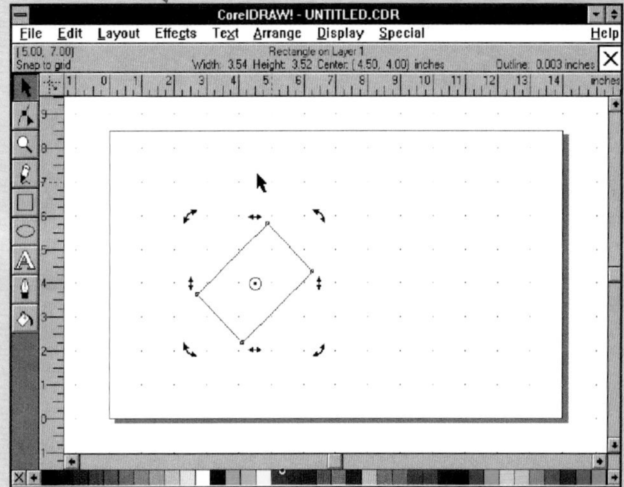

TASK 38

Filling an Object with Color

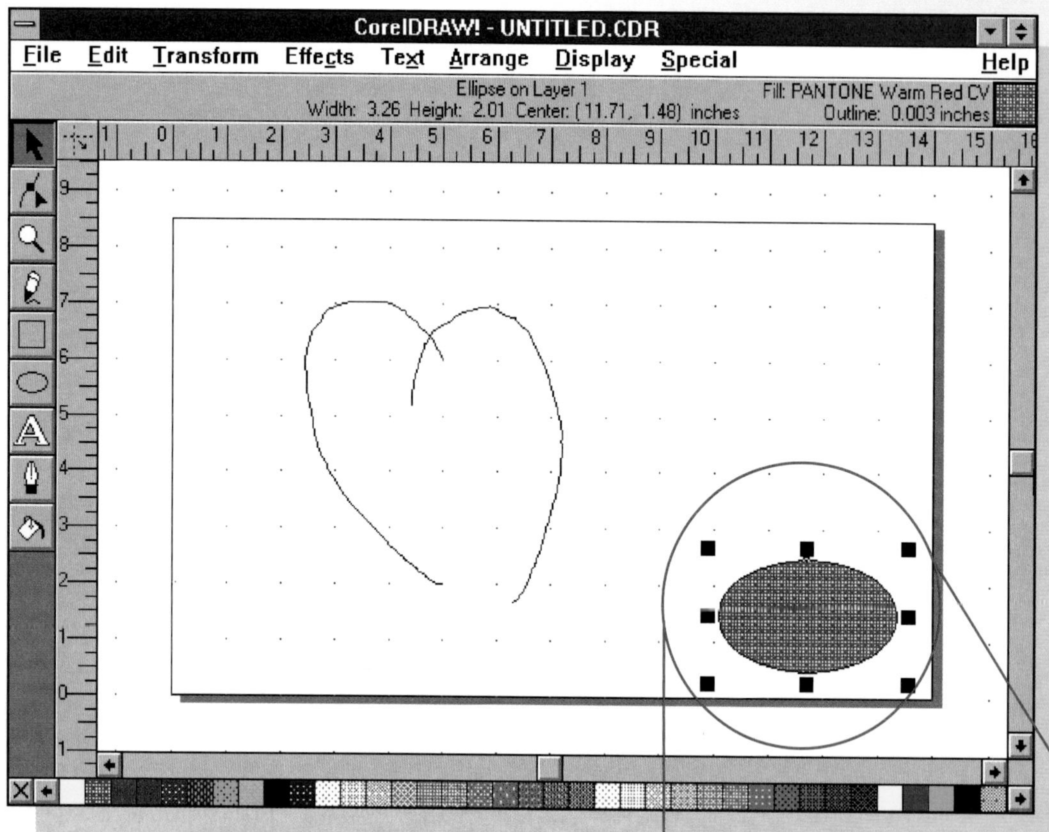

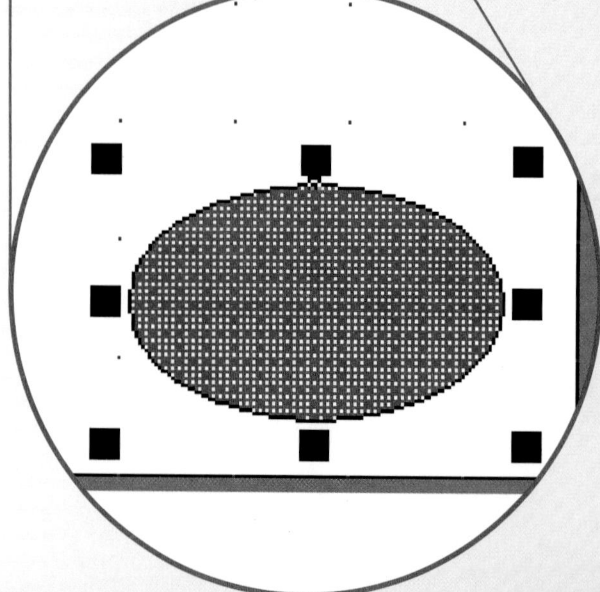

"Why would I do this?"

CorelDRAW's Color Palette, located at the bottom of the screen, contains hundreds of colors you can fill objects with. If you want to draw a red heart, or a green apple, it's easy using CorelDRAW's fill options.

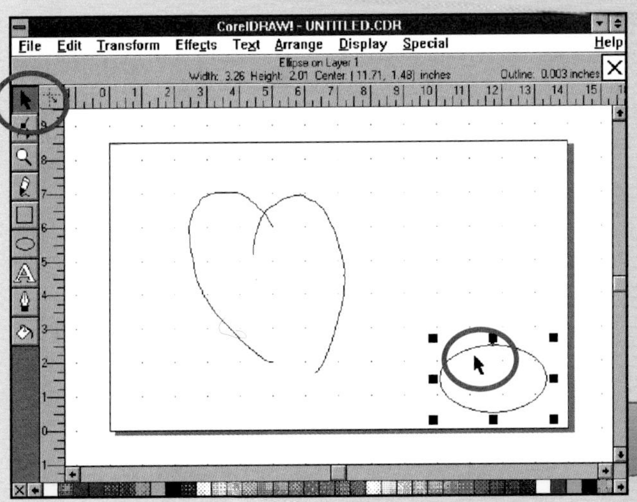

1 Click the **Pick** tool in the toolbox, and then click the object you want to fill. Sizing handles appear around the object.

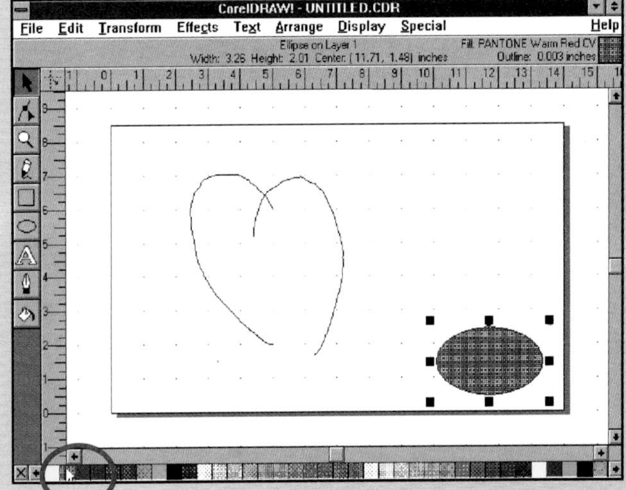

2 Using the left mouse button, click the color you want to use on the Color Palette at the bottom of the screen. This step fills the object with the color.

WHY WORRY?

If nothing happens when you click a color, check the Display menu to make sure you are not working in Wireframe view. A check mark should not appear by the Edit Wireframe option. Also make sure the object is completely enclosed.

TASK 39

Filling an Object with a Pattern

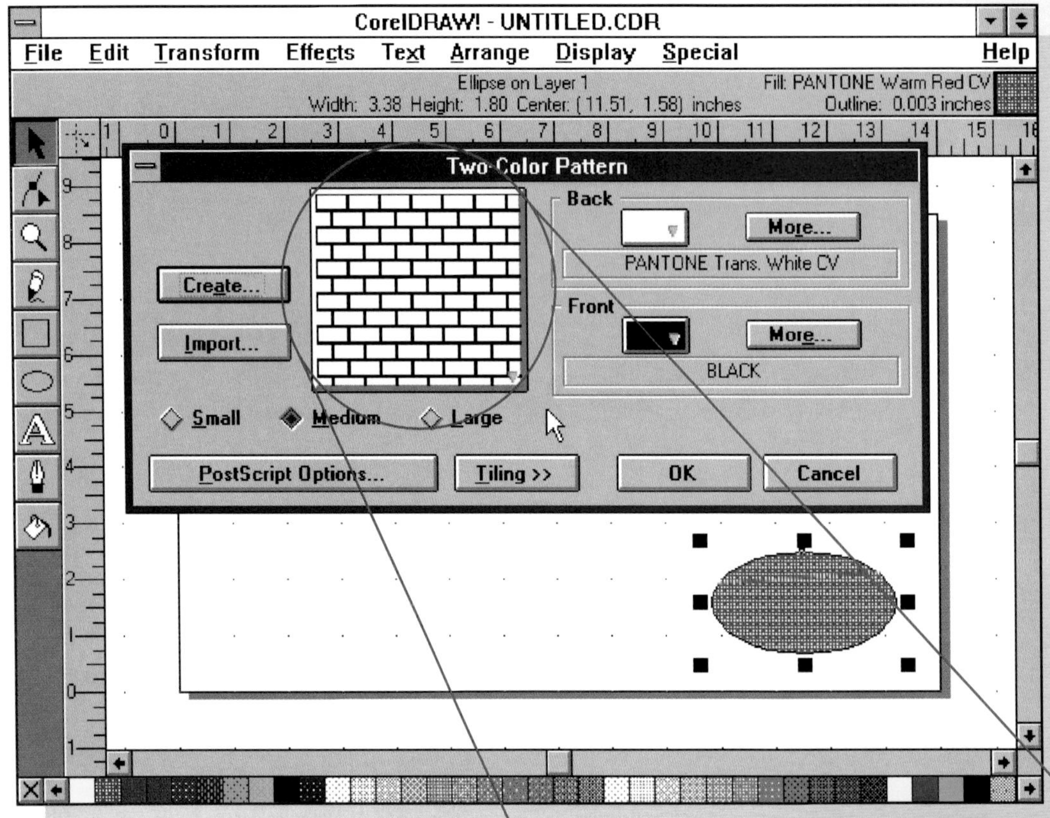

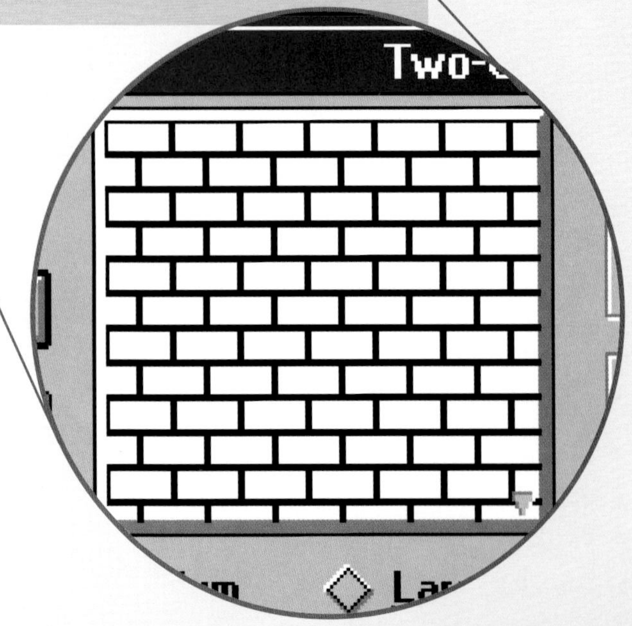

"Why would I do this?"

If you want to vary the appearance of the objects in your drawing, try using CorelDRAW's collection of two-color patterns. You can fill objects with patterns such as a brick wall, polka dots, and even plaid.

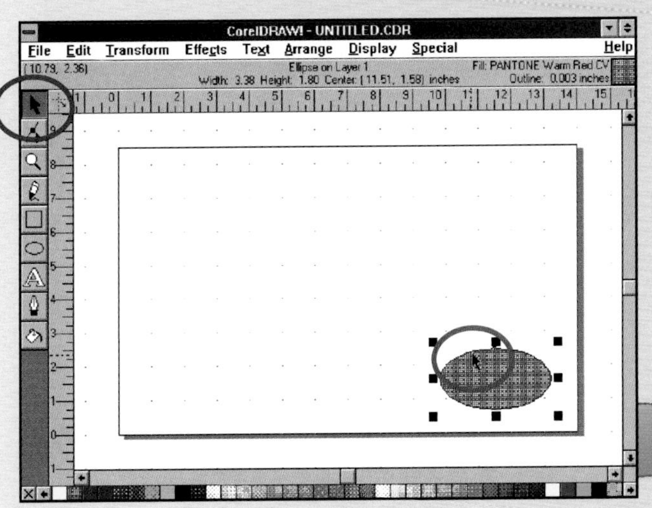

1 Click the **Pick** tool in the toolbox, and then click the object you want to fill with a pattern. Sizing handles appear around the object.

2 Click the **Fill** tool in the toolbox. This step opens the Fill fly-out menu. Then click the **Pattern fill** icon (checker board).

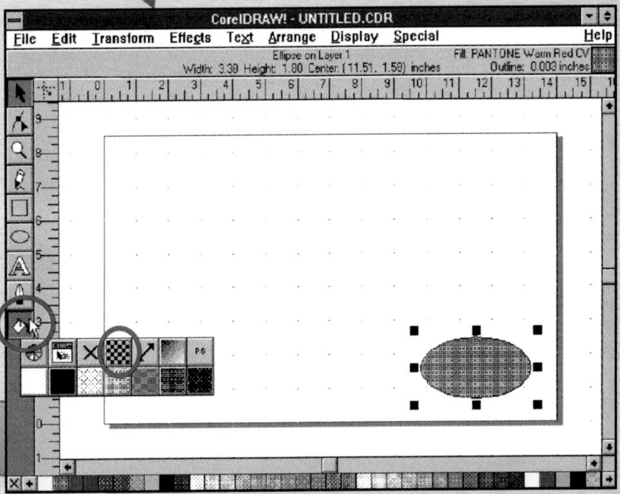

3 The Two-Color Pattern dialog box opens. You use this dialog box to choose the pattern for your object.

4 Click in the Pattern Preview box. This step opens the Two-Color Pattern options list.

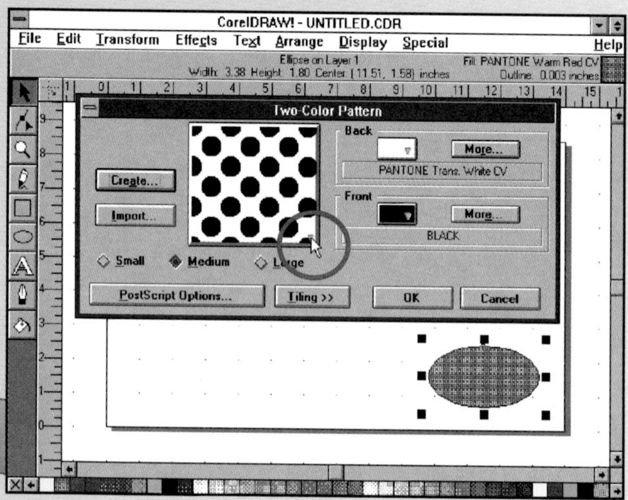

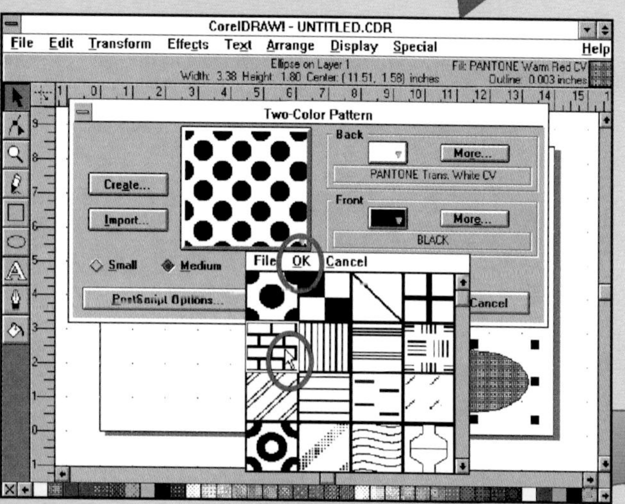

5 Click the **brick pattern**. Then click **OK**. This step selects the brick wall pattern. The brick wall pattern is shown in the Pattern Preview box.

NOTE

To change the colors of a pattern, select the Back and Front color buttons in the Two-Color Pattern dialog box. Each button opens a Color Palette from which you can choose colors for the pattern.

6 Click **OK**. This step completes the two-color pattern fill. The object fills with the brick wall pattern.

NOTE

If you rotate a pattern-filled object, the pattern does not rotate, only the object does.

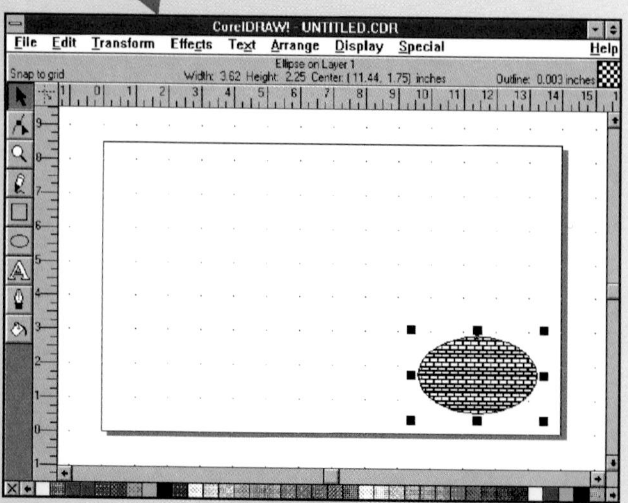

TASK 40

Removing an Object's Fill

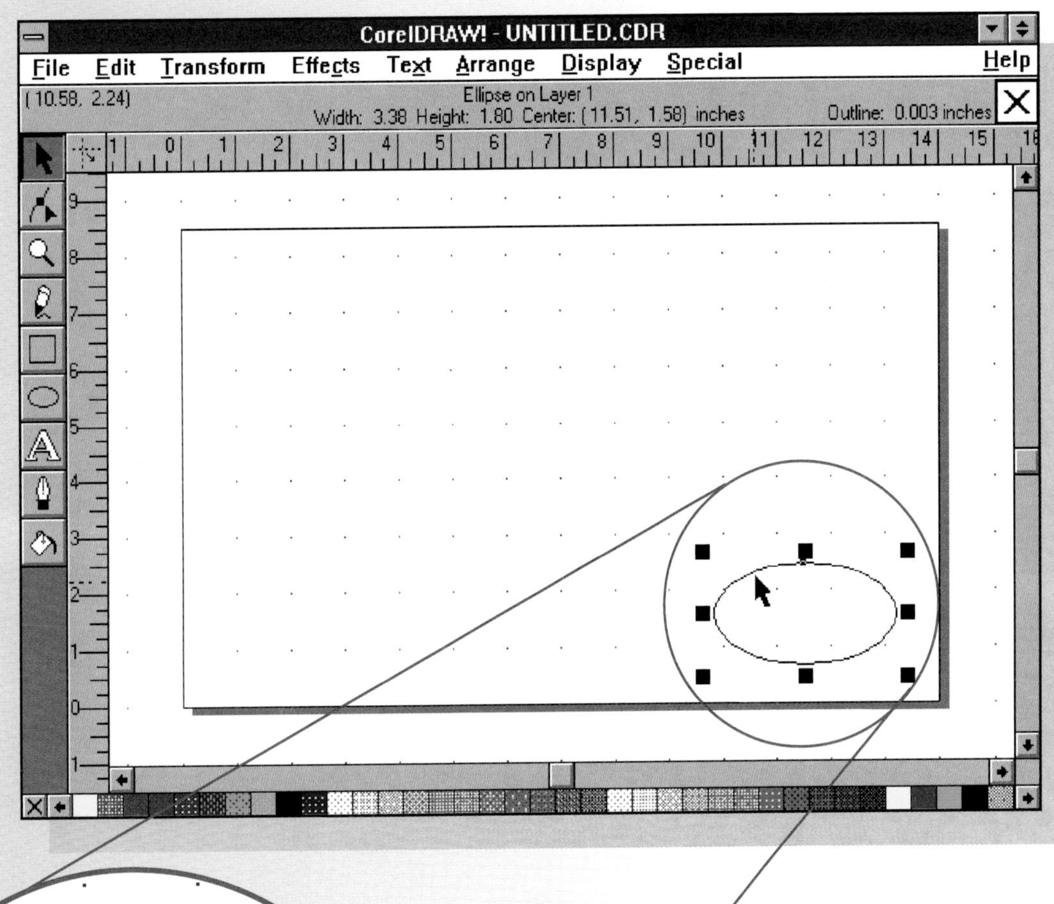

"Why would I do this?"

Many times you'll want to make an object transparent, showing only its outline. By clicking the × icon on the left end of the Color Palette, you remove any color or pattern from the selected object.

Task 40: Removing an Object's Fill

1 Click the **Pick** tool in the toolbox. Click the object that contains the pattern or color you want to remove.

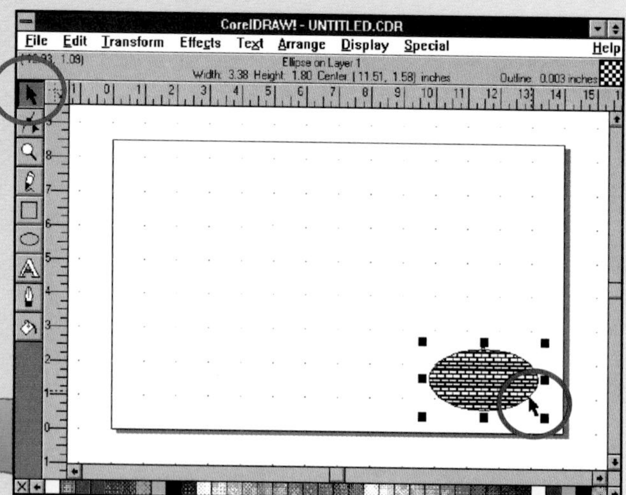

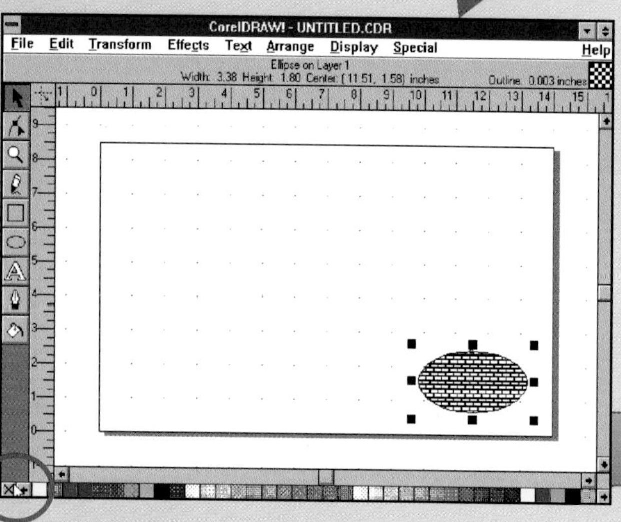

2 Click the × icon located on the left end of the Color Palette at the bottom of the screen.

3 The pattern or color in the object disappears.

NOTE

If you want to show an object without an outline and only a fill color or pattern, point to the × icon on the left end of the Color Palette and click the right mouse button. The object's outline disappears.

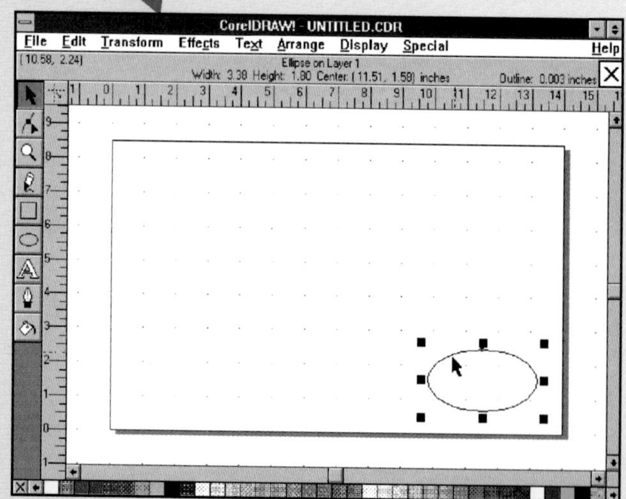

TASK 41

Changing the Outline of an Object

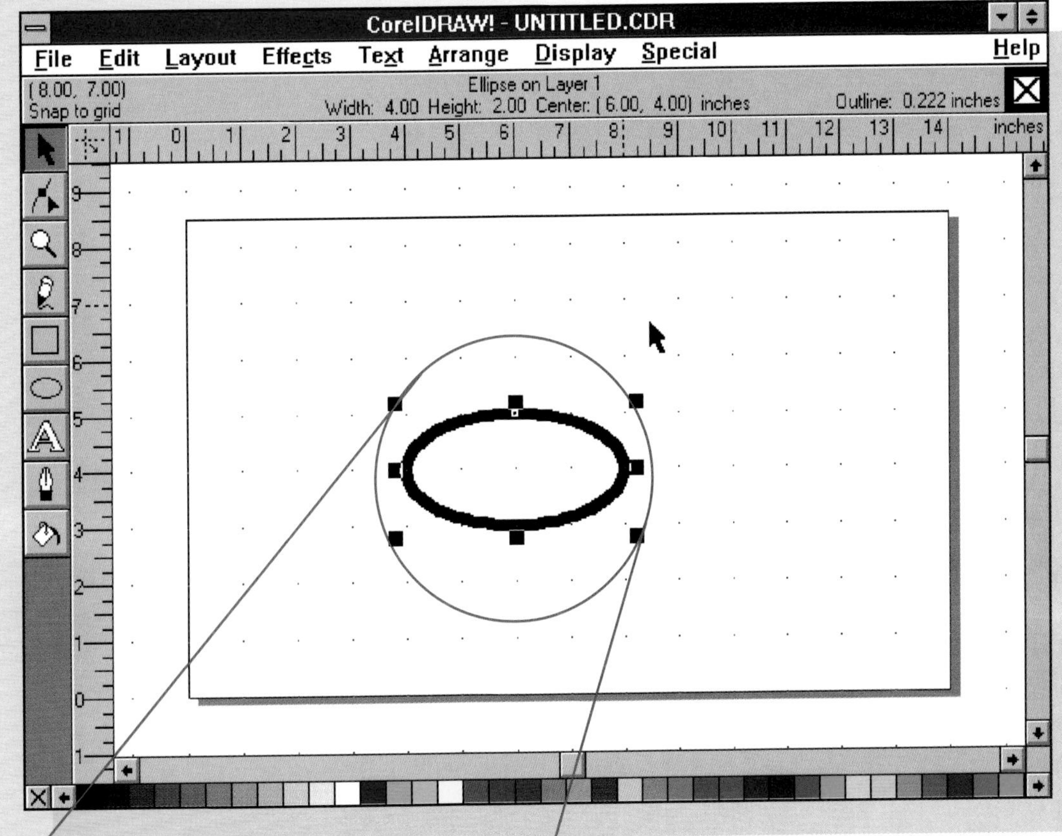

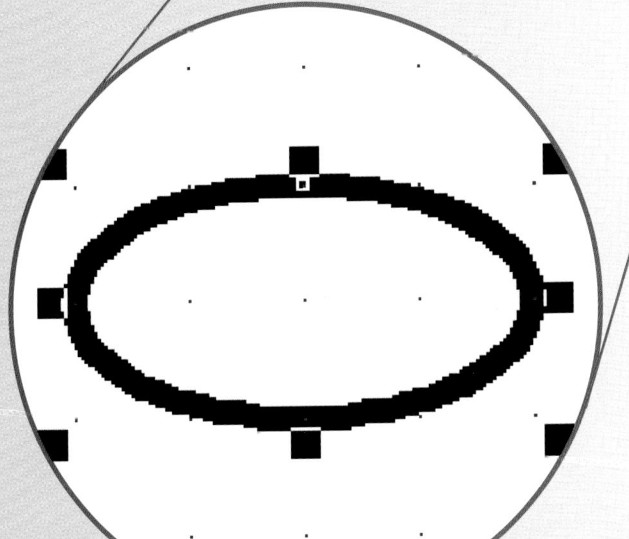

"Why would I do this?"

You can vary the thickness of lines and object outlines using the Outline fly-out menu. Your drawing might require a rectangle with a thick border and a circle with a thin border. Once you draw an object, you can adjust the thickness of its outline as needed.

Task 41: Changing the Outline of an Object

1 Click the **Pick** tool in the toolbox, and then click the object with the outline you want to change. Sizing handles appear around the object.

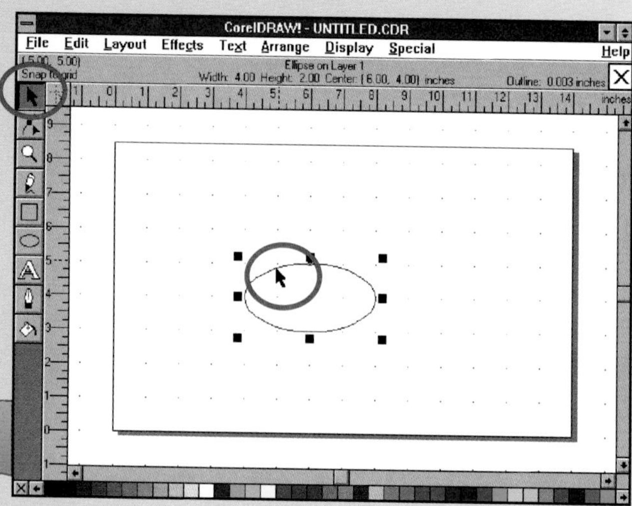

WHY WORRY?

If the skew and rotation arrows appear in place of the sizing handles, click the object.

2 Click the **Outline** tool in the toolbox. The Outline fly-out menu opens. Click one of the thick line styles on the top row of tools. This step selects a thick black line for the object's outline.

3 The object's outline immediately changes to a thick black line.

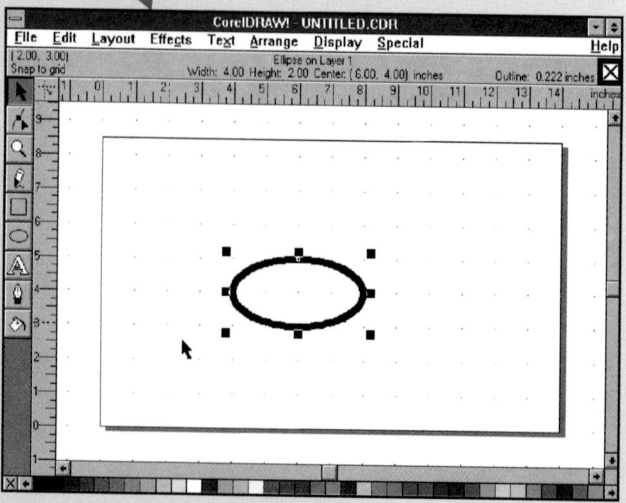

NOTE

To change the default line thickness, click in a blank part of the drawing window to deselect all objects. Then, choose a line thickness from the Outline fly-out menu. When a dialog box appears asking if you want to change the default line thickness on new objects, choose OK.

Choosing an Outline Color

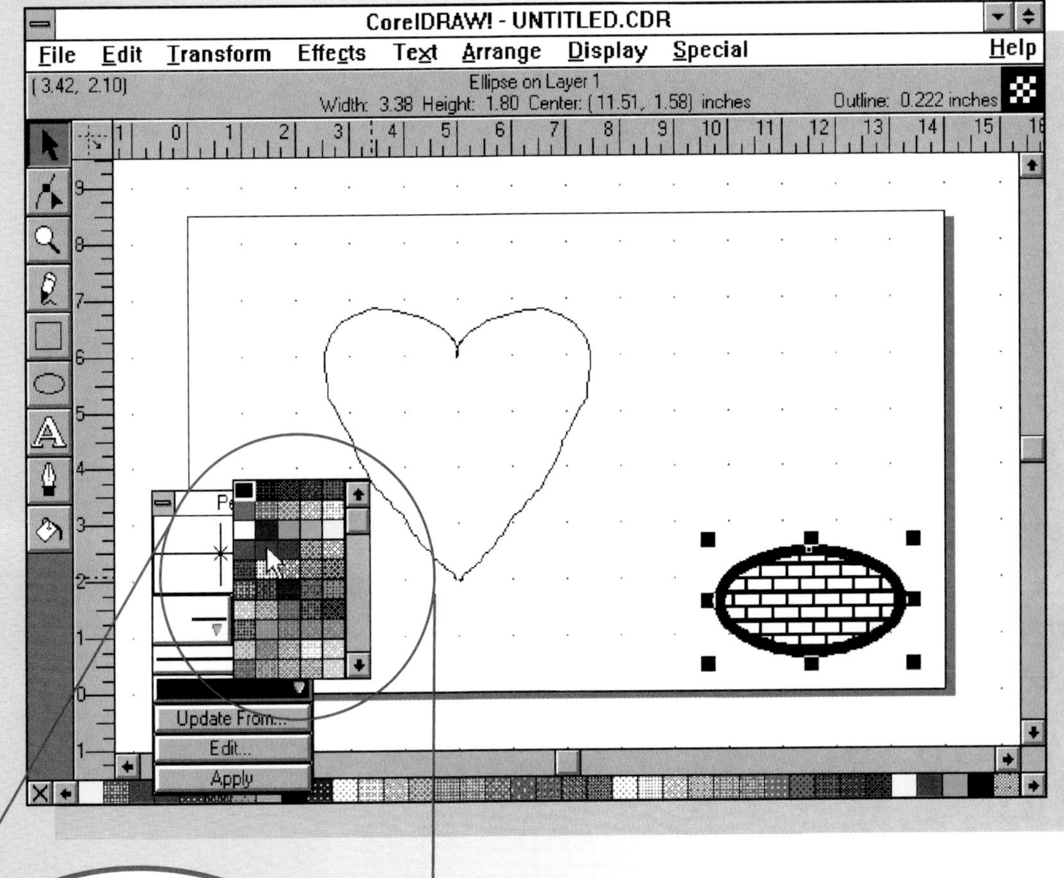

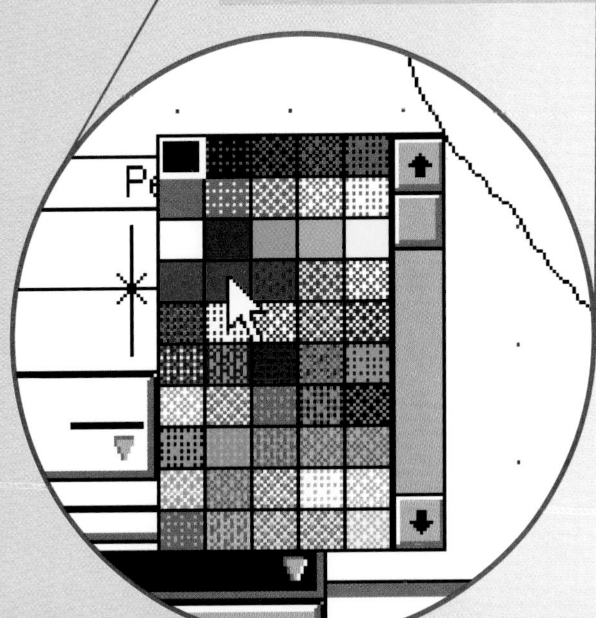

"Why would I do this?"

You can adjust the outline color of objects you draw the same way you adjust fill colors. You can create objects with outlines of any color available in the Color Palette.

Task 42: Choosing an Outline Color

1 Click the **Pick** tool in the toolbox, and then click the object that contains the outline you want to change. This step selects the object.

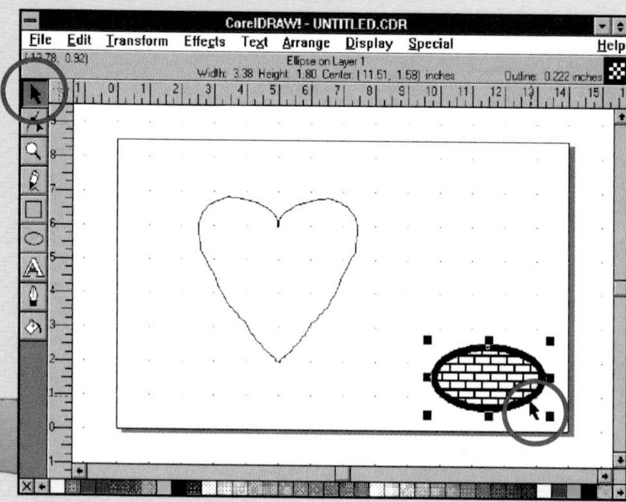

2 Click the **Outline** tool in the toolbox. Click the **Pen roll-up** icon on the Outline fly-out menu. This step opens the Pen roll-up window.

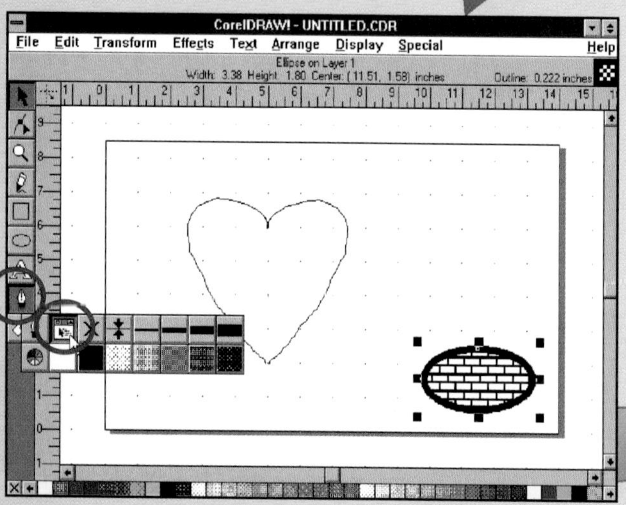

3 Click the **Color Selector** bar. This step opens the Outline Pen Color Palette.

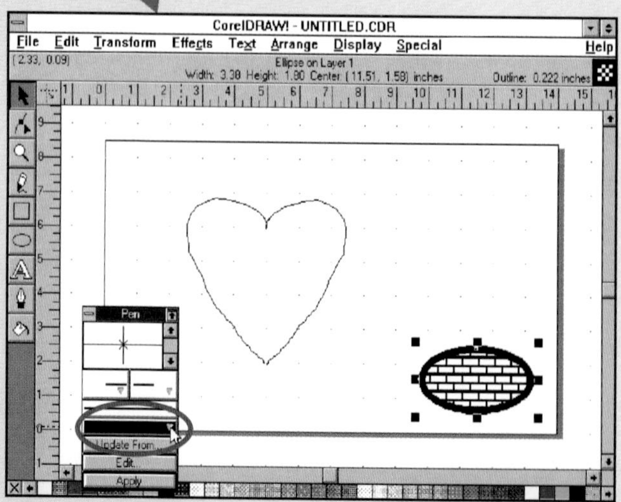

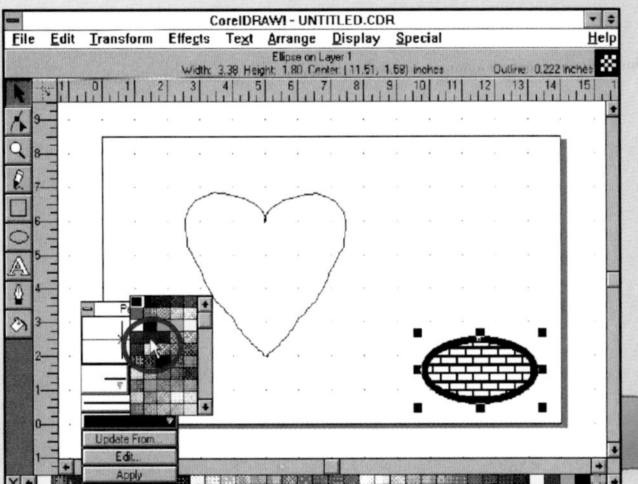

4 Click the color you want for the outline. This step selects the pen color. The Color Palette closes, and the Color Selector bar changes to the selected color.

5 Click **Apply**. This step applies the color change to the outline of the object.

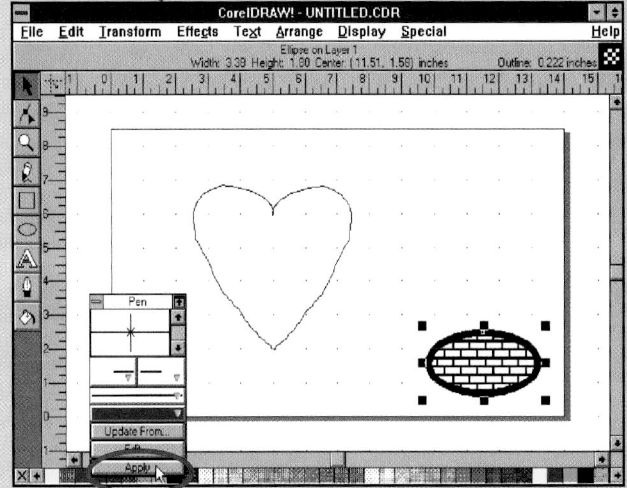

NOTE

You also can control the color of lines and objects by selecting the element with the Pick tool and clicking a color in the Color Palette using the right mouse button.

TASK 43

Adding Perspective to an Object

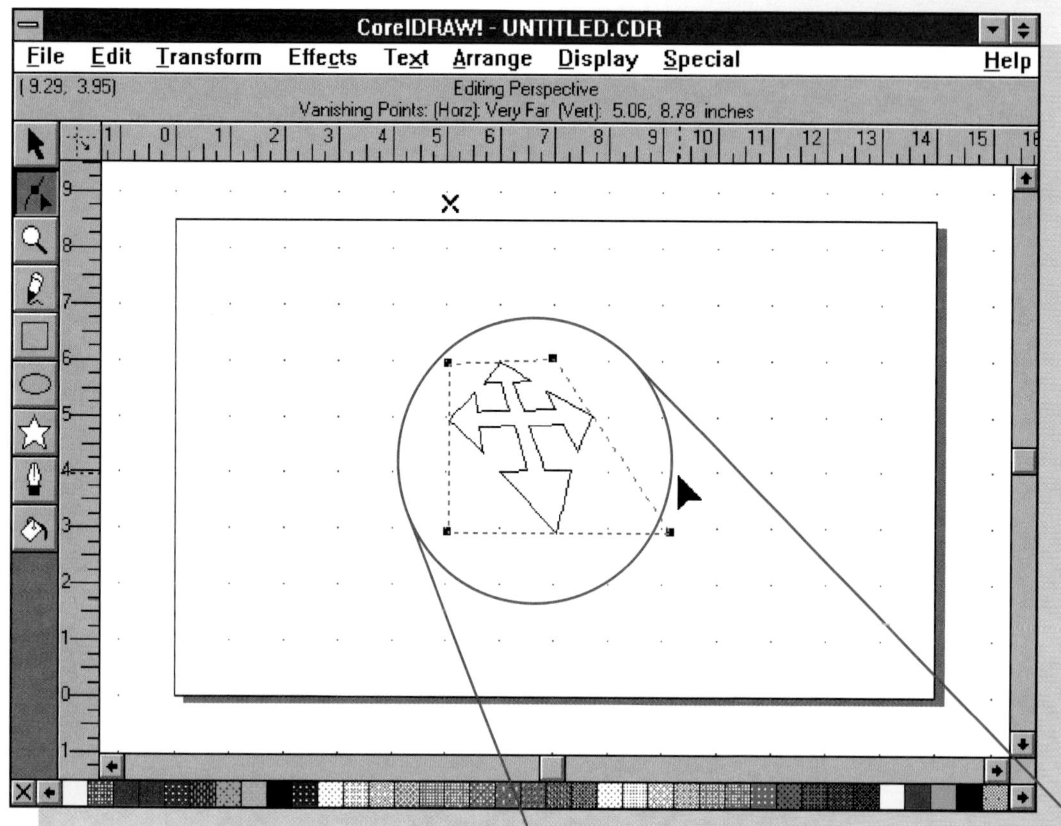

"Why would I do this?"

Using the Perspective command, you can tilt and angle an object so that it appears to come out of the page. Adding perspective to an object gives it a three-dimensional look, making part of the object look as if it were closer to you, and part of the object look farther away.

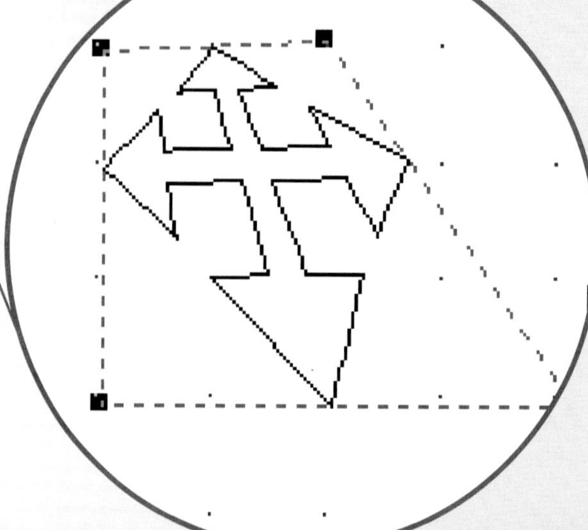

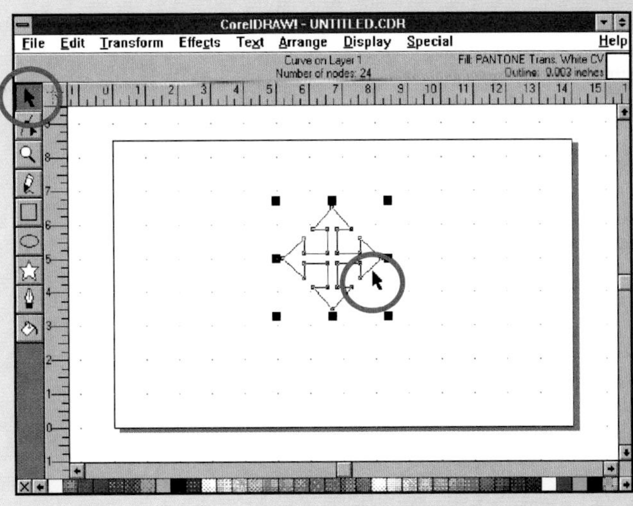

1 Click the **Pick** tool in the toolbox, and then click the object to which you want to apply perspective. This step selects the object.

2 Click **Effects** in the menu bar. Then click **Edit Perspective**. This step puts the object in perspective mode. Four nodes and a red dotted line appear around the object.

NOTE

In CorelDRAW 4, click Add Perspective on the Effects menu.

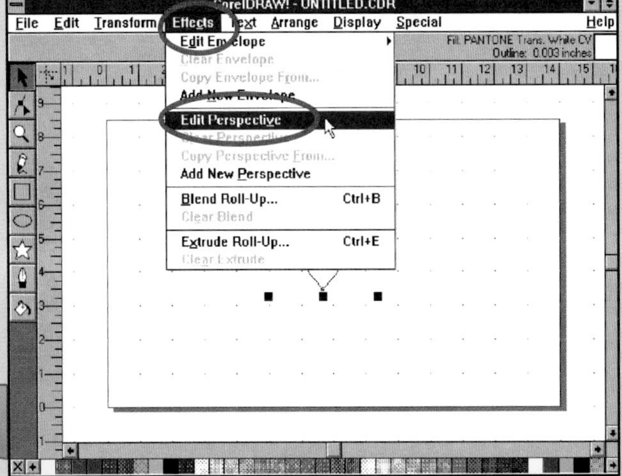

3 Position the mouse pointer on the **upper-right node** of the object. Drag the node to the left slightly. Then drag the **lower-right node** to the right slightly. The object now looks as if it is coming out of the page.

WHY WORRY?

You can undo the perspective you've added to an object by selecting Clear Perspective from the Effects menu.

TASK 44

Extruding an Object

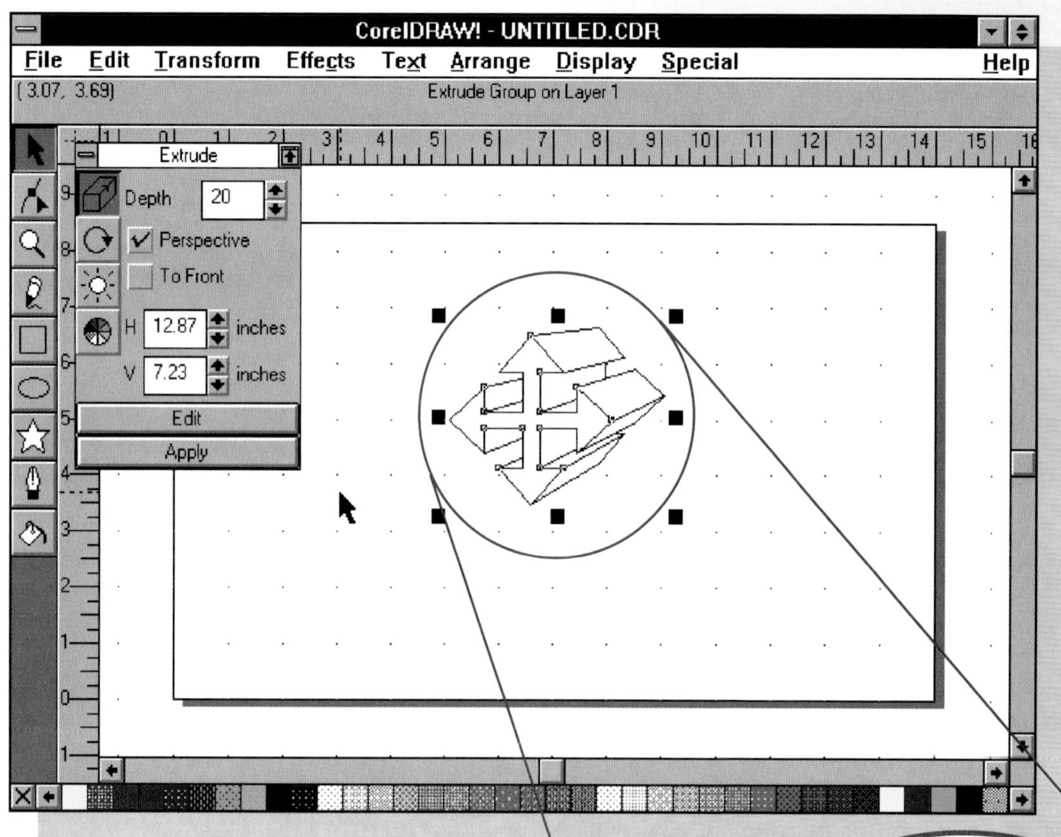

"Why would I do this?"

CorelDRAW's extrude feature takes a two-dimensional object and projects it back into the page to give it a three-dimensional appearance. You can create a two-dimensional object such as an arrowhead and extrude it to give it a three-dimensional, solid appearance.

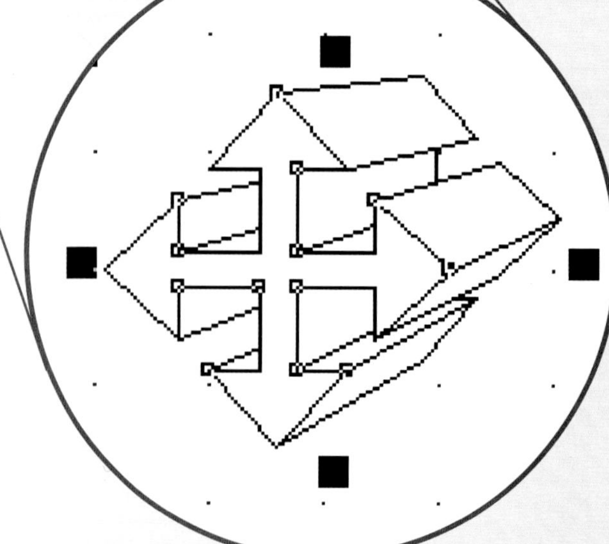

Task 44: Extruding an Object

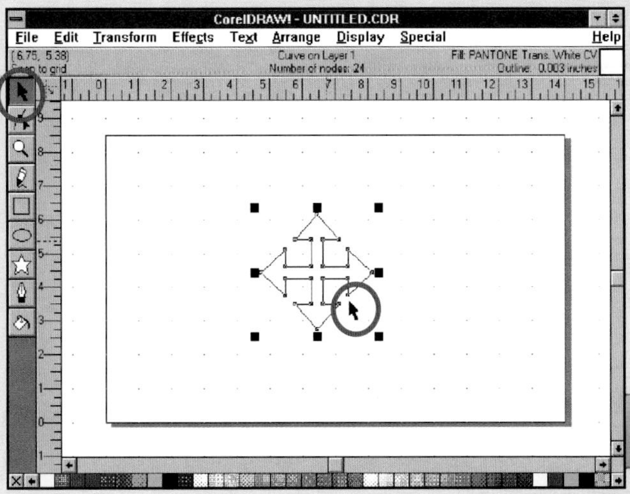

1 Click the **Pick** tool in the toolbox, and then click the object you want to look three-dimensional. This step selects the object.

2 Click **Effects** in the menu bar. Then click **Extrude Roll-Up**. This step opens the Extrude roll-up window. A blue-dotted outline appears slightly behind the object, showing you where the extrusion will appear. An ×-shaped control also appears near the object.

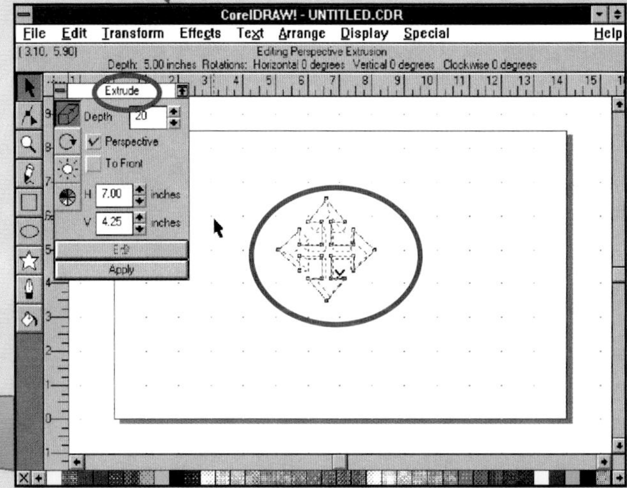

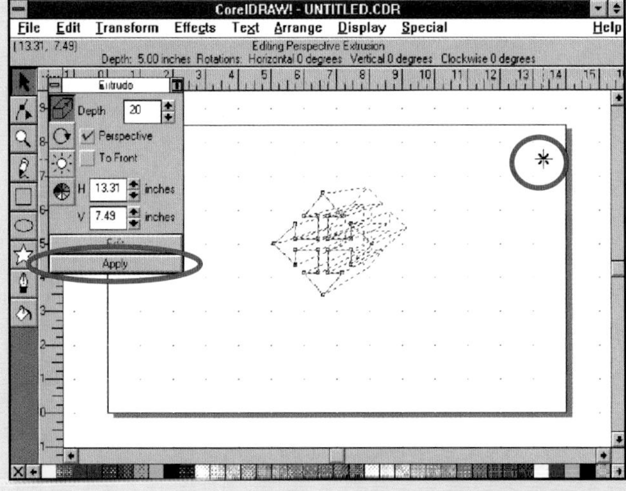

3 Drag the × control up and to the right. The blue-dotted outline shows that the symbol will appear as if it were projecting back into the page. Click **Apply** in the Extrude roll-up window. The extrusion is applied to the symbol.

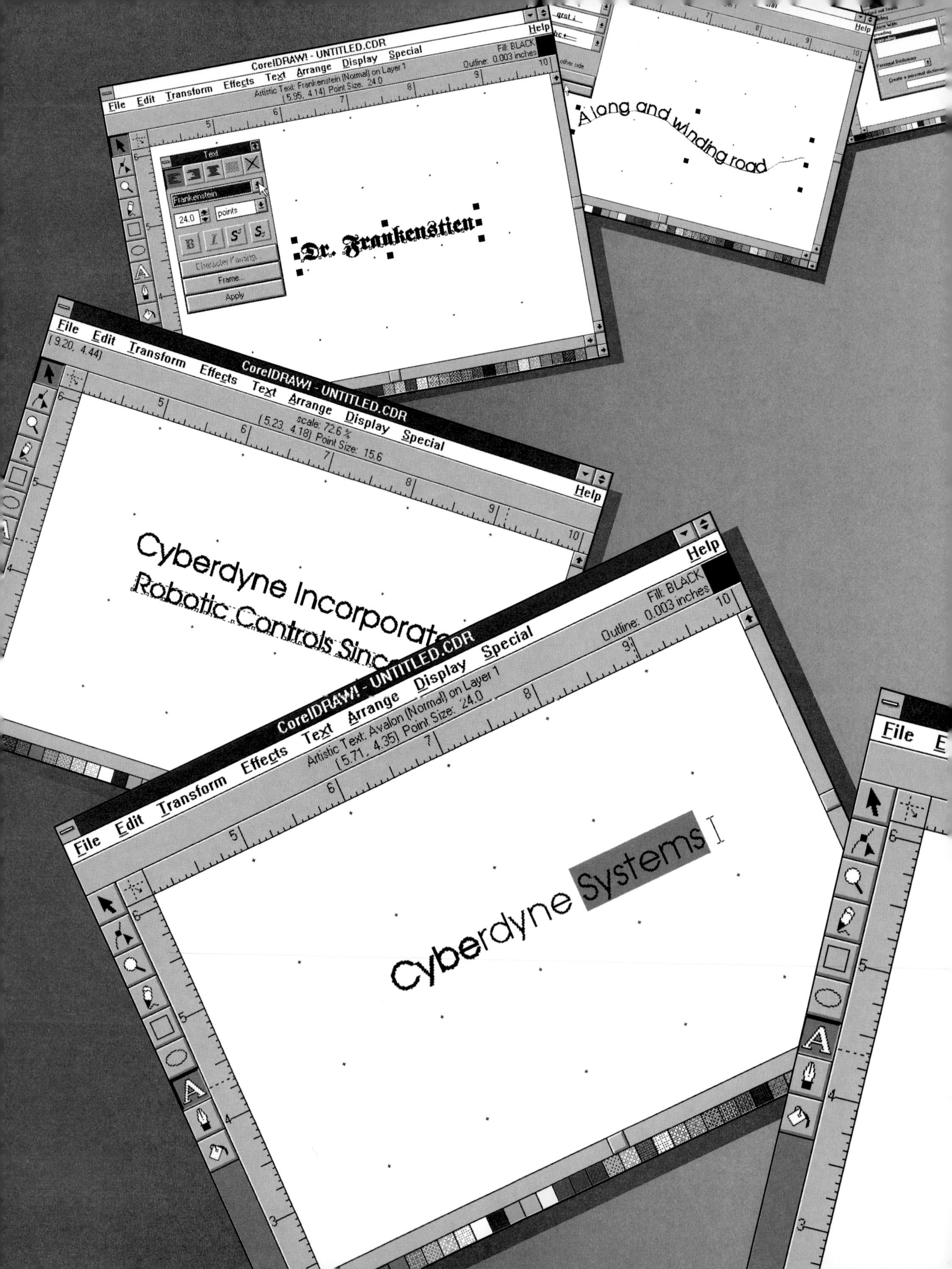

CorelDRAW! - UNTITLED.CDR
File Edit Transform Effects Text Arrange Display Special
Help
Artistic Text: Frankenstein (Normal) on Layer 1
(5.95, 4.14) Point Size: 24.0
Fill: BLACK
Outline: 0.003 inches
Text
Frankenstein
24.0
points
Frame...
Apply
Dr. Frankenstien
A long and winding road
CorelDRAW! - UNTITLED.CDR
File Edit Transform Effects Text Arrange Display Special
Help
(9.20, 4.44)
scale: 72.6 %
(5.23, 4.18) Point Size: 15.6
Cyberdyne Incorporate
Robotic Controls Sinc
CorelDRAW! - UNTITLED.CDR
File Edit Transform Effects Text Arrange Display Special
Help
Artistic Text: Avalon (Normal) on Layer 1
(5.71, 4.35) Point Size: 24.0
Fill: BLACK
Outline: 0.003 inches
Cyberdyne Systems
File

PART V

Adding and Editing Text

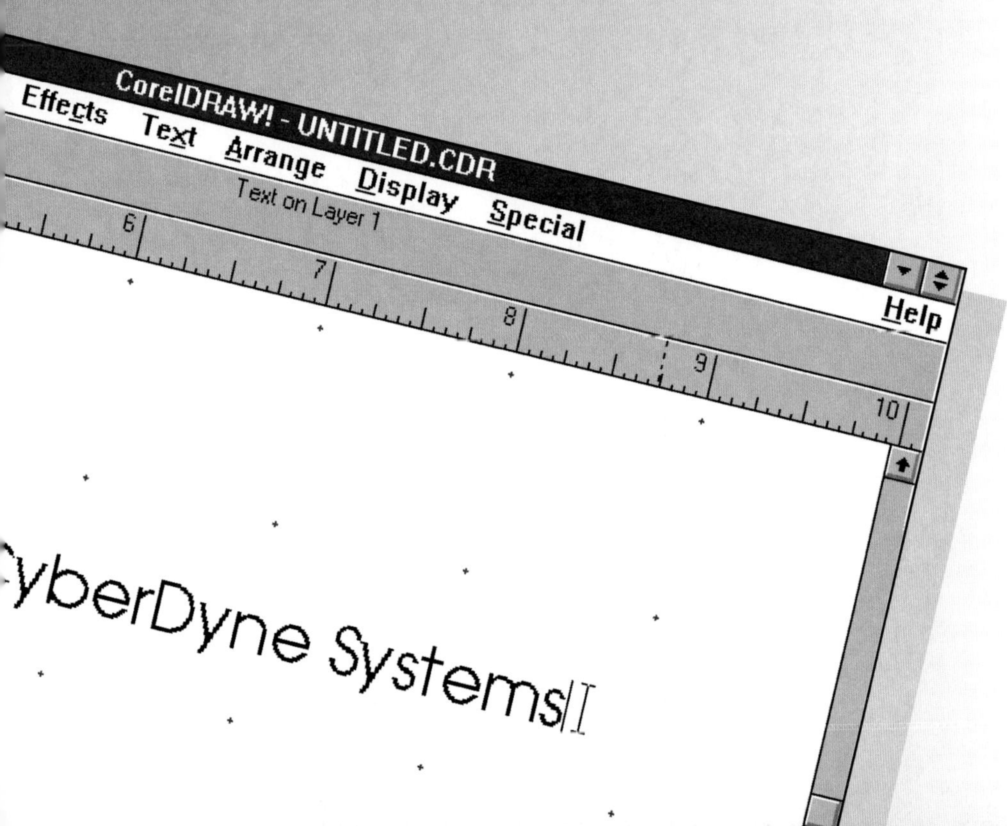

Many documents you create require text elements such as headlines, labels, and short descriptive paragraphs. And, different documents call for different styles of text. Using CorelDRAW's Text tool, you can add text anywhere in your drawing. The Text roll-up window provides a full range of formatting features that you need to get the text effect you're looking for.

In this part, you learn how to add Artistic text to your drawing, how to edit the text, and how to change the font of the text.

To add text to your drawing, you use the Text tool located in the toolbox. The Text tool enables you to type text directly in the drawing window.

Once you've typed the text you want, you can change it any way you like. In this part, you learn how to use the I-beam pointer to edit the characters of a text string and how to replace whole sections of a text string. A *text string* is just a line of characters you type, like this sentence.

You also learn how to change the font of a text string. A *font* is a set of characters (letters, numerals, and punctuation) that all have the same attributes. For example, the Courier font looks like it was typed with an old-fashioned typewriter. All the characters are a single line thickness, and the vertical portions of the characters have feet, called *serifs*. Cupertino, on the other hand, has thick round letters. CorelDRAW comes with hundreds of fonts, so you'll have plenty to choose from when you're ready to format the text in your drawing.

You learn to change the size, or point size, of the text you type. A font's size is measured in points. There are 72 points in one inch, so a 72-point font is one inch tall.

Like any other object in CorelDRAW, text is an object that can be resized, rotated, and filled with color. While you can increase or decrease the size of text by increasing or decreasing its point size, you also can change it's size by dragging the sizing handles of the text object. If you want to create a text object that is long and stretched out, you can drag its horizontal sizing handle.

YOU CAN CREATE A LINE OF TEXT THAT WEAVES AND CURVES.

Experiment creating three-dimensional text objects by adding perspective to the text and by applying the extrude commands to the object.

Once you have typed the text in your drawing, you can check for spelling mistakes using Corel's spell check command. To check the spelling of a text string, you simply select the text object and choose Spell Checker from the Text menu. The Spell Checker scans the text object for misspelled words, stopping when it finds a word not in its dictionary. You can then correct the misspelled word, or have Corel suggest a correction.

Stretch

Scrunch

You can create a line of text that weaves and curves by using Corel's Fit Text To Path command. You first draw a line or curve and then type the text string. Next, you select both the line and text string and choose the Fit Text To Path command, and the text is redrawn so it fits exactly along the line or curve.

TASK 45

Adding Artistic Text to a Drawing

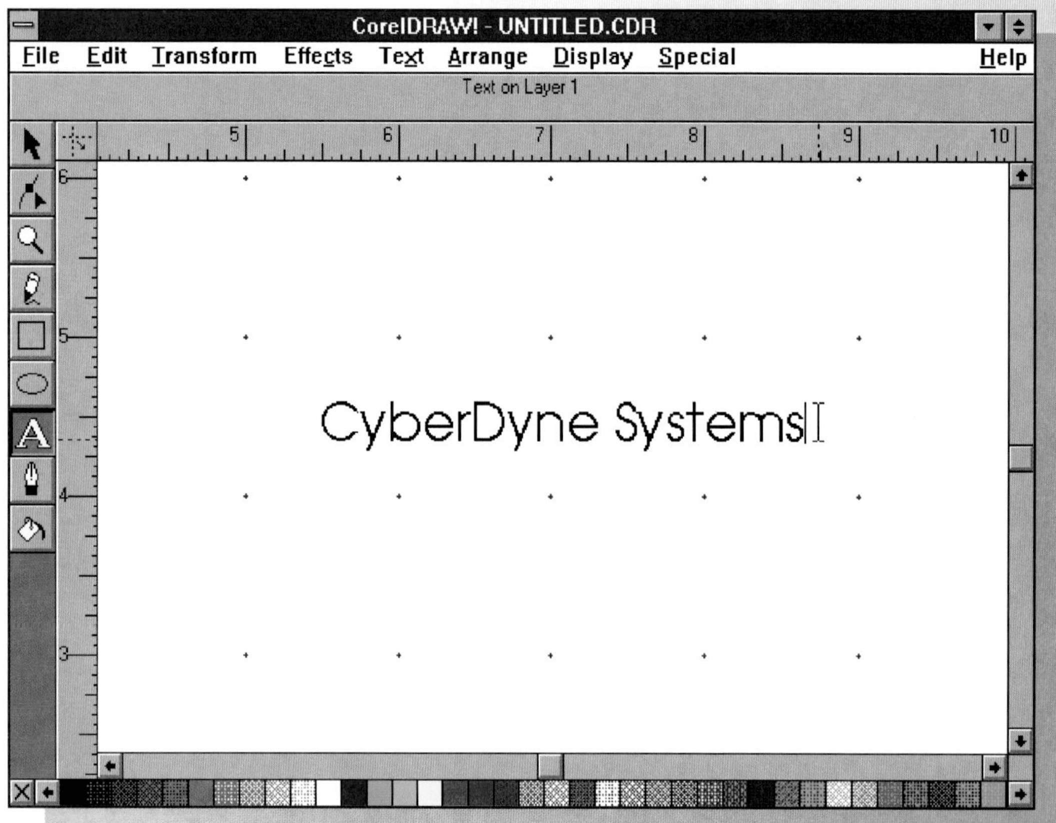

"Why would I do this?"

By adding text to your drawing, you can create complete documents such as sales brochures, company letterhead, greeting cards, and many more. CorelDRAW gives you great control over text. With hundreds of fonts, and the ability to stretch, rotate, and add color to text, you'll find that adding text to your documents is fun and exciting.

The text you type using the Text tool does not wrap like text in a word processor. You must press the Enter key to control line length.

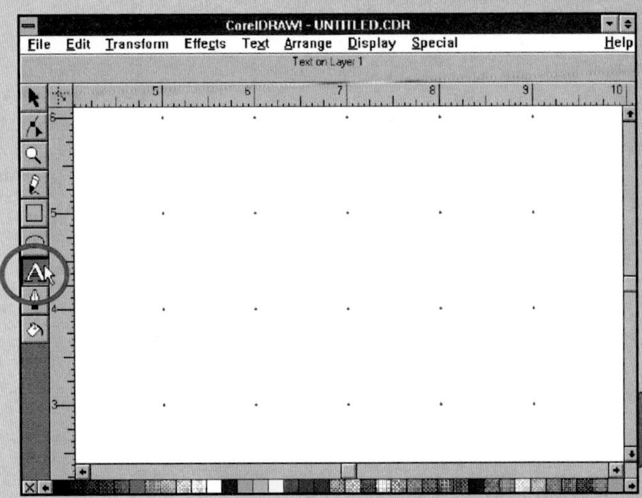

1 Click the **Text** tool in the toolbox. This step selects the Text tool. The pointer changes to a crossbar as you move it to the drawing window.

NOTE

You may find it easier to work with text with the drawing zoomed to actual size. To do this, click the Zoom tool in the toolbox. Click the Actual Size icon on the Zoom fly-out menu.

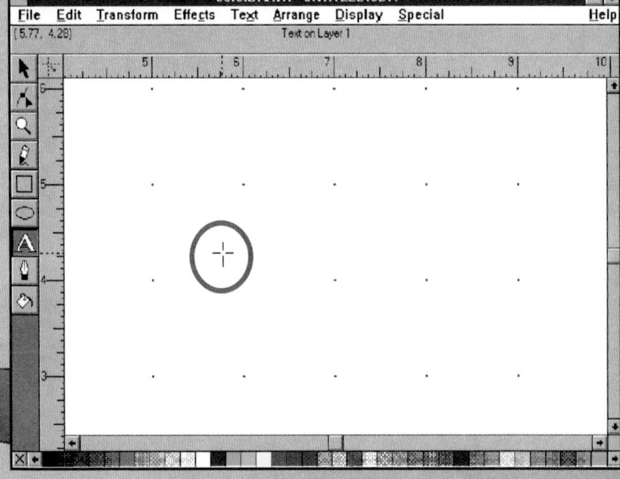

2 Position the mouse pointer where you want your Artistic text to begin and click the mouse button. This step readies the drawing window for you to enter text.

WHY WORRY?

If you are not sure where you want to place text in your drawing, go ahead and click any blank portion of the drawing window. You can then type your text there and move it later.

3 Type the text. This step adds text to the drawing window. The text is displayed in the default font and point size.

NOTE

As with the other tools in the toolbox, the text tool remains active until you select a different tool.

TASK 46

Editing Artistic Text

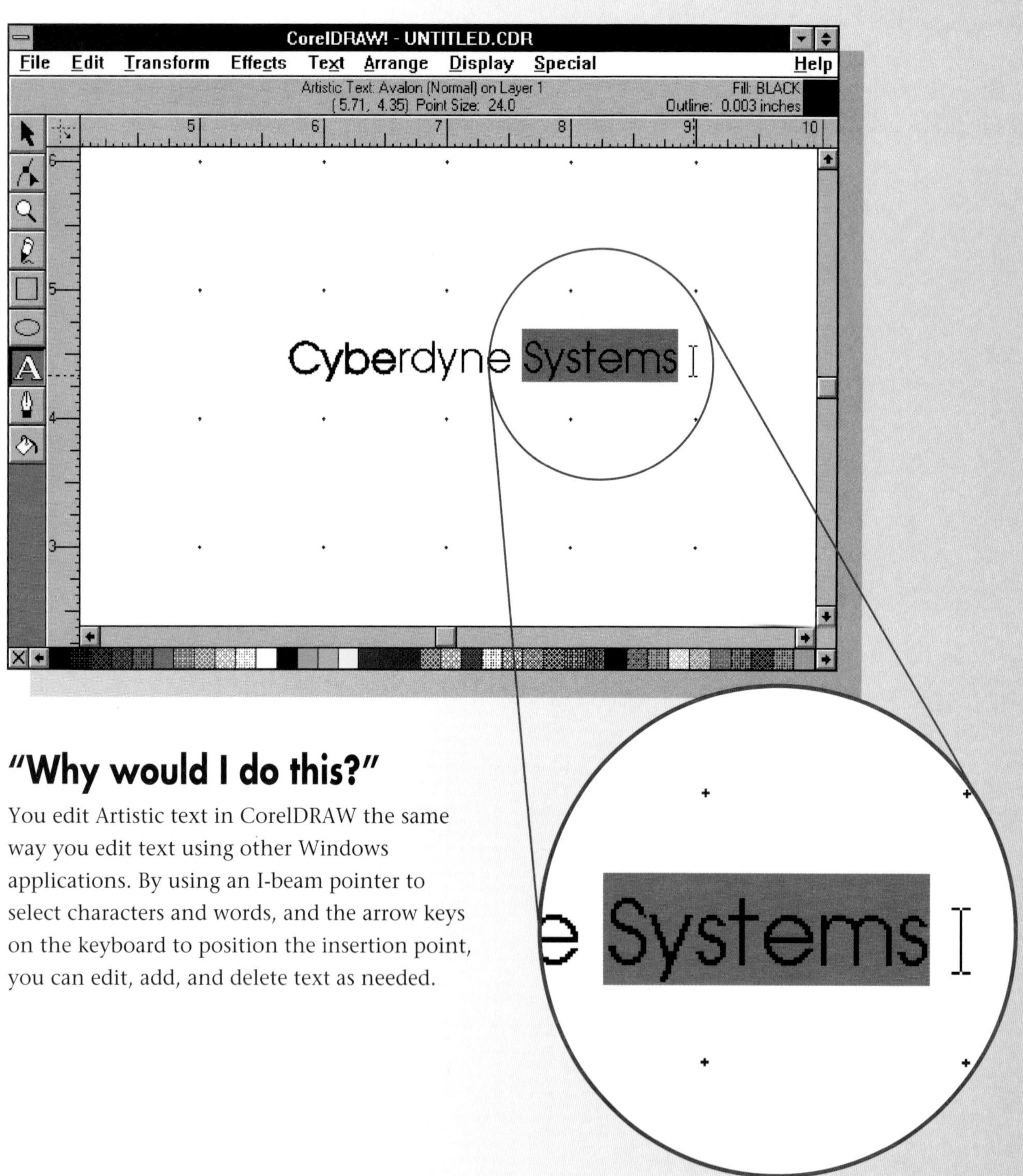

"Why would I do this?"

You edit Artistic text in CorelDRAW the same way you edit text using other Windows applications. By using an I-beam pointer to select characters and words, and the arrow keys on the keyboard to position the insertion point, you can edit, add, and delete text as needed.

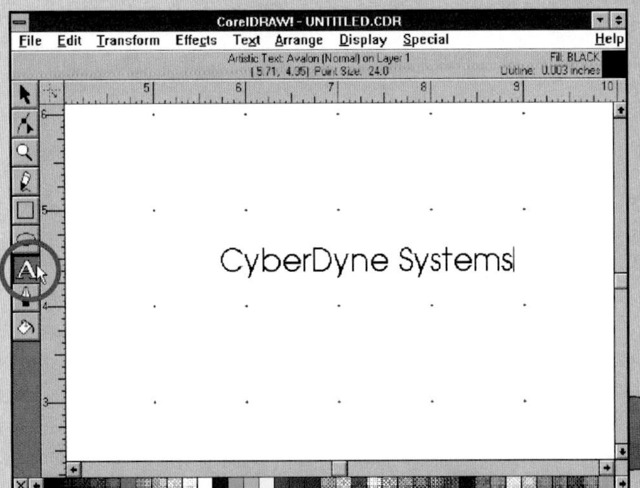

1 Click the **Text** tool in the toolbox. This step selects the Text tool. Move the pointer to the text you want to select.

2 When the pointer is in text, it changes to an I-beam. Click with the pointer in the text where you want to begin editing. This step positions the insertion point in the text string.

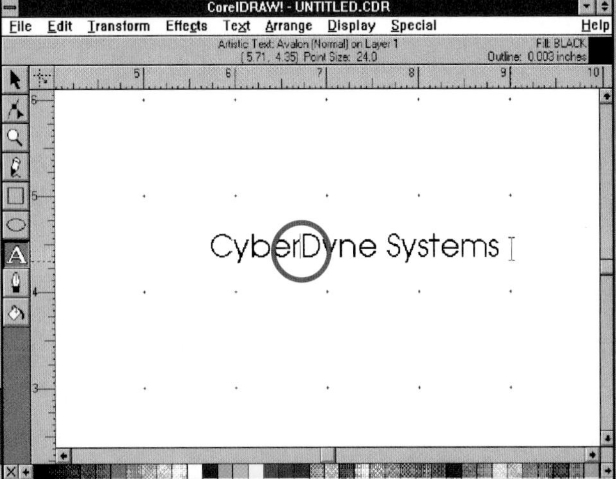

WHY WORRY?

If you find it difficult to position the pointer with the mouse exactly where you want it, click anywhere in the text and then use the left- and right-arrow keys to move to the letter to edit.

3 You can now use the **Delete** key to delete the character to the right of the cursor, or **Backspace** to delete the character to the left. Type any new characters as usual.

Task 46: Editing Artistic Text

4 To select a block of text with the mouse, click next to the first character to select and drag the pointer across the characters. As you drag, the text is highlighted. Release the mouse button when all the characters you want to select are highlighted.

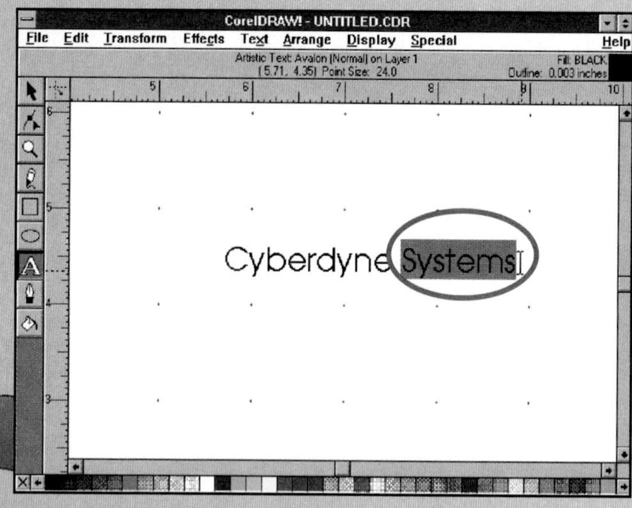

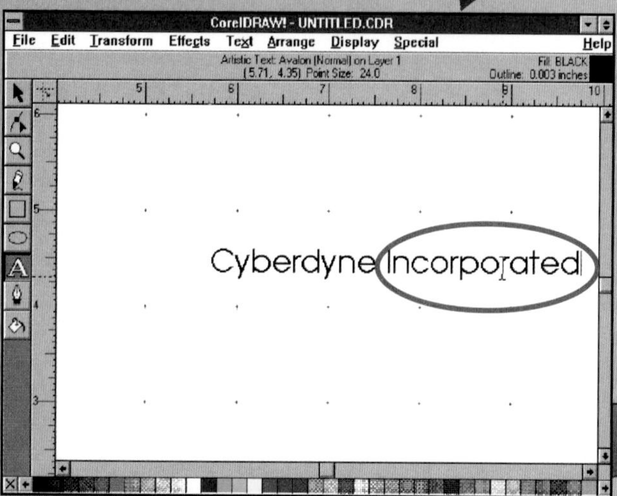

5 If you want to replace the highlighted text with new text, type the new text. This step replaces the highlighted text with the new text you type. If you just want to delete the highlighted text, press **Delete** or **Backspace**.

6 Click the **Pick** tool in the toolbox. This step completes the editing of the Artistic text. The Pick tool is selected. Sizing handles appear around the Artistic text.

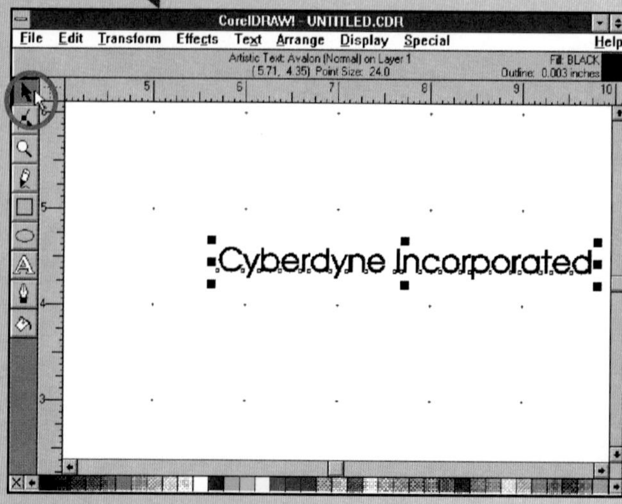

TASK 47

Resizing Artistic Text

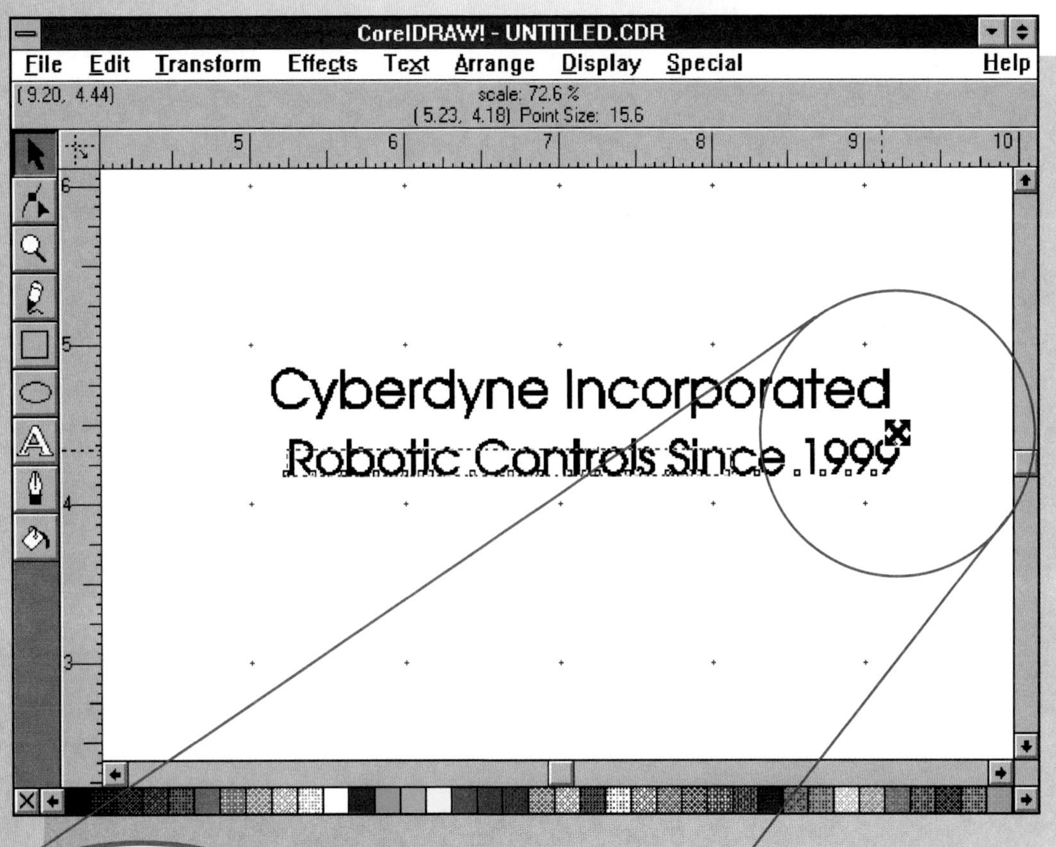

"Why would I do this?"

You can stretch and shrink Artistic text the same way you resize objects such as lines and circles. You can get some really interesting text effects by dragging the sizing handles of text objects. Also, you can give text perspective or a three dimensional look using Corel's Add Perspective and Extrude options.

Task 47: Resizing Artistic Text

1 Click the **Pick** tool; then click the text you want to resize. (If the text does not yet exist, add the text first and then perform this step.) This step creates an Artistic text string.

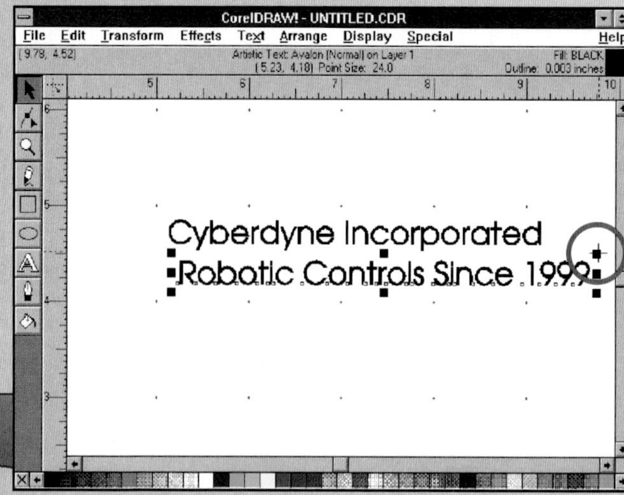

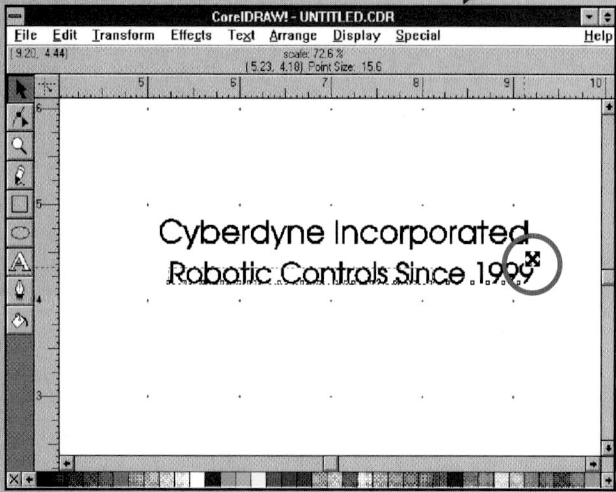

2 Position the pointer on one of the sizing handles of the text selected in step 1. Drag the sizing handle to resize the text. This step shrinks or enlarges the Artistic text, depending on the direction you drag the handle.

> **NOTE**
>
> You also can rotate Artistic text using the rotation arrows that appear when you select an object twice.

3 Release the mouse button. The text is resized to fill the bounding rectangle.

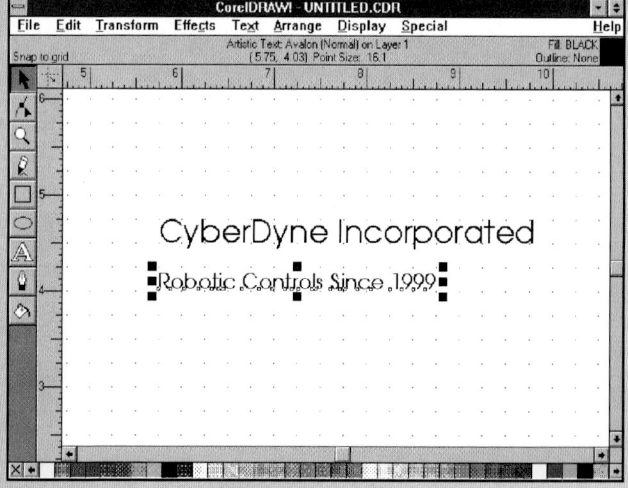

TASK 48

Formatting Artistic Text

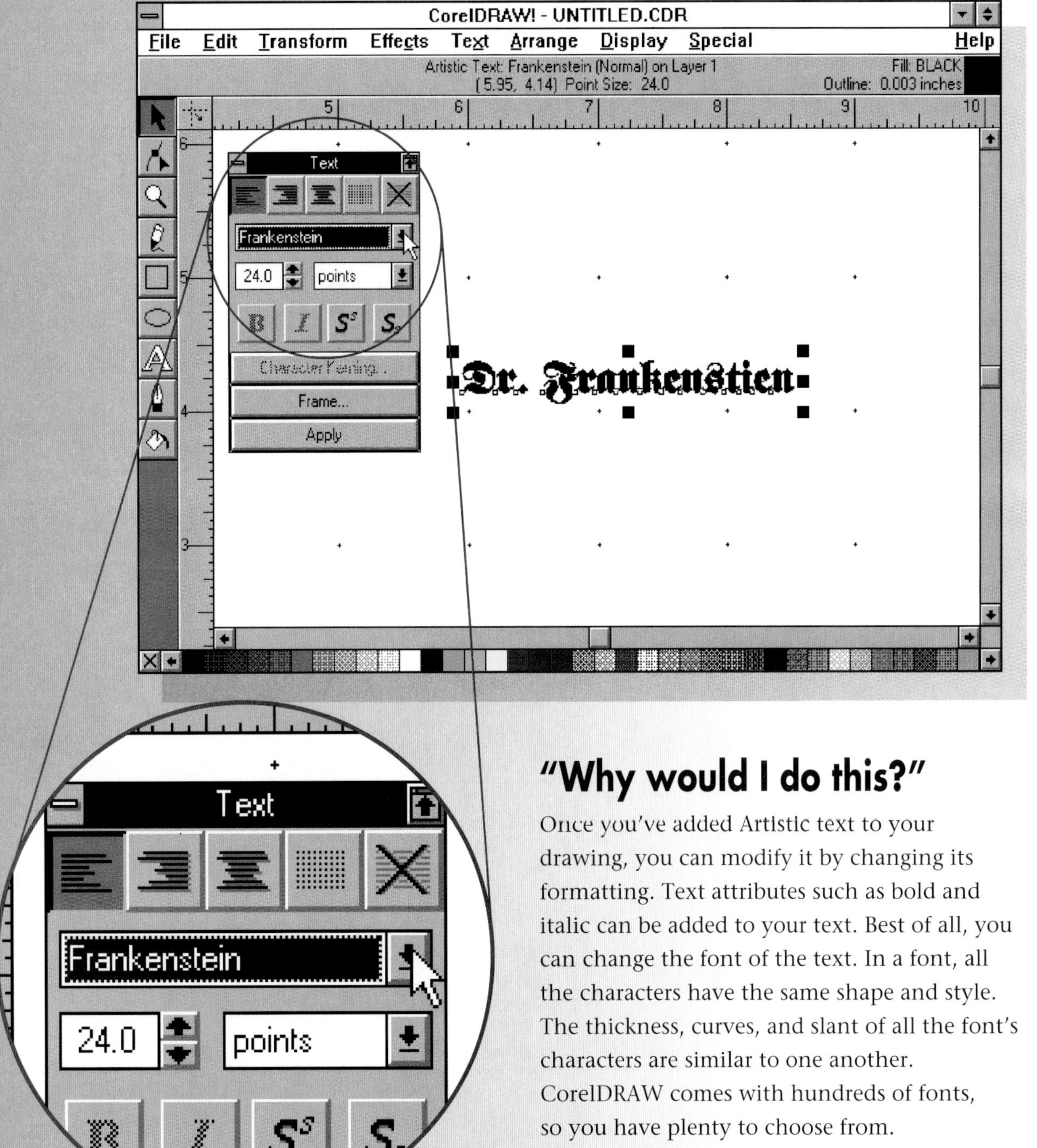

"Why would I do this?"

Once you've added Artistic text to your drawing, you can modify it by changing its formatting. Text attributes such as bold and italic can be added to your text. Best of all, you can change the font of the text. In a font, all the characters have the same shape and style. The thickness, curves, and slant of all the font's characters are similar to one another. CorelDRAW comes with hundreds of fonts, so you have plenty to choose from.

Task 48: Formatting Artistic Text

1 Using the **Text** tool, type new text to be formatted if you haven't already typed the text. Click the **Pick** tool to select the new text, or click the **Pick** tool and click the existing text.

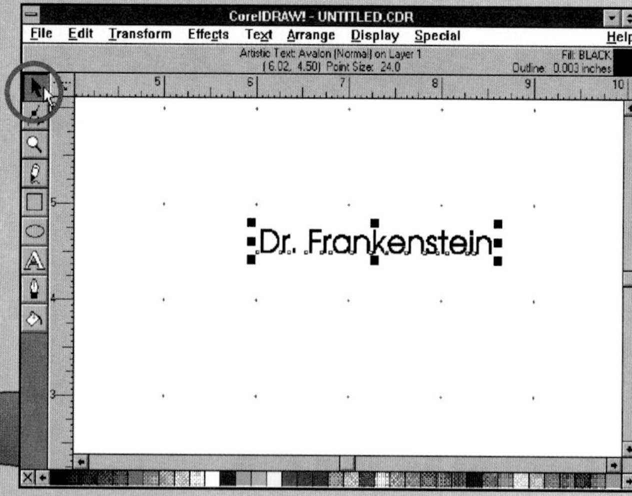

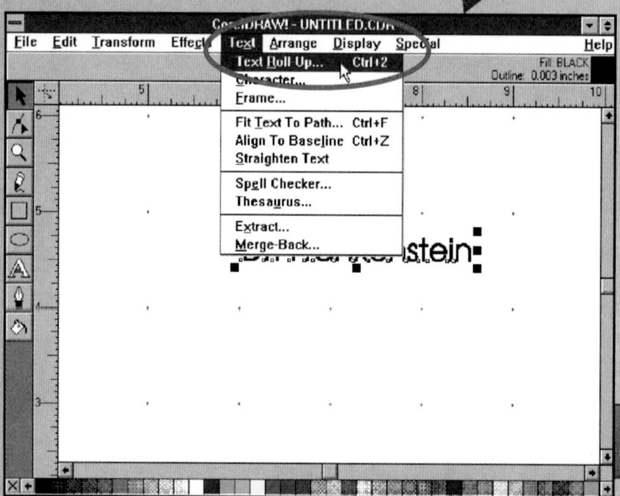

2 Click **Text** on the menu bar. Click **Text Roll-Up**. This step opens the Text roll-up window.

3 Scroll through the font list and click a font to use, such as **Frankenstein**. This step selects the font. The font name appears in the list box at the top of the roll-up.

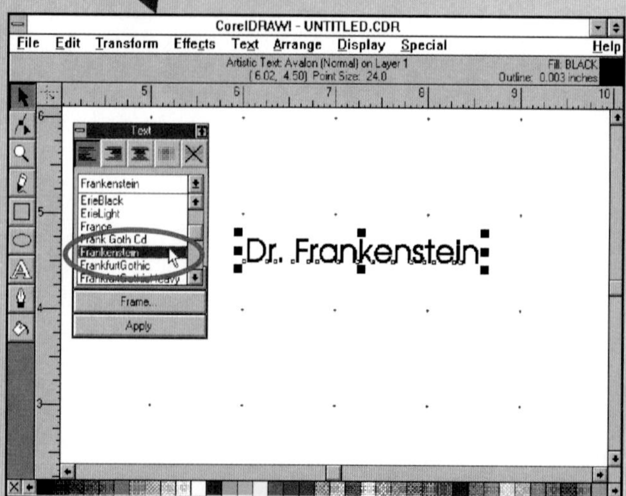

NOTE

If you installed CorelDRAW from disks and not a CD-ROM, only 75 CorelDRAW fonts will be available to you. Dozens more fonts can be installed from Corel's CD-ROM.

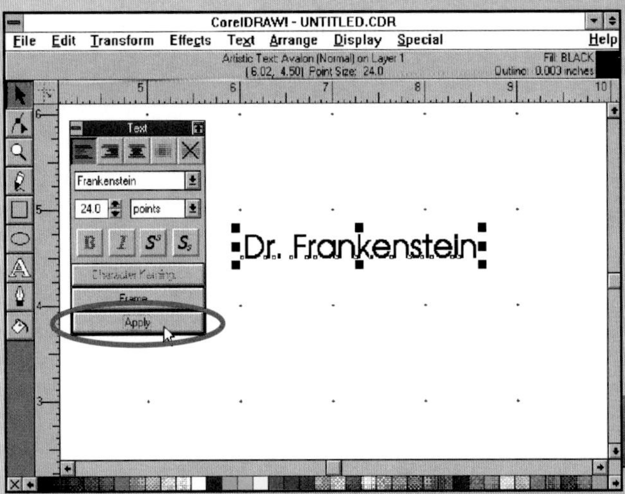

4 Click **Apply**. This step applies the font change to the selected text. The text you typed changes to the selected font.

5 Click the **up arrow** in the Text roll-up until the number reads the point size that you want for the text.

NOTE

Text size is measured in points. There are 72 points in one inch, so a 72-point font is one inch tall.

6 Click **Apply**. The text is changed to the point size you selected.

NOTE

You change the point size of individual characters by selecting the character and applying an new character size using the Text roll-up.

TASK 49

Fitting Artistic Text to a Path

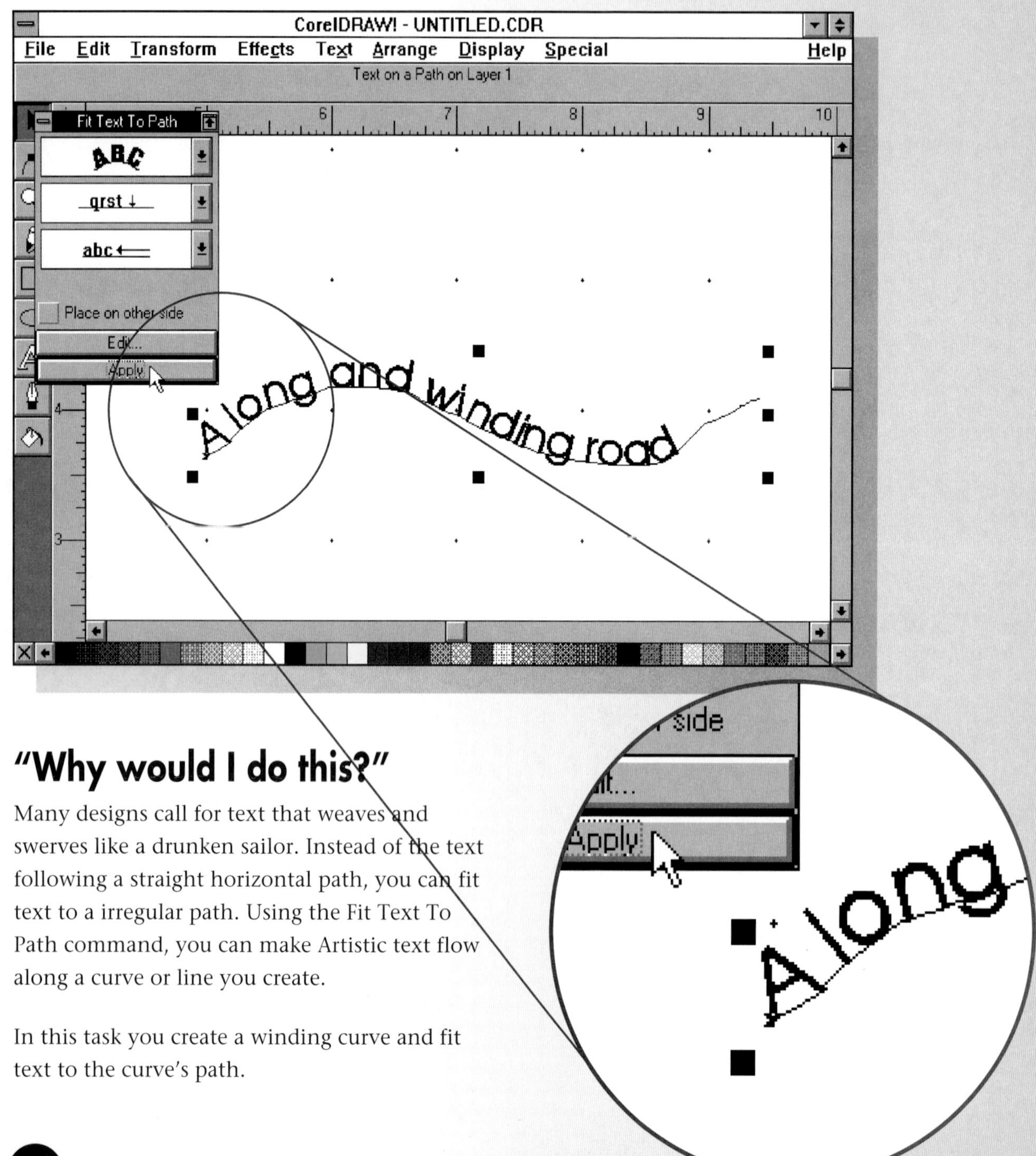

"Why would I do this?"

Many designs call for text that weaves and swerves like a drunken sailor. Instead of the text following a straight horizontal path, you can fit text to a irregular path. Using the Fit Text To Path command, you can make Artistic text flow along a curve or line you create.

In this task you create a winding curve and fit text to the curve's path.

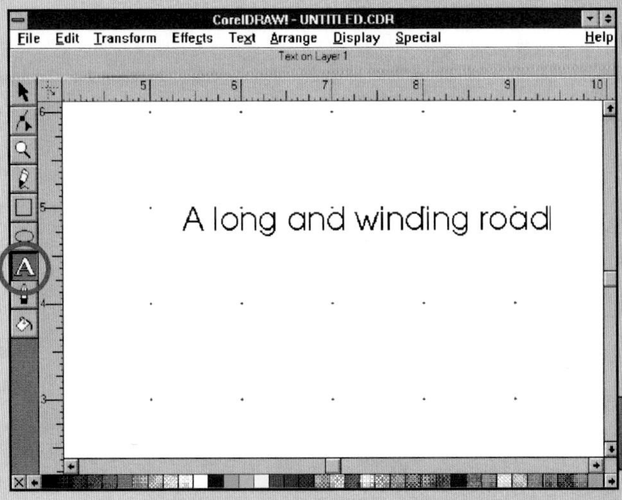

1 Using the **Text** tool, type the text you want to fit to the path. This step creates the text you'll fit to a path.

2 Using the **Pencil** tool, draw a curve in the shape that you want to fit the text to.

WHY WORRY?

If you want a smooth curve instead of a freehand curve, use the Bézier tool on the Pencil fly-out menu.

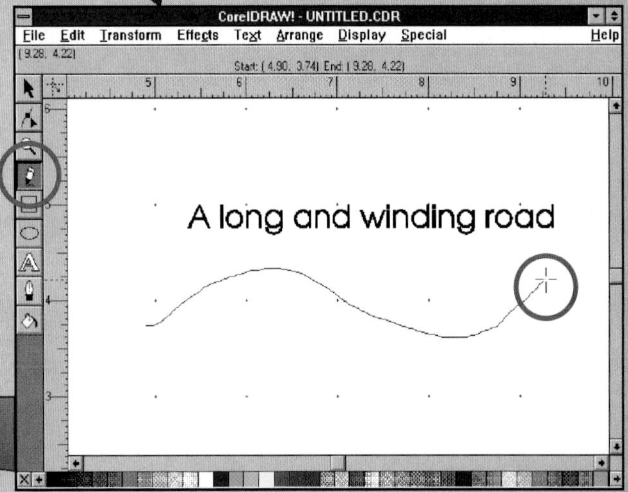

3 Click the **Pick** tool in the toolbox. This selects the curve that you want to fit the text to. Hold the **Shift** key and click the Artistic text created in step 1. This step selects the text and the line. To fit text to a path, you must select a text object and another object.

4 Click **Text** on the menu bar. Click **Fit Text To Path**. This step opens the Fit Text To Path roll-up window.

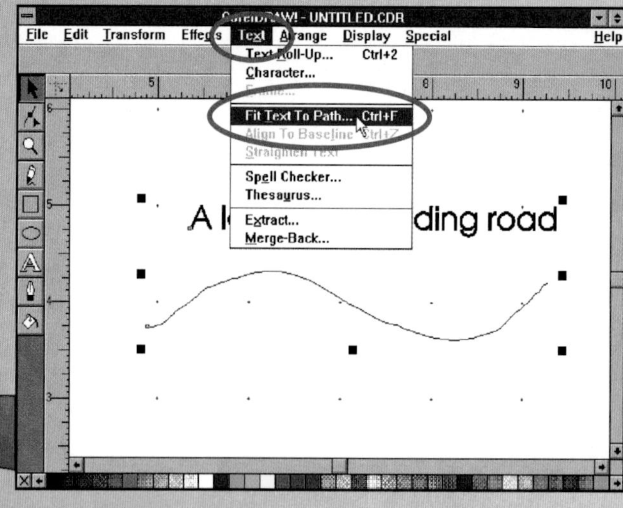

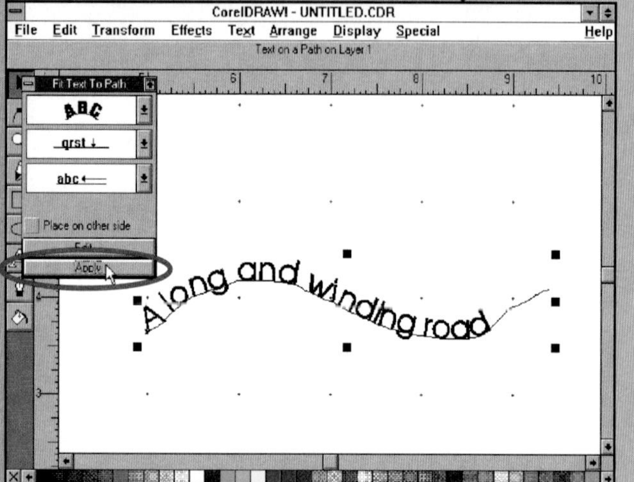

5 Click **Apply** in the roll-up window. The text is moved on top of the line, following its every curve and twist.

NOTE

You can delete the path by selecting Ungroup from the Arrange menu and then deleting the line

TASK 50

Spell Checking Text

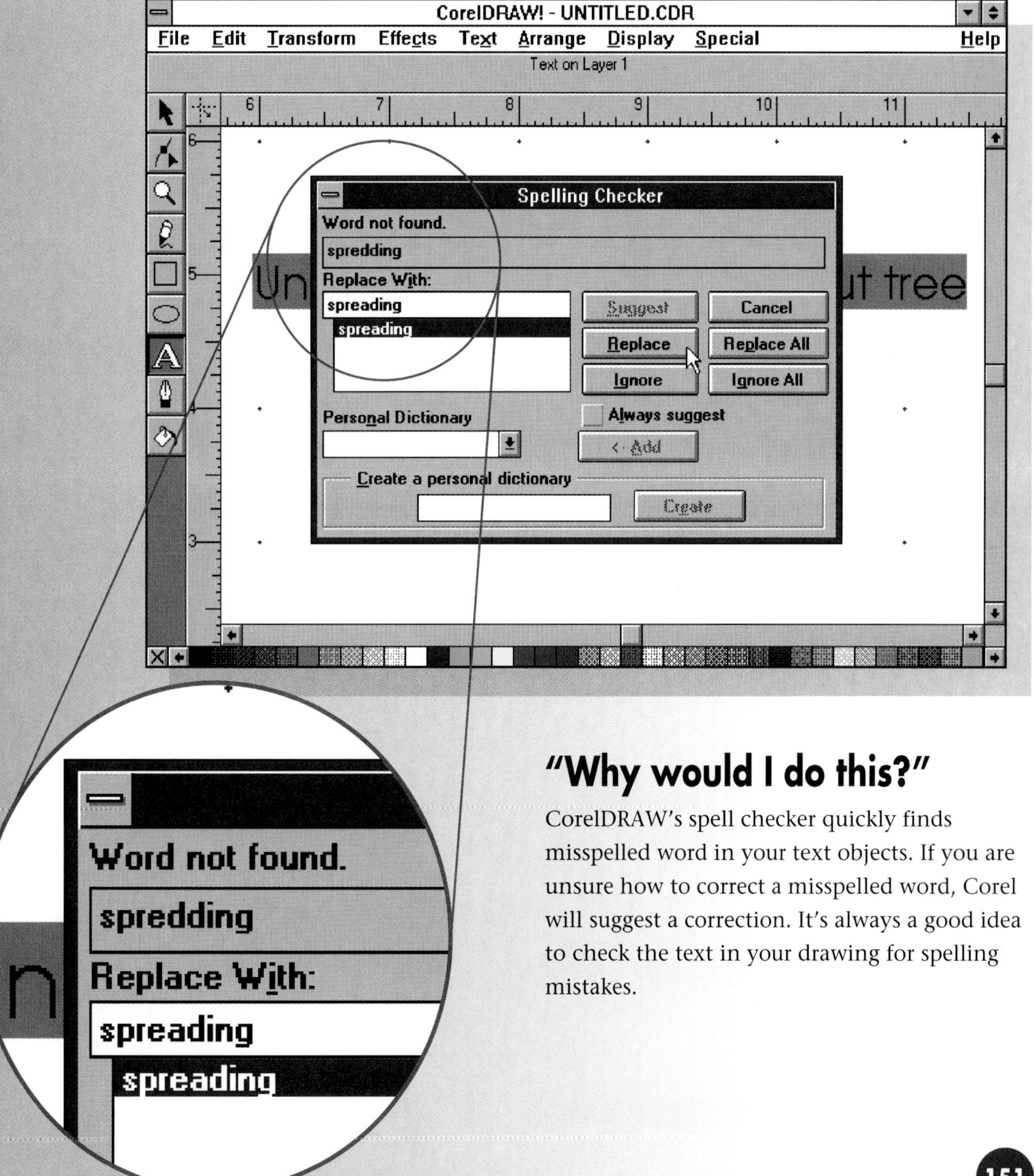

"Why would I do this?"

CorelDRAW's spell checker quickly finds misspelled word in your text objects. If you are unsure how to correct a misspelled word, Corel will suggest a correction. It's always a good idea to check the text in your drawing for spelling mistakes.

Task 50: Spell Checking Text

1 Use the **Text** tool to type new text, and then click the **Pick** tool to select the text to spell check. Or, to spell check existing text, click the **Pick** tool and then click the text.

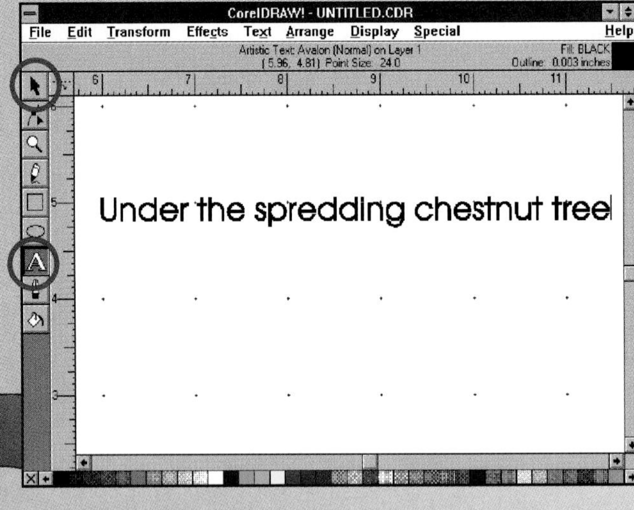

NOTE

You cannot spell check text that is fit to a path. Check the text's spelling prior to fitting it to a path. You can check text, however, that has been rotated, stretched, or manipulated in other ways.

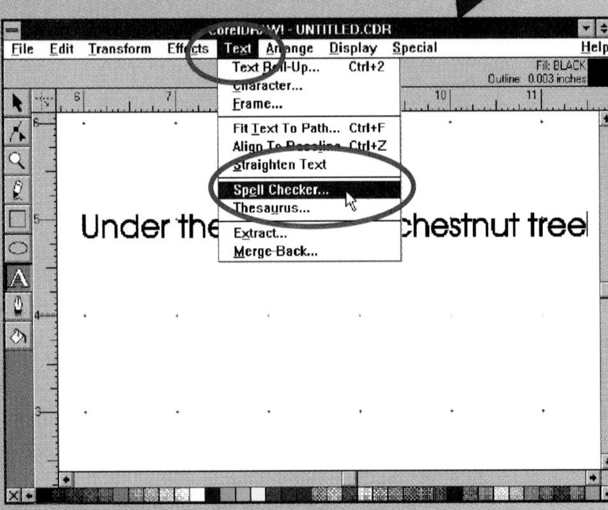

2 Click **Text** in the menu bar. Click **Spell Checker**. This step opens the Spelling Checker dialog box. The characters of the text object are highlighted.

3 Click **Check Text**. The text object is scanned for misspelled words. In this example, the word **spredding** appears in the Word Not Found box.

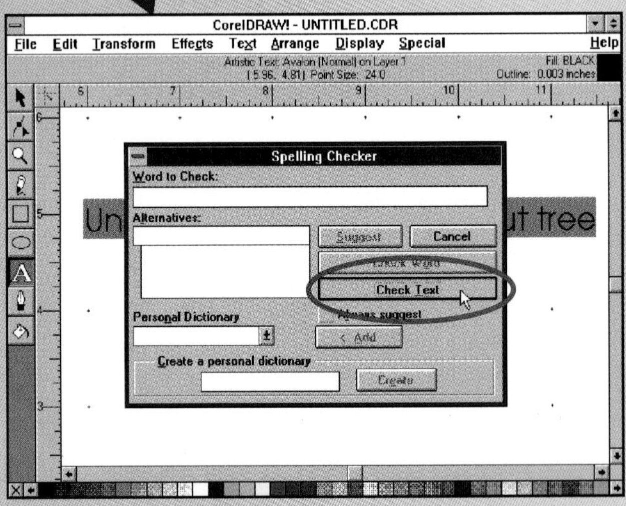

NOTE

CorelDRAW's spelling checker only checks the text of the selected text object. Make sure you check all the text objects in your drawing.

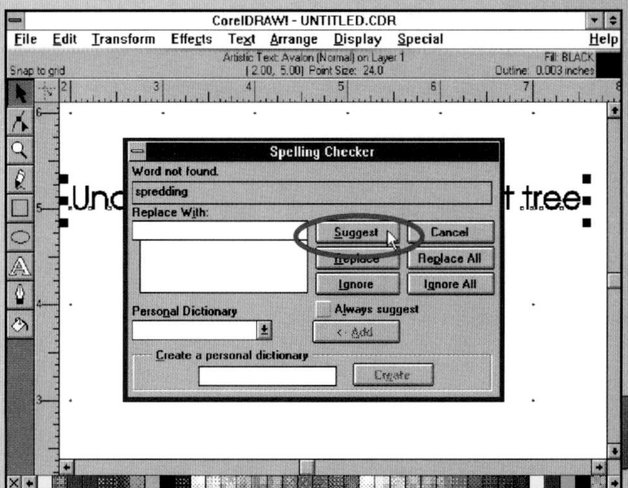

4 Click **Suggest** in the dialog box. The word **spreading** appears in the Replace With box. In this step, you requested a suggestion for the misspelled word that was found.

5 Click **Replace**. This step tells CorelDRAW to replace the misspelled word with the word listed in the Replace With box. The word **spredding** is replaced with **spreading**.

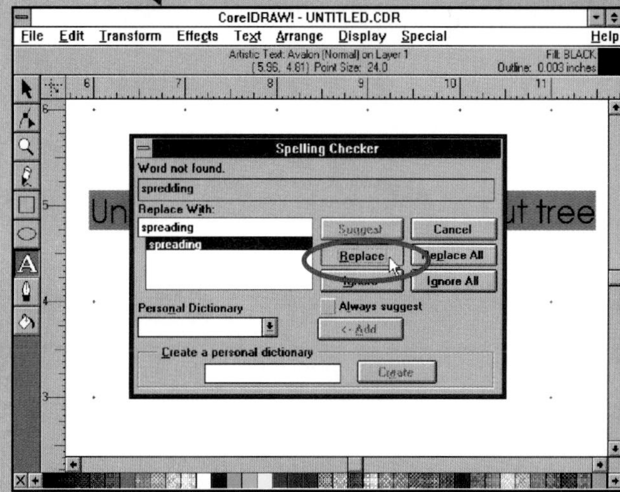

CorelPHOTO-PAINT!
File Edit Image Effects Mask Display Special Window
Help
NEW-1.PCX 100%
Color Selection
Canvas
Width: 800
Height: 800
Units: Pixels
Mode: 256 Color
Memory required: 1308 KB
Memory available: 17767 KB
OK
Cancel
Help
Tools
CorelPHOTO-PAINT!
File Edit Image Effects Mask Display Special Window
NEW-1.PCX 100%
Color Selection
Canvas
Help
CorelPHOTO-PAINT!
File Edit Display Font Options Window
New-1.pcx 100%
Tools
Help
File Edit Display Font

PART VI

CorelPHOTO-PAINT and CorelCHART Basics

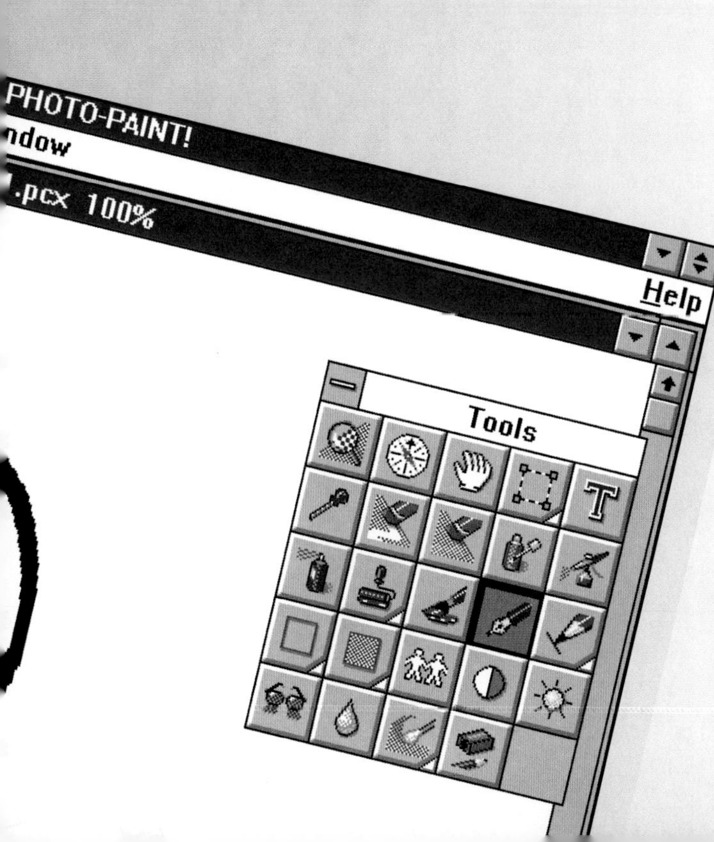

In this part, you'll learn the basics of CorelPHOTO-PAINT and CorelCHART. You'll learn to use PHOTO-PAINT special effects brushes to paint images in impressionist and pointillist styles. You'll also learn to use PHOTO-PAINT's smudge and smear tools to add special effects to your paintings. Near the end of this part, you'll learn to use CorelCHART templates to create charts and graphs quickly.

CorelPHOTO-PAINT enables you to create and edit bitmap images. A *bitmap image* is made up of thousands of tiny dots (pixels). When you paint a line or shape in PHOTO-PAINT, you turn on a path of pixels.

Objects in PHOTO-PAINT cannot be stretched and resized the way CorelDRAW objects can. When you draw an ellipse in CorelDRAW, a mathematical description of the ellipse is stored as part of the drawing file. Stretching the ellipse modifies the mathematical description. If you paint an ellipse shape in PHOTO-PAINT, the location of each dot forming the ellipse is stored. To change the shape of the ellipse in PHOTO-PAINT, you have to erase and paint the object again.

PHOTO-PAINT's special brushes, such as the Pointillist brush, help you create special effects in your painting. The Pointillist brush paints a path of multicolored dots, creating the pointillist effect that artists such as Seurat are famous for.

In addition to learning about PHOTO-PAINT's special brushes in this part, you'll learn about PHOTO-PAINT basics such as filling an area with color, changing paint colors, and erasing portions of your painting.

Once you've painted an image in PHOTO-PAINT, you'll want to experiment with the image enhancement tools in the Tool Palette. Using the Freehand Smear tool, you can smear paint colors together creating an effect similar to smeared oil paints on canvas. The Freehand Blend tool blends and softens an area of your painting, making the transition between colors appear fuzzy, not abrupt. To reverse the effects of the blend tool and make edges and transitions sharp, you can use the Freehand Sharpening tool. This part shows you how to use these tools and a few others.

To round out your exploration of the CorelDRAW suite of programs, several tasks at the end of this part teach you the basics of CorelCHART. With CorelCHART, you can create charts and graphs of numeric data. For example, you can create a pie chart showing the market share percentage of your company or a graph showing the growth of your child.

You'll learn to use CHART's templates to create charts such as pie charts, bar graphs, area graphs, and many more. You'll then modify the data of the template using the Data Manager. CorelCHART's Data Manager is a mini-spreadsheet that enables you to enter chart data in a series of rows and columns. Using the Data Manager, you can add titles and data labels to your chart. Finally, you'll learn to change the type of chart displayed in the Chart view. CorelCHART offers dozens of chart types, and as you'll see, you can use many chart types to display the same data.

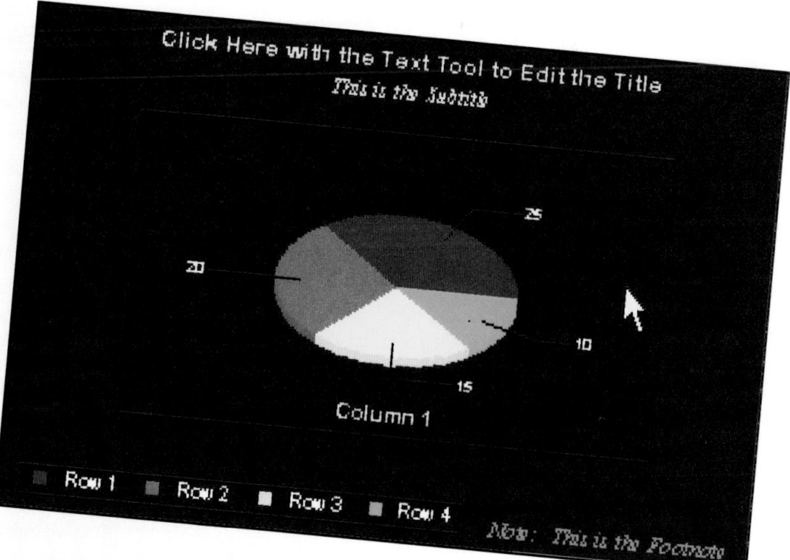

TASK 51

Starting CorelPHOTO-PAINT

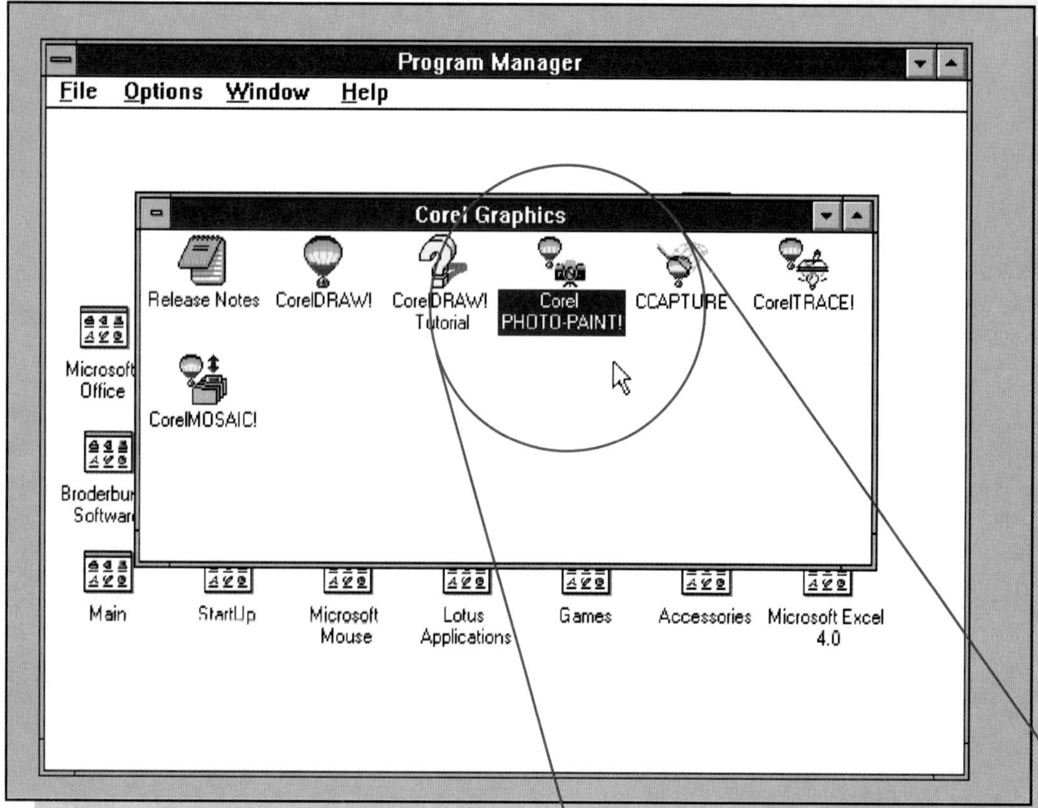

"Why would I do this?"

The CorelPHOTO-PAINT application is represented by an icon of a camera. Like other Windows applications, you can start CorelPHOTO-PAINT by double-clicking its icon.

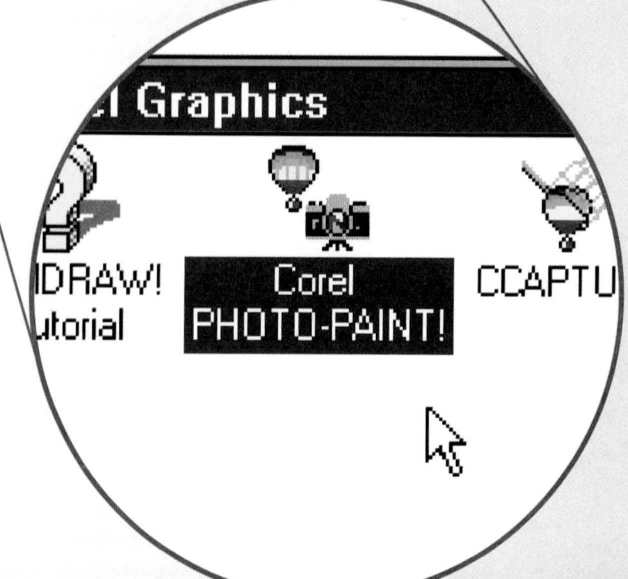

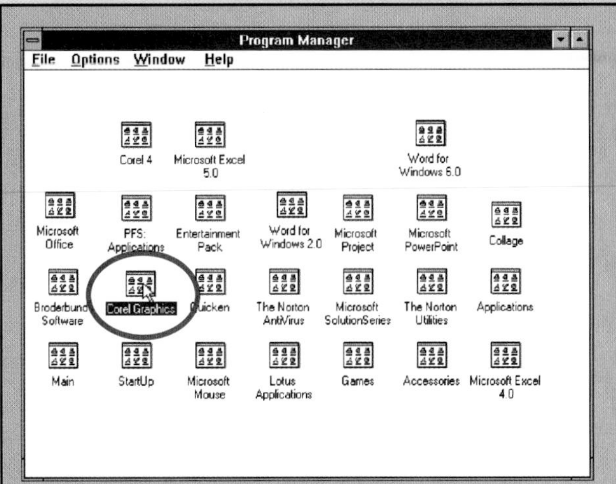

1 Double-click the icon labeled **Corel Graphics** (or **Corel 4** if you have CorelDRAW 4) in the Program Manager window. This step opens the Corel program group window.

2 Double-click the **CorelPHOTO-PAINT** icon in the Corel Graphics window. This step starts CorelPHOTO-PAINT.

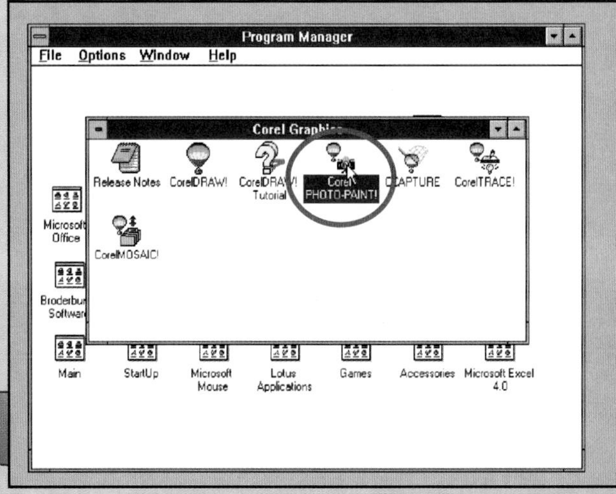

WHY WORRY?

If the CorelPHOTO-PAINT icon does not appear in the Corel Graphics program group, it was not installed. Run the CorelDRAW install program and install the CorelPHOTO-PAINT module of the set of Corel programs.

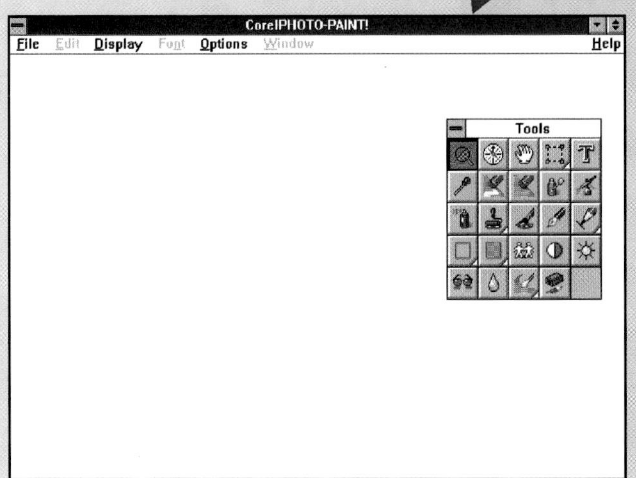

3 The main PHOTO-PAINT window appears on your screen. The CorelPHOTO-PAINT screen, unlike the CorelDRAW screen, does not contain a new file ready for you to use.

NOTE

To start CorelPHOTO-PAINT using the keyboard, press Ctrl+Tab until the Corel Graphics Program Group icon is highlighted; press Enter. Press the right-arrow key until the CorelPHOTO-PAINT icon is highlighted, and press Enter.

TASK 52

Creating a Picture File

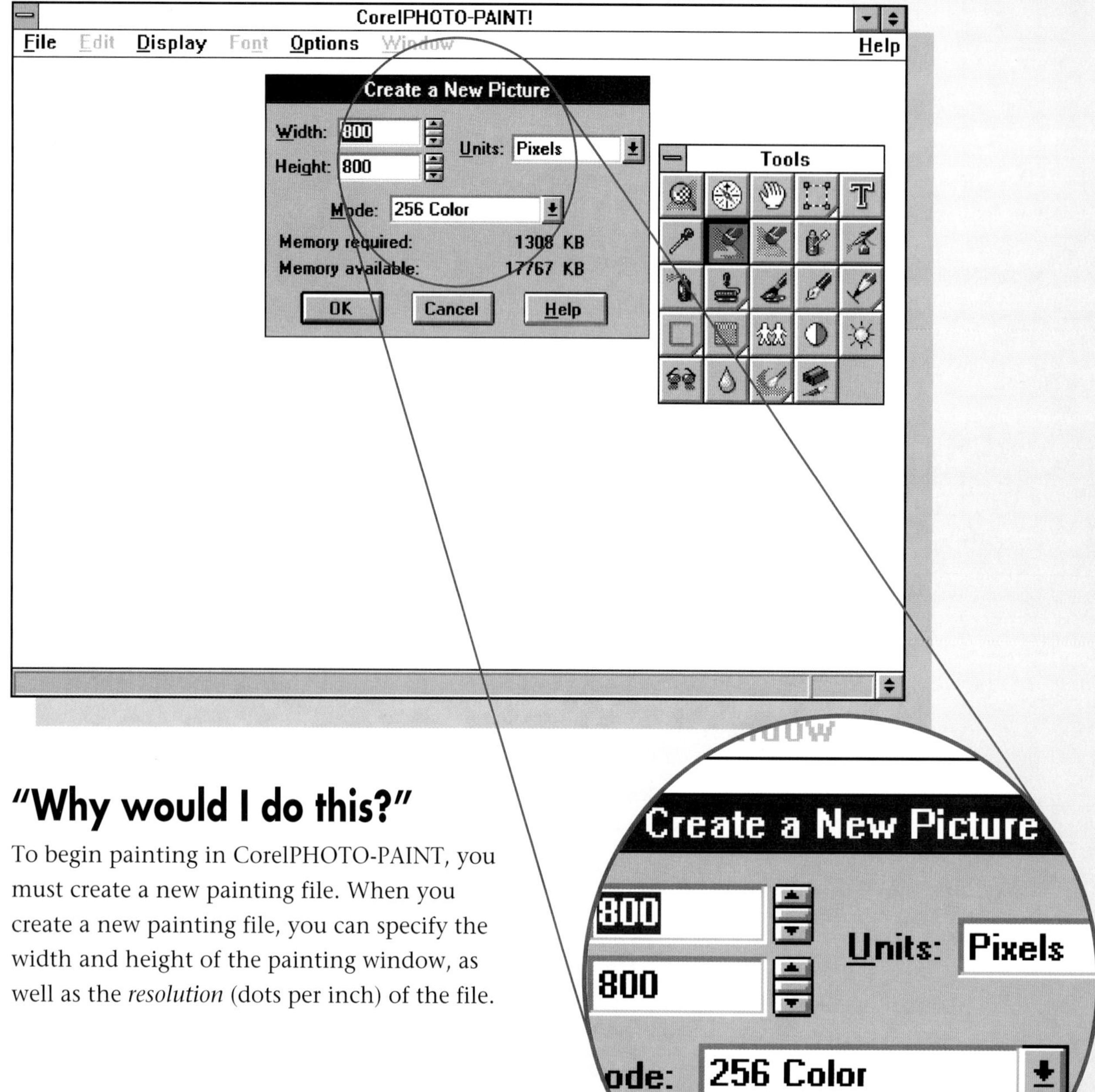

"Why would I do this?"

To begin painting in CorelPHOTO-PAINT, you must create a new painting file. When you create a new painting file, you can specify the width and height of the painting window, as well as the *resolution* (dots per inch) of the file.

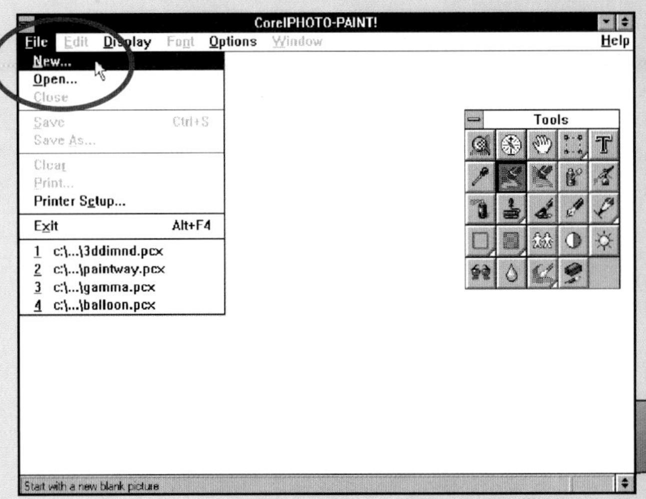

1 Click **File** on the menu bar. Then click **New** on the File menu. This step opens the Create a New Picture dialog box. The Create a New Picture dialog box shows the default width and height of a new picture painting area.

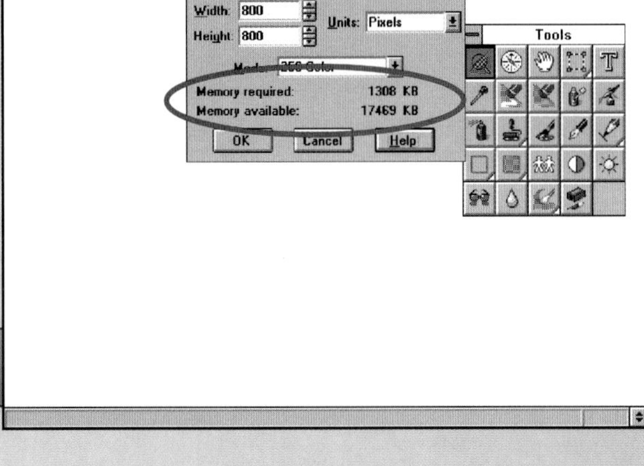

2 Notice the dialog box's Memory Required and Memory Available sections. As you increase the picture's size, the memory needed to create it also increases. The Memory Required number should not exceed the Memory Available number.

NOTE

Changing the Mode setting in the Create a New Picture dialog box also changes the memory required to create the image. For example, 24-bit color mode requires large amounts of memory.

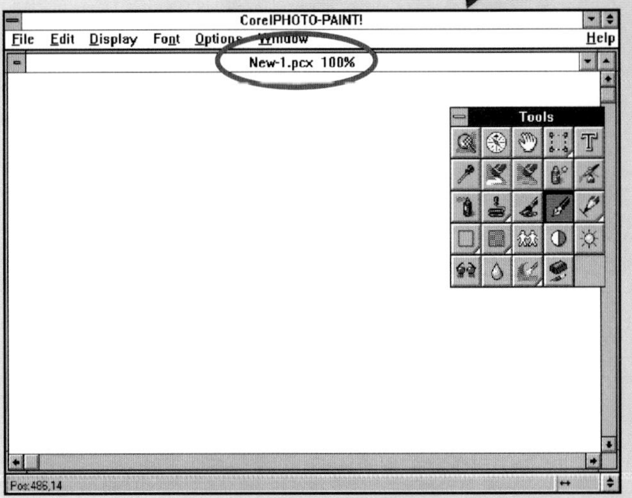

3 Click **OK**. This step creates a new blank picture window for you to paint in. The default file name, `New-1.pcx`, is displayed in the window title bar.

WHY WORRY?

A warning dialog box appears if the memory needed to create the new file exceeds the available memory in your computer. Click OK and change the dimensions or resolution in the Create a New Picture dialog box.

TASK 53

Painting with the Impressionist Brush (version 4)

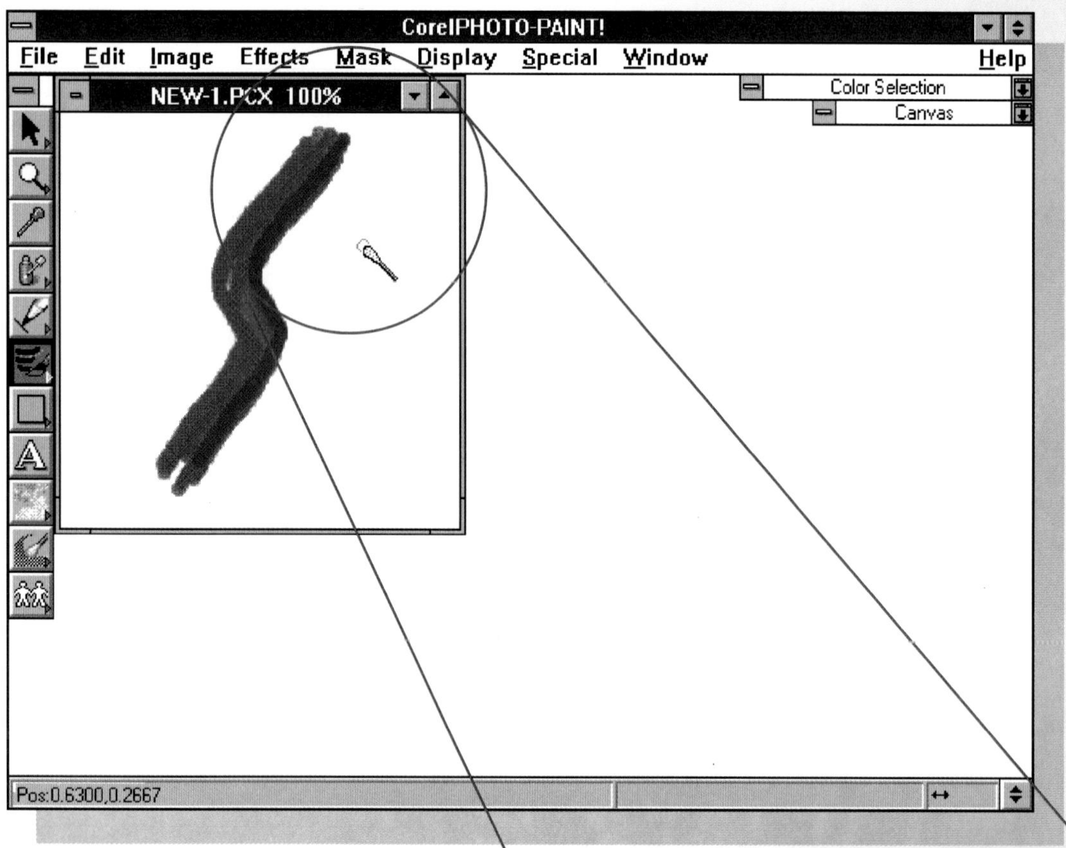

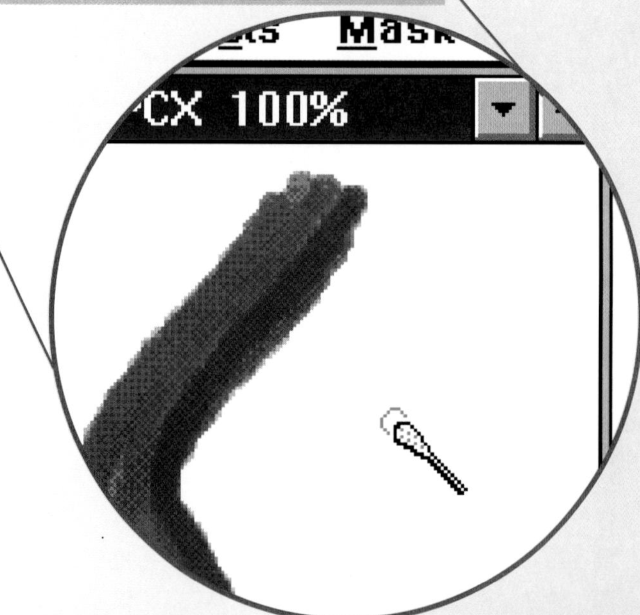

"Why would I do this?"

CorelPHOTO-PAINT 4 gives you numerous choices of paintbrush styles. The Impressionist brush helps you paint in a style similar to the great impressionists such as Monet. As you paint with the Impressionist brush, it applies a thick multicolored band of paint. The colors applied are chosen to work together. The Pointillist brush is only available in CorelPHOTO-PAINT 4.

Task 53: Painting with the Impressionist Brush (version 4)

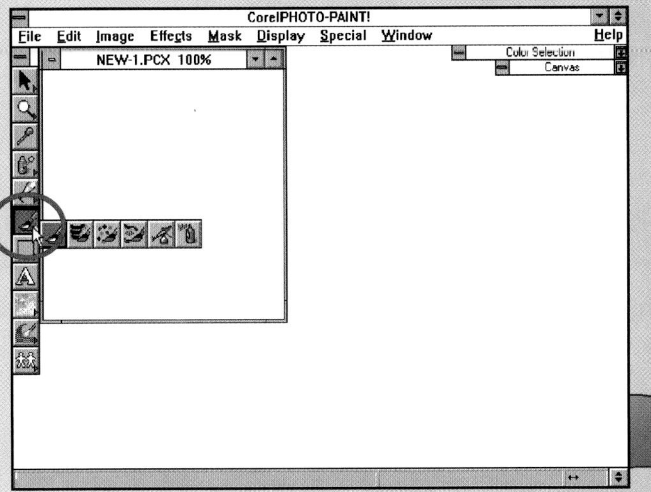

1 Position the pointer on the **Paintbrush** tool in the toolbox. Hold the left mouse button. The Paintbrush tool fly-out menu appears.

WHY WORRY?

If the Impressionist tool is already displayed in the toolbox, proceed with step 2 anyway. It does not hurt to reselect a tool from a fly-out menu.

2 Click the **Impressionist Brush** tool—the second tool in the fly-out menu. This step selects the Impressionist brush. The Impressionist brush icon replaces the Paintbrush icon in the toolbox.

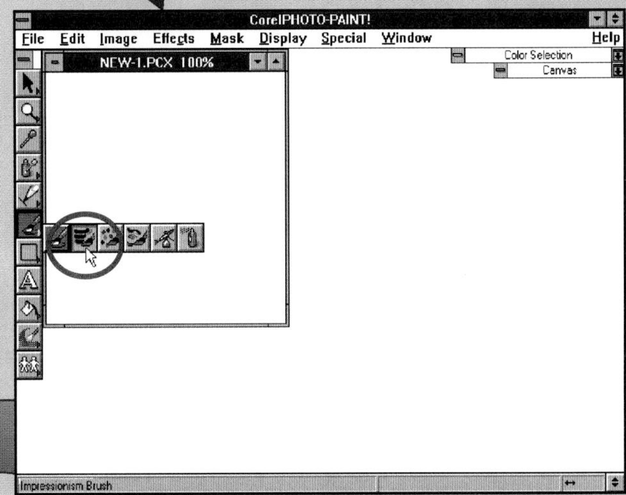

3 Move the pointer to the painting window. The pointer changes to the Impressionist brush. A small hollow circle at the tip of the pointer indicates the location and shape of the brush. Click the left mouse button and drag the pointer to paint. As you drag, a dotted-line path shows where the paint will be applied when you release the mouse button.

TASK 54

Painting with the Pointillist Brush (version 4)

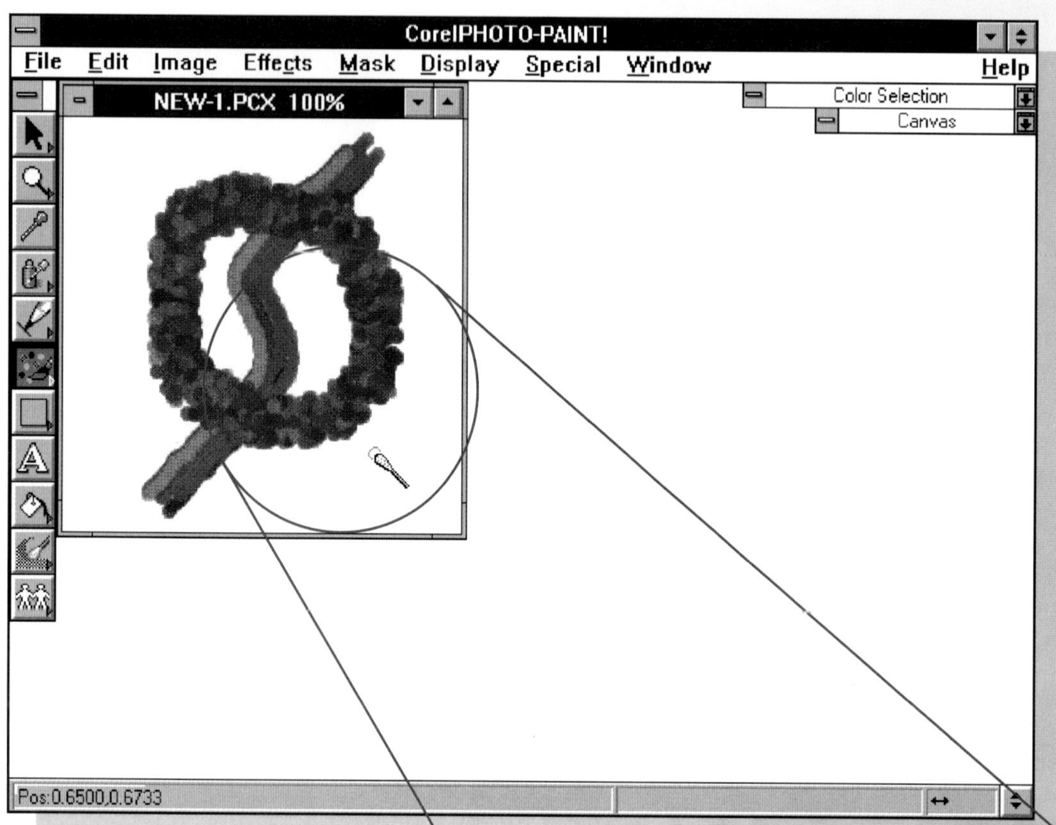

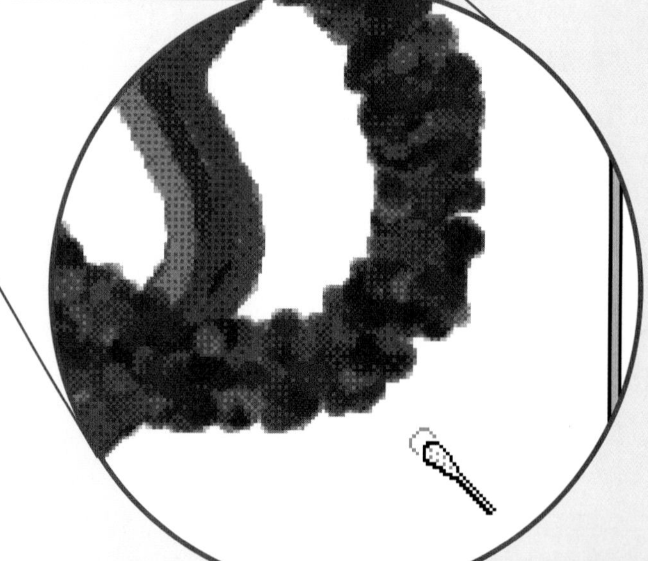

"Why would I do this?"

Like the Impressionist brush, the Pointillist brush creates a special effect. *Pointillism* is a painting style that uses clusters of small multicolored dots to create images. Using the Pointillist brush, you can paint images that are inexact and fuzzy, creating an effect similar to the work of artists such as Seurat.

Task 54: Painting with the Pointillist Brush (version 4)

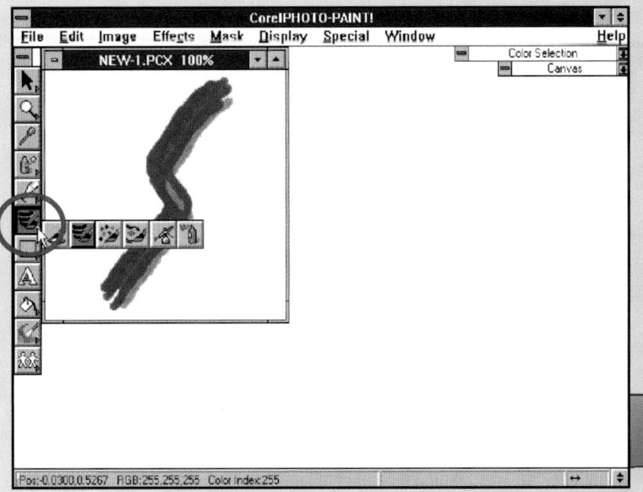

1 Position the pointer on the **Paintbrush** tool in the toolbox. Hold the mouse button. The Paintbrush tool fly-out menu appears.

WHY WORRY?

If the Paintbrush tool is not displayed in the toolbox, locate the Impressionist brush, the Pointillist brush, or the Artist brush, and proceed with step 2. All these tools are available on the Paintbrush tool fly-out menu.

2 Click the **Pointillist Brush** tool—the third tool in the fly-out menu. This step selects the Pointillist brush. The Pointillist brush icon replaces the Paintbrush icon in the toolbox.

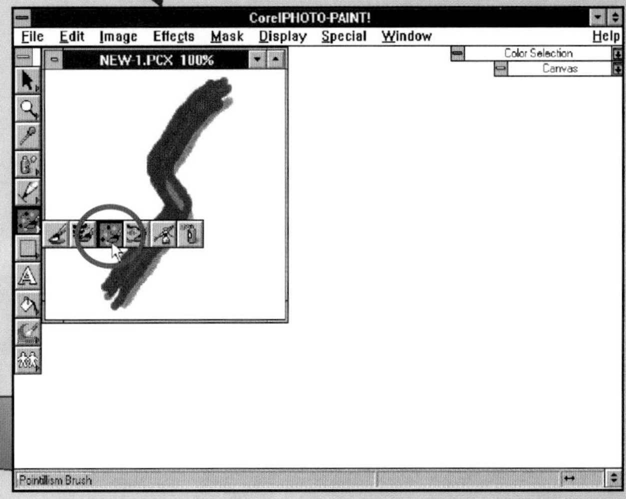

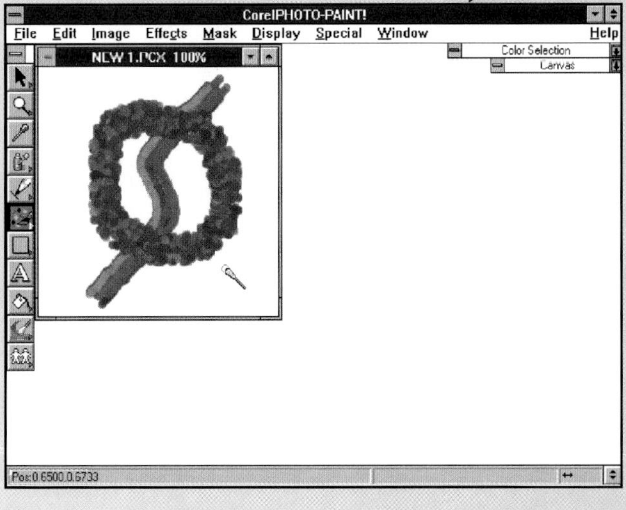

3 Move the pointer to the painting window. The pointer changes to the Pointillist brush. A small hollow circle at the tip of the pointer indicates the location and shape of the brush. Click the left mouse button and drag the pointer. As you drag, a dotted-line path shows where the paint will be applied when you release the mouse button.

TASK 55

Painting with the Pen Tool

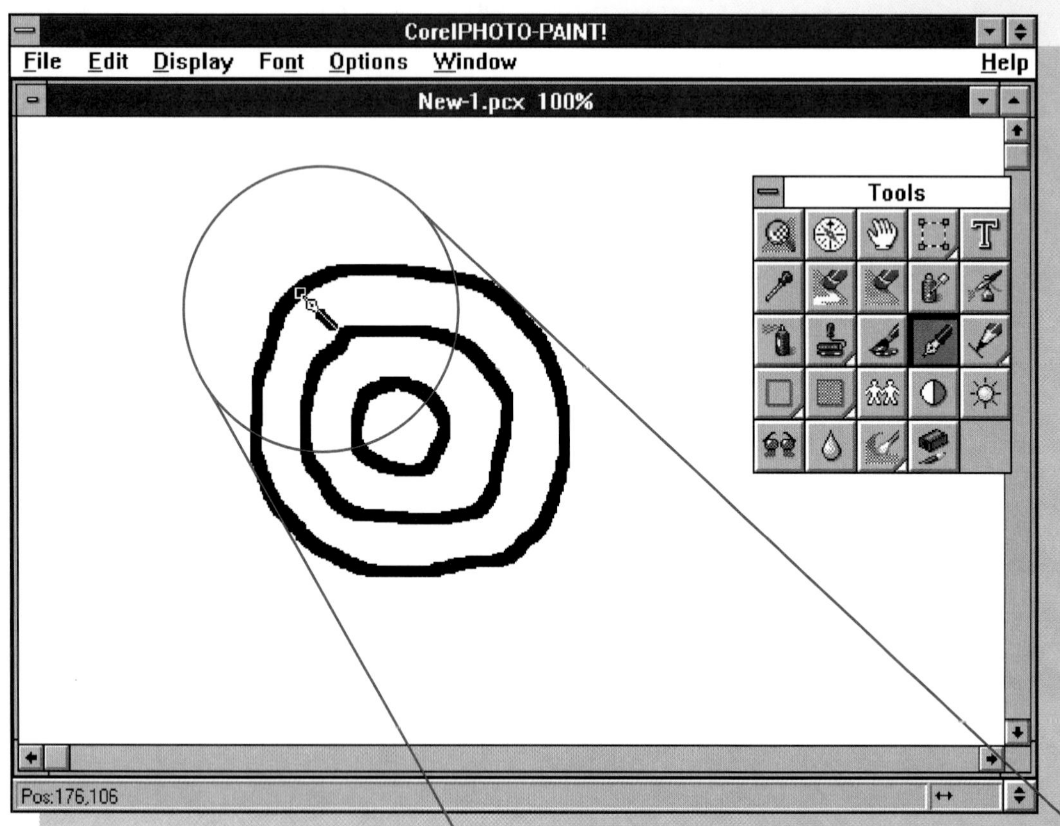

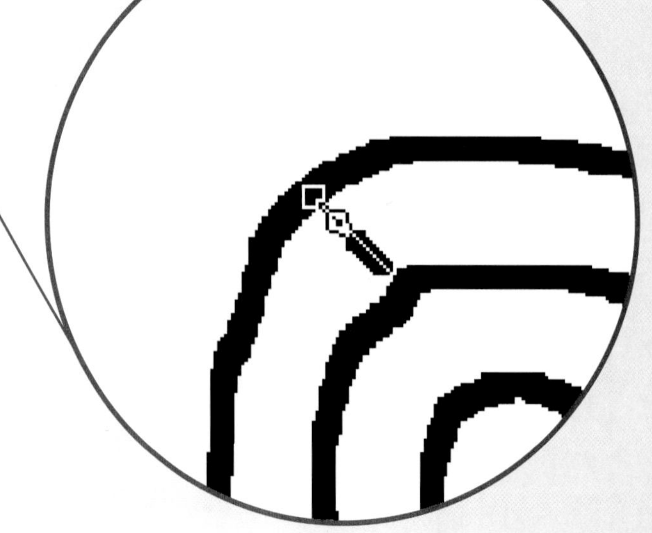

"Why would I do this?"

Using CorelPHOTO-PAINT's Pen tool, you can draw lines that have well-defined edges. Shaped like the tip of a fountain pen, the Pen tool draws smooth lines. If your painting requires solid-color lines that are smooth, use the Pen tool.

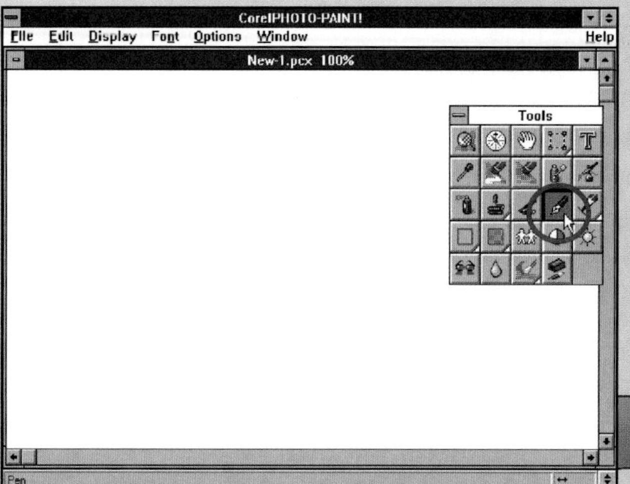

1 Click the **Pen** tool on the toolbox. This step selects the Pen tool.

NOTE

In PHOTO-PAINT 4, click the Line tool (shaped like a pencil) in the toolbox. A fly-out menu appears. Click the Pen tool on the fly-out menu.

2 Move the mouse pointer to the painting window. The mouse pointer changes to a fountain pen shape, with a hollow box at its tip. The box represents the size of the pen tip.

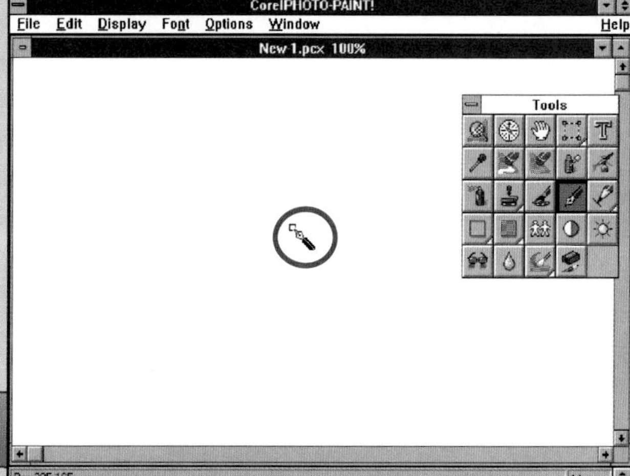

NOTE

If you want to change the shape of the Pen tool, double-click the Pen tool in the toolbox. The Brush Style dialog box appears. Select a new shape for the Pen tool and click OK.

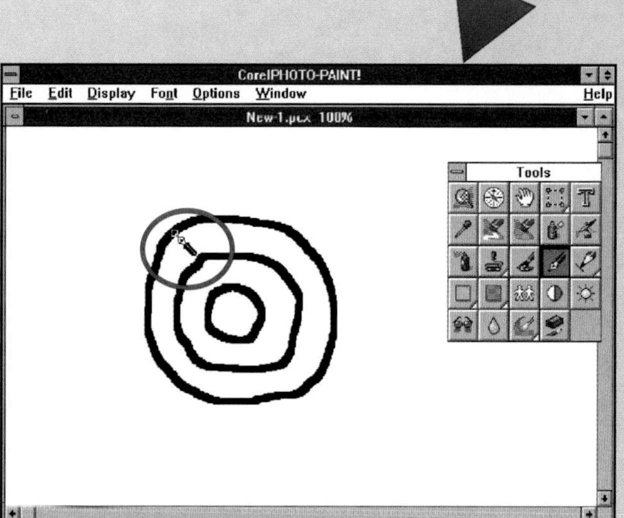

3 Hold the left mouse button. Drag the Pen tool around the painting area to paint. As you drag, a line is painted in the window.

TASK 56

Changing Paint Colors

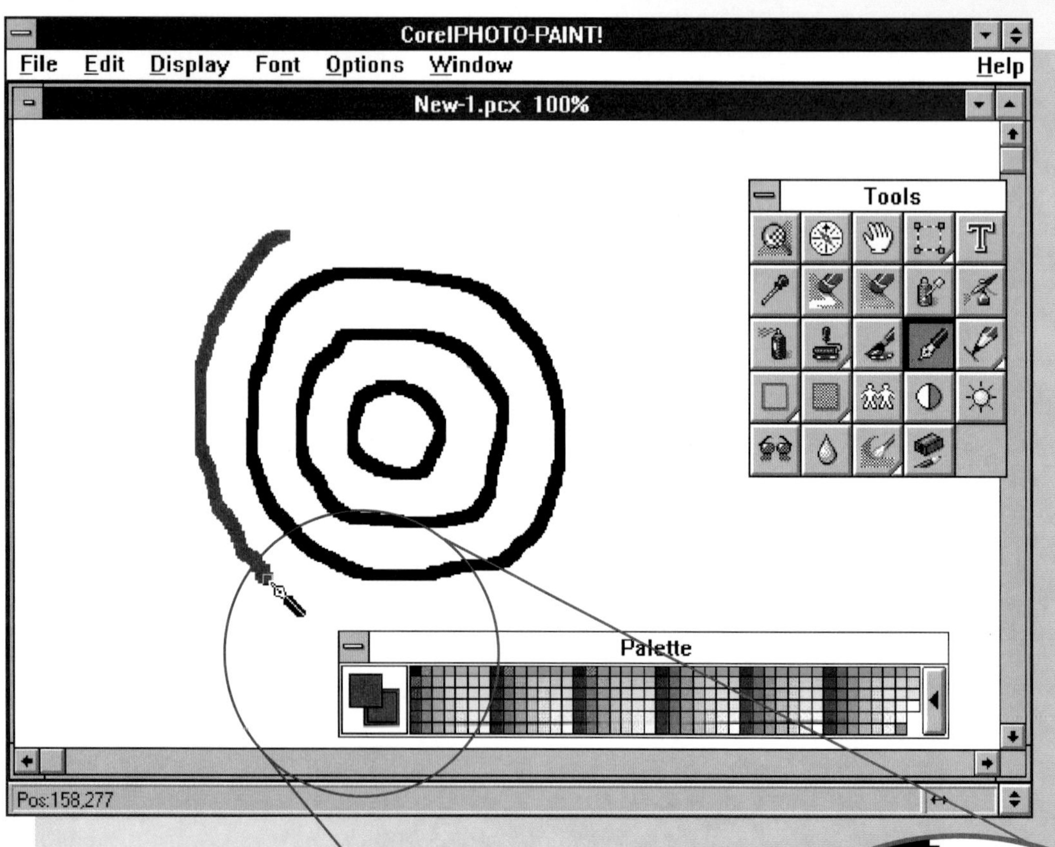

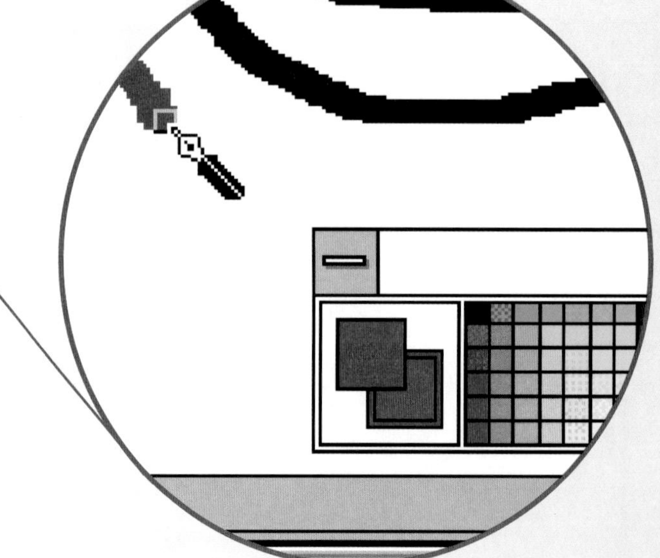

"Why would I do this?"

The color of the lines and strokes you paint is controlled by PHOTO-PAINT's Color Palette. The Color Palette is not displayed in the painting window by default. You must tell PHOTO-PAINT to display the palette by choosing Show Palette from the Display menu. Once the palette is opened, changing paint colors is as easy as pointing and clicking.

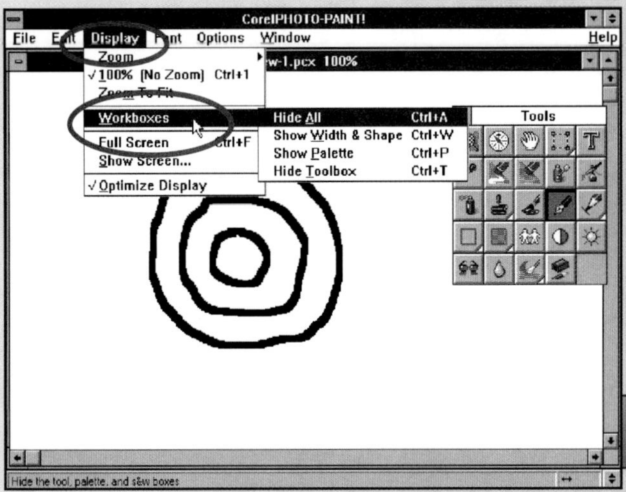

1 Click **Display** on the menu bar. Then click **Workboxes**. This step opens the Workboxes submenu.

2 Click **Show Palette** on the Workboxes submenu. The CorelPHOTO-PAINT Color Palette appears at the bottom of the screen.

NOTE

In PHOTO-PAINT 4, a Color Selection roll-up window is displayed by default when you start PHOTO-PAINT.

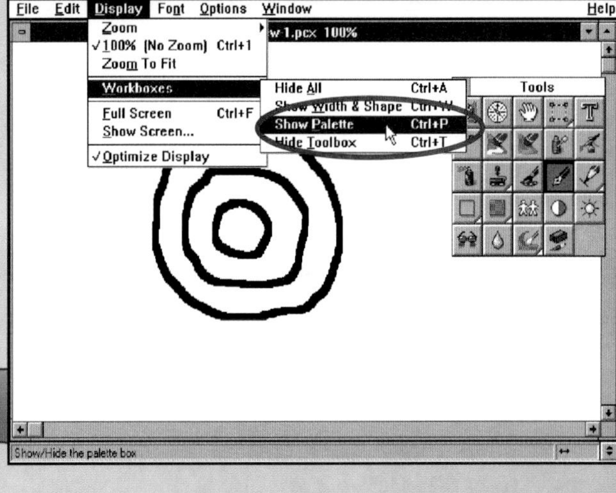

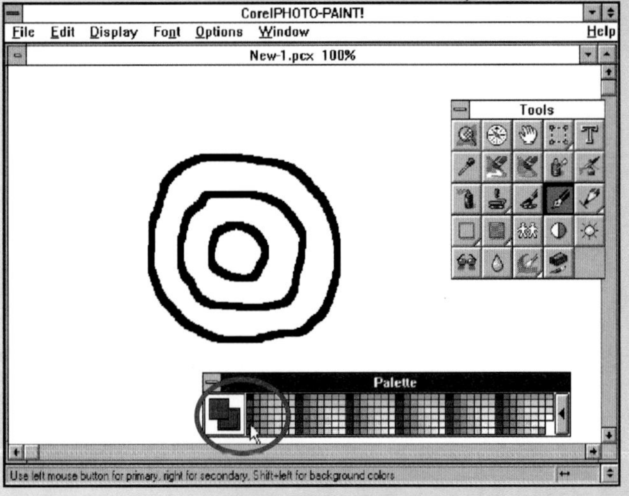

3 Point to **red** (or any other color) in the Color Palette (or the Color Selection roll-up in PHOTO-PAINT 4), and click the left mouse button. Move the pointer to the painting window and drag to create another line. The color of the line is now the color you chose. This step changes the color of the Pen tool's paint.

TASK 57

Filling an Area with Color

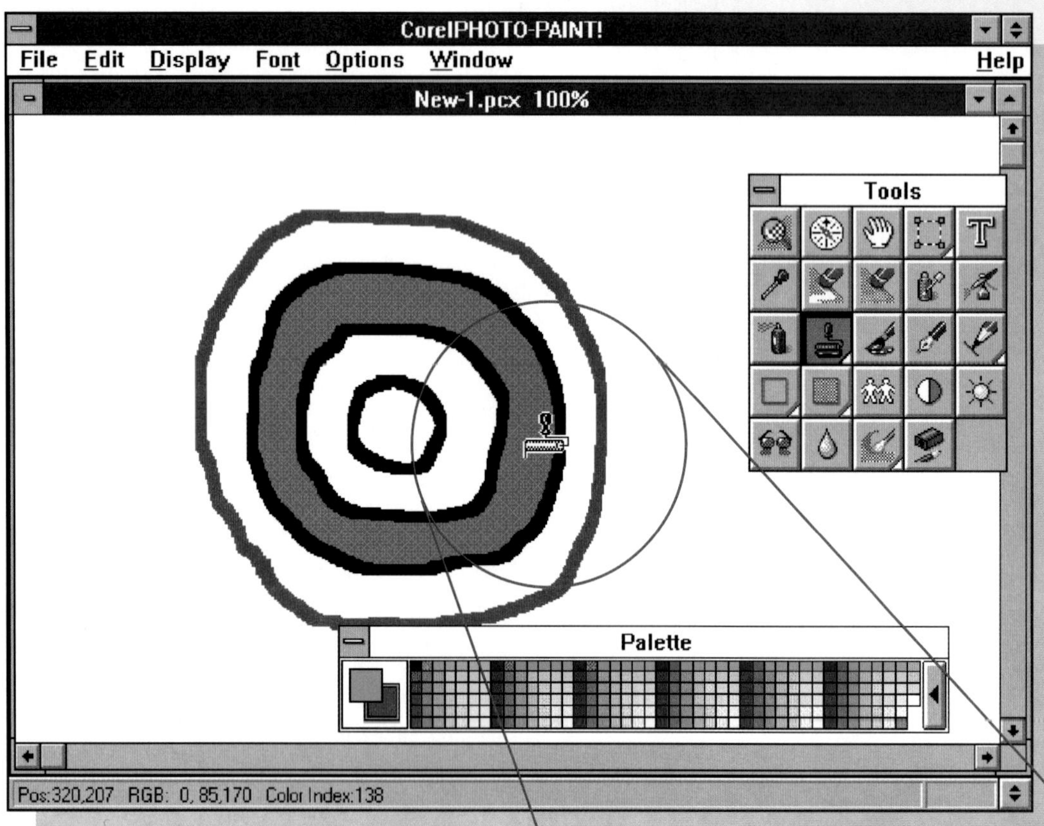

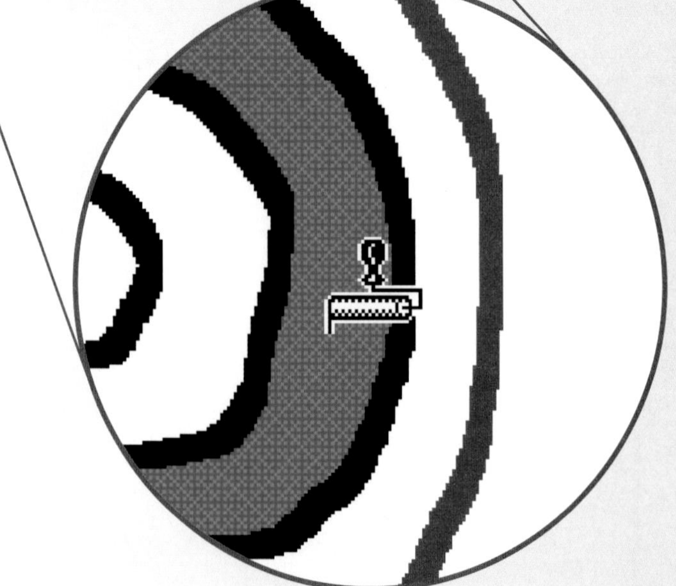

"Why would I do this?"

You can use the Flood Fill tool to fill an area of your painting with color. Other fill tools, located on the Fill tool submenu, can give your paintings different effects. The Tile tool, for example, adds a repeating pattern to the enclosed area; the Gradient tool adds a blend of color to the enclosed area.

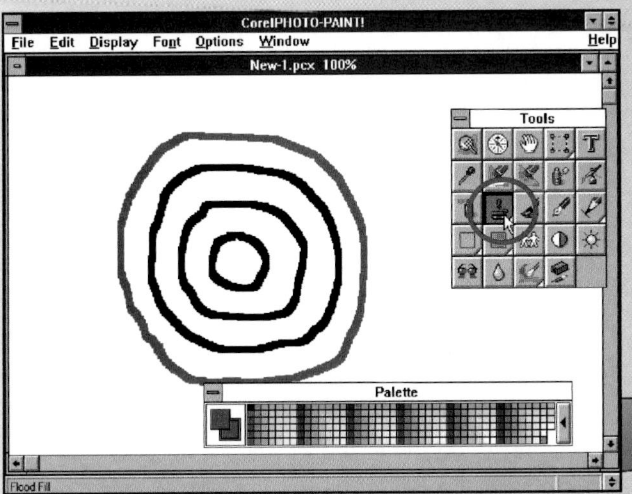

1 Click the **Flood** tool in the Tool Palette. This step selects the Flood tool.

WHY WORRY?

If a different fill icon appears in place of the Flood Fill icon, position the pointer over the fill icon and hold the mouse button. Move the mouse to the Flood Fill icon on the fly-out menu that appears. Release the mouse button.

2 Click a color in the Color Palette at the bottom of the screen, or in the Color Selection roll-up window in PHOTO-PAINT 4. The color indicator box changes to the color you select.

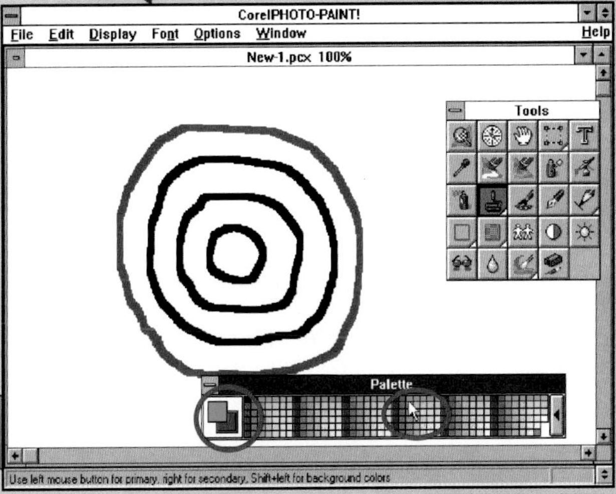

3 Position the pointer in the area you want to fill. The pointer changes to a paint roller icon when it enters the painting window. Click the mouse button. This step fills the area with the color selected in step 2.

TASK 58

Filling an Area with a Texture (version 4)

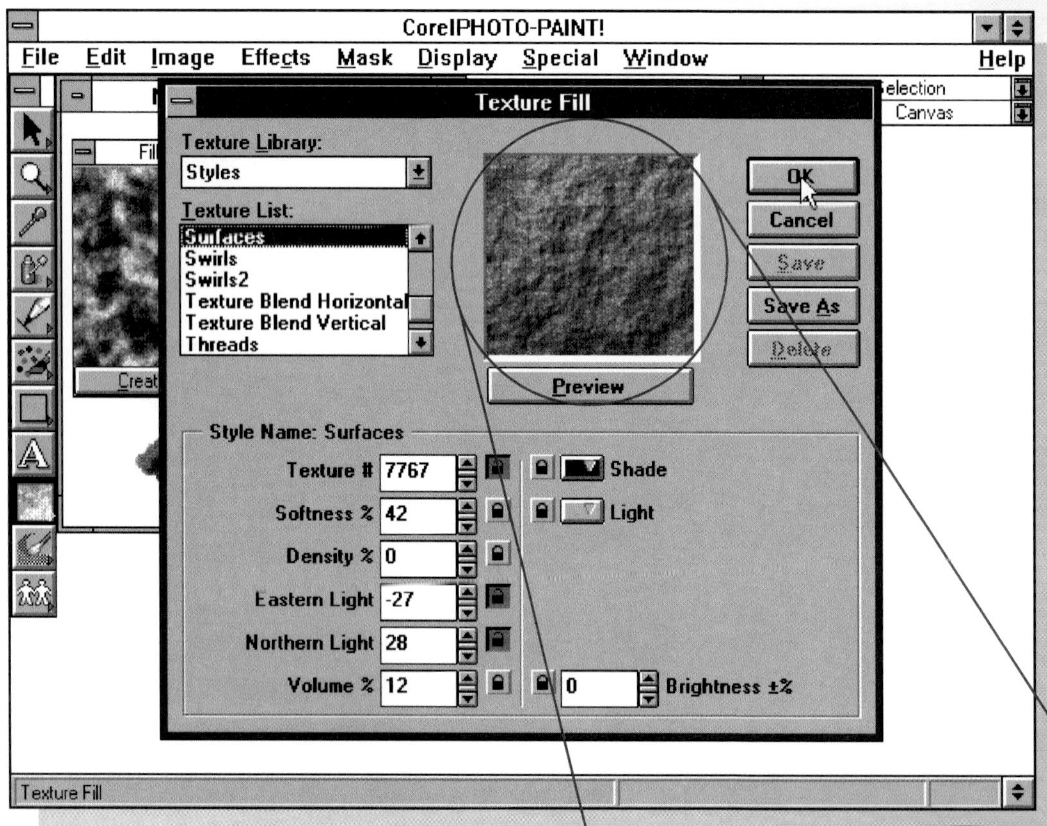

"Why would I do this?"

CorelPHOTO-PAINT 4 adds another fill option with the Texture tool. If you want to fill an enclosed area with a cloudy sky look, or perhaps a granite or marble texture, the Texture tool can do it.

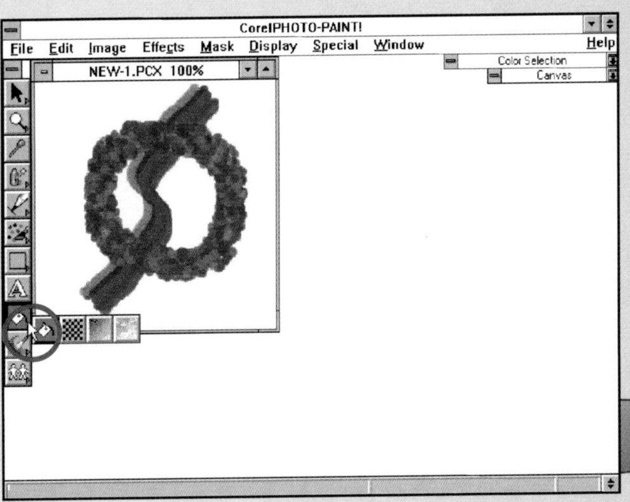

1 Click the **triangle** in the lower-right corner of the Flood Fill icon, located in the toolbox. The Fill tool fly-out menu appears.

2 Click the **Texture** tool on the fly-out menu. This step selects the Texture tool. Then double-click the **Texture** tool in the toolbox. The Fill Settings roll-up window appears, displaying the current texture setting of the Texture tool.

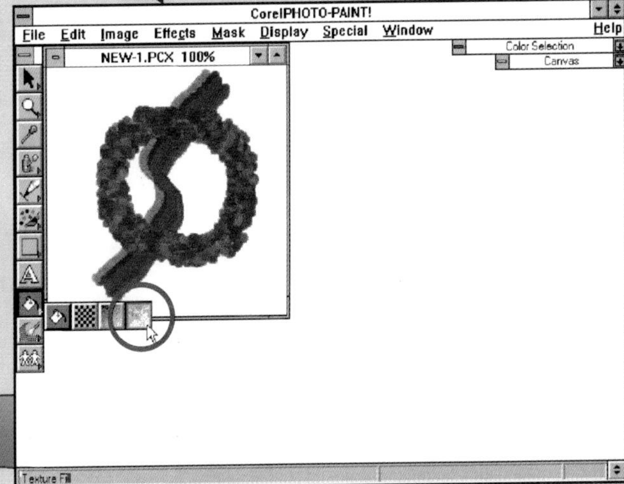

NOTE

You also can open the Fill Settings roll-up window by clicking Fill Setting roll-up on the Display menu.

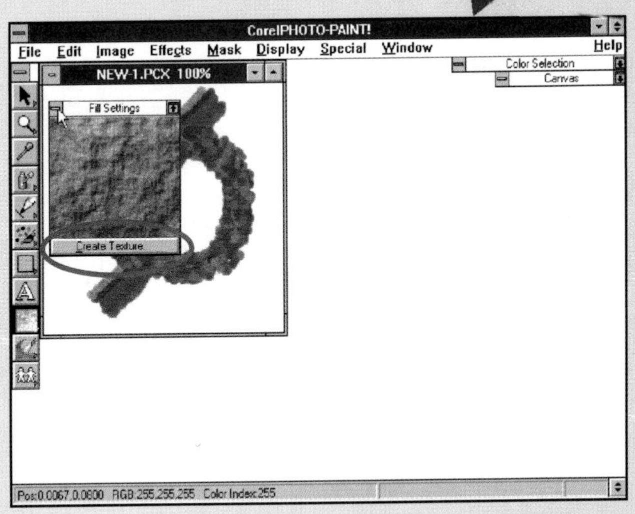

3 Click **Create Texture** on the Fill Setting roll-up window. The Texture Fill dialog box opens. The Texture Fill dialog box enables you to choose from many different textures available in CorelPHOTO-PAINT 4.

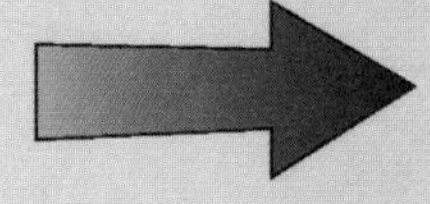

Task 58: Filling an Area with a Texture (version 4)

4 Scroll down the list of available textures, and click the selection for the type of text to use. The Texture Preview section of the dialog box displays the texture. Click **OK**. The Preview window shows the new Texture tool setting.

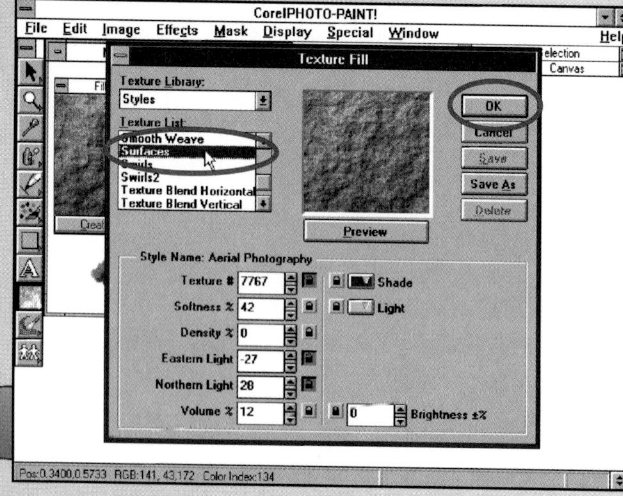

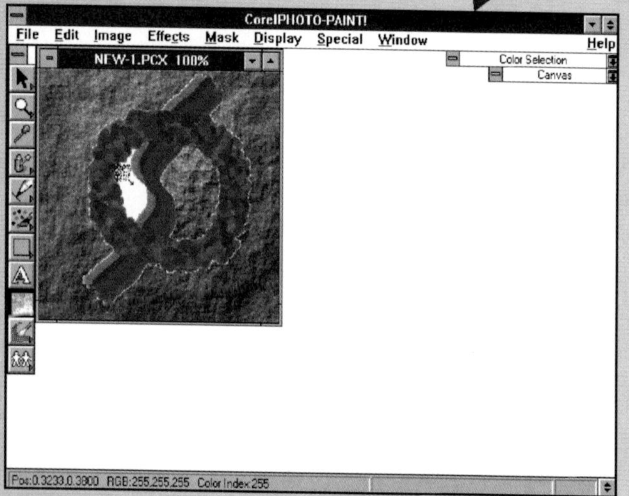

5 Move the pointer to the painting window. The pointer changes to the Texture Fill tool. Click the mouse button. The painting window fills with the new texture.

TASK 59

Blending an Area

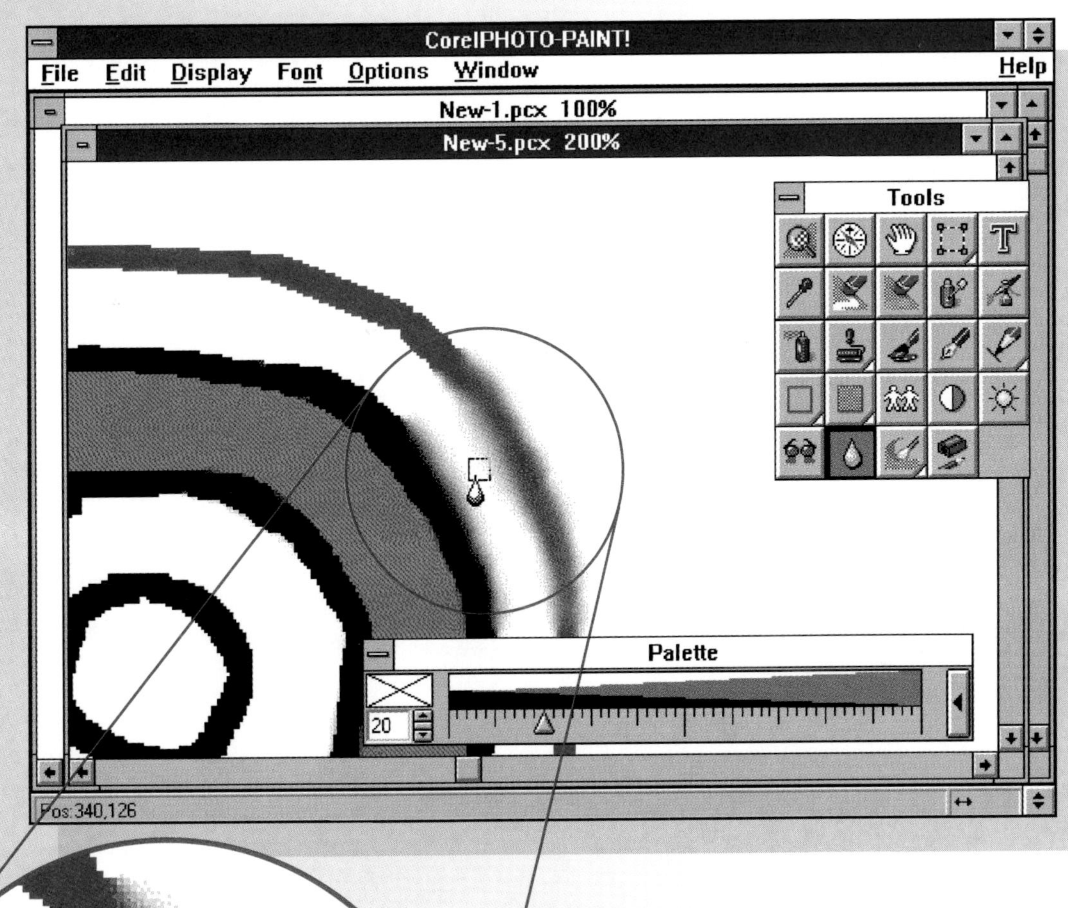

"Why would I do this?"

The Blend tool smoothes and softens an area of your painting. Using the Blend tool, you can smooth the transition between two colors of paint, softening the abrupt change between the colors.

Task 59: Blending an Area

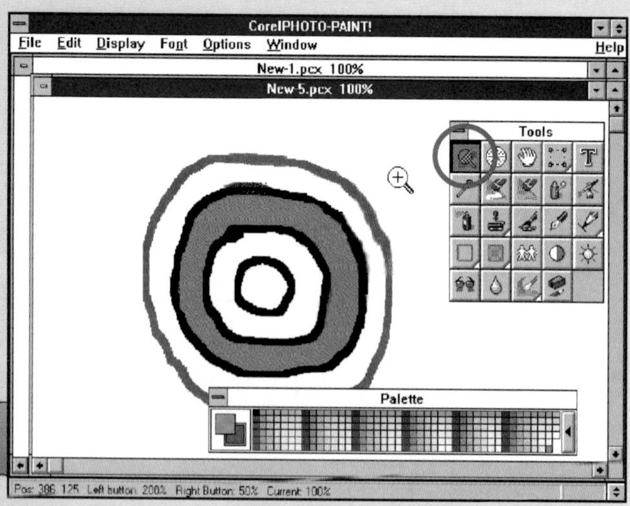

1 Click the **Zoom** tool in the toolbox. Position the pointer near the center of the painting window and click. The painting is enlarged to 200 percent. This step enlarges the painting so that you can better see the Blend effect.

NOTE

To reduce the size of the painting with the Zoom tool selected, click the right mouse button.

2 Click the **Freehand Blend** tool in the toolbox. The Freehand Blend Palette appears at the bottom of the screen.

WHY WORRY?

The Blend tool is not available in 256 Color mode. To use this tool, the painting mode must be 24-bit color or grayscale. Convert the painting mode by selecting Convert To on the Edit menu in PHOTO-PAINT 3, or on the Image menu in version 4.

3 Move the pointer to an area of the painting. The pointer changes to the Freehand Blend tool—a candle flame shape. Hold the mouse button and drag across the images in the painting. As you drag, the colors are blended together.

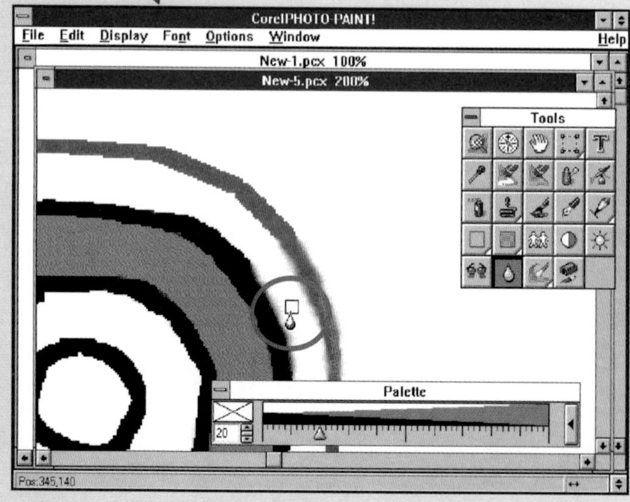

TASK 60

Smudging an Area

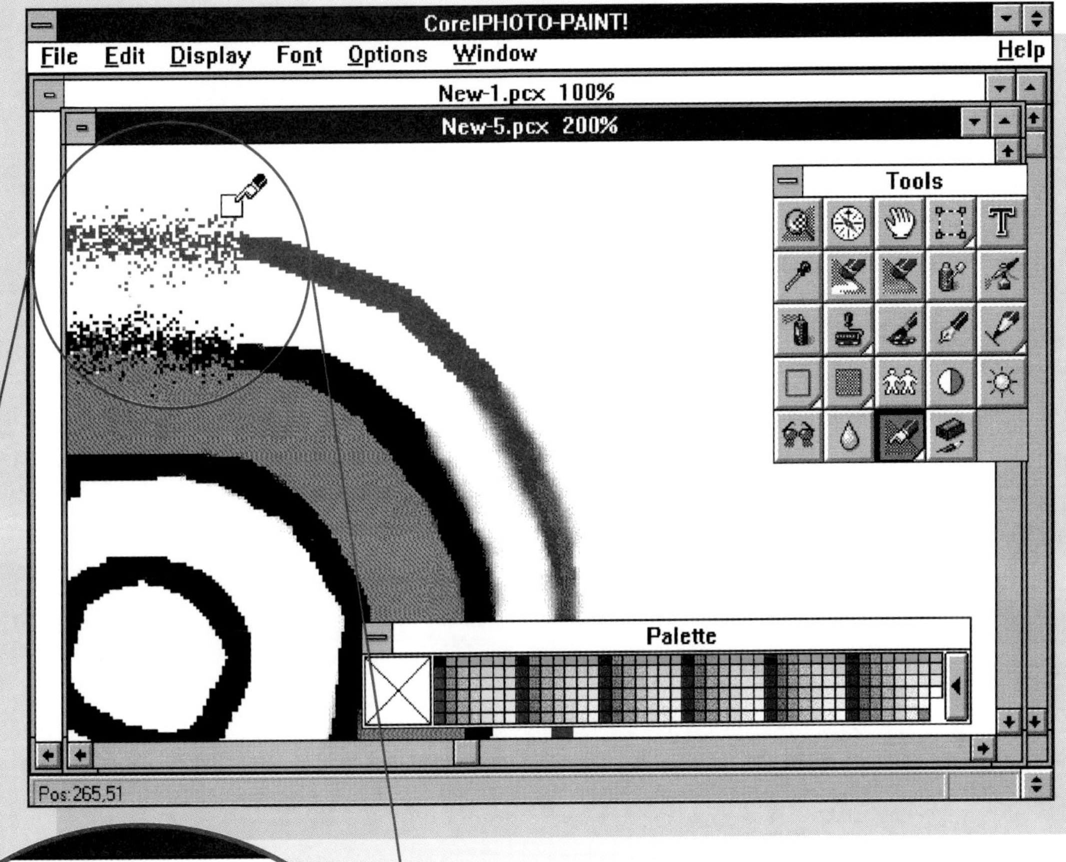

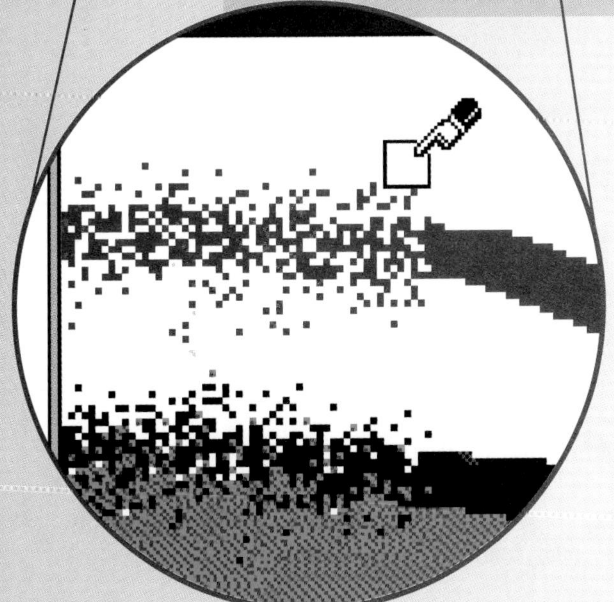

"Why would I do this?"

The Smudge tool randomly mixes dots of color in the painting. Smudging an area of your painting makes the area look coarse and textured, like sandpaper.

Task 60: Smudging an Area

1 Position the mouse pointer on the **triangle** in the lower-right corner of the Smear tool in the Tool Palette. Hold the mouse button. Drag the pointer to the **Smudge** tool. Release the mouse button. This step selects the Smudge tool.

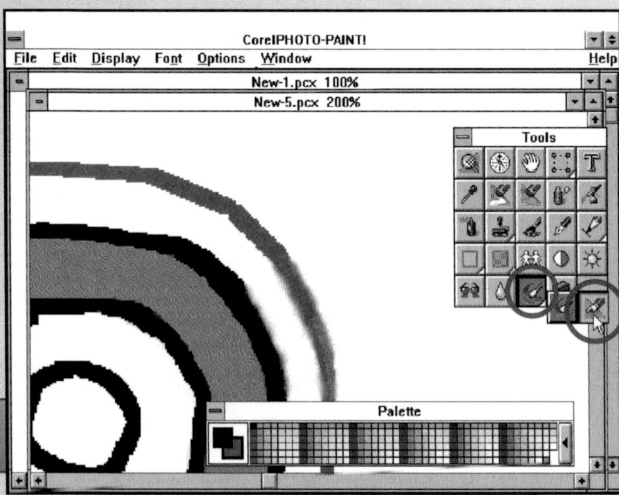

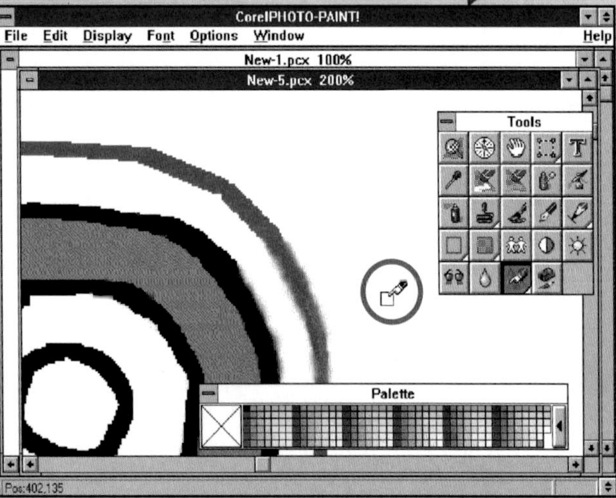

2 Move the pointer to the painting window. The pointer changes to the Smudge tool.

3 Drag across an area of the painting. As you drag, a dotted pattern appears beneath the Smudge tool's point. This step smudges the paint in your drawing.

WHY WORRY?

If you don't like the effect of the Smudge tool, click Undo on the Edit menu before performing any other operation. Any smudging you've done since you chose the tool will be undone.

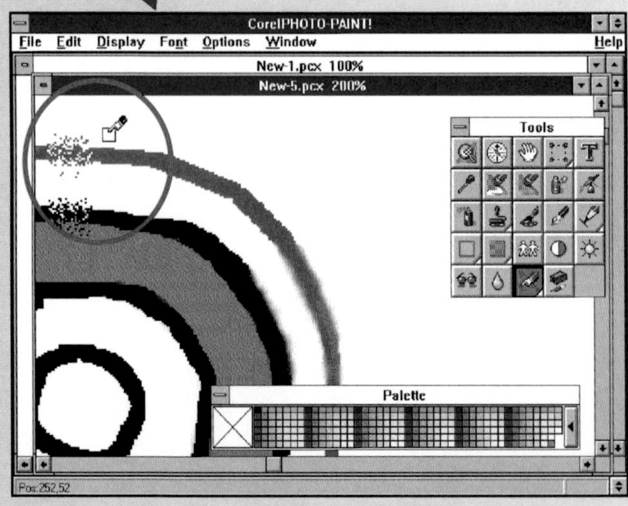

TASK 61

Smearing an Area

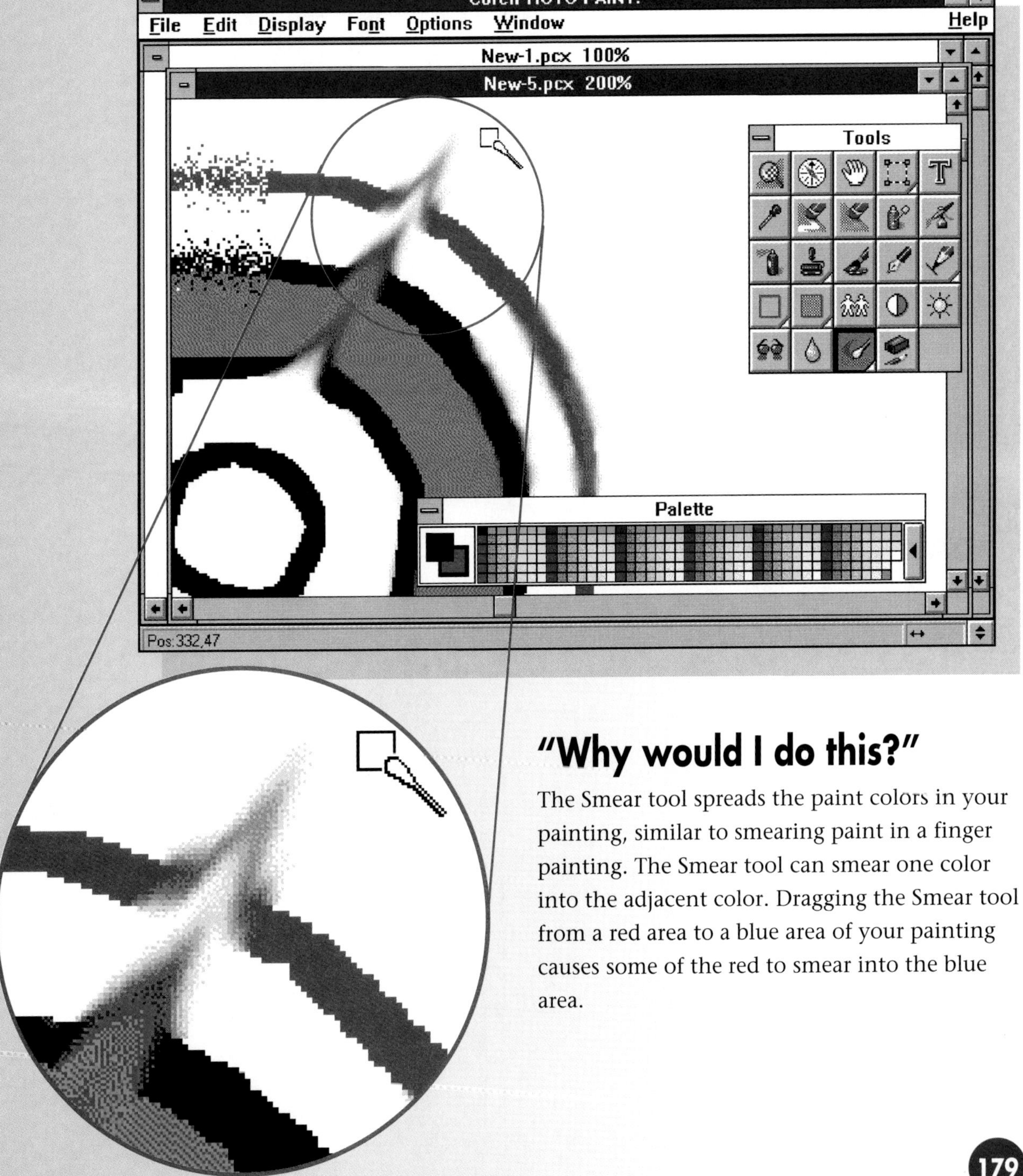

"Why would I do this?"

The Smear tool spreads the paint colors in your painting, similar to smearing paint in a finger painting. The Smear tool can smear one color into the adjacent color. Dragging the Smear tool from a red area to a blue area of your painting causes some of the red to smear into the blue area.

Task 61: Smearing an Area

1 Click the **Freehand Smear** tool on the Tool Palette. This step selects the Freehand Smear tool.

WHY WORRY?

If the Smudge tool is displayed in place of the Smear tool on the Tool Palette, hold the mouse button while pointing to the Smudge tool. A fly-out menu opens. Move the pointer over the Smear tool and release the mouse button.

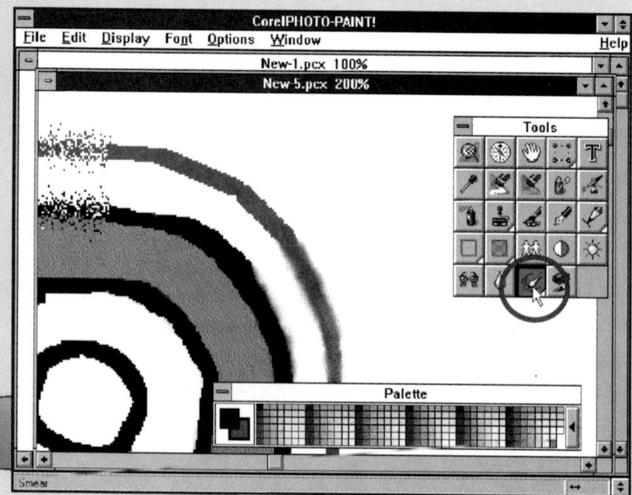

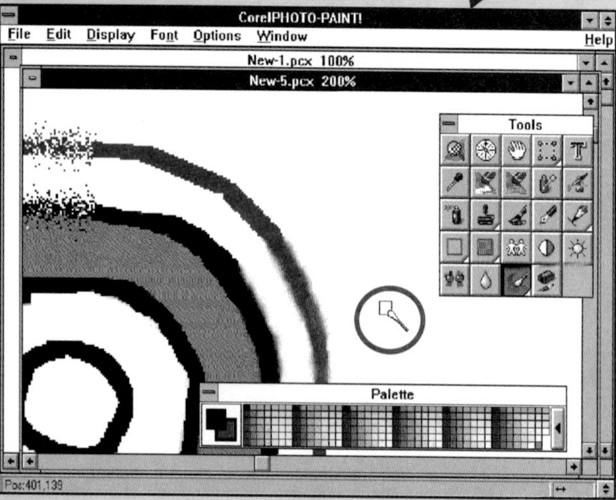

2 Move the pointer to the painting window. The pointer changes to the Freehand Smear tool.

3 Drag across an area of the painting. As you drag, the paint colors beneath the Smear tool tip are smeared together.

NOTE

The Smear tool is speed sensitive. The faster you move the Smear tool over the color area, the farther the color is smeared.

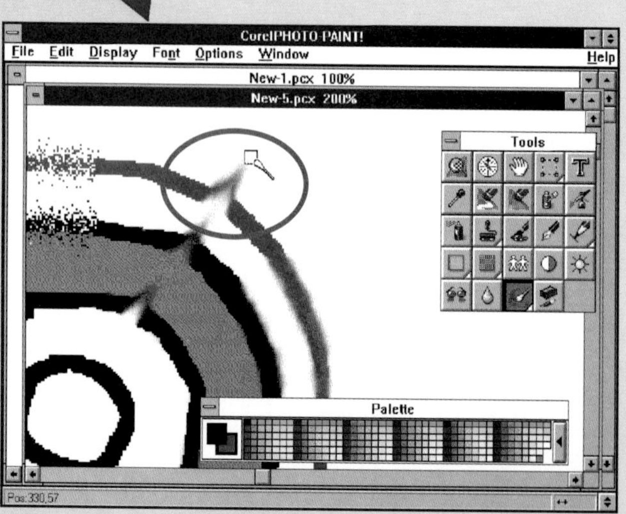

TASK 62

Sharpening an Area

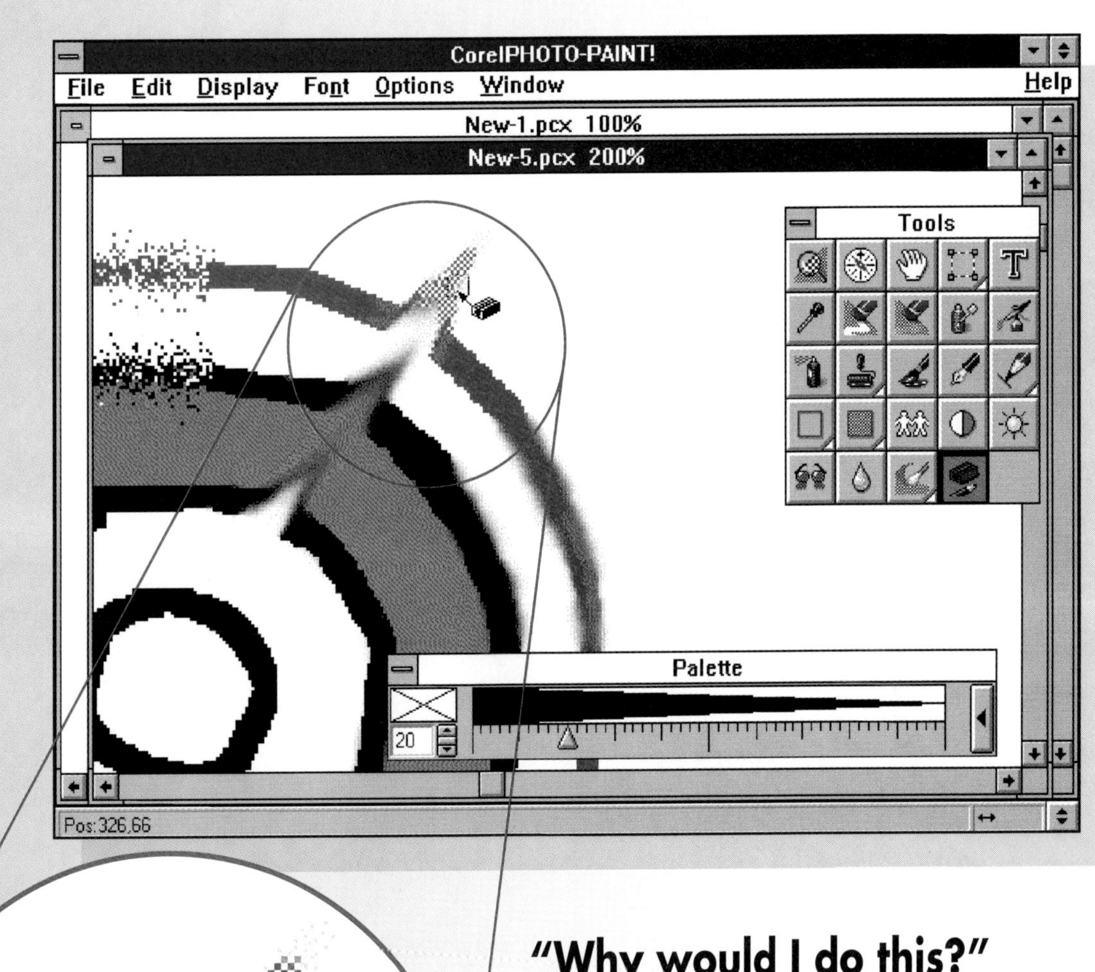

"Why would I do this?"

The Sharpen tool causes the edges and transitions between colors in your painting to become more defined. Dragging the Sharpen tool across a blurry edge causes the edge to look sharper.

Task 62: Sharpening an Area

1 Click the **Freehand Sharpen** tool in the Tool Palette. This step selects the Freehand Sharpen tool.

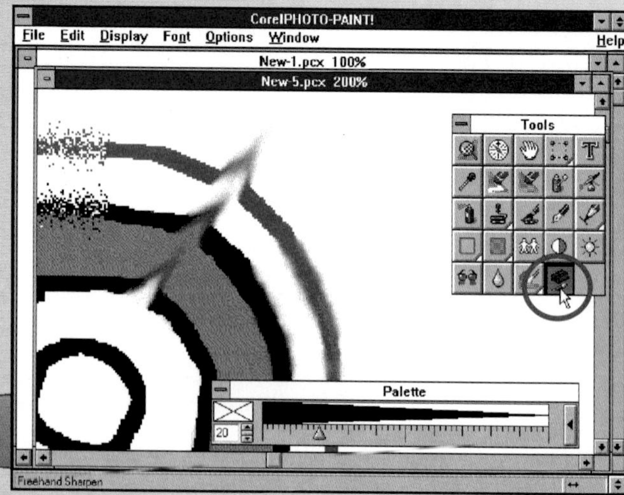

2 Move the pointer to the painting window. The pointer changes to the Freehand Sharpen tool.

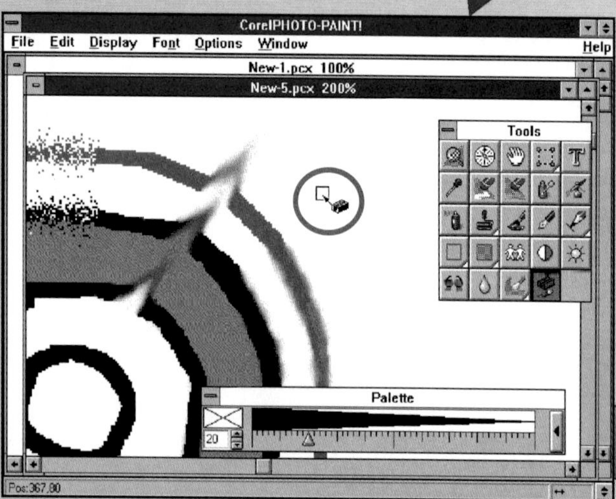

3 Drag across an area of the painting. As you drag, the paint dots beneath the Sharpen tool tip are sharpened.

NOTE

The Sharpen tool does not change the painting drastically. You may need to use the tool numerous times on one area to notice the effect of the tool.

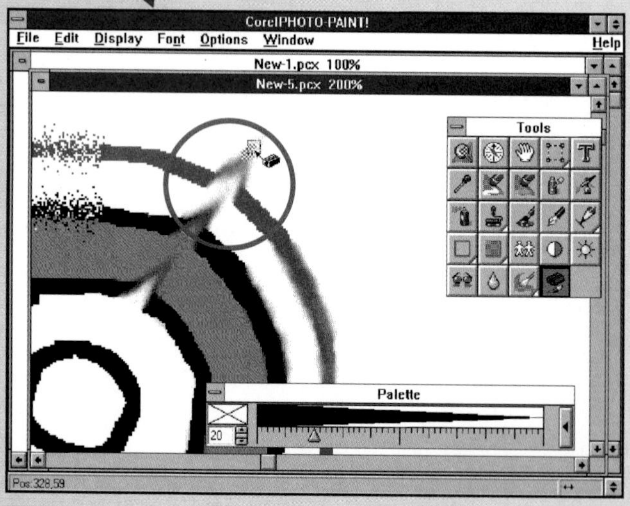

TASK 63

Erasing Part of a Picture

"Why would I do this?"

In CorelDRAW, you can select an individual object such as a line or circle and delete it. In CorelPHOTO-PAINT, you must erase instead of selecting and deleting. The Freehand Eraser tool erases a portion of your painting as you drag the tool in the painting window.

Task 63: Erasing Part of a Picture

1 Click the **Eraser** tool in the Tool Palette. This step selects the Eraser tool.

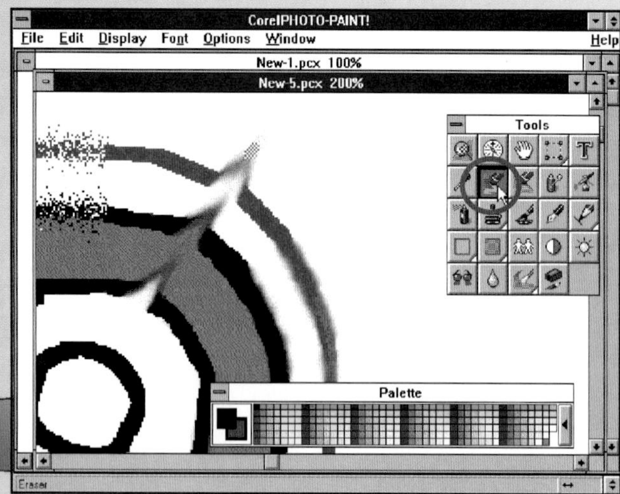

2 Move the pointer to the painting window. The pointer changes to the Eraser tool—shaped like a pencil eraser.

WHY WORRY?

You can erase the entire painting area by double-clicking on the Eraser tool.

3 Drag across an area of the painting. As you drag, the paint beneath the Eraser tool is erased.

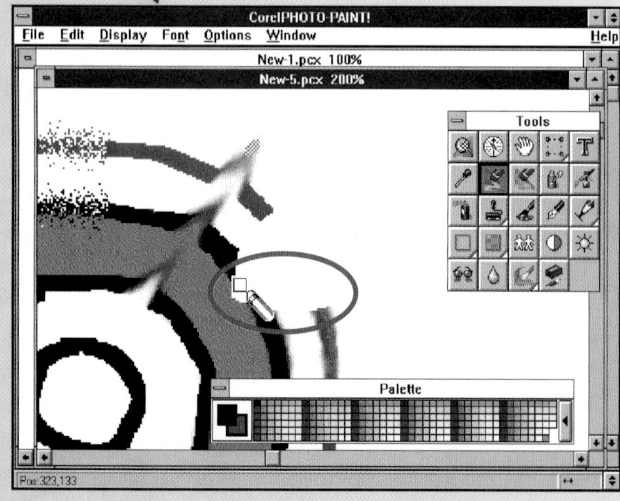

TASK 64

Starting CorelCHART

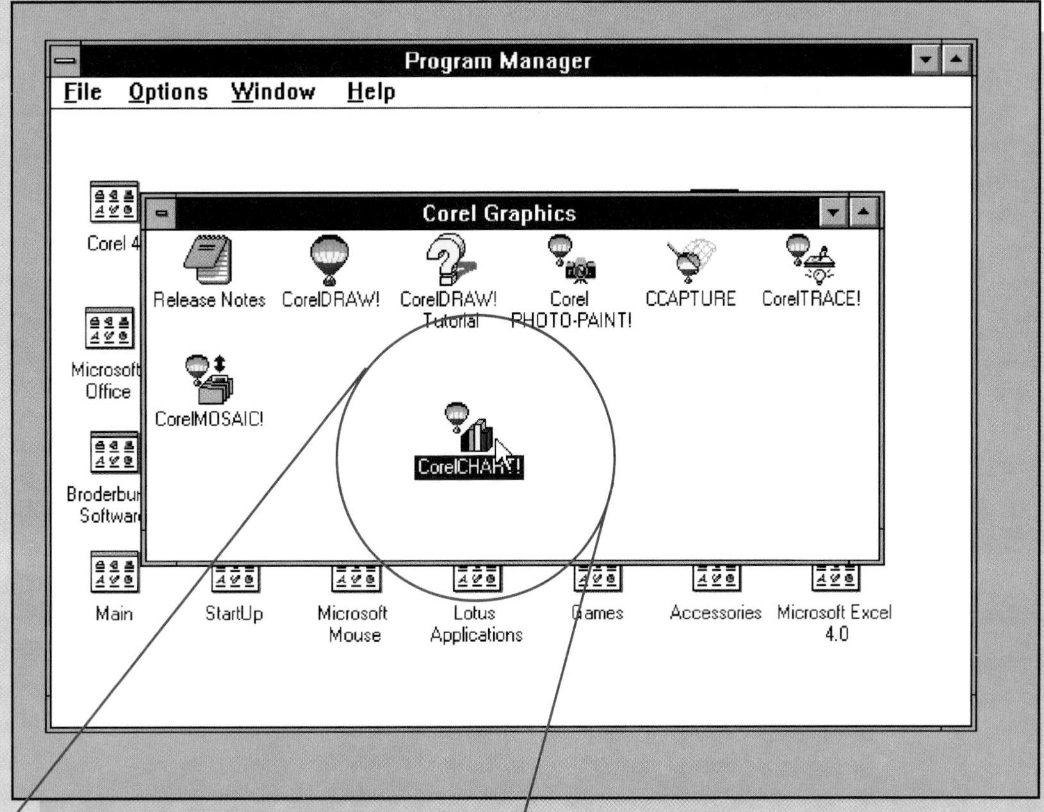

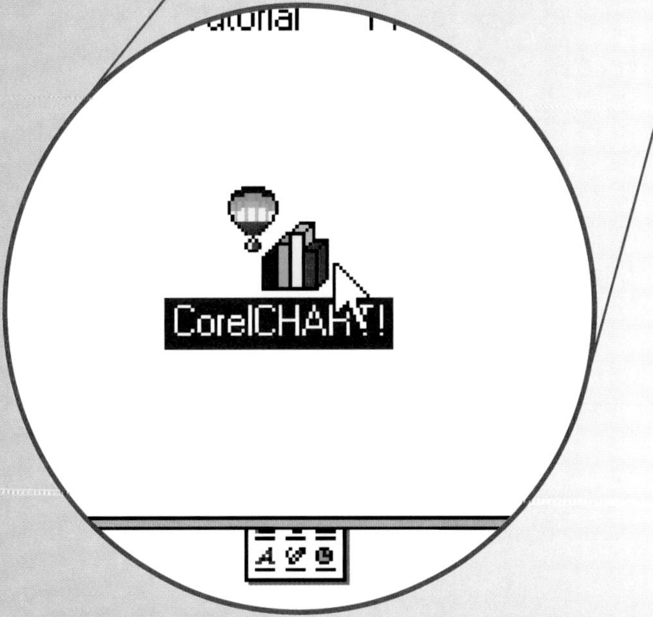

"Why would I do this?"

The CorelCHART application is represented by an icon of a 3-D Chart. Like other Windows applications, you can start CorelCHART by double-clicking its icon.

Task 64: Starting CorelCHART

1 Double-click the icon labeled **Corel Graphics** in the Program Manager window. This step opens the Corel Graphics program group window.

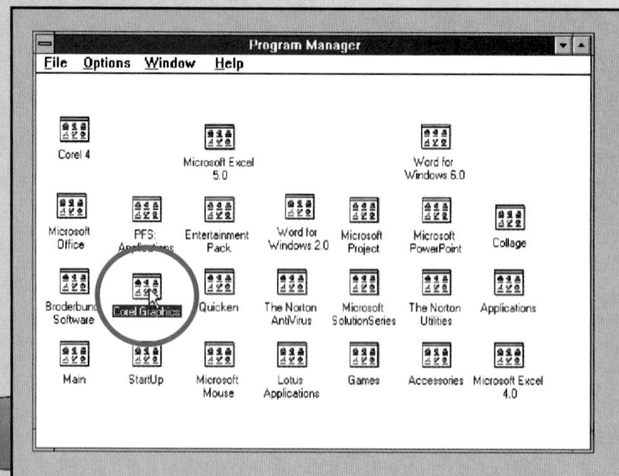

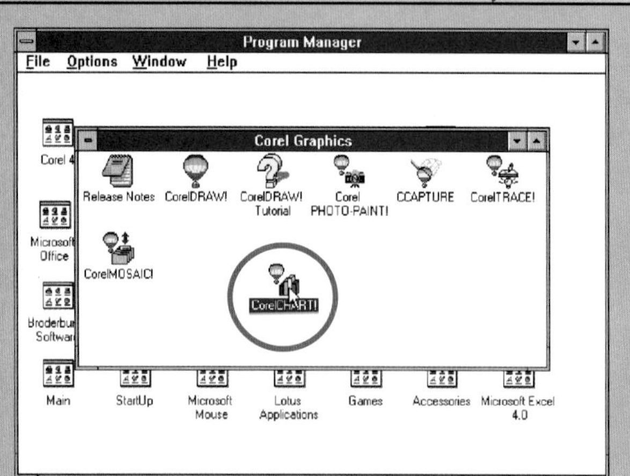

2 Double-click the **CorelCHART** icon in the Corel program group window. This step starts CorelCHART.

WHY WORRY?

If the CorelCHART icon does not appear in the Corel Graphics program group, it was not installed. Run the CorelDRAW install program, and install the CorelCHART module of the set of Corel programs.

3 The main CorelCHART window appears on your screen. Notice that the CorelCHART window does not contain a new file ready for you to work on, like CorelDRAW does when it is first started.

NOTE

To start CorelCHART with the keyboard, press Ctrl+Tab until the Corel Program Group icon is highlighted, and then press Enter. Press the right-arrow key until the CorelCHART icon is highlighted, and press Enter again.

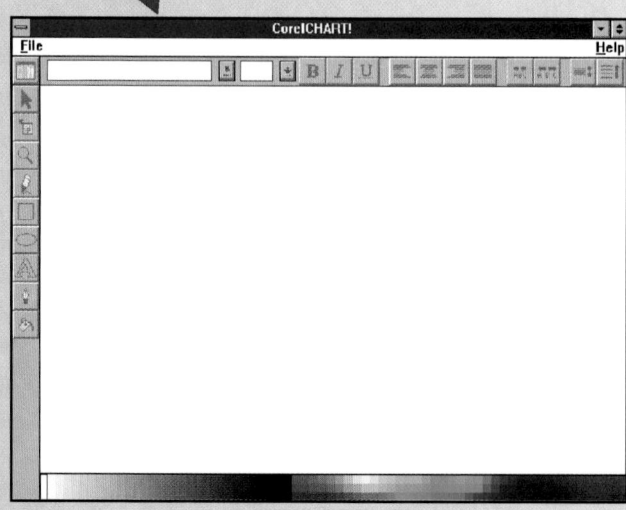

TASK 65

Selecting a Chart Template

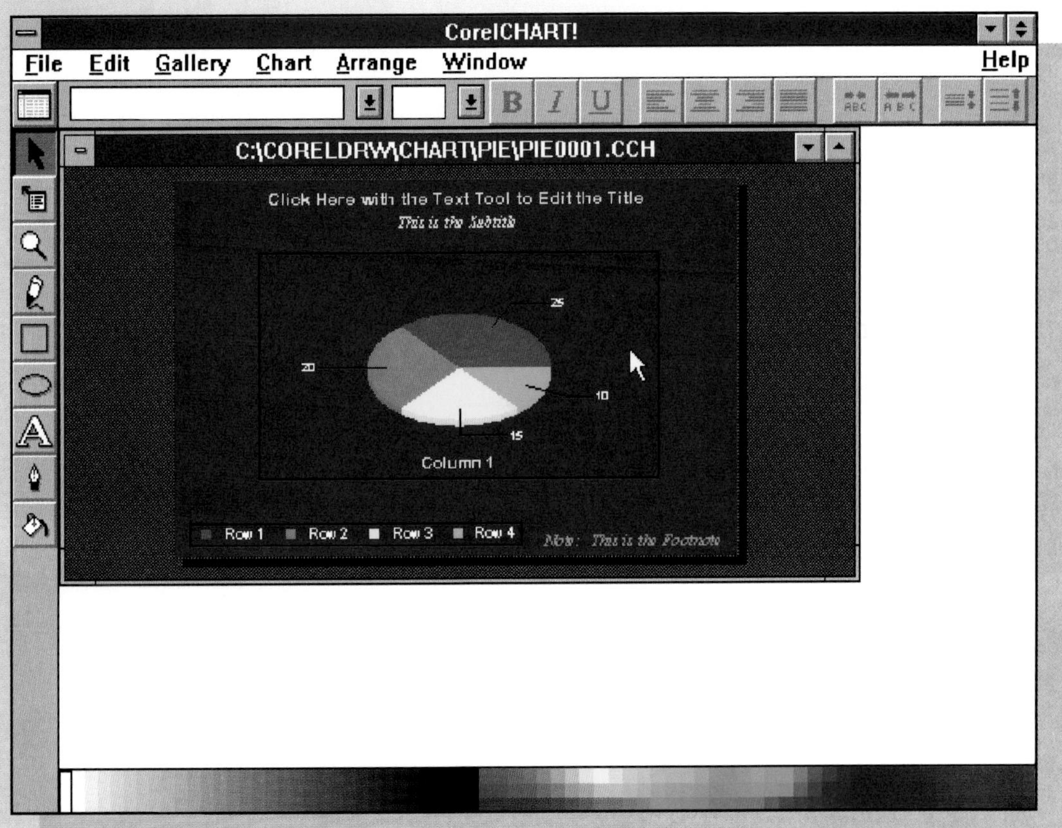

"Why would I do this?"

Rather than creating a chart from scratch, it is easier to start with one of CorelCHART's templates and modify the data and appearance of the chart to meet your needs. CorelCHART comes with dozens of templates to choose from, so you're likely to find one that is similar to the one you want to create.

Task 65: Selecting a Chart Template

1 Click **File** on the menu bar. Then click **Open.** This step opens the Open Chart dialog box.

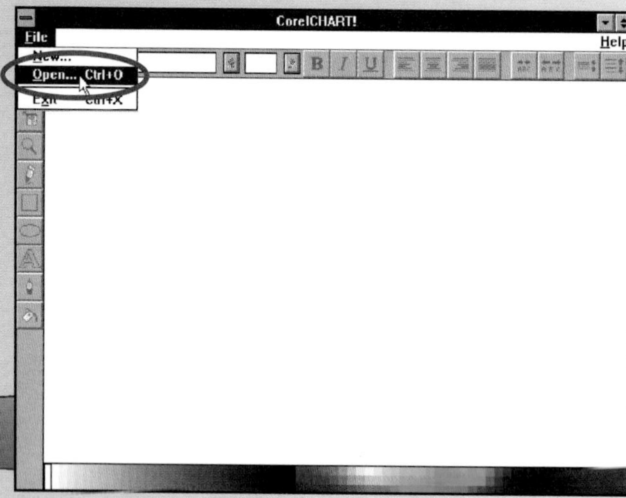

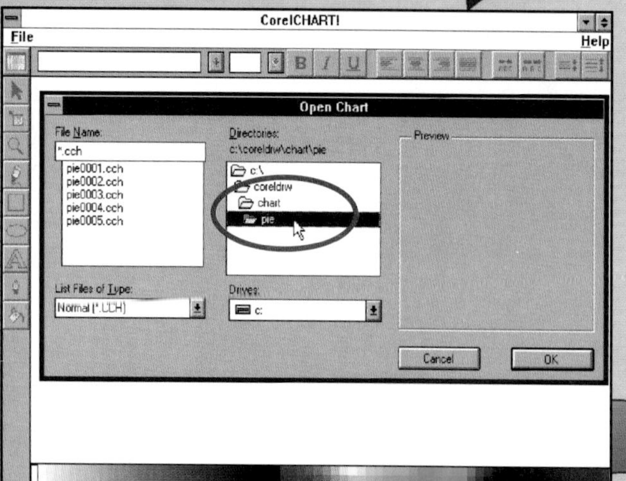

2 In the Open Chart dialog box, navigate the directories list and locate the Chart subdirectory under the coreldrw directory. Double-click **Chart** to reveal the chart type subdirectories. Double-click a chart-type subdirectory. The files in the chart-type subdirectory appear in the Files section of the dialog box.

3 Click a file name in the File Name list box, **pie0001.cch** in this example. Notice that the preview image of the chart appears in the Preview portion of the dialog box. Click **OK**. This step selects the chart template and opens it. The chart window opens.

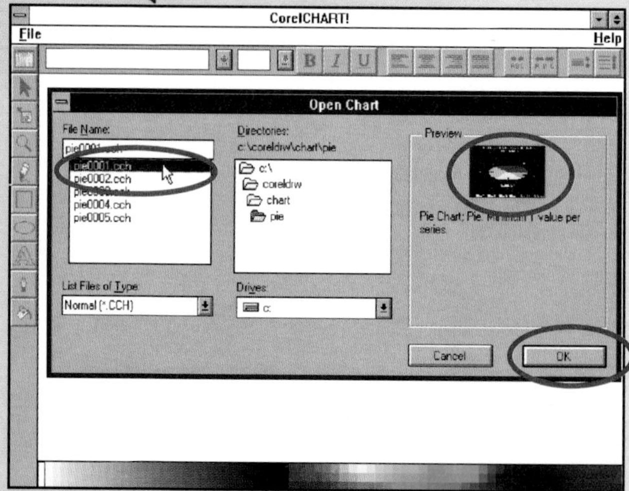

TASK 66

Switching between Chart View and the Data Manager

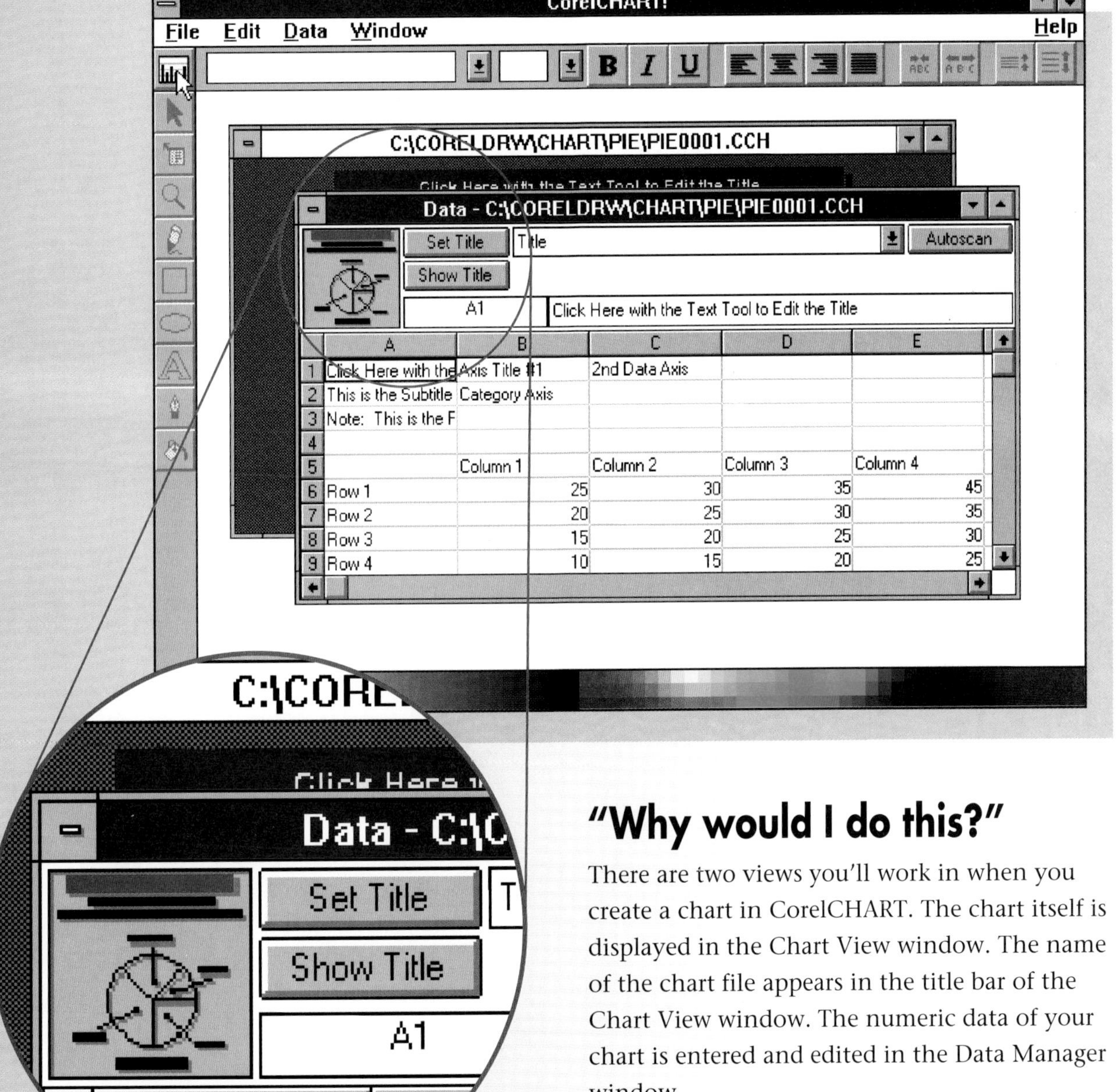

"Why would I do this?"

There are two views you'll work in when you create a chart in CorelCHART. The chart itself is displayed in the Chart View window. The name of the chart file appears in the title bar of the Chart View window. The numeric data of your chart is entered and edited in the Data Manager window.

Task 66: Switching between Chart View and the Data Manager

1 Click the **Data Manager View** icon located at the top of the toolbox. This step changes to CorelCHART's Data Manager view. The Data Manager window opens and is placed over the pie chart window. You enter your chart's numeric data in the Data Manager window.

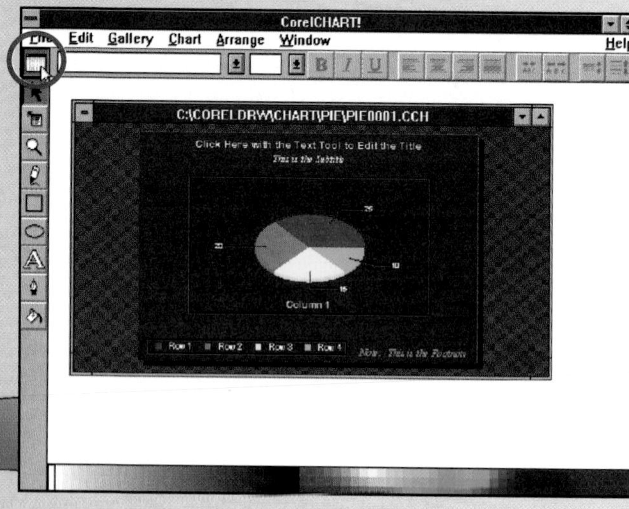

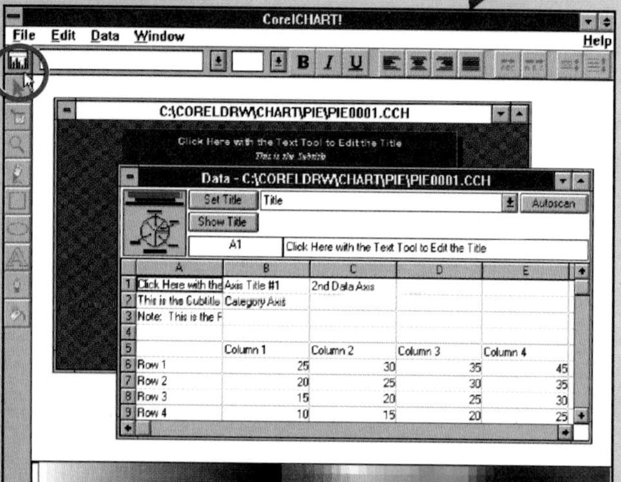

2 Click the **Chart View** icon located at the top of the toolbox. The chart window is displayed.

NOTE

You also can change between the Data Manager and the Chart view by selecting the window names that appear at the end of the Window menu.

TASK 67

Entering Text and Numbers in the Data Manager

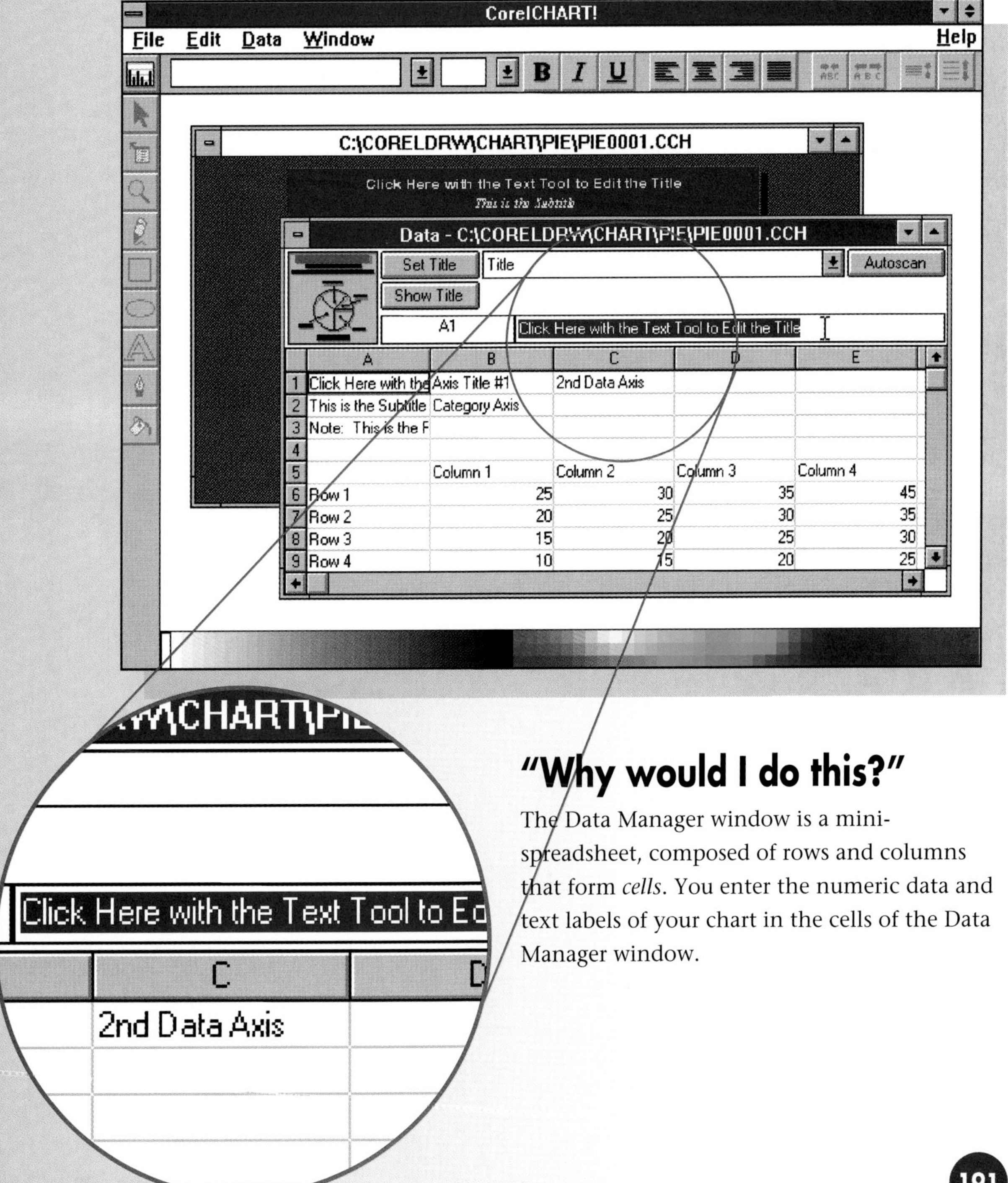

"Why would I do this?"

The Data Manager window is a mini-spreadsheet, composed of rows and columns that form *cells*. You enter the numeric data and text labels of your chart in the cells of the Data Manager window.

Task 67: Entering Text and Numbers in the Data Manager

1 Click cell **A1** in the Data Manager window. The text `Click Here with the Text Tool to Edit the Title` appears in the editing box of the Data Manager window. This step prepares the contents of cell A1 for editing.

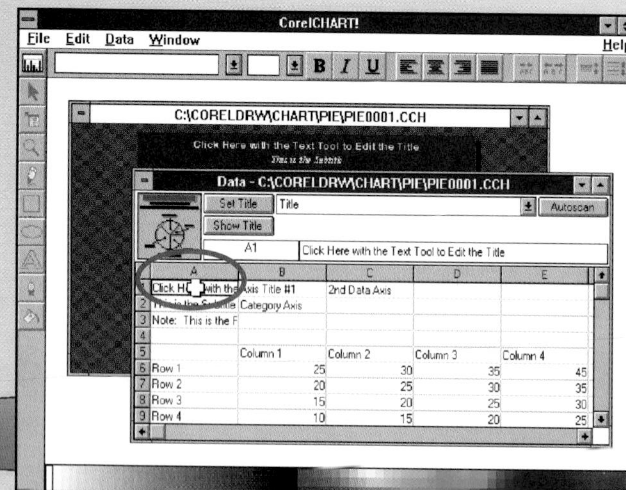

2 Position the pointer at the end of the text in the editing box of the Data Manager. The pointer changes to an I-beam shape. Drag over the text to select it. The text is highlighted as you drag over it.

3 Type a title for the chart, **1994 Sales by Region** in this example. The highlighted text is replaced by the text you type. This new text will be the title of your chart.

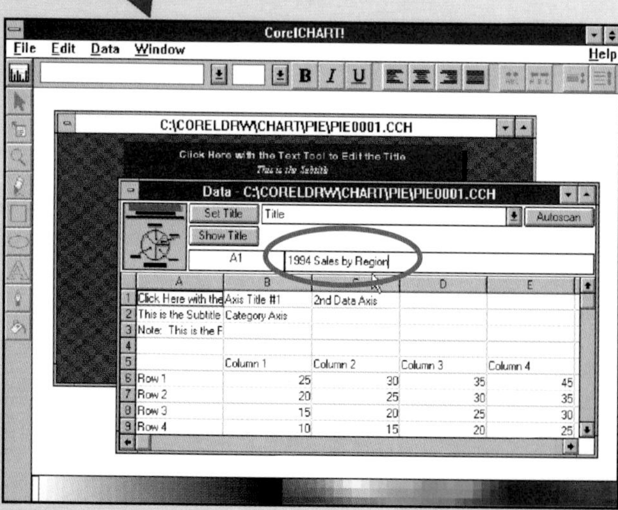

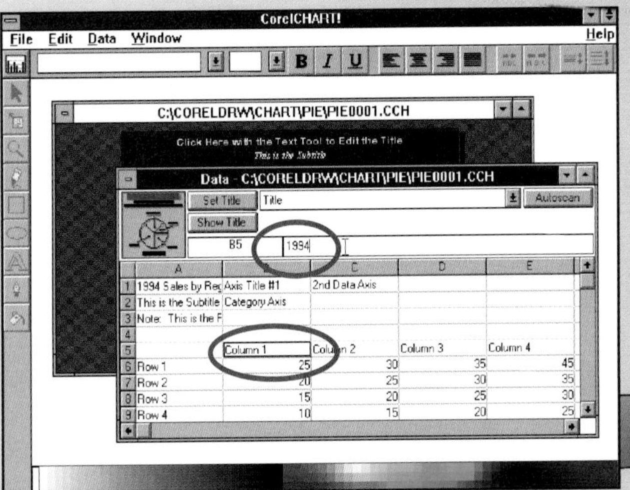

4 Click a column label cell, cell **B5** in this example. Highlight the contents of the editing line, and type a column name, **1994** in this example. This step enters the name of the column in the pie chart.

5 Click a row name cell, cell **A6** in this example. Highlight the contents of the editing line, and type a new row name, **North** in this example. Repeat this process for each row of data in your chart. This step enters the names of the wedges in the pie chart.

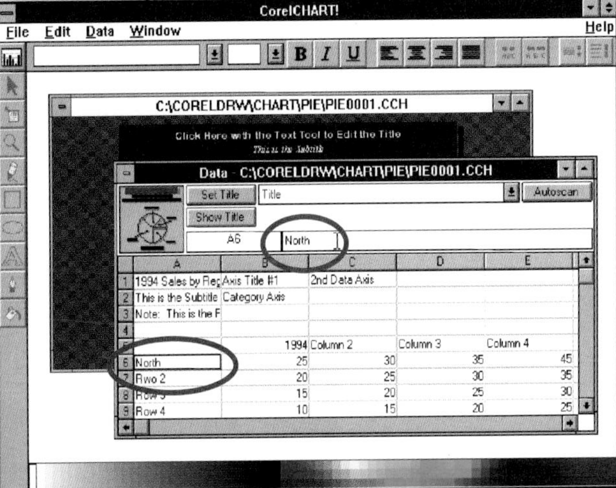

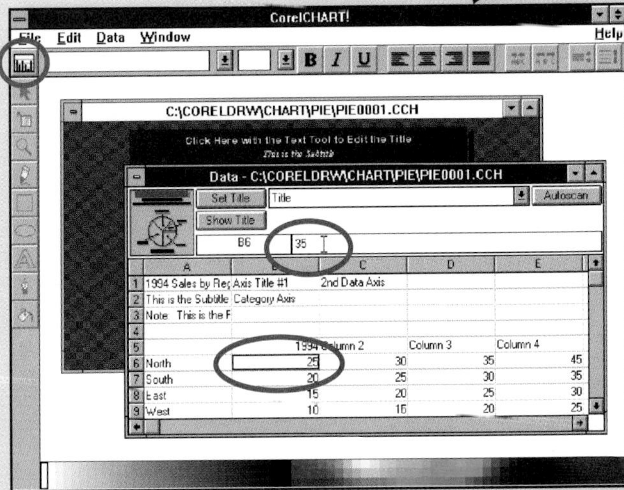

6 Click a data cell, cell **B6** in this example. Double-click the editing line to highlight the number. Type a new number for the cell. This step changes the number for the North region in this example. Click the **Chart View** icon in the toolbox to see the chart with the changes you've made.

TASK 68

Changing the Chart Type

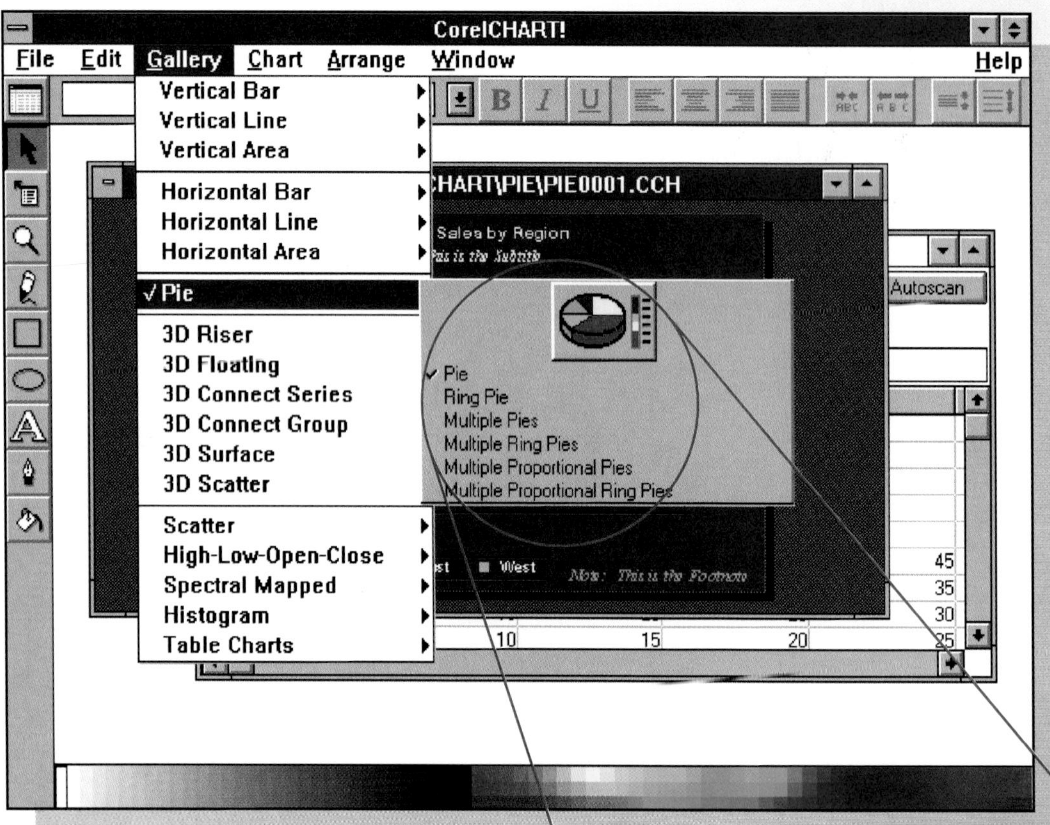

"Why would I do this?"

CorelCHART offers dozens of types of charts, from pie charts and three-dimensional column charts to scatter graphs and histogram plots. Once you have entered your data in the Data Manager, you can select different chart types to experiment with the data display.

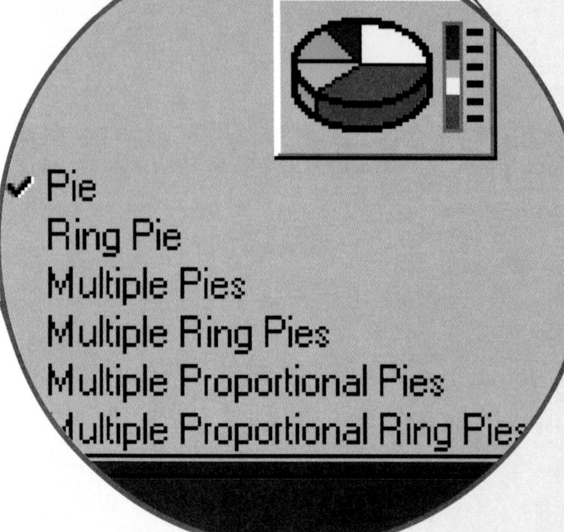

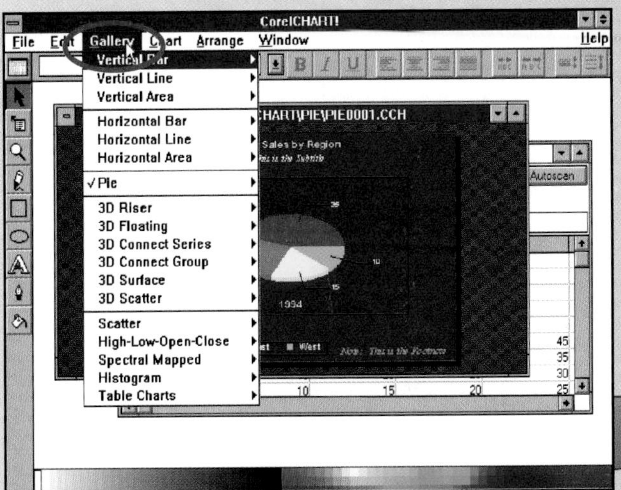

1 Click **Gallery** on the menu bar. This step opens the Gallery menu. The Gallery menu lists the chart types available to you.

2 Click a new chart type on the Gallery menu. The chart type submenu appears. Most chart types have several variations to choose from.

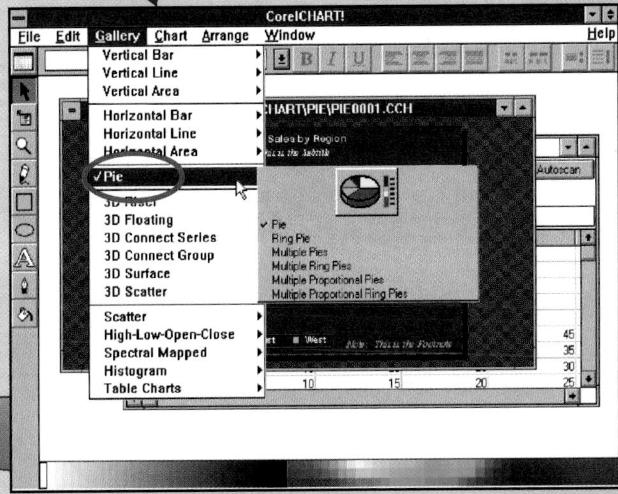

3 Click a chart type on the submenu. The Chart window changes to display the new chart type, six pie charts in this example.

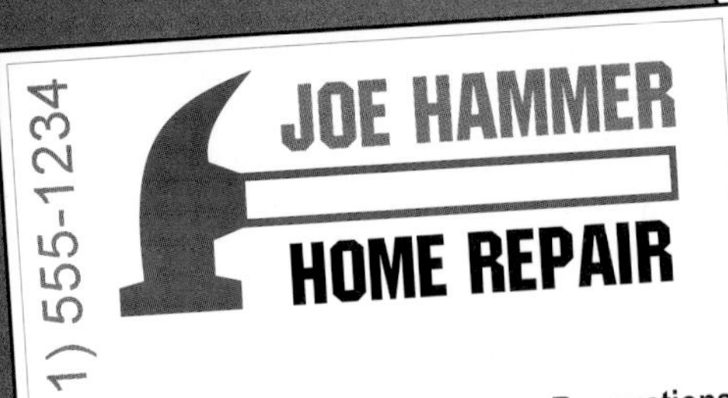

JOE HAMMER
HOME REPAIR
(111) 555-1234
Painting, Drywall, Plumbing, Renovations

Andes Tree Surgeons
1234 East Posadas Blvd., Santiago, Chile 234566-56

AIRCRAFT FOR SALE

Bud's Used Birds

Located behind the Twisty Freeze on Clancy Ave.

A10 $1,200,000

Best deal on the lot. Will consider trade for tanning bed.

Piper Cub 210 $1,200,000

Bud's mother's plane. Only flown on Sundays.

Cobra $1,200,000

Runs good. Needs some rotor work. Good wood hauler.

MiG $1,200,000

We bought too many. Straight from our Soviet Comrades.

F-16 $1,199,995

Just back from one-year lease. Like new. Some rips in upholstery.

PART VII

Sample Documents

- Creating a Logotype
- Creating a Company Letterhead
- Creating a Business Card
- Creating a Sales Bulletin
- Creating a Greeting Card

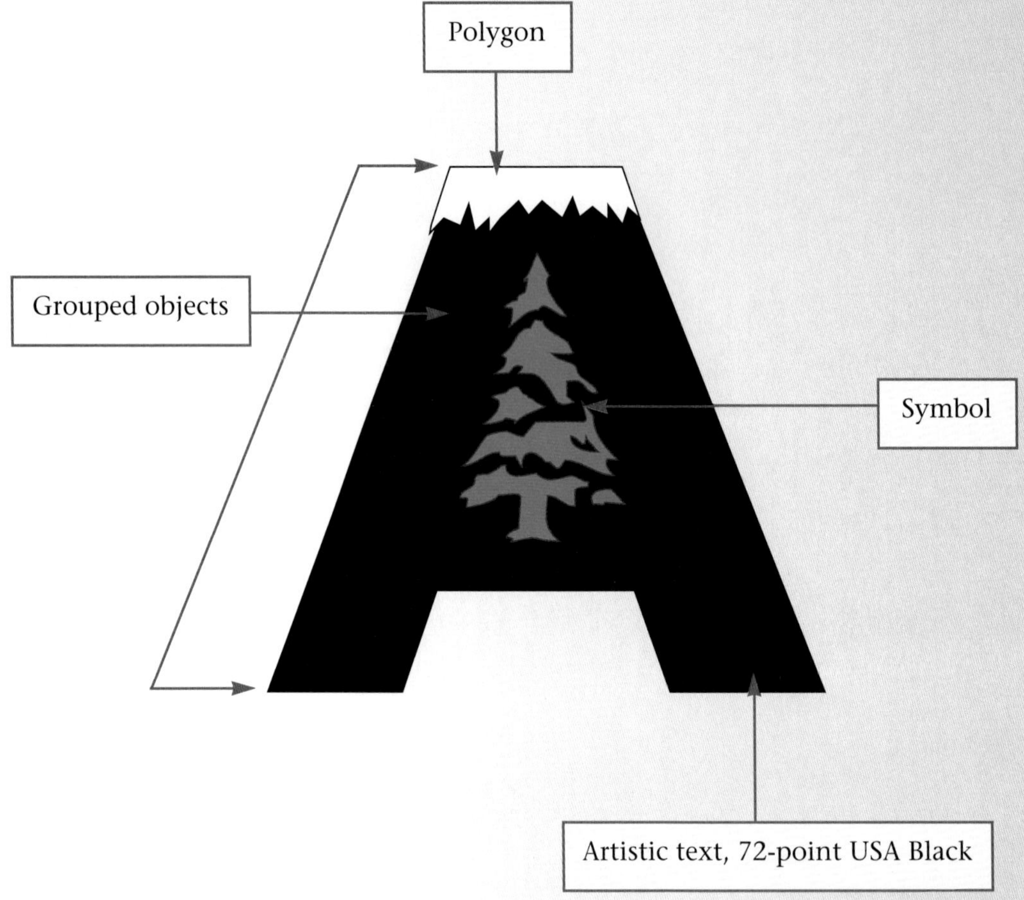

You can create professional-looking logos in CorelDRAW by combining text and symbols. In this sample, you'll create a logotype by replacing the triangular white space in a capital letter A with a symbol of a tree. Once you've drawn the logo, you can group the objects together and resize the grouped logo as needed.

Creating a Logotype

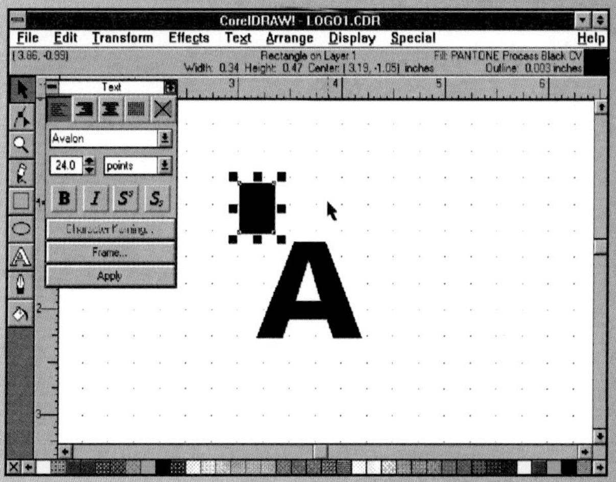

1 Create a capital letter A in USA Black font, 72 points. Change the display to Actual Size. Place a black-filled rectangle over the triangle in the A. See these tasks:

Adding Artistic Text to a Drawing	page 138
Formatting Artistic Text	page 145
Viewing an Object at Actual Size	page 89
Drawing a Rectangle or Square	page 56

2 Place a .5-inch tall symbol #6 from the Plants category in the drawing window. Change the symbol's fill to green. Place the symbol in the letter A. See these tasks:

Adding a Symbol	page 68
Filling an Area with Color	page 170
Moving an Object	page 98

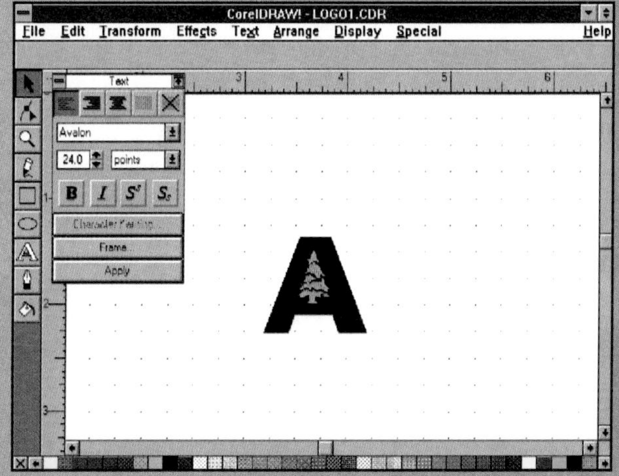

3 Draw a polygon shaped like a snow cap using the Polygon tool. Fill the polygon with white color. Select all the objects in the logo and group them together. See these tasks:

Drawing a Polygon	page 65
Grouping Objects	page 82

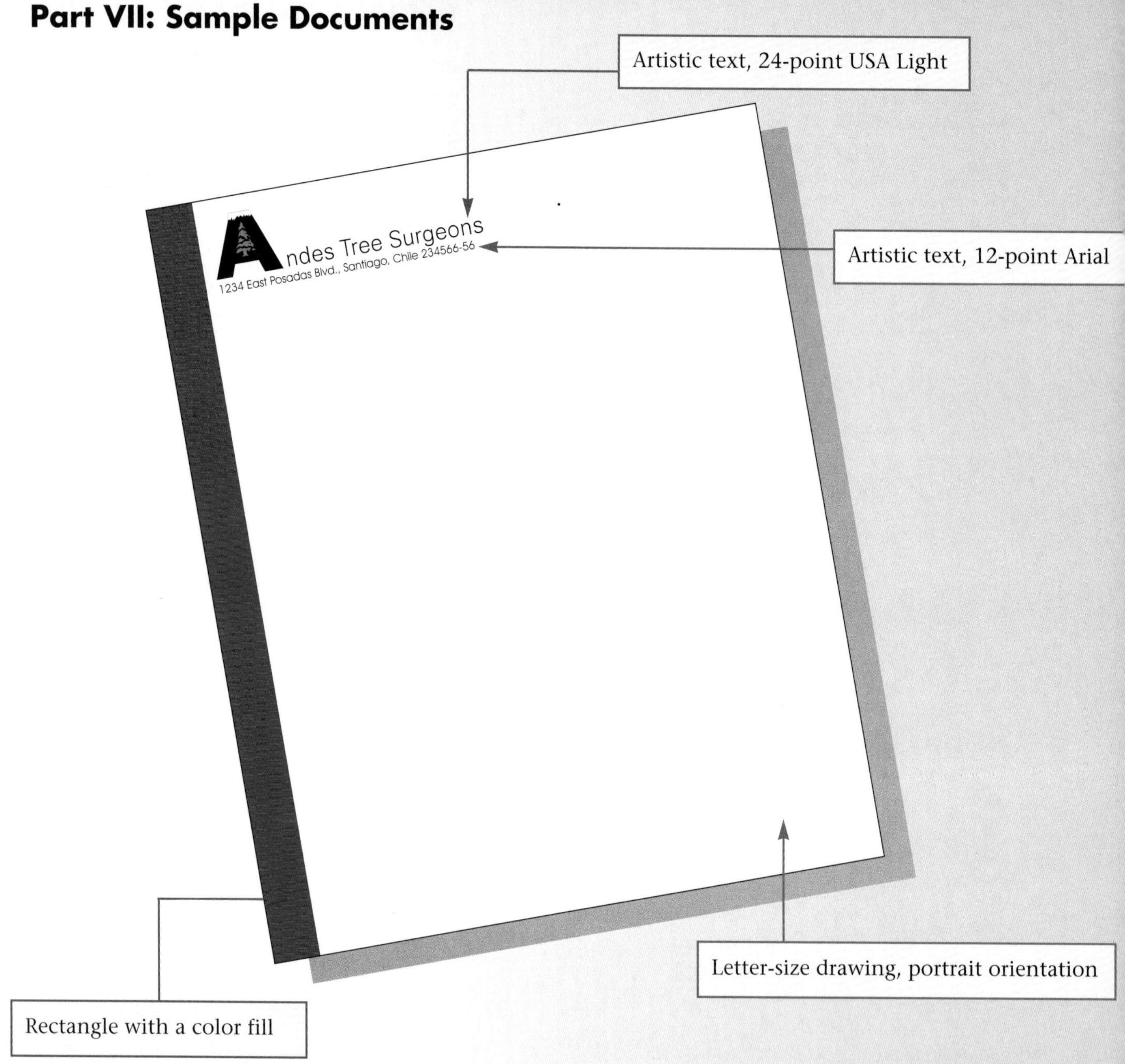

A company's letterhead should reflect the personality and objective of the company. For example, a bank's letterhead is likely to be conservative, evoking a feeling of trust and longevity. Adding graphics and logos to a letterhead helps convey the company's purpose.

In this sample, you'll use the logo created in the first sample as the foundation of a company letterhead.

Creating a Company Letterhead

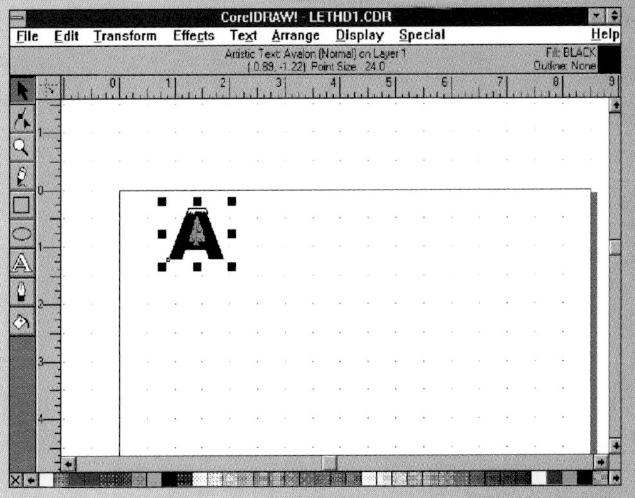

1 Copy the logo created in the first sample to a new drawing. Change the page setup to display a letter-size page in portrait orientation. Move the logo to the top of the page. See these tasks:

Copying an Object	page 100
Specifying the Paper Size and Orientation	page 25
Moving an Object	page 98

2 Add the text **ndes Tree Surgeons** after the logo in 24-point USA Light font. Place the text next to the logo at the top of the page. Add the address text in Arial, 12 point. See these tasks:

Adding Artistic Text to a Drawing	page 138
Formatting Artistic Text	page 145

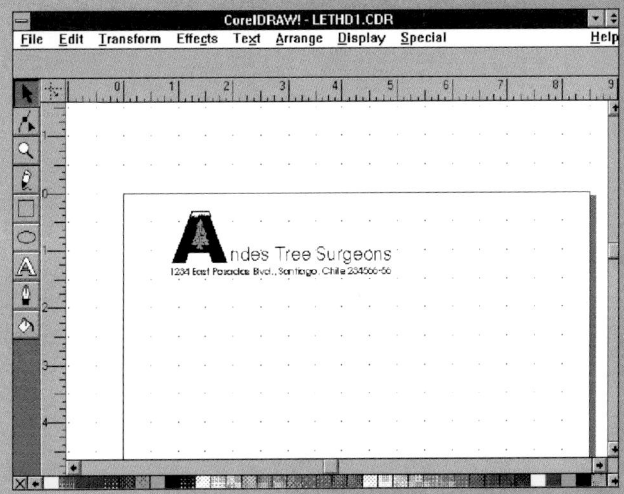

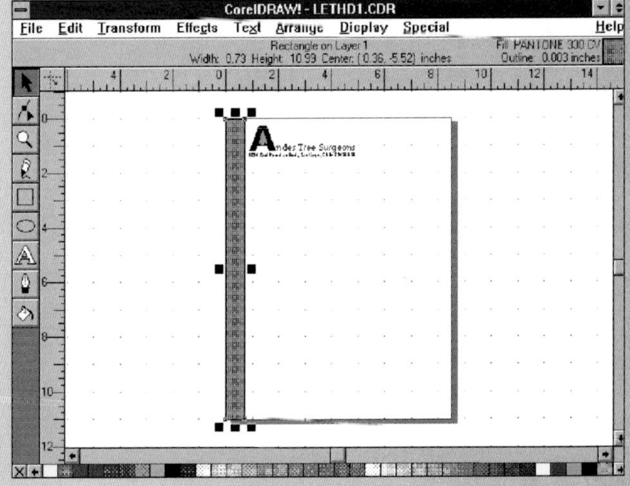

3 Draw a long rectangle down the entire left edge of the page. Fill the rectangle with a green color. See these tasks:

Drawing a Rectangle or Square	page 56
Filling an Object with Color	page 118

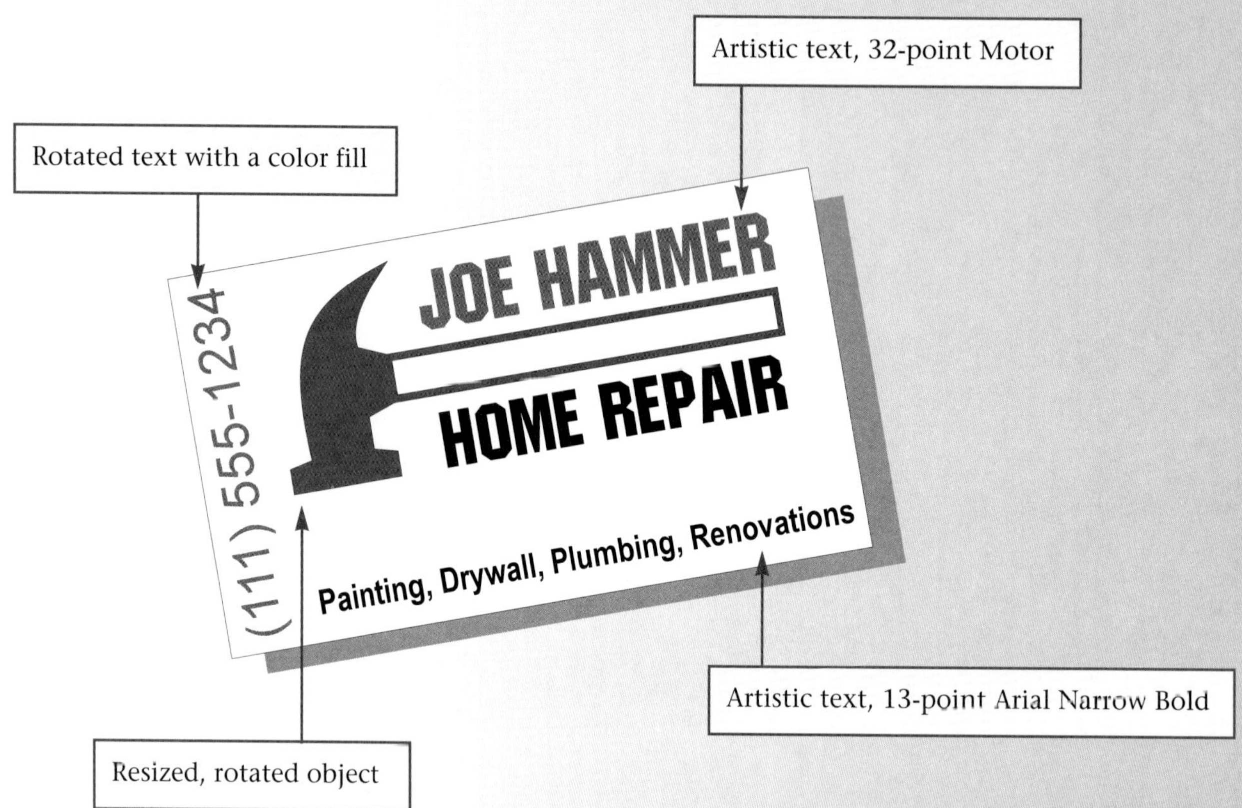

Creating a unique business card is easy using CorelDRAW's numerous fonts and symbols. Once you've designed your card in CorelDRAW, you can take it to a quick printer to have it reproduced in quantity. Or you can buy card stock perforated to business card size to print your business cards on a laser printer.

In this sample, you'll create a standard size business card using text and symbols.

Creating a Business Card

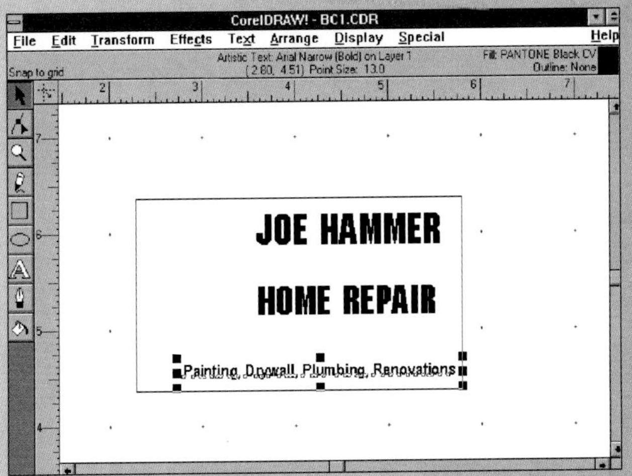

1 Draw a rectangle 3.5 inches long by 2 inches high. Add artistic text JOE HAMMER, and HOME REPAIR in Motor font, 32 point. Add other text in Arial Narrow Bold, 13 point. See these tasks:

Drawing a Rectangle or Square	page 56
Adding Artistic Text to a Drawing	page 138

2 Type the phone number, change its fill to brown, and rotate it as shown. Change the fill color of JOE HAMMER to brown. See these tasks:

Adding Artistic Text to a Drawing	page 138
Formatting Artistic Text	page 145
Filling an Object with Color	page 118

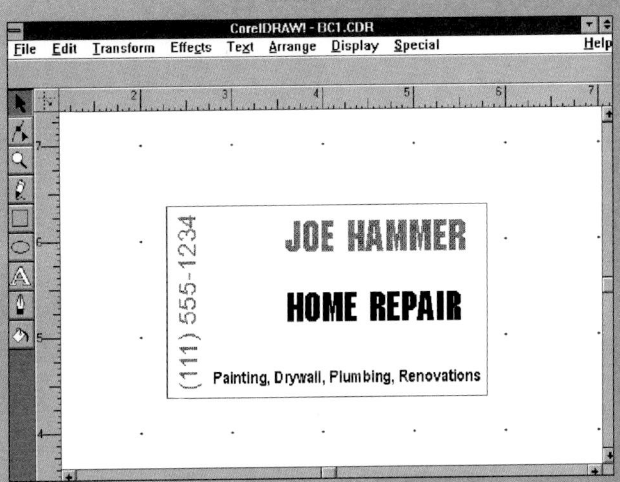

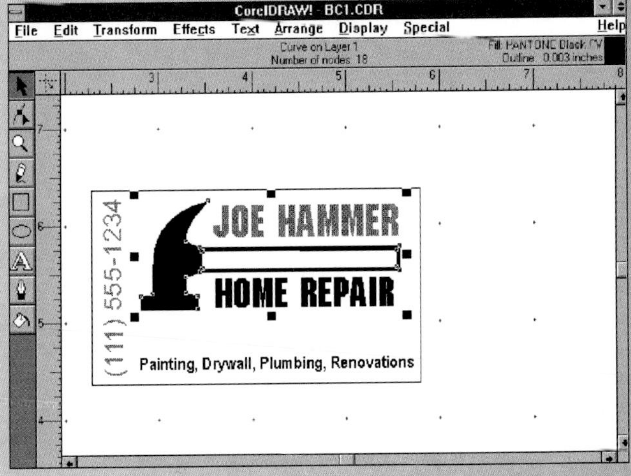

3 Place a 1.5-inch symbol #2 from the Tools category in the drawing window. Rotate the symbol 90 degrees to the left. Stretch the symbol lengthwise to 175% of its original size. See these tasks:

Adding a Symbol	page 68
Rotating an Object	page 115
Resizing an Object	page 109

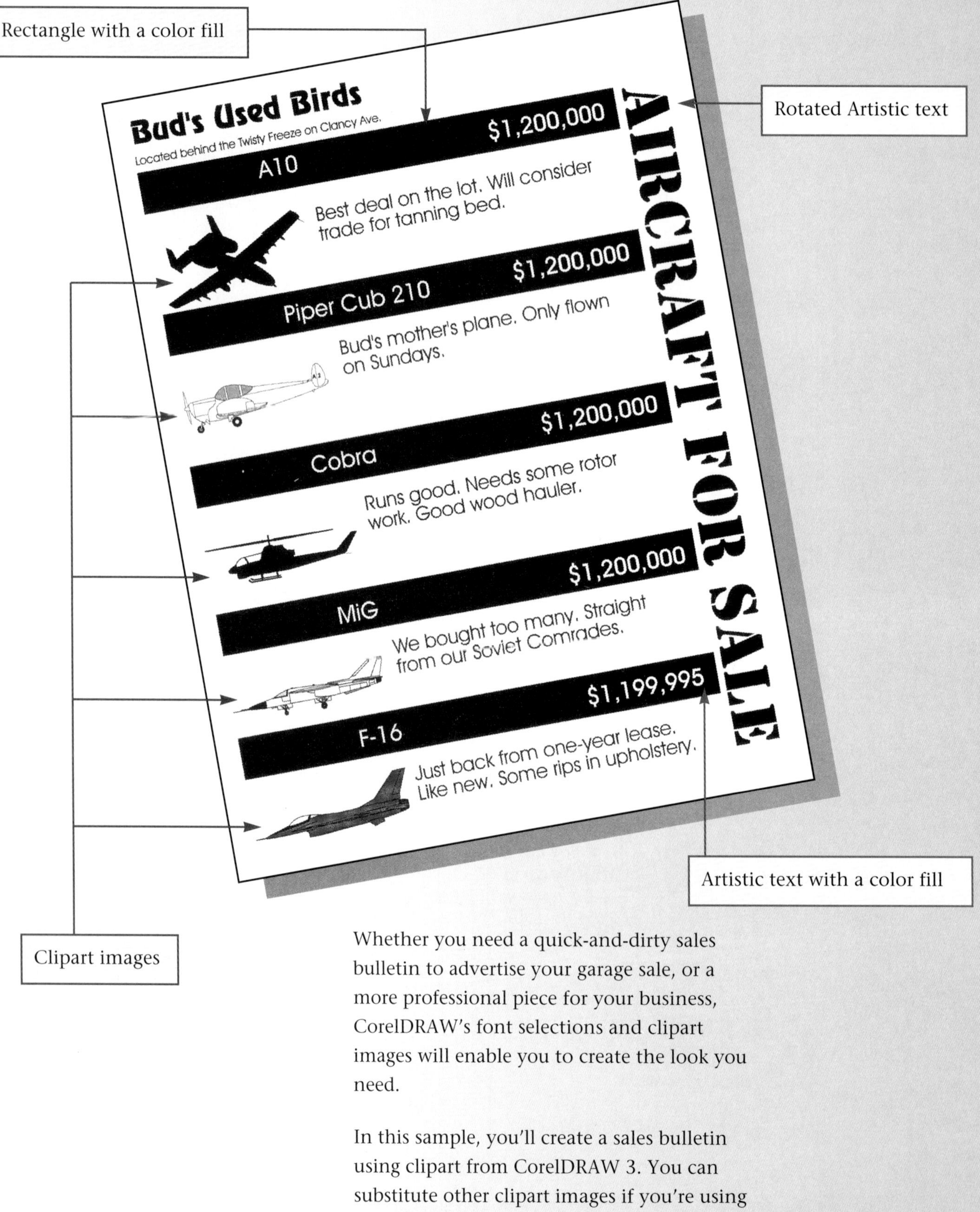

Rectangle with a color fill
Rotated Artistic text
Bud's Used Birds
Located behind the Twisty Freeze on Clancy Ave.
AIRCRAFT FOR SALE
A10
$1,200,000
Best deal on the lot. Will consider trade for tanning bed.
Piper Cub 210
$1,200,000
Bud's mother's plane. Only flown on Sundays.
Cobra
$1,200,000
Runs good. Needs some rotor work. Good wood hauler.
MiG
$1,200,000
We bought too many. Straight from our Soviet Comrades.
F-16
$1,199,995
Just back from one-year lease. Like new. Some rips in upholstery.
Artistic text with a color fill
Clipart images

Whether you need a quick-and-dirty sales bulletin to advertise your garage sale, or a more professional piece for your business, CorelDRAW's font selections and clipart images will enable you to create the look you need.

In this sample, you'll create a sales bulletin using clipart from CorelDRAW 3. You can substitute other clipart images if you're using CorelDRAW 4.

Creating a Sales Bulletin

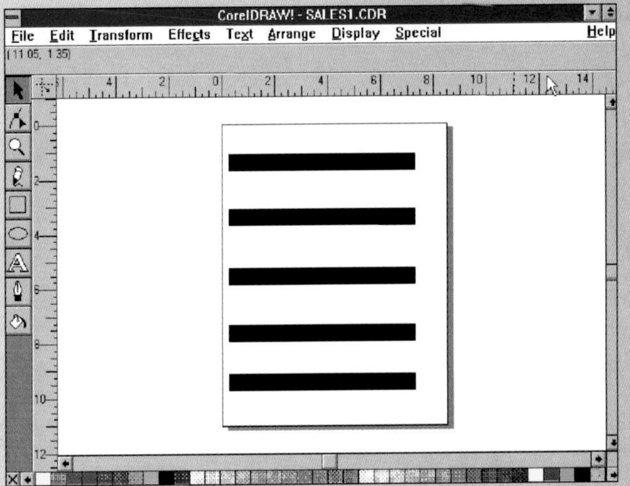

1 Draw five black-filled rectangles 7 inches long by .5 inches tall on the page, spaced 1.25 inches apart in a new drawing with a letter-size page in portrait orientation. See these tasks:

Specifying the Paper Size and Orientation	page 25
Drawing a Rectangle or Square	page 56
Filling an Object with Color	page 118

2 Add the white-filled Artistic text to the rectangles. Add other Artistic text as shown. See these tasks:

Adding Artistic Text to a Drawing	page 138
Filling an Object with Color	page 118
Rotating an Object	page 115

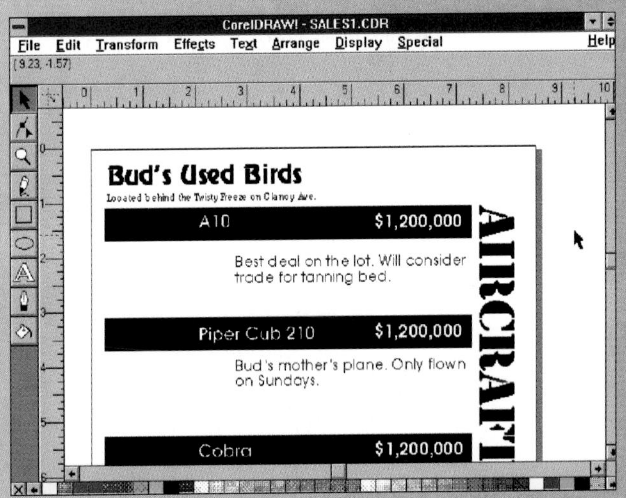

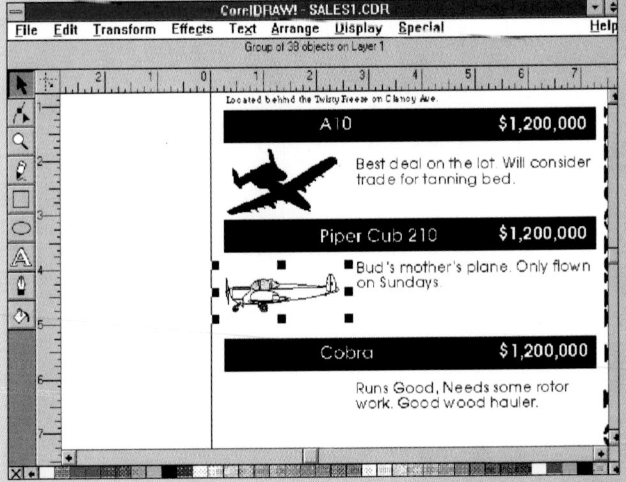

3 Import the file A10blk.CDR from the Aircraft Clipart subdirectory. Import 4 other images to complete the drawing. Place the images along the left side of the page. See these tasks:

Importing a Clipart Image	page 71
Moving an Object	page 98

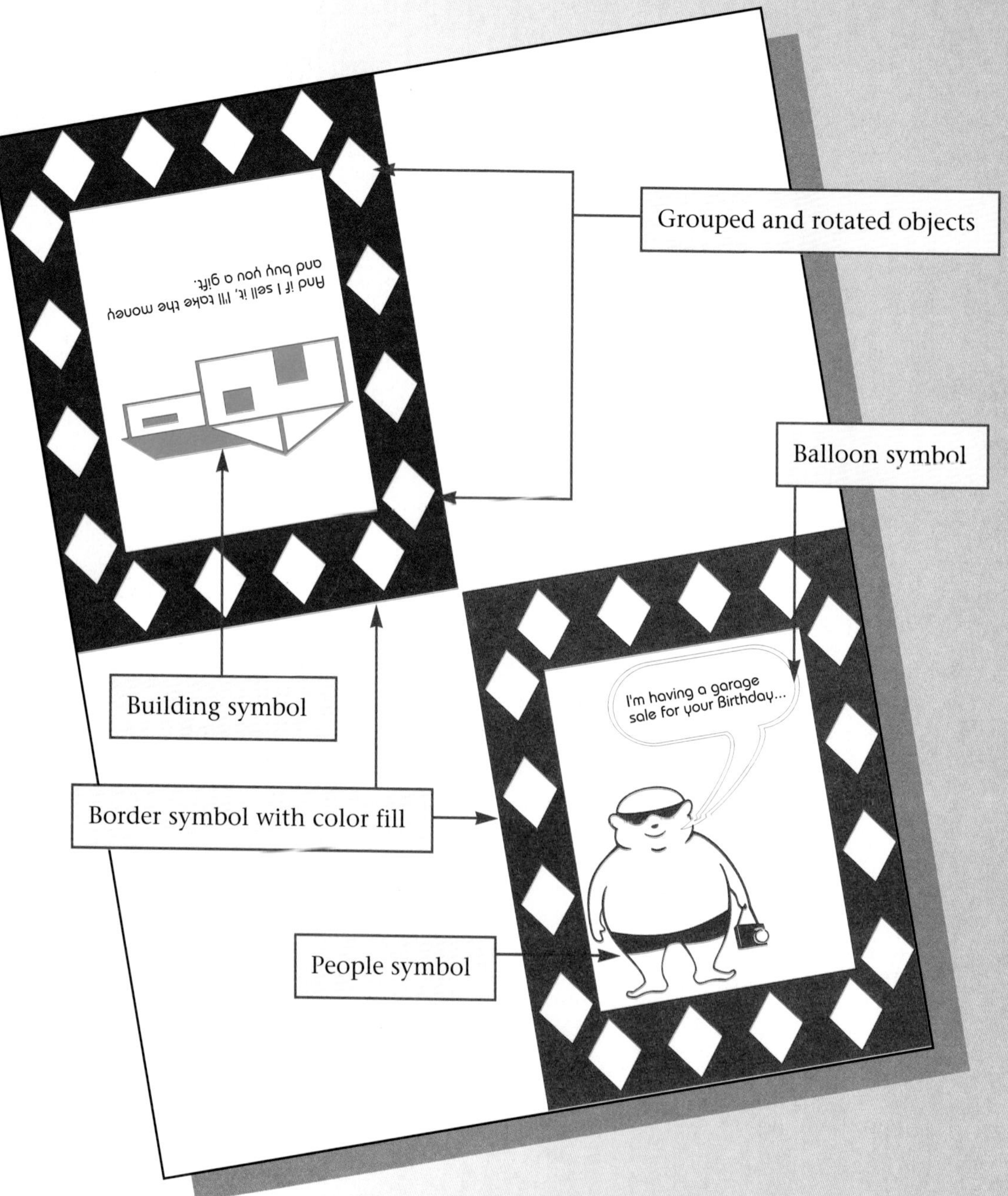

You can have fun creating your own greeting cards using CorelDRAW. By combining text, symbols, and clipart, you can create a custom greeting card for any occasion. You can design the card in black and white and print it on colored paper, or add color to the design and print the card on a color printer.

The card in this sample is designed to be folded top-to-bottom first, and then side-to-side.

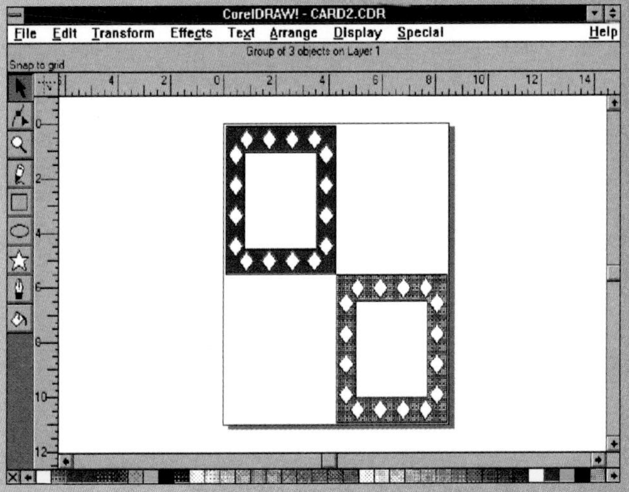

Creating a Greeting Card

1 Add two symbols #6 (#83 in version 4) from the Border2 category to a new letter-size page in portrait orientation. Resize both symbols to fit one quarter of the page, as shown. Fill symbols with color. See these tasks:

Adding a Symbol	page 68
Resizing an Object	page 109
Filling an Object with Color	page 118

2 Add symbol #37 (#69 in version 4) from the People category, symbol #22 (#45 in version 4) from the Building category, and symbol #45 (#77 in version 4) from the Balloon category to the drawing. See this task:

Adding a Symbol	page 68

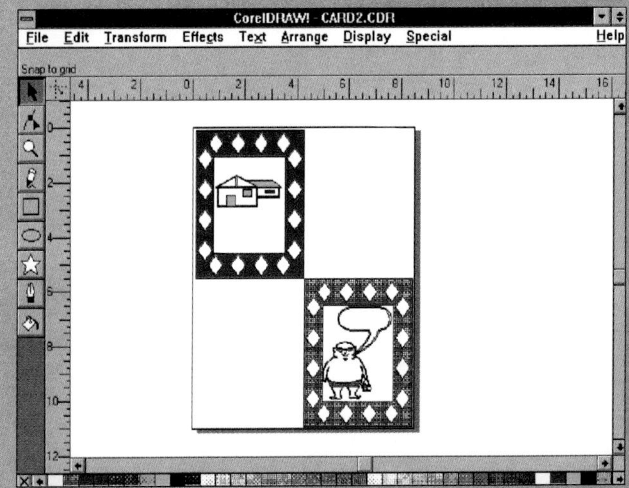

3 Add the text **I'm having a garage sale for your Birthday...**. Add **And if I sell it, I'll take the money and buy you a gift.** to the card's top border. Group and rotate the objects in the top portion of the card 180 degrees. See these tasks:

Adding Artistic Text to a Drawing	page 138
Grouping Objects	page 82
Rotating an Object	page 115

Index

E

F

G

H-K

L-M

N-O

P-Q

R

S

T

U-V

W-Z

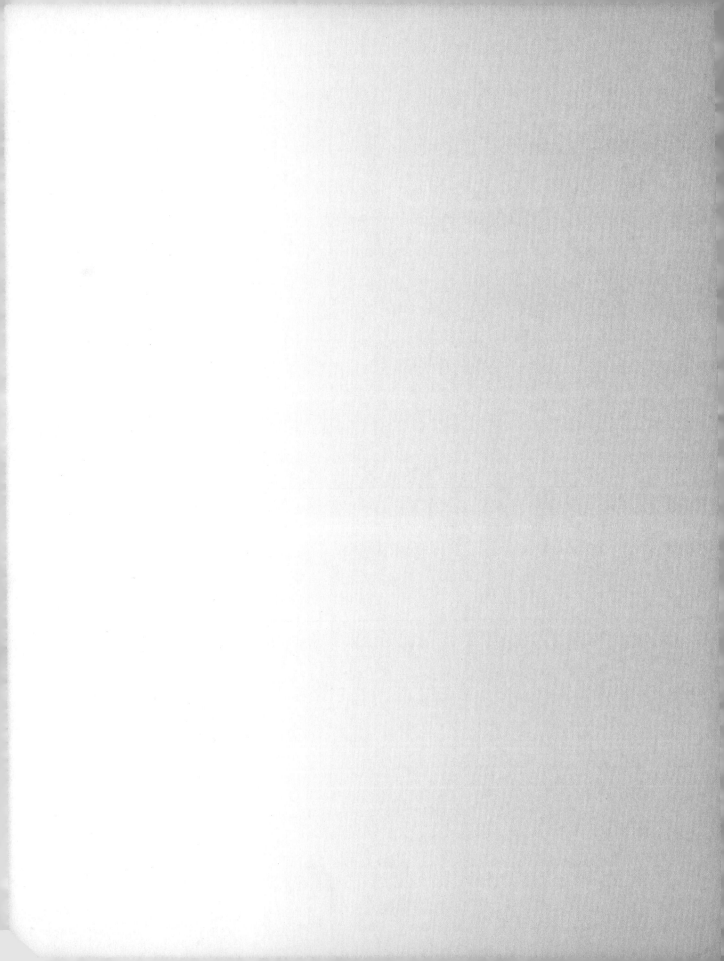